# THE COMPLETE GUIDE TO
# Foliage Planting

# THE COMPLETE GUIDE TO
# Foliage Planting

WARD LOCK

## A WARD LOCK BOOK

First published as *Foliage Plants in Garden Design*
by Ward Lock, 1992
This edition first published in the UK 1997
by Ward Lock
Wellington House
125 Strand
LONDON
WC2R 0BB

A Cassell Imprint

Text copyright © Sandra Bond (*Hostas*) 1992, Nigel J Taylor (*Ornamental Grasses, Bamboos, Rushes & Sedges*) 1992, Michael Jefferson-Brown (*Hardy Ferns*) 1992, Myles Challis (*Large-Leaved Perennials*) 1992

Distributed in the United States
by Sterling Publishing Co., Inc.
387 Park Avenue South, New York, NY 10016–8810

Distributed in Canada
by Cavendish Books Inc.
Unit 5, 801 West 1st Street
North Vancouver, B.C. Canada V7P 1PH

A British Library Cataloguing in Publication Data block for this book may be obtained from the British Library

ISBN 0 7063 7581 5

Line drawings by Carole Robson (*Hostas*; *Ornamental Grasses, Bamboos, Rushes & Sedges*), Michael Jefferson-Brown (*Hardy Ferns*) and Rosemary Wise (*Large-Leaved Perennials*)
Planting plans by Taurus Graphics (*Hostas*)
Typeset by RGM, The Mews, Birkdale Village, Southport, PR8 4AS
Printed and bound in Spain by Graficas Reunidas, Madrid

## ACKNOWLEDGEMENTS

The publishers are grateful to the following for granting permission to reproduce the colour photographs: John Newbold (pp. 6, 27 & 86); Simeon Bond (pp. 11, 30, 46, 51, 59, 62, 66, 67, 79 & 95); Ali Pollock (p. 14); John Fielding (pp. 19, 22, 34, 39, 54, 71, 75, 83, 87, 101, 117, 129, 157, 161, 168, 169, 176 & 180); Roger Phillips (pp. 42, 74 & 90); Dr Ulrich Fischer (pp. 70, 82 & 91); Neoplants Ltd (p. 78); Nigel Taylor (pp. 96, 105, 112, 120, 133, 136, 144, 145, 149, 152, 153, 156, 164, 165, 173, 177, 181 & 185); Tim Sandall/*The Gardener* (pp. 108, 125 & 141); Photos Horticultural Picture Library (pp. 186, 222, 254 & 258); Michael Jefferson-Brown (pp. 190, 211, 239, 259, 262, 263, 266, 267, 270 & 271); Bob Challinor (pp. 194, 199, 203, 206, 215, 219, 226, 231, 234, 243, 246, 247, 250, 251, 255, 273, 278, 299, 303, 306, 315, 318, 322, 327, 331, 334, 335, 338, 342, 343 & 346); Myles Challis (pp. 274, 283, 347, 350, 354, 358 & 359); Michael Nicholson (pp. 287, 290, 295 & 355); David Crampton (p. 310); and Garden Picture Library (p. 351). The publishers are also grateful to the John Lewis Partnership for granting permission to undertake photography at the Longstock Water Garden and also to Mr. J. Bond for granting permission to undertake photography at the Savill Garden, Windsor Great Park. Front cover right to left clockwise: Andrew Lawson; Clive Nichols (*Sambucus* 'Sutherlands Gold', *Carex stricta* 'Bowles' Golden', *Hosta* 'Buckshaw Blue', Hadspen House Garden, Somerset); Jerry Harpur (garden owner Gunilla Pickard); Jerry Harpur (*Parthenocissus quinquefolia*); Andrew Lawson; Andrew Lawson; Andrew Lawson. Back cover: Andrew Lawson.

# Contents

**Hostas**
*Sandra Bond*                                      6–95

Foliage in design                                     8
Hostas as garden plants                              10
The importance of colour in garden
   design                             32
The use of hostas as container plants                44
Cultivation                                          47
Plant directory                                      58


**Ornamental Grasses, Bamboos, Rushes &
Sedges**
*Nigel J Taylor*                                   96–185

The truth about grasses                              98
Why grow grasses?                                   103
Using grasses in the garden                         107
Cultivation and propagation                         138
Plant directory                                     140

**Hardy Ferns**
*Michael Jefferson-Brown*                        186–273

Introducing ferns                                   188
Ferns as foliage plants                             197
Using ferns in the garden                           204
Creating a fernery                                  217
Growing hardy ferns                                 229
Round-the-year maintenance                          238
Plant directory                                     244


**Large-Leaved Perennials**
*Myles Challis*                                  274–361

Introducing large-leaved perennials                 276
The value of architectural plants
   in the garden                     279
Companion planting                                  285
Large-leaved perennials and water                   298
The tropical touch                                  307
Large-leaved perennials in containers               323
Plant directory                                     329


Index                                               362

# Hostas

## Sandra Bond

*H. sieboldiana* contrasting in form with
*Miscanthus sinensis* 'Silver Feather' and the
unusual *Campanula bononiensis*.

# Foliage in Design

Foliage plants have an important place in garden design; they set the scene and can act as the framework to plants with less determinate form. Foliage comes in all shapes and sizes, evergreen and deciduous, and it is the interplay between the similarities and contrasts that result in effective design.

A totally evergreen garden can appear very static, rather dull and lacking in surprise, whereas a garden with no evergreens is deprived of winter 'bones' so the aim should be for balance and harmony. The shape, size and colour of foliage all influence design; contrasting and complementary leaf shapes have a part to play – a large round leaf underplanted with a small round leaf, a plain leaf against a frilly one. Very large plain leaves rest the eye and act like full stops; they can complement the scheme (although large pinnate leaves need much more care in use and should not be over-used).

A bamboo towering above a group of hostas introduces not only a contrast in size and shape but in density of leaf. It appears airy and graceful and sets off the solidity of the hosta to perfection. Vertical plants are a vital element in designing a garden. Too many and the effect can be heavy; not enough and the planting looks flat and uninteresting. Low level accents can be achieved by irises, day lilies, grasses, Solomon's seal, and higher ones by the larger bamboos, grasses such as *Miscanthus sinensis* 'Variegatus' and some ferns.

In the ideal plan all plants should harmonize, in reality it is better to make small groups into pleasing compositions at different times but the restrictions of soil, climate and aspect must always be considered. In the long term plants that suit the conditions will make the most satisfactory gardens. Hostas will grow in the sun but with very few exceptions will not look their best: the leaves will develop brown edges, they will become dormant early, and as there are so many plants that revel in dry sunny conditions, why struggle? Hostas are basically shade plants, some tolerate more sun than others and some even need more but they are not sun lovers. It is far better to accept the physical limitations and to design accordingly. What are often seen as difficult situations can, with the right plant material, become a positive advantage. Foliage and form are not enough if the plants will not flourish; it is far better to grow them in containers if the required conditions cannot be met. A very wide range of plant material can be grown this way. Good design goes hand in hand with plant knowledge; the combination of artistic flair with an understanding of fundamentals can result in designs of outstanding beauty. Remember when planning and planting that schemes need time, as plants do not generally reach maturity in a season.

## Hostas as important foliage plants

Hostas have a restful quality; they act like full stops and create a cool oasis and are one of the most important foliage plants. There is an enormous range in size, shape and colour and although they are also flowering plants it is the foliage that is the dominant element in design.

Hostas are generally easy, long-living perennials that associate with many other plants. As their season of interest is from spring through to autumn, the most successful use in small gardens is often in the context of mixed planting. A framework of trees and shrubs will give the light shade conditions that hostas revel in; bulbs can give colour in the very early months before the leaf canopy develops and contrast in form for the rest of the season can come from grasses, ferns and other perennials, giving an interesting all-year-round garden.

Existing shade, such as in the shadow of a building, is ideal for foliage borders; they need not be dull as foliage comes in many shapes and colours. The variation in the hosta leaf can be exploited, the plain green, grey, gold and blue leaves being just as important as the variegated ones, although there is no doubt that variegated hostas are planted far more in gardens, despite the fact that an assortment of variegated leaves is not easy to mix successfully. Used well, variegation in plants acts like a highlight, and a predominantly shady green corner of ferns, for example, can be brought to life by the addition of a green and white hosta such as *H.* 'Francee'.

## Variation in hostas

Hostas come in a wide range of sizes from miniatures 5 cm (2 in) high to towering 1.2 m (4 ft) mounds, but the very tiny hostas do not have the impact upon design that their larger brethren have. Some mounds are spreading, others upright and this is another aspect that can be exploited. *H.* 'Krossa Regal', for example, is vase-shaped and can be planted as an accent among lower-growing plants, whereas a smaller variety such as *H.* 'Ginko Craig' looks much better planted in larger numbers as an edging.

The leaves come in four basic shapes: round, lanceolate, heart-shaped and triangular. Some are wafer-thin while others are thick in texture; some have flat margins, others wavy. The leaf can be cupped, twisted, puckered, dimpled or flat, and present many different surface appearances: matt, glossy, leathery or glaucous, and each leaf surface giving a different effect as the light catches it. If all these variables are considered with the many combinations of leaf colour (blue, cream, gold, green, grey and white) and size it is not so surprising that there is now a very large range of hostas available.

Although hostas are primarily foliage plants they do flower, their elegant flower spikes or scapes usually appearing through the latter half of the summer. The flowers range from white to deep violet, and some are delightfully fragrant. *H.* 'So Sweet', one of the newer varieties, has beautiful scented white flowers in late summer above a green and cream-edged mound of foliage and, like all scented hostas, has been developed from *H. plantaginea*. One of the present breeding aims is to increase the range of fragrant hostas as this is a very worthwhile improvement.

Gardeners can exploit the diversity of hostas to achieve many different effects, but it must be remembered that the immature plant often bears little resemblance to the mature hosta: the leaf is narrower, the colour is not fully enhanced and the variegation less pronounced. Hostas should be left alone for the first three or four years to grow and mature; constant chopping up means that the mature leaf form is never allowed to develop.

# Hostas as Garden Plants

In their native habitat hostas do not grow in deep shade but on the margins of deciduous forests, on rocky outcrops and even in the open in damp grasslands. They are partly hidden in the vegetation and in order to flower and set seed they need some sun. They are not being used as foliage plants, so the visual appearance of the leaves is not important. Gardeners growing hostas as foliage plants would like to keep the foliage in pristine condition, and the ideal for most hostas is filtered shade, adequate moisture and feeding; full sun and dried roots is a recipe for disaster – leave these sorts of situations to Mediterranean-type plants. Green and gold hostas will stand more sun as long as they are not dry at the roots, but blue hostas maintain their colour far longer with more shade. The blues have developed a bloom to the leaf to protect against spring sun before the leaf canopy develops and this disappears as the summer advances when it is no longer needed, but if these are grown in the shade of trees and shrubs then the blueness is retained for most of the summer. This is why blues look much bluer in shade.

Some hostas can be grown in dry shade as long as they are established and, ideally, mulched and naturally strong-growing. The less the shade the more essential that the moisture level is adequate. The plants will not be as luxuriant but some will grow surprisingly well where little else will. In very cool climates where the temperatures are rarely high and the sun weak many hostas can be grown in the open as long as there is adequate moisture. A few very thick-leaved hostas such as H. 'Sum and Substance' will stand full sun but these are the exceptions. If in doubt plant in the shade.

Micro-climates often exist in gardens. A large shrub rose, for instance, will create a partially shady, cooler spot underneath, even though the roses are in full sun, and hostas can take full advantage of this. H. 'Halcyon' associates wonderfully with old-fashioned pink and white shrub roses and their abundance of foliage lets the hosta grow in a relatively shady position. As long as the sun of late spring is not abnormally strong H. 'Halcyon' is quite happy until the leaf canopy develops. It is the versatility of the hosta that has made it one of the most popular perennial plants today.

Hostas can be used in various ways in gardens – in hosta borders, in shady corners, on the margins of ponds, as ground cover, on alpine beds and in containers. They can be used on their own or in association with a wide range of plants that enjoy the same conditions.

## Hosta borders and walks

Very keen growers of hostas tend to have a hosta border or even a hosta walk. There is so much variation in hostas that they can be grown together, contrasting and complementing each other. I personally prefer a shrub and tree backdrop and a modest use of other flowering and foliage perennials that maintain the cool effect but add contrasts of form rather than colour.

**Gold and greens. H. 'Geisha' with the cascading mounds of Hakonechloa macra 'Aureola', the gold tones picked up by the mats of Lysimachia nummularia 'Aurea'.**

The shade provided needs to be light rather than dense so that some light filters through, and the competing roots from other plants not so greedy that they take all the moisture and goodness from the soil. Such conditions could exist in light deciduous woodland and the border or walk created by edging a path with hostas. A shady house or garden wall border will also give an ideal site as long as it is not bone dry. If planting hostas in a prominent position in the garden it is probably best to use them with discretion as they are primarily summer plants and hosta borders will by their very definition not be interesting in the winter. It is possible to use bulbs that like shade as underplanting, but it is important to remember that hostas like a rich diet and this does not suit snowdrops, for example.

Enthusiasts who become collectors of hostas are happy to accept the need to create near to ideal conditions, erecting artificial means of shade to achieve this without the worry of competing tree roots and problems of seasonal variation. At its most attractive this can be a specially constructed tunnel or pergola with light but closely spaced members to give filtered light; wooden laths are often used in the USA, especially in nursery demonstration areas. They can be made into handsome structures. Trade growers usually use net tunnels covered in plastic and giving 50 per cent shade, as these are far cheaper and give enough light for golds to colour and enough shade for the white-edged varieties not to burn. Artificial protection achieves other benefits such as wind protection – wind can burn leaves just as the sun can – and late frosts are not as damaging in shady areas.

By growing hostas in close proximity, cultural needs are met far more easily and frost cloth can be rolled over the plantings if unseasonal weather occurs in late spring when the emerging shoots are most prone to damage.

If a large number of hostas is grown together great care is needed in the juxtaposition of the different varieties. Making the most effective use of hostas by leaf colour is discussed more fully in the next chapter, but the most satisfactory grouping is to place the gold and green-gold variegated forms at the opposite end from the white variegated ones, and to use greens and blues in between. Highlights among the blues can come from H. 'Frances Williams', a blue with a wide yellow-beige edge, or H. tokudama 'Aureo-nebulosa' with a cloudy yellow centre to its bluish leaf. H. 'Bright Lights', an even brighter gold-centred H. tokudama form, would fit beautifully where a border is changing from gold to blue. H. 'Snow Cap' and H. 'Regal Splendor' could be planted nearer the white end; these two very new hostas which will become popular, have white edges to blue-green leaves. There are so many attractive hostas of varying shades of plain golds, blue and greens to set off the variegated ones, and green hostas are just as effective as the variegated forms and much under-used.

When variegated hostas are associated with each other great care is needed and it is important to keep to a limited spectrum and a similar leaf shape. H. fortunei 'Aureo-marginata', a medium green with a yellow margin is reflected on a much smaller scale by H. 'Golden Tiara' and if plain yellow and green varieties are placed in the same group a satisfactory picture will be achieved. There is an enormous variation in the shades of blues and greens and this can be exploited by picking up the subtle differences in adjoining plants.

Sometimes less than satisfactory groupings have to be made as the collector needs to find a home for the latest treasure. Lance-shaped hostas can be the most difficult to place but if used together the similarity of leaf shape acts as a common denominator, over-ruling any discordant elements.

Some hostas are so dramatic, they make wonderful specimens. A single plant of *H*. 'Sum and Substance', which has enormous chartreuse-gold leaves, can be placed as a 'full stop' in a predominantly gold planting of much smaller varieties such as *H*. 'Golden Prayers' which should be used in larger numbers as an underplanting. Hostas at the edge of the border look much better if planted in generous numbers of a limited range, as they give the border cohesion.

If hellebores, pulmonarias and small daffodils are planted towards the back of the border these will give interest in the spring; *Narcissus* 'Thalia' is especially effective with the emerging shoots of hostas.

# Shade gardens

Hostas are ideal shade plants and can be planted in areas that often present problems. In recent years many gardeners have realized that hostas not only grow in shade but they thrive there, and the part of the garden that was the least favourite place can become the most attractive in the garden. Instead of bemoaning the problems of shade, some gardeners start to plant more trees and shrubs in order to create new shade beds for the increasing number of hostas, hellebores and ferns, to name but a few of the plants that they now wish to collect.

Moist shade is far easier to deal with than dry shade but because the sun does not dry out the soil at the same rate of evaporation as in the open, dry soil in shade is usually cooler, and with the addition of humus and mulch many hostas can be planted with a wide range of other plants.

Figure 1 is of a woodland glade with some parts drier than others, and the plants have been selected accordingly. The shade is cast by existing deciduous trees and shrubs and by the planted evergreen shrubs,

which in this instance are viburnums, sarcococcas, skimmias and camellias as the soil is neutral. The hostas act as foils to the shrubs and are associated with other perennial plants which enjoy the same conditions.

DRY SHADE

It is possible to have a bed in dry shade that is as interesting as the rest of the garden; it will not be very colourful as very few brightly coloured plants thrive but it will be all the more effective because it is restful and in keeping with the ambience of shade. Many established gardens have a large tree where very little seems to thrive but in many instances the ground can be completely covered virtually up to the bole. Trees that leaf very late are not suitable for hostas as the leaf canopy will not give protection to the young hosta foliage, and those that have extensive surface roots can be too greedy; planting just beyond the overhanging branches will be more successful if the tree is a dense evergreen such as a large holly.

Good soil preparation is needed. Organic matter helps to retain moisture; this can be manure or home-made compost, and leaves should not be cleared away but allowed to rot down to make leaf mould. When planting, adequate holes must be made among the surface tree roots and as much moisture-retaining composts incorporated as possible. The plants need to be thoroughly watered in and ideally mulched to retain the moisture, but if no mulch is available pulling dry soil over the wet is better than nothing, and will prevent direct transpiration.

The first season of planting is critical. Plants must make adequate root systems so that they will be able to withstand future periods of drought – often the only moisture that penetrates is that in the months when the tree is not in leaf. Old, established clumps of hosta have stood droughts remarkably well without any

watering although the leaves have become smaller in places where the lack of rainfall has been extreme and the water table has dropped to very low levels. Many strong-growing hostas will be perfectly happy; they will not be as large but will make more than satisfactory mounds.

Figure 2 shows a suggested planting plan for a dry, shaded bed. In my garden I have a very large oak tree; the soil below its wide canopy is dry but the accumulated leaf mould of many years has helped to improve the structure. The only plants originally growing there were a large colony of double snowdrops and some woodland anemones which I have left. *Luzula sylvatica* 'Marginata', *Geranium macrorrhizum album* and *Helleborus foetidus* were planted near the tree trunk and have established a complete ground cover. *H. undulata* 'Albo-marginata' (*H.* 'Thomas Hogg'), *H. undulata* 'Univittata', *H.* 'Francee' and *H.* 'Ginko Craig' were all then planted in groups where their white-variegated foliage gives highlights. Blue and green hostas used include *H. lancifolia*, *H.* 'Candy Hearts', *H.* 'Blue Boy', *H.* 'Blue Wedgwood' and *H.* 'Halcyon' for areas near the edge of the bed and *H.* 'Blue Angel' (a *H. sieboldiana* type that does not have cupped leaves) and *H. fortunei* 'Hyacinthina' for larger mounds. Very cupped hostas such as *H. tokudama* and *H.* 'Sea Lotus Leaf' are best not planted under the drip of trees as their leaves collect debris that falls from the tree.

Plants for winter–spring interest include bergenias, which need to be carefully placed slightly away from the hostas, hellebores, pulmonarias, snowdrops, and

**Frontyard bed in the garden of Warren and Ali Pollock in Wilmington, Delaware, USA. Hostas left to right are 'Antioch', 'Roseanne' (a new yellow), *fortunei* 'Aureo-marginata' with 'August Moon' behind and 'Sum and Substance' at top left.**

*Iris foetidissima*. Additional vertical accents are from the repetitive planting of *Iris foetidissima* 'Variegata', an invaluable plant for the winter garden and a fine contrast in form and colour against blue and green hosta clumps. As the season advances Solomon's seal (*Polygonatum × hybridum*), dicentras and foxgloves are followed by aconitums and Japanese anemones, and then a carpet of cyclamens.

The degree of moisture varies enormously in areas of shade. Nothing will grow under very dense established evergreen trees such as a yew as moisture never penetrates, but in areas that are dry in the summer and get some winter rainfall, there are many plants that will associate with the hostas and are invaluable. *Arum italicum* 'Pictum' is particularly effective in the winter and spring garden with its delightful silvery veined leaves which completely disappear when the drumsticks of red berries (which are poisonous) push up in the autumn. *Euphorbia amygdaloides robbiae* with its dark green leathery evergreen leaves, luzulas and symphytums will clothe areas that are just too dry for the hostas. Some of the *Dryopteris filix-mas* forms will grow surprisingly well in dry shade and make interesting contrasts with the hostas, as will *Tellima grandiflora* with its creamy green spires of tiny flowers.

Invaluable evergreen carpeters, which can act as 'markers' to the hostas in the winter months so that a fork is not inadvertently pushed into the crowns, include *Ajuga reptans*, epimediums (although these need their old leaves cut away in the spring so that the flowers can be appreciated), small leaved ivies, lamiums, pachysandras, tiarellas and vincas (periwinkle). All will colonize dry shade as long as they are given a good start and a mulch applied when the soil is moist or it has been watered.

If the soil is dry because of walls or buildings it is much easier to plan, as the angle of the sun will

15

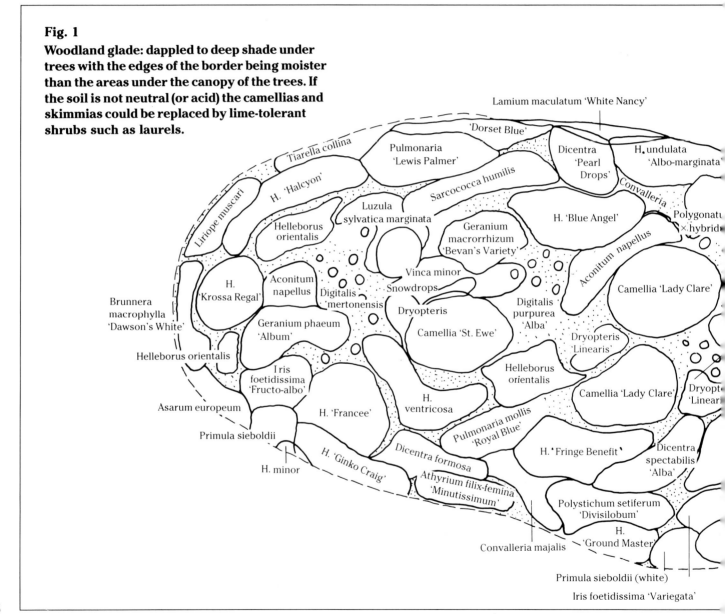

**Fig. 1**
**Woodland glade: dappled to deep shade under trees with the edges of the border being moister than the areas under the canopy of the trees. If the soil is not neutral (or acid) the camellias and skimmias could be replaced by lime-tolerant shrubs such as laurels.**

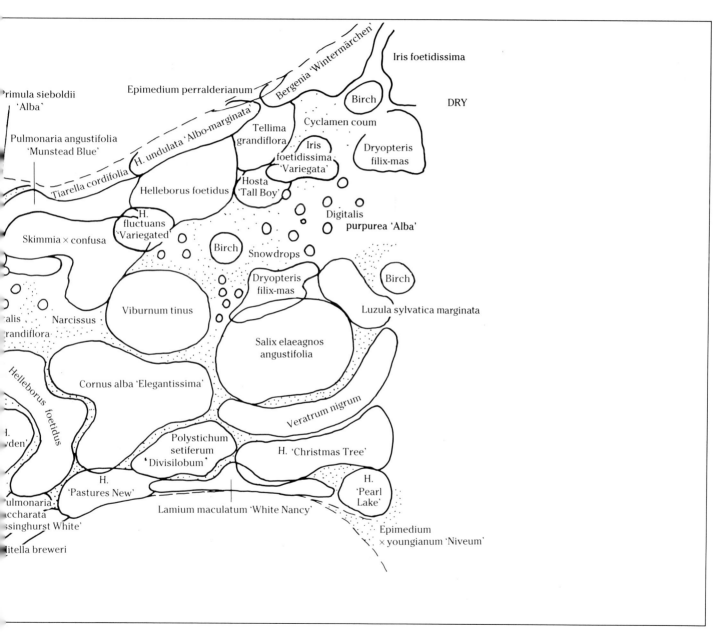

Primula sieboldii 'Alba'

Epimedium perralderianum

Bergenia 'Wintermärchen'

Iris foetidissima

Birch

DRY

Pulmonaria angustifolia 'Munstead Blue'

H. undulata 'Albo-marginata'

Cyclamen coum

Tellima grandiflora

Iris foetidissima 'Variegata'

Dryopteris filix-mas

Tiarella cordifolia

Helleborus foetidus

Hosta 'Tall Boy'

H. fluctuans 'Variegated'

Digitalis purpurea 'Alba'

Skimmia × confusa

Birch

Snowdrops

Dryopteris filix-mas

Birch

Viburnum tinus

Luzula sylvatica marginata

alis grandiflora

Narcissus

Salix elaeagnos angustifolia

Helleborus foetidus

Cornus alba 'Elegantissima'

Veratrum nigrum

H. 'den'

Polystichum setiferum 'Divisilobum'

H. 'Christmas Tree'

H. 'Pastures New'

H. 'Pearl Lake'

ulmonaria accharata ssinghurst White'

Lamium maculatum 'White Nancy'

Epimedium × youngianum 'Niveum'

itella breweri

17

**Fig. 2**
**Dry shade under the canopy of an established tree such as an oak which gets winter rain but where very little moisture penetrates in summer.**

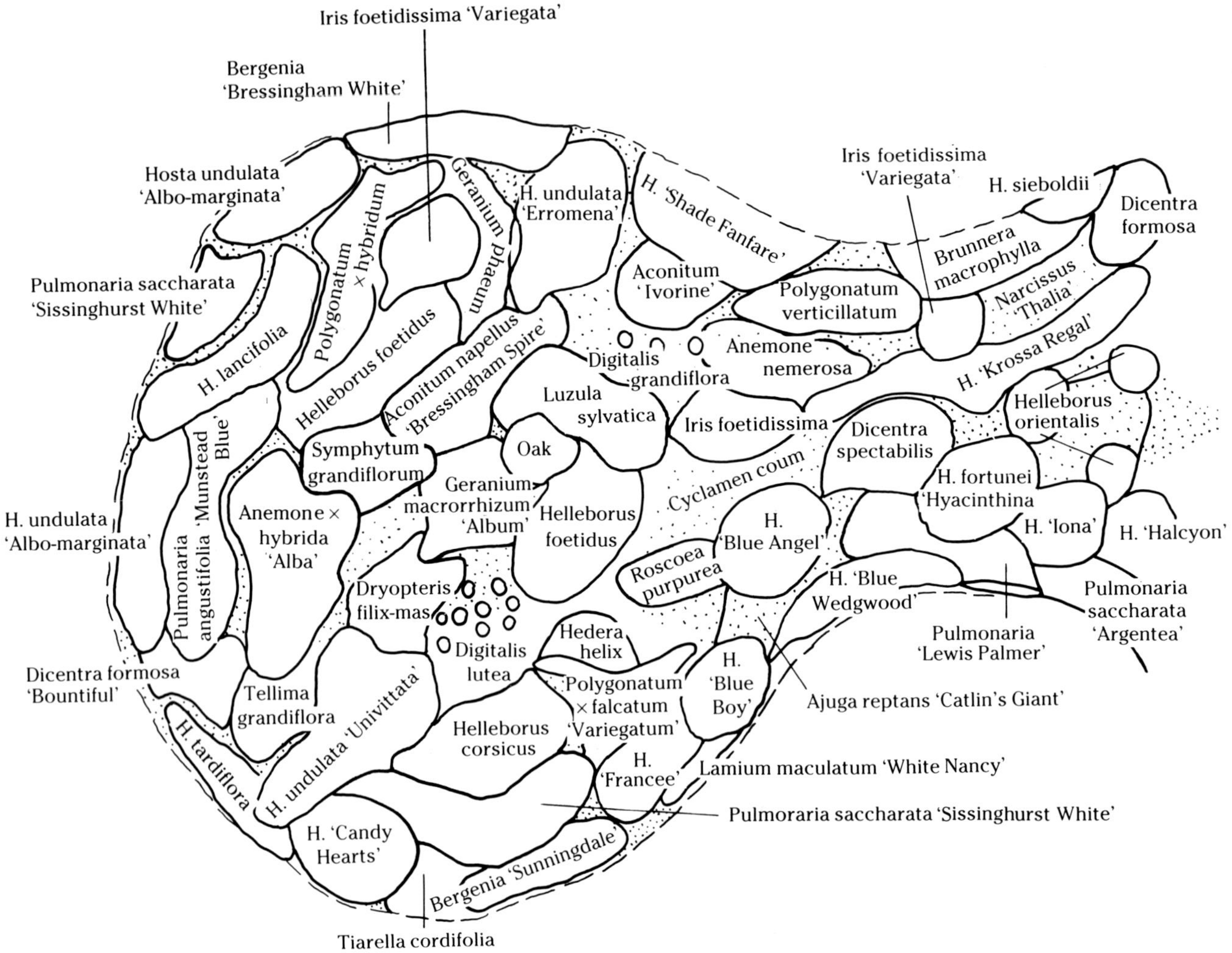

determine the degree of shade at any given time in the year and many more hostas can be successfully established as long as adequate soil preparation and watering are given. Gold and gold-variegated hostas are best planted in areas of more light but most of the others will be happy. Some, especially the blues, happily grow in areas where the sun never penetrates. The leaves will be fewer but larger, and the flowers more sparse.

## MOIST SHADE

Moist dappled shade is the ideal habitat for hostas and the range of plants that can be used in association with them is very large. Many of the plants that will tolerate dry shade will luxuriate in damper conditions, although not all are suitable. Here the massed effects of drifts of plants blending with each other and with the hostas will achieve their zenith. The principle of planting in drifts applies as much on the large scale as on the small. All planting schemes need linking plants, groups which are often at the edge to tie the design together. Hostas are one of the best of the perennial plants for this purpose. Chosen carefully they can bring order to chaos, but the slightly wild effect should not be lost altogether; the ideal looks natural, but has been carefully contrived by the selection of the plant material. This is the place for blues and greens with a judicious use of variegated forms.

Figure 3 is for a cool scheme which could also be used in a damp border in the white garden, the purist removing the flowers from the hostas. *Matteuccia struthiopteris*, the ostrich feather fern, is a superb architectural plant as long as it is not placed in a windy situation and associates beautifully with many hostas,

Previous page:
**H. undulata 'Univittata' at Wakehurst Place, Sussex, UK. This will establish in dry shade.**

providing a contrast in form and leaf. The white edges of H. 'Francee' and H. 'Ginko Craig' are accentuated against the lacy plumes and the lower-growing fern *Polystichum setiferum* 'Divisilobum' with its much darker green fronds sets the hostas off to perfection. The finely cut foliage of *Aruncus aethusifolius*, with tiny creamy-white spires of flowers reminiscent of an astilbe, peeps out from under the mound of H. 'Francee'. *Heuchera cylindrica* 'Greenfinch' (*Heuchera* 'Green Ivory' would be equally effective) with its taller spikes of greenish bells completes the picture as it is far happier in cool, moisture retentive soil although it will grow in drier soils.

In a sheltered, moist, partially shaded corner *H. montana* 'Aureo-marginata' (this hosta is the first to emerge and can be damaged by frost) could be the focal plant for a late spring group with *Dicentra spectabilis* 'Alba' which seems to need moister soil than some of this family, *Primula* 'Dawn Ansell', a lovely double primrose that flowers for weeks in spring, *Geum rivale* 'Album', a diminutive water avens, and *Milium effusum* 'Aureum' (Bowles' golden grass). Astrantias, ferns, *Smilacina racemosa*, *Primula sieboldii* (preferably a white form) *Lilium martagon* 'Album' and *Kirengeshoma palmata* would all associate with the hostas for continued interest through the season. H. 'Ground Master' and H. 'Golden Scepter' could be used as edging hostas in generous numbers as these also emerge earlier than most.

A completely different effect is achieved by planting *H. sieboldiana* or one of the many other large blue hostas in generous drifts with *Astrantia maxima* which has glistening pink flowers, Solomon's seals, and pink and white astilbes (they flower for much longer in partial shade and do not need as much moisture as when planted in the sun). Plants for interest early in the season are plum-coloured *Helleborus orientalis*, *Ophiopogon planiscapus nigrescens* and pink

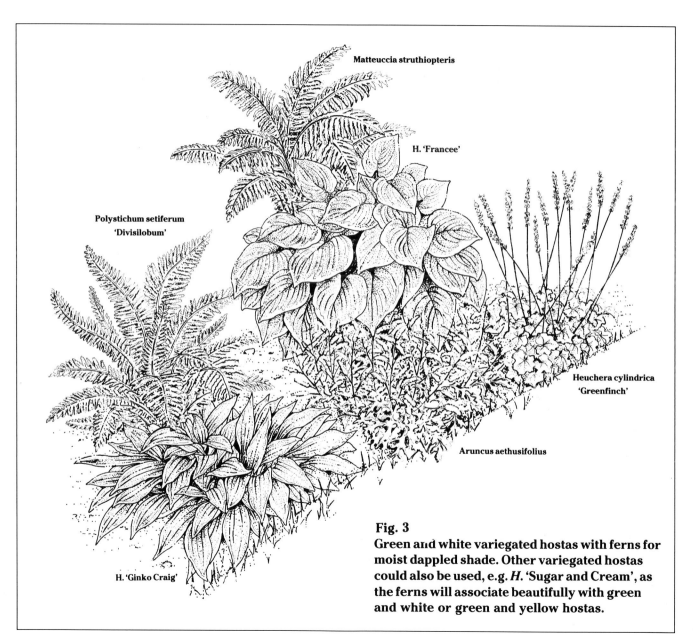

Matteuccia struthiopteris

H. 'Francee'

Polystichum setiferum
'Divisilobum'

Heuchera cylindrica
'Greenfinch'

Aruncus aethusifolius

H. 'Ginko Craig'

**Fig. 3**
Green and white variegated hostas with ferns for
moist dappled shade. Other variegated hostas
could also be used, e.g. *H.* 'Sugar and Cream', as
the ferns will associate beautifully with green
and white or green and yellow hostas.

erythroniums. *H.* 'Halcyon' underplanted with *Pulmonaria longifolia* or one of the newer very silvery pulmonarias such as *P. saccharata* 'Tim's Silver' and *Astrantia major* 'Rubra' could also weave in and out towards the front of the border. *Viola labradorica* with its small purple leaves and propensity for self-seeding is excellent for ground cover under the mounds of blue hostas, as are the tiarellas and *Ajuga reptans*.

Plants for vertical accents include bamboos such as *Phyllostachys nigra* and *Sinarundinaria nitida* (*Semiarundinaria nitida*) or, on a smaller scale, aruncus, cimicifugas, filipendulas and veratrums. The variegated hosta for this border could be *H.* 'Christmas Tree' planted in front of a group of *Veratrum nigrum*. The tall stems of near-black flowers would create a dramatic focal point in late summer and echo the purplish black tones of *Ajuga reptans* 'Atropurpurea', *Ophiopogon planiscapus nigrescens* and *Viola labradorica* which are used for ground cover. The hosta enthusiast could add many more smaller hostas with blue-green foliage such as *H.* 'Hadspen Blue', *H.* 'Blue Moon', *H.* 'Dorset Blue and *H.* 'Blue Boy' and a few with variegated leaves such as *H.* 'Frosted Jade' and *H.* 'Iona'.

## HOUSE BORDERS

Shady patios and corners of buildings need bold, architectural planting. It is often better to use only one hosta variety and to contrast this with other plants. If very dry the choice of plants is more restricted than if the moisture is adequate, but, as can be seen from the plants shown in Figure 2, there is still a good range to pick from.

The colour of the walls behind should be considered and often schemes of a restricted colour palette are the

**H. crispula with the rare orchid Dactylorhiza elata for a moist shady position.**

most effective. A large green hosta underplanted with *Polystichum setiferum* 'Divisilobum' and lily-of-the-valley with a backdrop of variegated green and white ivy creates a cool oasis against a red brick wall. A very simple little bed in the shady corner of two walls could be edged with box and planted with cimicifugas and *H.* 'Fringe Benefit' or with *Digitalis ambigua*, *H.* 'Shade Fanfare' and ferns.

Shady house borders are often the ideal place for a hosta and fern border, the individual plants being selected in relation to the dryness of the soil. Many ferns happily grow with hostas and provide delightful contrasts, so that both groups of plants are visually enhanced.

Fragrant hostas such as *H.* 'Royal Standard', *H.* 'Sugar and Cream', *H.* 'Summer Fragrance', and *H.* 'So Sweet', which form part of the planting shown in Figure 4, should be grown close to doors and windows so that they can be appreciated. Most of the newer scented hostas are happy in partial shade as they flower much earlier than *H. plantaginea*, which must have a very warm spot to flower and is not suitable for colder areas. Smaller-growing daffodils could be planted towards the back of the border, the unfurling shoots of the hostas hiding their leaves as they die down.

# Ponds and streams

Hostas look particularly effective near water and although they are not bog plants they will luxuriate just above this level, where their toes are in contact with a constant supply of water and the crowns are above the wet level so that they do not rot off. Many other large-leaved perennials need similar conditions and make excellent companion plants for hostas. The largest is *Gunnera manicata* but in a smaller garden

23

rheums, darmeras (peltiphyllums) or rodgersias could give a similar effect. Tall vertical accents are provided by grasses, sedges, ligularias, filipendulas and moisture-loving irises such as *I. laevigata*, *I. sibirica* and *I. pseudacorus* (see pages 28–9). Pink and white astilbes with large blue mounds of *H. sieboldiana* 'Elegans' is very effective. Waterside areas need lush planting – massed groups of a limited range of plants is far more effective than many ones or twos, a principle which applies as much to a large lake as to a tiny garden pond.

Most bog plants grow in full sun or partial shade but with a few exceptions the hostas are happier with some shade. Therefore it is better to choose strong-growing varieties and to plant them on the shady side of larger plants so that they will be protected from the intensity of the midday sun. The best hostas for standing up to the sun are the golds and a few green ones. Thick-textured golds such as *H.* 'Sum and Substance' and *H.* 'Midas Touch' will be happy in moist soil in all but the hottest climates but for the rest it is better to give them the filtered light of larger plants above the wettest level of the bog. Green hostas can be particularly good *en masse*, *H. undulata* 'Erromena',

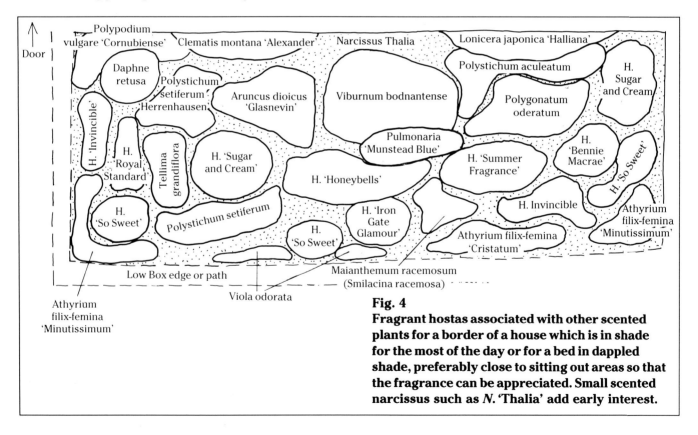

**Fig. 4**
**Fragrant hostas associated with other scented plants for a border of a house which is in shade for the most of the day or for a bed in dappled shade, preferably close to sitting out areas so that the fragrance can be appreciated. Small scented narcissus such as *N.* 'Thalia' add early interest.**

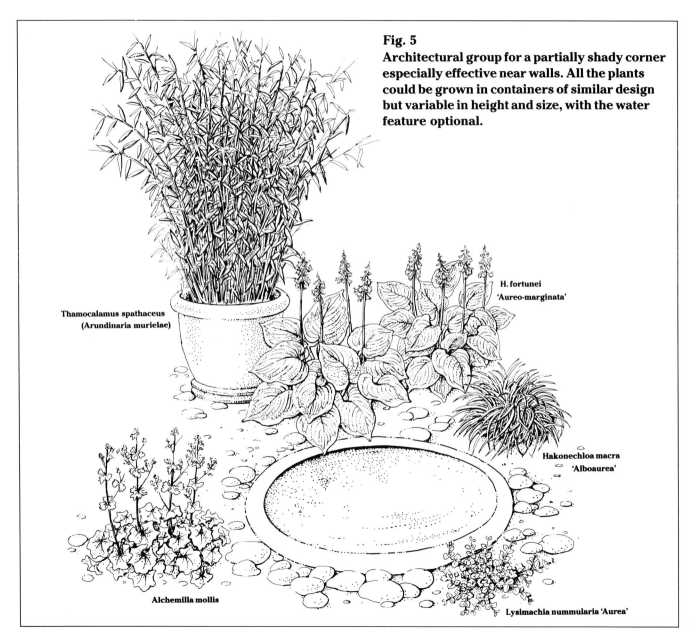

**Fig. 5**
**Architectural group for a partially shady corner especially effective near walls. All the plants could be grown in containers of similar design but variable in height and size, with the water feature optional.**

H. fortunei
'Aureo-marginata'

Thamocalamus spathaceus
(Arundinaria murielae)

Hakonechloa macra
'Alboaurea'

Alchemilla mollis

Lysimachia nummularia 'Aurea'

25

*H.* 'Tall Boy' and *H. montana* cooling down the brilliance of day lilies, primulas and astilbes.

Even without the advantage of a natural stream or a pond, there is no need to forgo the pleasure of associating hostas with water in your garden. A small dish filled with water or a large round boulder with a hole drilled in it for a fountain could be the focal point for a simple foliage group (Fig. 5). A bamboo planted in a container to restrict its spread can provide the backdrop to a group of *H. fortunei* 'Aureo-marginata' underplanted with *Alchemilla mollis* and the little gold-leaved creeper, *Lysimachia nummularia* 'Aurea', all mulched with small cobbles to help retain moisture and prevent damage by slugs and snails. *Ligularia przewalskii* 'The Rocket' could be used instead of the bamboo as long as there is sufficient moisture.

# Ground cover

Hostas are very useful under trees and shrubs as ground cover. They make dense clumps or spreading mats and can be left alone for many years. The best types are those with a vigorous habit; stoloniferous hostas are particularly useful for covering large areas. Aesthetically it looks far more effective to use a few varieties in large numbers than a vast medley in ones or twos. For shade and semi-shaded areas hostas are invaluable. They will happily grow where little else will and make excellent ground cover once established. For a balanced effect in the winter useful evergreen ground cover includes ajugas, bergenias, *Helleborus foetidus, Iris foetidissima,* pulmonarias, tellimas and tiarellas. Hostas that tolerate dry shade are particularly useful as the soil can often be dry under the higher foliage canopy.

Shrub roses can make quite dense canopies and colonies of hostas can exist happily underneath in the dappled shade. The blues are very effective with old roses, and large mounds of *H. sieboldiana* will hide the bare stems at the base of the roses, while complementing the flowers, especially the mauves, pinks and whites. On a smaller scale drifts of *H.* 'Halcyon' and hardy geraniums bring cohesion to the rose bed.

One of the most successful uses of hostas as ground cover is in areas of acid soil where they are used extensively under rhododendrons, pieris, camellias and other ericaceous shrubs. They will not only fill the spaces between the shrubs but, with other woodland plants, will extend the season of interest.

**Hostas useful for ground cover and mass planting**

| | |
|---|---|
| *clausa normalis* | 'Royal Standard' |
| *fortunei* (most) | 'Shade Fanfare' |
| 'Francee' | *sieboldiana* (and forms) |
| 'Fringe Benefit' | *sieboldii* |
| 'Gold Edger' | 'Sugar and Cream' |
| 'Ground Master' | 'Sum and Substance' |
| 'Hadspen Blue' | *undulata* 'Albo-marginata' |
| 'Halcyon' | *undulata* 'Erromena' |
| 'Honeybells' | *undulata* 'Univittata' |
| 'Invincible' | *ventricosa* |
| *lancifolia* | 'Wide Brim' |

Hostas can be left alone to mature and, other than initial establishment, the occasional feed and, if troubled by slugs and snails, the spreading of pellets, they will need no further attention for years.

**A damp border in the garden of John Newbold illustrating contrasts in form from *Rheum palmatum*, *Iris pseudacorus* 'Variegata' and *H. undulata* 'Albo-marginata' ('Thomas Hogg').**

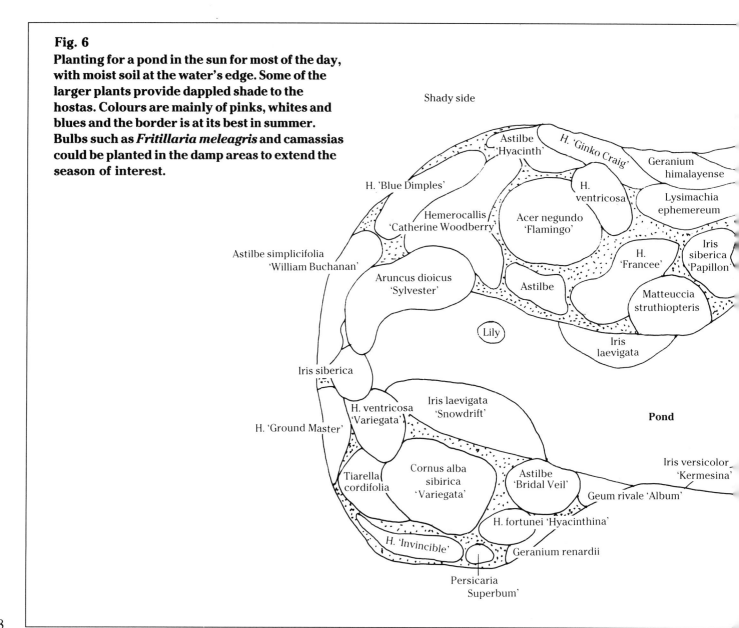

**Fig. 6**
**Planting for a pond in the sun for most of the day, with moist soil at the water's edge. Some of the larger plants provide dappled shade to the hostas. Colours are mainly of pinks, whites and blues and the border is at its best in summer. Bulbs such as *Fritillaria meleagris* and camassias could be planted in the damp areas to extend the season of interest.**

Shady side

Astilbe 'Hyacinth'

H. 'Ginko Craig'

Geranium himalayense

H. 'Blue Dimples'

H. ventricosa

Lysimachia ephemereum

Hemerocallis 'Catherine Woodberry'

Acer negundo 'Flamingo'

Astilbe simplicifolia 'William Buchanan'

H. 'Francee'

Iris siberica 'Papillon'

Aruncus dioicus 'Sylvester'

Astilbe

Matteuccia struthiopteris

Lily

Iris laevigata

Iris siberica

H. ventricosa 'Variegata'

Iris laevigata 'Snowdrift'

Pond

H. 'Ground Master'

Iris versicolor 'Kermesina'

Tiarella cordifolia

Cornus alba sibirica 'Variegata'

Astilbe 'Bridal Veil'

Geum rivale 'Album'

H. fortunei 'Hyacinthina'

H. 'Invincible'

Geranium renardii

Persicaria Superbum'

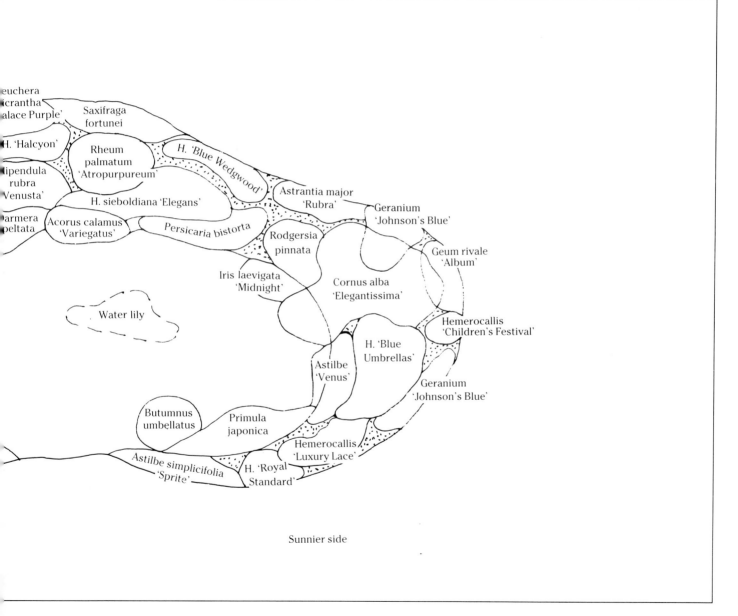

euchera
icrantha
alace Purple'

H. 'Halcyon'

ipendula
rubra
'Venusta'

armera
peltata

Saxifraga
fortunei

Rheum
palmatum
'Atropurpureum'

H. sieboldiana 'Elegans'

Acorus calamus
'Variegatus'

H. 'Blue Wedgwood'

Persicaria bistorta

Astrantia major
'Rubra'

Rodgersia
pinnata

Iris laevigata
'Midnight'

Geranium
'Johnson's Blue'

Geum rivale
'Album'

Cornus alba
'Elegantissima'

Water lily

Hemerocallis
'Children's Festival'

H. 'Blue
Umbrellas'

Astilbe
'Venus'

Geranium
'Johnson's Blue'

Butumnus
umbellatus

Primula
japonica

Astilbe simplicifolia
'Sprite'

H. 'Royal
Standard'

Hemerocallis
'Luxury Lace'

Sunnier side

29

# Alpine beds

The shady parts of rock gardens and raised beds make excellent sites for many of the smaller-growing and often not very vigorous hostas. Most would be completely lost in the larger border and need to be seen in closer proximity for the beauty of their leaves and flowers to be appreciated. Alpine beds are often covered in chippings and this can help to give a cool root run and reduce the problem of slugs and snails. They generally need a fair amount of shade and will often grow happily in a rocky crevice where they can look particularly effective. Most need to be established in pots and with the very small ones it is advisable to keep a piece growing in a pot to guard against loss, whether from slugs, unseasonal weather or accidental removal in winter when weeding.

Small ferns, hepaticas, mossy saxifrages, cyclamens, erythroniums, trilliums and a host of other shade-loving alpines are complemented by the addition of hostas, the choice being determined by the degree of moisture in the soil.

**Smaller hostas generally under 25 cm (10 in) in height**

'Amanuma'
'Blond Elf'
'Blue Blush'
'Blue Moon'
'Blue Skies'
'Carrie Ann'
'Celebration'

'Chartreuse Wiggles'
'Dawn' ('Sunset') (see 'Hydon Sunset'*)
'Dorset Blue'
'Duchess'
'Elfin Power'
'Fresh'
'Ginko Craig'
'Goldbrook Grace'
'Golden Prayers'
'Green with Envy' (see 'Hydon Sunset'*)
'Hadspen Heron'
'Hakujima' (see 'Saishu Jima'*)
'Harmony'
'Hydon Sunset'
'Lemon Lime'
'Little Aurora' (see 'Golden Prayers'*)
'Little White Lines'
*minor*
'Pixie Power' (see 'Elfin Power'*)
'Royalty'
'Saishu Jima'
'Shining Tot'
*sieboldii* (most forms)
'Squiggles' (see *H. sieboldii* 'Shiro-kabitan'*)
*tardiflora*
'Thumb Nail' (see *H. venusta*\*)
'Tiny Tears'
'Vanilla Cream'
*venusta*
*venusta* 'Variegated'

*in Plant Directory, pages 58–94

**A fragrant group suitable for a partially shady house border. *H.* 'So Sweet' (white flowers) and *H.* 'Iron Gate Glamour' with ferns and *Pachysandra terminalis* 'Green Carpet'.**

31

# The Importance of Colour in Garden Design

The more subdued palette is far more effective in creating areas of tranquillity; part of a garden or a border can be planted in individual colour schemes to achieve this. The white garden is in fashion at the moment, often in a separate enclosure delineated by yew hedges to intensify the paleness of the flowers. A blue scheme allows the eye to recede, making a garden seem larger, whereas red immediately draws the eye – a red border is exciting but not tranquil.

The main quality of most foliage plants is that they are restful and create peaceful gardens. Hostas are not brash plants and generally look far more effective when planted within a scheme using a limited colour range, although the plainer-leaved ones are valuable in toning down fussy borders and bringing discipline into the garden.

Different colour schemes can be used in the same area by planting for a winter and summer effect, the bright spring garden of hellebores, pulmonarias and bulbs becoming a cool oasis of greens and creams when the light of the summer becomes more intense. The subdued light of a low sun is totally different from the harsher effect of the midsummer rays, and canopies of summer foliage will soften and filter. Colour varies from season to season, day to day, hour by hour and even from person to person: colour is a subjective thing. The interplay of light on hosta foliage changes with the texture or colour of the plant, and some colours work far better with each other – the greys and blues with shades of pink, and whites or yellow with blues and white.

## USING VARIEGATED LEAVES

Many hostas have variegated leaves, the edges can be green, blue, yellow, cream or white, the centres the same colours and they can be in nearly every combination. If you need a gold centre with a green margin, H. 'Gold Standard' or H. 'September Sun' would be suitable, if a blue edged in creamy yellow is required, then H. 'Frances Williams' would be perfect.

Variegated leaves are dominant and must be used with care; they need plain neighbours or those that echo the colour scheme. Too much variegation gives a jumbled up hodge podge, the eye does not know where to focus, but a single green and white hosta rising from a mass of filigree ferns is restful. Sometimes within a limited spectrum variegation used in different scales is very effective. Try H. undulata 'Albo-marginata' (H. 'Thomas Hogg') against Euonymus fortunei 'Emerald Gaiety', the larger leaf of the hosta echoed by the much smaller leaf of the shrub. This contrast in size or shape is very important when mixing variegated plants together. A backdrop of gold-edged ivy leaves clothing a wall would be complemented by a hosta with gold variegation but not by H. 'Francee' which has a very crisp white edge.

White variegated hostas are best not used with yellow or yellow-variegated ones as the whole effect is dissipated, although schemes using hostas which are yellow edged in spring, then cream- or white-edged later, can be devised, the yellow tones echoing the spring garden and the whiter ones the summer effect.

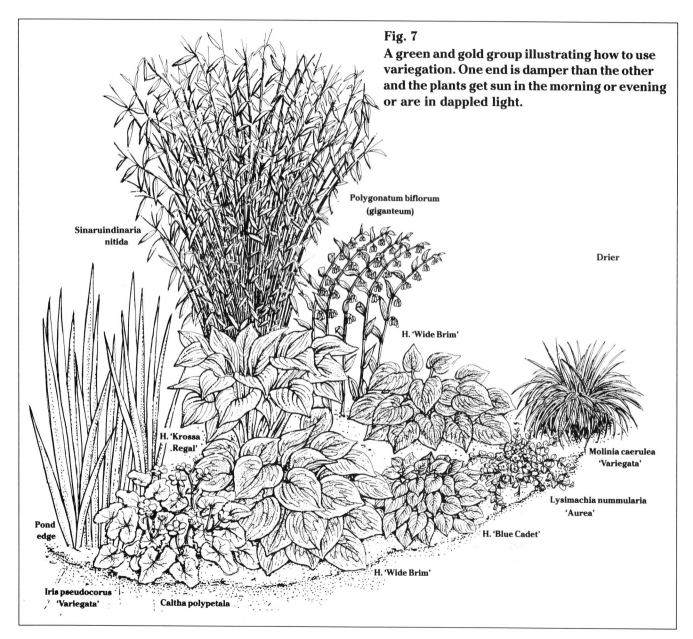

**Fig. 7**
**A green and gold group illustrating how to use variegation. One end is damper than the other and the plants get sun in the morning or evening or are in dappled light.**

Sinaruindinaria nitida

Polygonatum biflorum (giganteum)

Drier

H. 'Wide Brim'

H. 'Krossa Regal'

Molinia caerulea 'Variegata'

Lysimachia nummularia 'Aurea'

H. 'Blue Cadet'

Pond edge

H. 'Wide Brim'

Iris pseudocorus 'Variegata'

Caltha polypetala

It is the hosta that has strong white variegation all season that needs some plain neighbours and to be associated with plants that have white, not yellow variegation.

Variegated plants are not a panacea for interesting gardens. Used carefully they make focal points and can look very effective but used indiscriminately they often look a mess. White flowers with white variegation or yellow spires with gold variegation are complementary: *Ligularia prewalckii* 'The Rocket' planted with *H. fortunei* 'Aureo-marginata' and *Iris pseudacorus* 'Variegata' is a very dramatic and successful group. In summer the tall, black-stemmed yellow spires of the ligularia intensify the gold margin on the hosta as the gold stripes of the iris are beginning to fade to green. Earlier, the most dominant plant would have been the iris, its vividly striped gold and green leaves seen against the cut-leaved mound of the green ligularia and the rounded form of the hosta. A far more subtle effect is *Aruncus dioicus* 'Glasnevin' planted with *H.* 'Sugar and Cream'. The green of both plants leans towards the yellow, the flowering spires of the aruncus are not pure white but have creamy undertones as does the margin of the hosta, so both plants complement each other perfectly.

Figure 7 is an example of how to use variegated plants and it would be equally suitable for a border with a gold and green theme. The bed is in partial shade, one end bordering a pond or with an area of boggy soil which is planted with *Iris pseudacorus* 'Variegata' and *Caltha polypetala*, the plain green round leaves perfectly accentuating the iris. *H.* 'Wide Brim' with creamy gold bands has very similar varieg-

**A superb clump of *H. sieboldiana* 'Elegans' with lush moisture-loving perennials in the garden of Derek Fox in Essex.**

ation to the iris but in a completely different leaf form and it also has plain neighbours, the vase-shaped *H.* 'Krossa Regal', the arching bamboo and, for earlier interest, the giant Solomon's seal bedecked with bells of greeny white flowers and a similar habit, but on a smaller scale, to the bamboo. As the season advances the creamy yellow edge of the hosta becomes lighter, accentuating the striped cream and green leaves of the molinia and setting off its airy panicles to perfection.

Although molinias are usually grown in full sun, they are perfectly happy in dappled light as long as they get sun for part of the day and, like hostas, they do better in fertile soil. Their variegation is particularly effective with a range of variegated hostas that have creamy yellow margins such as *H.* 'Shade Fanfare' and *H. fluctuans* 'Variegated'.

# White gardens

Hostas with white in their foliage grow far better in the shade, and therefore even in quite dark corners a lightening effect can be created. They will usually flower sparsely so that even the purist will have few flower stems to cut off if they are of the wrong tone. Some hostas have white flowers but when designing with them it is the colour of the foliage that must be of prime importance: a large gold mound with white blooms would be discordant in a green and white or grey and white scheme, whereas *H.* 'Francee', which is not white flowering but has excellent green and white foliage, would look far more effective in such a scheme. Blue-grey foliage is often part of a white garden and therefore most blue hostas are useful; some even have white flowers.

Even within white gardens there are subtle tones of other colours – few white flowers are paper white;

35

most have tints of yellow, pink or blue and hostas can be selected to pick up the different shades, using blue foliage with lavender and pinky tones or greens and creams with the yellow-tinged whites. In shadier places hostas are invaluable; they are the ideal companions for a wide range of white-flowering perennials such as *Dicentra spectabilis* 'Alba', *Pulmonaria* 'Sissinghurst White', *Astrantia major* 'Shaggy', *Polygonatum falcatum* 'Variegatum' and *Chelone obliqua* 'Alba' to name but a few. When well grown, *H. crispula*, with its lovely undulating white-margined,

green leaves planted with Solomon's seal and lily-of-the-valley is a picture. *Miscanthus sinsensis* 'Variegatus', with its green and white arching foliage, *Iris foetidissima* 'Variegata' and *Iris foetidissima* 'Fructo-alba' bedecked in autumn with delightful white fruit, could be added to provide invaluable vertical accents. *H.* 'Snowden' and the scented *H.* 'Royal Standard' are two of the best of the white-flowering hostas to plant in drifts.

Figure 8 is a very simple but effective white and green foliage scheme in a shady corner. A small group

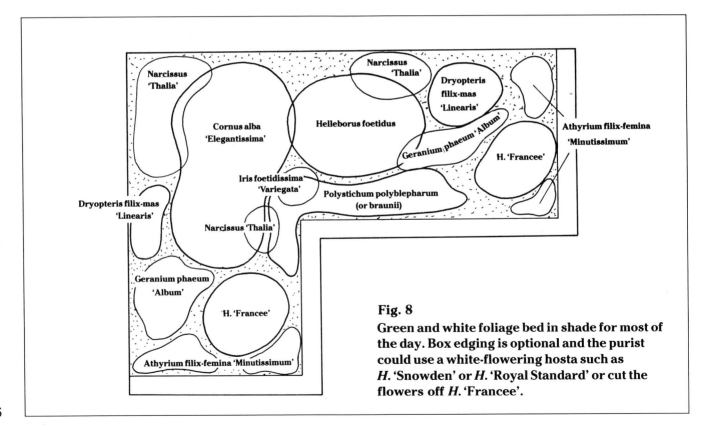

**Fig. 8**
**Green and white foliage bed in shade for most of the day. Box edging is optional and the purist could use a white-flowering hosta such as *H.* 'Snowden' or *H.* 'Royal Standard' or cut the flowers off *H.* 'Francee'.**

of *Cornus alba* 'Elegantissima' is underplanted with *Helleborus foetidus*, the red stems of the shrub contrasting with the red rims of the flowers of the hellebore in early spring. *Narcissus* 'Thalia', a delightful fragrant daffodil, flowers just as the leaves of the hostas are starting to emerge, *H.* 'Francee' has pronounced reddish shoots on emergence and as the cornus becomes covered in green and white leaves, the hosta pushes up its foliage mound of green and white. The ferns give contrasts in leaf form and *Geranium phaeum album* carries light airy white flowers in summer.

### White- or near white-flowered hostas suitable for a white garden

'Blue Angel'
'Blue Seer' (see *H. sieboldiana* 'Elegans'\*)
'Carrie Ann'
'Emerald Isle' (see *H. sieboldii*\*)
*kikutii* 'Pruinose'
'Louisa' (see *H.* sieboldii\*)
'Love Pat'
'Osprey'
*plantaginea*
'Royal Standard'
'Sea Lotus Leaf'
*sieboldiana* (some)
*sieboldii* 'Alba'
'Snow Cap'
'Snowden'
'Snowflakes' (see *H. sieboldii* 'Alba'\*)
'So Sweet'
'Sugar and Cream'
*tokudama*

\* in Plant Directory, pages 58–94

# Green gardens

There are many different shades of green: *H. montana* has large shiny leaves, *H.* 'Black Hills' comes with very dark, seersuckered foliage and *H.* 'Jade Scepter' is a pale chartreuse. A predominantly green foliage scheme relies on contrasts of leaf form for the different effects, and vertical accents from plants such as day lilies, irises and grasses are very important. Leaves will dominate the scheme although flowers are perfectly acceptable. Green borders can be very restful, especially near buildings or in shady corners. Bricks, paving cobbles and wood are complemented by the simplicity of a green scheme but the foliage must be interesting.

The summer effect could include hostas, alchemillas, ferns, ligularias, bamboos and grasses with evergreen effects from *Itea ilicifolia*, *Osmanthus heterophyllus*, *Viburnum tinus*, hellebores, liriopes, pachysandras and sarcococcas. If the soil is acid rhododendrons, camellias and *Trochodendron aralioides* will also flourish. Many of these plants have greenish flowers and this can further exploit the green theme.

Imagine a backdrop of *Garrya elliptica*, *Hedera colchica* 'Paddy's Pride' and *Hydrangea petiolaris*, with evergreen interest from *Daphne laureola*, *Helleborus corsicus*, green and white shades of *Helleborus orientalis* and the shiny green foliage of *Iris foetidissima*. The green stems of *Cornus stolonifera* 'Flavirama' could be underplanted with *Narcissus cyclamineus* 'Jenny' and *H. fortunei* 'Aureomarginata'. *Liriope muscari*, *Ajuga reptans* 'Alba', mitellas, asarums and smaller-growing bergenias would serve to clothe the spaces between the smaller hostas. *Dryopteris filix-mas* 'Linearis', with its slender, erect, finely cut fronds and *Digitalis lutea*, a perennial foxglove with small creamy yellow flowers, would be the perfect foil to the hostas. The border is subdued, an oasis of green.

# Gold gardens

The best-known gold-leaved hosta is *H. fortunei* 'Aurea' which, although yellow in spring, fades to green with maturity. Most of the newer gold hostas stay gold all season. They need some sun to colour but not too much – dappled light is ideal. Without any protection they will scorch and become papery white, while in too much shade they will turn chartreuse. Sometimes this colour is very useful in deep shade as it gives a lightening effect and gold hostas can be planted in shade to achieve it. As a general rule the thicker the leaf then the more sun they need to colour. *H.* 'Sum and Substance', *H.* 'Midas Touch', *H.* 'Gold Edger', *H.* 'Golden Medallion' and *H.* 'Gold Regal' will all grow in sunny spots, in all but the hottest climates as long as the site is moist, but *H.* 'Piedmont Gold' with its thinner leaf texture must have some shade.

A border of only gold hostas would be monotonous but used with green and green and gold variegation they can be effective. There are many yellow-flowering plants that associate with hostas, particularly hemerocallis, ligularias, alchemillas, and some irises. Figure 9 is a scheme for a moist bed in dappled shade, perhaps on the edge of a pond, or the planting could be adapted to a formal design for a courtyard garden. Most of the plants except for the hostas will also grow in sun as long as the soil is damp and this can be exploited by planting the hostas on the shady side of the *Ligularia przewalskii* 'The Rocket' and the *Miscanthus sinensis* 'Zebrinus'. *Cortaderia selloana* 'Gold Band' would be equally effective although it needs more sun than the miscanthus.

The ligularia has an excellent mound of large, round, serrated green leaves and in late summer very tall black stems carry bright yellow flowers, a dramatic accent plant in a bog garden or near a formal pond in a modern setting, perhaps mulched with large cobbles. It is the perfect foil to *H.* 'Gold Standard', which needs some shade so that it does not scorch but if the light is too poor it will not colour. *Alchemilla mollis*, an invaluable plant with rounded velvety leaves, on a smaller scale than the ligularia, has sprays of lime green flowers for weeks in midsummer. Its tendency to self seed can be exploited, letting it weave in and out of the border. The graceful mound of the miscanthus has the gold bands on its narrow green leaves emphasized by the two gold hostas. In a formal scheme these could be planted as a separate group with alchemillas and day lilies and covered in cobbles. Golden daffodils and winter aconites would provide early interest.

A mixed planting of green and gold would be effective for a bed which has sun in the morning or the evening. *Cornus alba* 'Aurea', *Iris foetidissima* and *Bergenia* 'Bressingham White' would all provide winter interest before the hostas emerge in the spring. *H.* 'Sum and Substance', a strong architectural mound could be used as a specimen. Other large, gold hostas could include *H.* 'Sea Gold Star', *H.* 'Midas Touch' and *H.* 'Zounds'. (*H. tokudama* 'Aureo-nebulosa' and *H.* 'Frances Williams' could be included but it is important that the variegation should not be dominant.) *H.* 'Golden Prayers', *H.* 'Gold Edger' and *H.* 'Hydon Sunset' would all contribute as edgers and gound cover. *Alchemilla xanthochlora*, greener and smaller growing than *A. mollis*, would contrast perfectly with *H.* 'Chinese Sunrise' while the slight green tone inside the white border of *H.* 'Moonlight' could be accented by the dark, glossy fronds of *Polystichum braunii*.

**H. 'Gold Standard', excellent in the garden and in a pot. It should be positioned so that it receives just enough sun to colour, but not enough to scorch.**

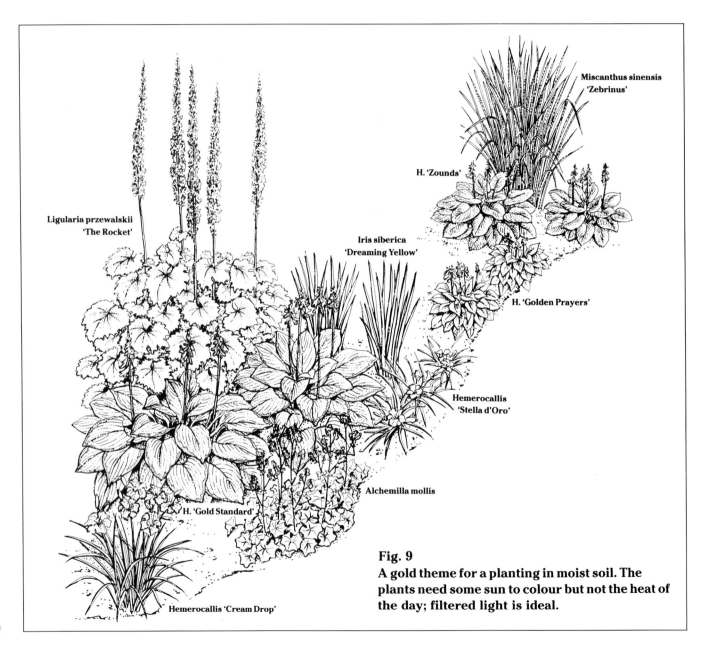

Miscanthus sinensis
'Zebrinus'

H. 'Zounds'

Ligularia przewalskii
'The Rocket'

Iris siberica
'Dreaming Yellow'

H. 'Golden Prayers'

Hemerocallis
'Stella d'Oro'

Alchemilla mollis

H. 'Gold Standard'

Hemerocallis 'Cream Drop'

**Fig. 9**
**A gold theme for a planting in moist soil. The plants need some sun to colour but not the heat of the day; filtered light is ideal.**

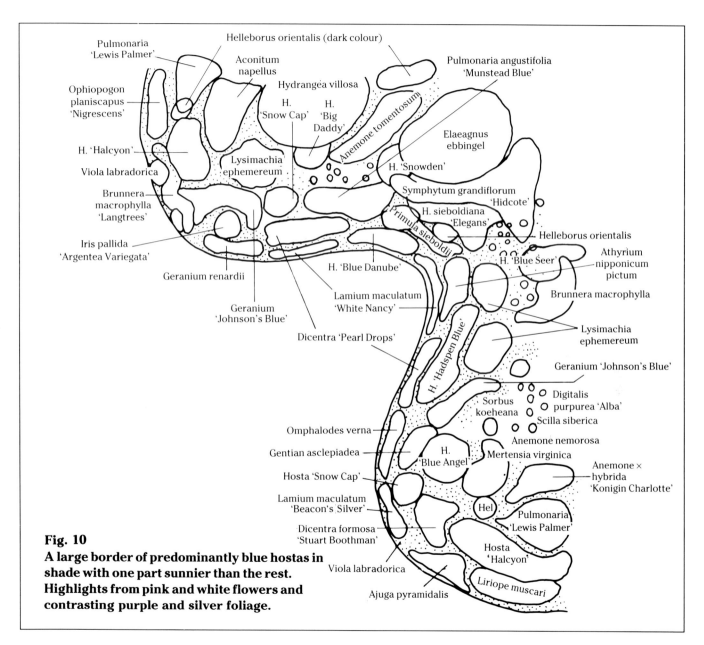

**Fig. 10**
**A large border of predominantly blue hostas in shade with one part sunnier than the rest. Highlights from pink and white flowers and contrasting purple and silver foliage.**

# Blue gardens

There are many excellent blue-foliaged hostas, but they need to grow in partial or full shade to maintain their colour. Planted in full sun they will be green by the end of the season as the surface coating on the leaf will have disappeared. In cool areas blue hostas will often retain their colour to the end of the season and the hotter the climate the more shade they will need to stay blue. The choice of plain blue hostas is wide-ranging, but those with variegation are as yet few. The best known is *H.* 'Frances Williams' but others to look out for include *H. tokudama* 'Aureo-nebulosa', *H.* 'Regal Splendor', *H.* 'Snow Cap', and *H.* 'Pizzazz'.

The effect of blue foliage is rather different from a blue sunny border where flowers predominate and the composition is tempered by airy flowers and spires. Blue foliage needs contrasts in colour such as *H.* 'Halcyon' planted with *Heuchera micrantha* 'Palace Purple' and *Ajuga pyramidalis* 'Metallica Crispa' or contrast in form such as from *Liriope muscari*, the blue flower spikes and strappy leaves perfectly set off by the rounded mounds of the hostas. *Lysimachia ephemereum*, not always the easiest plant to place, reveals its refined beauty in association with blue hostas and with *Athyrium niponicum pictum*, its lacy fronds tinged with greys and purples. Whites, pinks, lilacs and purples lighten the effect as do golds and whites in a blue-gold scheme.

In Figure 10 *Elaeagnus ebbingei* provides an evergreen silvery green backdrop, while the bluish-tinged pinnate leaves of the sorbus and the hydrangea's felted greyish foliage complement the lower level. The spring-flowering perennials such as pulmonarias, hellebores and scillas as well as those for the later season such as aconitums are planted towards the back of the border. Blue-foliaged hostas, white foxgloves and lilies dominate the summer scene. Ideally this type of planting needs to be able to be viewed from a distance, the blues and whites in a glade of evergreen shrubs and deciduous trees, against a shady wall covered in greenery or a yew hedge. Many of the plants are allowed to intermingle, dicentras skirting the unfurling leaves of the hostas and as they die down the willow gentian (*Gentiana asclepiadea*), aconitums and *Anemone tomentosa* 'Robustissima' take their place.

The spring garden could be further enlivened by golden daffodils and often the most successful effects are achieved by an early blue and gold garden giving way to blues, purples, pinks and white. Schemes with blue need fine tuning as the effect of light can intensify or dissipate the many shades. Some blues look wonderful together and others do not work at all. The inclusion of flowers of different hues and generous groups of hostas will usually bring cohesion, the hostas acting as foils and links to any discordant elements among the other plants.

**Complete ground cover, the blueness of
*H.* 'Halcyon' intensified by the green and gold.**

# The Use of Hostas as Container Plants

Most hostas make superb pot plants, complementing a wide range of ornamental containers. I have been growing considerable numbers of specimen hostas in containers for many years, mainly for exhibiting, and have developed a love-hate relationship with a few of them. Some grow better in pots than in the garden but others are certainly a problem to maintain after the first four or five years.

Great care should go not only into the selection of the hosta but into the container and the position in the garden. Regardless of the ornamental container used it is far easier to grow a hosta in a plastic pot of a size relevant to the growth of the plant, and to put this inside a decorative container, with cobbles or some other medium placed over the pot to hide the inner container. In winter the hosta can be removed and something more interesting put in its place. If repotting or other care is required this is much easier to carry out from a cheap plastic pot than trying to remove a specimen from what could be a very valuable container.

Ideally the hosta needs to be in a place out of the wind and not in the heat of the sun; early morning or evening sun is far less damaging and some even need it to colour. A solitary pot is more prone to the elements as it does not have the protection of neighbouring plants. Containers can be placed anywhere in the garden, but tend to be near the house as this simplifies watering.

Hostas with cascading mounds are particularly effective and can often stand alone or as a pair to emphasize a particular feature. *H.* 'Green Fountain' looks very elegant, its shape shown off to perfection in a pot, but it needs plenty of room or will be easily damaged. Others need to be placed in groups, each plant carefully chosen to set off its neighbour. The backdrop should always be considered as part of the scheme. *H.* 'Gold Standard' will make a superb specimen in a large container. Green on unfurling and brilliant gold with a green rim if given dappled light later on in the season, it could look spectacular placed against a green background or dark coloured brick walls. But near a pink colour-washed wall it would be horrendous; far better to use a plain green or blue variety in this situation – *H.* 'Snowden', with large grey-green leaves and lovely white flowers would not be out of place and it seems to grow better in a large container than in the ground.

Variegated hostas need the same care in placing as they do in the garden. The easiest are those with white variegation – *H.* 'Francee' grows very well in a container and will look good against most backgrounds – but green and yellow or blue and yellow variegation need far more thought. Generally it is better to have only one variety in a pot and if it is felt that the container is large enough for other plants to be included then these must be chosen with care. Small ferns, creeping Jenny, periwinkles or trailing ivies will all complement the hosta.

Gold hostas are not the easiest to place and some do not grow well in pots other than in the short term. *H.* 'Sum and Substance', with enormous chartreuse-gold leaves like dinner plates, could look sumptuous against a bamboo in a corner that gets some sun as long as the container is simple and of large dimensions.

Town gardens often have shady corners or even areas where no sun penetrates; the soil if there is any, is often very poor and the only satisfactory way to grow plants is in containers. They may range from tiny pots to large raised beds. Hostas are the ideal plants for these gardens, especially in association with other shade-loving plants such as ferns, bamboos, cut-leaf acers, and large-leaved evergreens. The most popular container hosta in Japan is *H. fluctuans* 'Variegated', still rare in the west but spectacular in a large round glazed pot, an excellent focal point in a courtyard.

Containers do not have to be limited to pots: special planters made from brick, railway sleepers or timber can be an integral part of a terrace area. These should be treated the same way as a small border and are only suitable for hostas if in shade for the hottest part of the day. On a much smaller scale a deep stone sink is suitable for the tiny hostas.

When the area to plant is small a careful choice of the plant material and containers must be made. Containers need to be balanced not only with the hostas but with each other. Containers can soften modern architecture and, when used with discretion, complement period buildings, but too many styles and different materials filled with a medley of plants is just as lacking in cohesion as a similar planting in the garden.

Effective little groups can be made by standing the pots on cobbles or by incorporating small water features such as that shown in Fig. 5. (page 25). Fragrant varieties such as *H.* 'Summer Fragrance', *H.* 'So Sweet', *H.* 'Invincible', and *H.* 'Sugar and Cream' grow particularly well in large containers and if placed near sitting out areas, the air will be deliciously scented in late summer when they come into bloom.

Hostas in containers are far more demanding of regular attention than in the ground (see next chapter for cultivation advice) but this can pay dividends especially in early years, when a suitable pot-grown plant will grow far better than one of a similar size planted in the ground. Nearly all except those with *H. sieboldiana* and *H. tokudama* in their parentage grow well in pots.

The following hostas are particularly recommended for pots, some growing better in a container than in the ground.

| | |
|---|---|
| *fortunei* (all) | *lancifolia* (and forms) |
| 'Francee' | *minor* |
| 'Goldbrook' | *nakaiana* (and related |
| 'Gold Standard' | hybrids) |
| 'Golden Prayers' | 'Reversed' |
| 'Golden Tiara' | *sieboldii* (and related |
| 'Green Fountain' | hybrids) |
| 'Halcyon' | 'Snowden' |
| 'Hydon Sunset' | 'So Sweet' |
| 'Invincible' | 'Summer Fragrance' |
| *kikutii* (and forms) | *undulata* (all) |
| 'Krossa Regal' | |

## Hostas for flower arrangers

Most hostas are useful in flower arrangements, but some are better than others, as very thin leaves are hard to condition and do not last as long in water. The choice is wide but for a basic collection most arrangers like a variety of leaf sizes and colours. Many grow their plants in pots as it is certainly easier to be sure of a supply of undamaged leaves, so necessary for floral work.

The same principles of colour, shape and texture apply in an arrangement as in the garden. It is usually

better to use the foliage of one hosta variety than many different ones, and the simplicity of the leaf is an excellent foil to frilly flowers.

All parts of a hosta can be used, the leaves, flowers and seed heads, although to most arrangers it is the foliage that is of paramount importance. It is always better to pick material early in the morning or late in the evening and to immerse the stems, cut on the slant, in water placed in a cool place until they are needed. The leaves can even be completely immersed in water for short periods without coming to any harm. Flowers and seeds heads can also be dried or preserved in silica gel. Some, such as *H.* 'Christmas Tree', have black seed pods and others, such as *H.* 'Celebration', are red; these could also be varnished for winter arrangements.

Hostas described in the Plant Directory (see pages 58–94) which are particularly suitable for floral work are marked with an asterisk (although not all are yet readily available).

**A white garden group on the stand of Goldbrook Plants at Chelsea 1991. *H.* 'Gloriosa' (with the narrow white edge) and *H.* 'Ginko Craig' are the perfect complement for *Zantedeschia aethiopica* 'Crowborough'.**

# Cultivation

## In the garden

In earlier chapters we have looked at the requirements of shade and moisture for hostas when grown to perfection. Hostas grown in less than ideal conditions can still make satisfactory garden plants, but some effort is amply repaid. Once a strong root system is established, many hostas will stand a surprising amount of neglect. They are long-lived, relatively easy to cultivate and can be left undivided for many years.

### PLANTING OUT

Hostas are dormant in the winter and although they can be moved and planted nearly all the year round as long as care is taken, the ideal time is in the spring when the new shoots are about to emerge and new roots will quickly establish as the soil warms up. Planting in autumn in moist soil before the advent of frosts is successful with strong vigorous divisions, but not to be recommended for those that need more attention to establish themselves well. It is far better to leave these in a greenhouse or cold frame so that they do not become frosted and rot off.

Pot-grown plants are often easier to establish and the effort of potting on new divisions, especially if very small, and giving them optimum care for a year or two can result in far better plants in a shorter time. Very small-growing hostas and those that are highly variegated and lack chlorophyll, especially if expensive, should always be grown on for a year or two.

Hostas bought in pots can be planted all through the summer months as long as they are kept watered. The advantage of doing this is that because they are planted in leaf they are more likely to be in the right place in the scheme and the effect is immediate. Once planted they should be left alone to mature. It takes time for the mature leaf form to develop and constant splitting up or disturbance means that some gardeners never appreciate the beauty of a mature clump.

### SOILS AND SITES

Hostas prefer free-draining but moisture-retentive soil with adequate organic matter. The most difficult soils are those that are sandy or solid clay; the ideal is a rich loam. Neutral to slightly acidic soils result in the most luxuriant leaf colour, especially for green- and blue-leaved hostas, but as long as the soil is not thin, overlying chalk, hostas will grow happily in limey soils. Sandy soils need an abundance of organic matter to be added and clay benefits from being opened up to improve the drainage; digging in pea shingle and adding manure will in time result in a very satisfactory planting medium for hostas as clay soils are usually fertile and once the roots are established sufficient moisture is usually available.

Peaty loams or even free-draining raised beds which have adequate moisture and are not in the baking sun make ideal homes for many of the smaller and often stoloniferous hostas.

Large, strong-growing hostas need more soil preparation than tiny varieties. The planting hole should relate in size to the vigour of the hosta, and an adequate provision of manure or compost added. The newly planted hosta does not want to come into direct contact with the organic matter as too much feed before the plant has grown can result in brown, soft leaves and even death if the cell structure is destroyed. Organic matter is best placed in the bottom of the hole with a layer of loam, leaf mould or a proprietary compost placed over it. If the hosta is an open-ground division then it should be spread over a slight mound, the roots spread out with the crown near the surface and firmed in.

If planting from a container, freeing some of the roots, especially if curling round in the pot, helps establishment. A slight mound is not required but firming in is important. It should be planted at the same level as in the container. After watering in, mulching will help to retain moisture and in the first season of growth it is important that the plant continues to have adequate moisture. Drooping leaves tell their own story but young plants do not want to be drowned.

Failing a supply of organic matter hostas can be planted in good quality compost, ideally one that has a rough structure, and fed on a great variety of fertilizers and foliar feeds. It is best to remove flower scapes from young plants so that all the plant's energy can go into making a good root system.

### FEEDING

Hostas grow much faster if they are fed and watered regularly. Feeding in the early days should be little and often, such as a fortnightly feed of Phostrogen at half strength or, if in areas of limey water, a liquid feed containing iron. A very easy way to make sure the plant has adequate feed is to incorporate slow-release pellets in the compost in the planting hole, but never exceed the stated dose – very few pellets are required. It is better to use less than the recommended dosage as too much feed to very young plants can be harmful. When established, especially if the hosta is large and vigorous, a mulch of well-rotted manure or compost in the autumn will be appreciated, but not over the crown which is better protected with a layer of bark or peat. The smaller the hosta the less food and water it

requires, but general conditions become more important. *H. sieboldiana* forms will happily grow in clay soils as long as the planting site is well-prepared, but the much smaller *H. venusta* would probably turn up its toes and die.

# Growing in containers

Cultivation of hostas in containers is slightly different from in the open ground, although some of the same principles apply. A newly acquired division or a small container-grown hosta must not be placed in an enormous pot as the closed environment of the container can often result in failure. Any container can be used as the final home as long as it is not shallow, drains well – root rot can cause just as many problems as a failure to water – and the planting medium it contains is open in structure, to allow the roots oxygen as well as water and nutrients.

### PLANTING UP AND POTTING ON

A proprietary coarse, peat-based compost containing 25% grit and slightly acidic is ideal, but home-made mixtures of rich loam mixed with peat, bark or leaf mould to which 25% grit or perlite has been added can be satisfactory as long as a feeding routine is followed. Up to a third of very old horse manure or garden compost can also be used in the formulation but it must be old and not fresh. The easiest way to feed is to incorporate slow-release pellets into the compost as the fertilizer is activated by water and warmth, the plant taking up the amounts it requires as it grows. Slow-release pellets need to be applied every spring but do not give more than the recommended dosage. Any additional feeding can be given in liquid form when watering, which should be into the compost and not on to the hosta leaves as these will mark.

If the compost is slightly lower than the top of the

pot, it is much easier to give a thorough soaking every other day or so. The compost should be moist but not saturated, and although rain will help to keep the leaves clean in periods of drought great care must be taken with overhead watering. It must be done when the sun is not out or there will be scorch damage; droplets of water on the leaves act like magnifying glasses and cause unsightly brown spots. Glaucous foliage suffers the most from watermarks, especially if the water is limey and it is not possible to remove the lime deposits without removing the surface bloom. If the water used is limey it may be necessary to counteract this by using products with extra iron in order that the compost does not become too alkaline. The health of the plant is not really affected, only its visual appearance, and the leaves, especially green ones, become rather pale.

## CONTAINERS

It is far easier to keep a hosta happy in a plastic pot as these retain moisture, and in the growing season it is very important that the container does not dry out; in a terracotta pot failure to water results in the porous pot taking the moisture out of the hosta's root system. If a large clump is to be planted in a container then the pot must obviously be of adequate size, but most people start with a newly acquired, relatively small plant, and this will grow much better if it is potted on in stages, rather than put in a large pot straight away.

This does not mean you cannot use that large decorative pot you want to place strategically in your garden, but you may need to place a smaller pot inside it for a year or so, and when the plant is nearly filling this with roots, move up to a larger size. This pot-within-a-pot arrangement may be the best of both worlds if a favoured decorative pot is of terracotta or other porous material, since as well as hiding a less attractive plastic pot, it also gives the hosta roots a non-porous home which will not leach precious moisture from them. Having a container within a container, with shingle or a similar medium filling the gap between the two also helps to create a humid environment and acts as a deterrent to slug and snail damage. A further advantage is that in winter it is very easy to lift out the hosta and use something in its place while the hosta is dormant. The hosta can be placed in a cold-frame, unheated garage or shed and nearly forgotten about until spring as it needs very little water and is best kept on the dry side, but it should not be allowed to dry out to the extent that the compost shrinks from the sides of the pot.

In areas of extreme frosts, hostas are often grown in containers which are planted in the ground and then removed to protected areas in the winter. It is very important that water does not come into direct contact with the crown of the containerized hosta when it is in the frozen state and some form of protection must be given such as a mulch and covering with plastic or frost cloth or it must be buried in the ground.

It is best not to place containers in too hot a position as they can rapidly heat up in summer and in extreme cases root damage can occur. The pot inside a pot should help to prevent this.

Potting on is best done in the spring and, if the plant has become pot-bound, root pruning will encourage new, younger feeding roots. Tip the plant out of the pot, lay it on its side and, with a sharp knife – a carving knife is ideal – cut a thin slice off the bottom. Unravel some of the stronger-growing roots and repot in new compost. As long as the knife is clean there should be no infection but a sound precaution is to clean the knife between dealing with each plant.

## DIAGNOSING PROBLEMS

Most hostas reach maturity after four or five years and even if the pot is large problems can develop with some varieties. Some hostas exhibit problems at a much earlier age than others and even in the same variety in the same sized container, given exactly the same cultural care, one can develop problems before another. Most hostas are perfectly happy in a large pot for a considerable number of years – in fact, some seem to grow better in pots. Observations from growing hostas for exhibiting over the past nine years indicate there is a general pattern but there will always be exceptions to the rule.

If your hosta appears to be late in emergence (remembering not all hostas come up at the same time) and the leaves appear small, possibly deformed, then it is time to investigate the root system. Take a knife and cut the rootstock in half, and you will probably find a very congested, hard root core. There will probably be two tiers of roots, the individual crowns are no longer able to make roots into the compost and if the divisions are pulled apart you will find under the crown a thick mass that is very hard and woody. Such a plant, if left alone, will just deteriorate and finally die, but if split up and repotted or the individual pieces planted in the garden, some, though probably not all, will recover and develop into healthy new plants. Root congestion like this can also happen in the ground if plants are neglected, although it is less common.

Sometimes part of the plant seems to be growing properly but the odd crown has leaves that are smaller and twisted, and if this plant is cut up as soon as is practical (it can be done in a greenhouse when the plant is growing), virtually all the individual pieces will recover and after a season or so return to normal.

If the roots have rotted off this again can indicate that the crowns are congested but also may be caused by other problems such as pests and diseases. When dealing with the individual pieces it is important to remove any damage and cut away any rot. A dose of fungicide can be beneficial before repotting.

Very strong-growing hostas are the most difficult to grow long term in containers; they will never reach full maturity of leaf and they will always be smaller than specimens in the open ground. The large clumps of *H. sieboldiana* and *H.* 'Frances Williams' seen at international flower shows will have come from the ground and only been grown short-term in a container, usually no longer than a season before they will be returned to the ground.

RECOMMENDED VARIETIES

Generally hostas that make small crowns and fine roots give no trouble and make the most satisfactory container plants; indeed they often grow better. All the *H. fortunei* types are ideal and even after ten years a *H.* 'Francee' of mine, now growing in a 20-litre pot, is still a superb specimen.

There will always be exceptions but for long-term pot culture I would not recommend hostas that have *H. sieboldiana* in their make-up, e.g. *H.* 'Frances Williams' and *H.* 'Big Mama'. Some of the Tardiana group are also difficult (although *H.* 'Halcyon' can make an excellent pot plant), as are the large-leaved golds such as *H.* 'Midas Touch', *H.* 'Piedmont Gold', *H.* 'Golden Sunburst', and *H.* 'August Moon'. Hostas that make very thick roots are best grown in the ground after four years, as only in the ground will they develop the full potential of their foliage. *H. sieboldiana* forms have been used in the development of many hybrids so a watchful eye would need to be kept on any of that parentage which you grow in containers when young.

**H. 'Christmas Tree' with *Carex comans* in the foreground. The white hydrangea, *Cornus alba* 'Elegantissima' and bamboo in the background contribute to an effective group for the white garden.**

# Pests

### SLUGS AND SNAILS

Unfortunately a hosta leaf is caviar to a slug or a snail and measures must be taken to protect the plants from these pests. There are a large number of different species of slugs and snails and some do more damage than others. The small brown and grey slugs are a far greater nuisance than their larger relatives, and of the snails the garden snail and the strawberry snail are the most serious. The latter is much smaller, with a pale brown, flattened shell and hides in the crown of the plant, making it very hard to kill. Nothing looks worse than a plant that is reduced to lace curtains although the odd hole or so does not spoil the garden effectiveness and is nearly impossible to avoid if your garden is a paradise to these pests.

There is only one answer and it may take a season or two of constant warfare before vigilance and preventive measures can be reduced to the odd battle or so. First and foremost it is important to be tidy, to clear away all possible breeding sites – rotting vegetation is the perfect home for a slug or a snail. If mulches are applied around your plants, these pests must be eradicated first or your efforts to get your hostas to grow well will be defeated.

The most effective control is certainly slug pellets, but for those gardeners who do not wish to use them there are other preventive measures. Slug pellets contain either metaldehyde or methiocarb; methiocarb is more toxic than metaldehyde, which breaks down more quickly in the soil. They are usually blue, a colour unattractive to birds, and they also contain animal repellent substances. They are very effective and slugs and snails do not usually recover, but they must be applied frequently. The easiest way to scatter them is to put one flower pot inside another, fill the inner pot with pellets and use the drainage holes in the pots to sprinkle the pellets thinly over the whole garden; animals are less likely to eat them than when in heaps and control is far more effective. They can be placed in shelters created by a stone which protects them from rain and then the dead slugs and snails can be easily removed before animals can eat them.

Pellets must be used on a very regular basis, always after rain, and at intervals no greater than every ten days; they need to be spread very early every season, before the shoots emerge in the spring and applications should continue right through the growing season to reduce the breeding cycle. Gradually there will be fewer adults produced, although some years will always be worse than others. In spells of dry weather damage is usually less because the slugs will stay deep in the soil and snails will withdraw into their shells.

A reasonably effective method which is more acceptable to gardeners with pets is to use a liquid product. There are a number on the market but they must be watered very thoroughly on to the plant and its surroundings and used at frequent intervals. Most are based on aluminium sulphate, which is relatively nontoxic. Other products, such as slug tape and slug gels, exist but although probably effective for protection round a few prized plants, they are not the answer for slug- and snail-infested gardens.

There are non-chemical methods, but unfortunately most will only give some measure of control. A torch light inspection at night will allow physical removal of the offenders as they come out at night to feed but, although effective this is time-consuming in any but the smallest garden. Destroy the slugs and snails collected – throwing them over the hedge only means they will return!

Damage can be limited by surrounding the plants with a rough material that slugs do not like travelling over. Eggshells, coal ashes or gravel are all deterrents, but it is no good whatsoever putting this over occupants in residence.

Natural predators can help also to reduce the problem: birds, hedgehogs, frogs and toads should be encouraged. I have found toads particularly effective and find they do not seem to pick up poisoned slugs and snails; I have a thriving toad population, despite using a considerable number of pellets. Although these natural predators help, they are not usually present in large enough numbers to stop all damage to leaves.

Failing all else, as some gardens seem to have far more slugs and snails than others, it is far easier to protect plants in pots. Even slug pellets can be tucked out of site in the rim of the pot and removed and replaced at frequent intervals; most domestic pets or birds will not investigate inside. Pots stood on gravel or paving with the foliage of each not touching can often escape unscathed without any need for slug and snail control. If damage is spotted lifting up the pot or going out at night will usually reveal the culprits, which can then be removed. When hostas are dormant it is a good idea to tip the plant out of the pot to see if any eggs have been laid and to remove them before they develop and become the next generation of pests.

Some hostas are more resistant to damage than others. Thick, leathery leaves are less attractive to slugs and snails than thin papery ones. H. 'Sum and Substance', for example, has a very large, extremely thick leaf that also stands well above the ground when mature, and suffers much less than many other varieties. H. 'Celebration', H. sieboldii forms and other small, thin-leaved hostas are the most vulnerable. The following are worth considering and although less prone to slug damage than most, some can certainly be damaged by snails, the tiny snails being a very difficult problem.

## Hostas least damaged by slugs and snails

| | |
|---|---|
| 'Barbara White' | *hypoleuca* |
| 'Big Daddy' | *kikutii* 'Pruinose' |
| 'Blue Angel' | 'Krossa Regal' |
| 'Blue Cadet' | 'Love Pat' |
| 'Blue Umbrellas' | 'Midas Touch' |
| 'Bold Ruffles' | *nigrescens* |
| 'Christmas Tree' | 'Pizzazz' |
| *fluctuans* 'Variegated' | *rupifraga* |
| *fortunei* 'Aureo-marginata' | 'Sea Lotus Leaf' |
| | *sieboldiana* (and forms) |
| 'Frances Williams' | 'Snow Cap' |
| 'Fringe Benefit' | 'Spritzer' |
| 'Gold Edger' | 'Sum and Substance' |
| 'Gold Regal' | Tardiana group |
| 'Golden Sculpture' | *tardiflora* |
| 'Green Fountain' | *tokudama* (and forms) |
| 'Green Piecrust' | 'Zounds' |
| 'Green Sheen' | |

### RABBITS, HARES AND DEER

The only way is to fence. Rabbits can reduce a specimen hosta to the ground at a sitting. Every time new leaves are pushed up it will return for another meal until the hosta leaves will eventually get smaller and smaller and disappear. Rabbit fencing must be close-meshed (small ones can get through very small holes), buried below ground and at least 90 cm (3 ft) high. Fencing against deer, also very partial to hosta leaves, needs to be at least 2 m (6½ ft) high. In some respects it is not surprising that hosta leaves are such a favourite food, as they are used in cooking by the Japanese.

### MICE AND VOLES

Mice can eat hostas, especially in winter and those that are mulched are usually more vulnerable. It is a Catch

53

22 situation: mulching can protect against frost, retain moisture and result in better growth but it is also a home for mice, slugs and snails. Voles are not a general problem but if you have them then you will soon become aware that they are fond of hosta roots. A large specimen hosta of mine became a winter repository for at least thirty acorns and all the roots under the crown were eaten. Wire mesh guards will protect the roots.

VINE WEEVILS

These are far more of a problem when growing plants in pots than in the ground. If any larvae – they are white and C-shaped – are discovered they should be killed immediately as they eat roots. The adults can notch the foliage and this can be unsightly.

Plants frequently repotted do not seem to have the same problems as those that are left in the same compost for a number of years. A number of proprietary soil pest killers can be incorporated in the compost and preventive measures taken every few months. Recent research developments will probably result in satisfactory biological controls based on a nematode becoming the solution to the problem. If it is suspected that weevil larvae are in the roots, you must shake off all the compost, destroy the larvae and repot in fresh compost. Hostas are not the favourite food of a vine weevil and it is usually only a problem in neglected plants. Woodlice can also notch the petioles and the leaves but they are not a serious problem.

OTHER PESTS

Hostas are generally trouble-free and although sap-sucking insects can cause visual damage they do not usually harm the plant in the long term. The easiest control is a strong jet of water to wash off the offenders. This is more often a problem under protection than in the garden.

# Diseases

Hostas are relatively free of any problems and as long as they are given good culture and kept free from slug and snail damage they are likely to flourish for many years, but occasionally a virus infection will result in leaves with mosaic-like markings, chlorotic spots or a stunted appearance (this can also be caused by crown congestion). It is important to realize that late frosts, leaf scorch and mineral deficiency can show the same symptoms but if a viral infection is suspected the only answer is to destroy the plant. Insects or a propagating knife can transmit the virus to perfectly healthy plants. Some of the Tardiana group seem more prone to virus, as do *H.* 'Sea Sprite', *H. opipara* and *H. crispula.*

Spots on leaves have a number of causes. Leaf spot disease can be treated by spraying with Benomyl or Thiram as it is caused by fungi, but most spots on hosta leaves are caused by frost or sun damage. A slight frost will not destroy the leaf but break down some of the cell structure and the damage will not be obvious immediately. The sun, especially if the leaves are wet, can cause brown burn spots where the individual water droplets have acted like a lens. Insects can cause pinhead spots, as can chemicals, and fumes and oily residues may also damage the leaf surface. Brown edges to leaves are usually the result of frost or wind damage, although seasons that are abnormal, whether spells of extremes temperature and of drought, seem to contribute. There is nothing wrong in removing the odd damaged leaf although it is a mistake to remove all of them.

**H. 'Tall Boy' in the RHS garden, Wisley, where the mass planting is very effective when in flower. Good ground cover.**

Crown rot, which can be caused by a fungus, can occur, especially in places with high temperatures. If the leaves turn yellow and the crowns detach from the middle, the plant must be pulled apart, only the healthy pieces retained and each piece treated with a fungicide before being repotted in new pots and fresh compost. Sometimes poorly drained soil or too dense a compost which has been over-watered, can cause the same problem, especially with *H. sieboldii* forms which do not have a very vigorous root system and a tendency to crown congestion. At Chelsea Flower Show in 1989, when the temperature in the marquee exceeded 38°C (100°F), some of the hostas developed the early signs of crown rot; they were packed with moss around the crowns to hide the pots and this inhibited air circulating around the plants; a gap is now left around the stems to prevent this happening.

Having described some of the possible threats to hostas, it is worth reiterating that, other than damage caused by slugs and snails and late frosts, most gardeners will never meet any other problems. Compared with many garden plants, most hostas are easy, problem-free perennials that grow surprisingly well in a number of situations.

# Propagation

### DIVISION

Spring, when the crowns are just beginning to emerge, is the ideal time to split. If the clump is mature the easiest way is to take a sharp spade and slice a piece off, leaving the rest in the ground. This piece can then be cut up further or pulled apart into individual crowns. Some hostas pull apart easily; others need a sharp kitchen knife. The plant left in the ground will quickly recover; by the end of the season you will not notice the missing piece, and the clump will maintain its mature leaf form. The rest will give you pieces to grow on but they will take a few years to return to adult leaf form and must be treated like newly acquired plants. If only a few plants are needed then the slice taken off can be replanted as it is and this will not go back to a juvenile leaf form but any woody root must be cut away and the plant treated in the same way as those being divided from containers.

Some hostas are very slow to make divisions and a number of other methods have been tried, mainly by nurserymen, to induce the plant to make propagating material. The Ross Method was originally developed in USA and the details published in the *American Hosta Journal*. It is easier to carry out this technique on a thick, single crown hosta growing in a pot although it can be used quite satisfactorily on plants in the ground. I have found the best time is in spring or early summer when the plant is in active growth. The soil or compost is scraped back to reveal the basal plate of the stem; the roots are below this. A thin, sharp straight knive is inserted into the stem just above the basal plate and the knife pushed down through the plate into the roots (Fig. 11). Another cut can then be made at right angles to the first. Where the stem has been damaged the tissue will mend by callousing, a scar will form and this encourages a growth bud which in turn will become a new division. The hosta should be tended carefully and although slight yellowing of the leaves often occurs, the plant continues to grow.

A slight adaption of this method is to push the knife in as far as the middle of the crown only and to slice down, repeating the process round the stem. A very thick stem can have six to eight slits, but two or three would be plenty for a less developed plant. Instead of one large crown the plant should develop a number of smaller plants, according to the knife cuts. The resulting new crowns need to be grown on usually for at least one season before they are split up, to give them time to develop their own root systems.

## OTHER METHODS

Hostas can be grown from seed but generally they will not come true. Most people who have bought packets of seed or collected their own are very disappointed with the resulting progeny. Many new hostas are being raised by deliberate or accidental crossings but for every new hosta raised many thousands of seedlings are culled. The proportion of variegated seedlings arising, for example, from *H.* 'Frances Williams', is infinitessimal, most plants turning out to be blues, greens and a tiny percentage of golds. It is better not to pass on seedlings by name until they have been registered and this should only be for plants that are worthy.

The most common method of propagation of the newer hostas today is micropropagation. Without the advent of tissue culture, the newer hostas would not have become as popular as they have. Many thousands can be propagated in a matter of months and a nucleus stock built up by the nurseryman. These young plants need special care in their early days and most should not be planted out in the garden until they have had two seasons of growth. They have been propagated in sterile conditions and need a period of adaption to the outside world.

Many hostas are inately unstable, they sport readily and in the tissue culture laboratory this is magnified, with the result that the very technique of propagating is giving rise to many more new varieties. If proved worthy these are in turn propagated. Three very fine hostas which will be in great demand in years to come that have arisen in this way are a cream-edged *H.* 'Honeybells' called *H.* 'Sugar and Cream', a cream-edged *H.* 'Krossa Regal' (*H.* 'Regal Splendor') and a gold-centred *H.* 'Halcyon' (*H.* 'June').

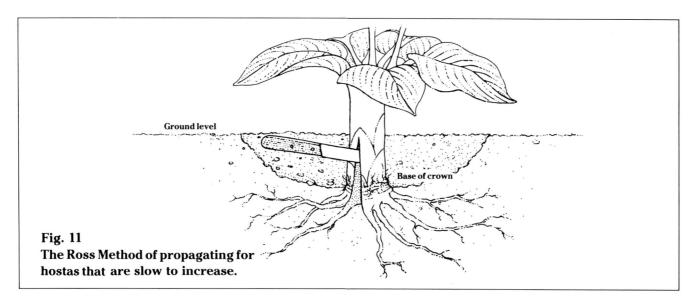

Ground level

Base of crown

**Fig. 11**
**The Ross Method of propagating for hostas that are slow to increase.**

# Plant Directory

This is by no means a comprehensive list of the hostas available as there are now over 1100 registered names, but it is a selection of those that are readily obtainable and of those that are in specialist nurseries and likely to be popular in the future. I have included some of the old favourites, species that I feel should be more widely grown, and some of the newer cultivars that have a future in the garden or for the flower arranger. Present breeding aims are for increased pest resistance and sun tolerance, fragrance in the flowers, new colour breaks such as blue and white variegation and an ever-increasing range of small hostas which should appeal to the alpine gardener and those with tiny plots. I have listed a selection of the many kinds and although some are expensive, the advent of propagation by tissue culture means they will not be expensive tomorrow and some will become as common in gardens of the future as *H.* 'Frances Williams' is today.

Not all are easy to grow but if they are distinctive and desired by certain gardeners who are prepared to take care then I feel they have a part to play. An example is *H.* 'Reversed', loved by flower arrangers who know it, and if grown in a pot in dappled shade it can look spectacular, but it is certainly not a good landscape plant.

Most hostas in cultivation are not species, although the name may suggest otherwise. I have left those that have historic associations with their well-known name even if we now know they are not species, but for more recent cultivars I have followed the practice of the international registration body for hostas in USA. As we learn more about hostas it is inevitable that nomenclature changes will be made. The gardener often finds this confusing but in the long term taxonomic accuracy will help to resolve the problems.

Many hostas have suffered from errors of nomenclature since their introduction. The species are chiefly natives of Japan but some come from China and Korea and partly because of their variability in the wild they have been wrongly identified. Mature plants often look very different from the juvenile form and this again causes confusion, and plants are frequently sold under erroneous names. Some older hybrids have also been described as species but with the present enormous interest in the genus a start has been made in trying to solve some of the many points of confusion.

There is much argument at the moment over identification within the Tardiana group raised by Eric Smith, and it is quite possible that in the future changes must be made. The original cross was of *H. tardiflora* and *H. sieboldiana* 'Elegans' and the resulting progeny were given a TF number, the first generation being designated TF 1×, the second TF 2× and the third, of which only one seems to exist, TF 3×1. Some of the progeny of the second generation also indicate that a *H. nakaiana* form could have become involved in the cross: e.g. *H.* 'Blue Belle' (TF 2×22) and *H.* 'Eric Smith' (TF 2×31). The problem of identification in this group is complex. Many of the plants are very similar to each other, and were distributed under number when very young, the names being given later, some in Europe and some in USA, with the result that we now have either more than one plant with the same name or the same plant with two or more names. I believe we may discover that *H.* 'Blue Moon' and *H.* 'Dorset Blue' have been mixed up in the trade as they are very similar;

*H.* 'Dorset Blue' is the more vigorous. *H.* 'Blue Dimples' and *H.* 'Blue Wedgwood' are certainly muddled up, something that is very easy to understand when their relevant numbers were TF 2 × 8 and TF 2 × 9 and they look very like each other in the immature state. I have only listed a selection of superior hybrids in the group, of which, *H.* 'Halcyon' is the best known and most widely planted.

The following list of hostas includes a brief description of each and where applicable special cultural requirements. Parentage has sometimes been included as this can be a useful guide to a hosta's appearance and its growing characteristics. The dimensions given denote height × spread (H/S) of the

***H.* 'Spritzer' (a young plant) with *Hakonechloa macra* 'Alboaurea', *Carex testacea* and ferns edging a path, seen against a backdrop of *Cornus alba* 'Aurea' and *Elaeagnus ebbingei*.**

mature foliage mound, this being the dominant element in the garden although it will vary in different climatic regions. The spread indicates the required planting distances. Those marked * are especially suitable for flower arranging.

### *H.* 'Allan P. McConnell'

H/S 13 × 20 cm (5 × 8 in)

Attractive small green leaves with a narrow white margin. 38 cm (15 in) purple scapes with lavender flowers in midsummer. Useful for edging or on a shady rock garden.

### H. 'Amanuma'
H/S 15 × 30 cm (6 × 12 in)
A *H. nakaiana* seedling. A small green mound with slightly wavy leaves; lavender flowers from early summer onwards on 38 cm (15 in) purple-dotted scapes.

### H. 'Antioch'
H/S 50 × 90 cm (20 × 36 in)
Form of *H. fortunei* 'Albo-marginata'. Medium to large cascading mound of cream-edged green heart-shaped leaves. Lavender flowers in midsummer. Similar to *H.* 'Spinners' which is larger, *H.* 'Moorheim' ('Moorheimii') and to *H.* 'Goldbrook' which is smaller and has a wider gold edge turning cream. Looks wonderful in partial shade planted with ferns and *Geranium phaeum album* where it lightens a dark corner.

### H. 'August Moon'
H/S 65 × 90 cm (26 × 36 in)
Young foliage is pale green which deepens to gold if grown in dappled shade and develops large corrugated golden leaves when mature. 90 cm (3 ft) pale lavender, trumpet-shaped flowers in mid-summer. Vigorous and fast-growing. Will grow in sun in cooler climates. A number of sports have arisen, and some will have a future in the garden: *H.* 'Abiqua Moonbeam' ('Mayan Moon') is blue-green with lime green margins; *H.* 'Lunar Eclipse' has a white edge to the gold leaf; *H.* 'September Sun' is a gold with a dark green edge, a very attractive new variety.

### H. 'Barbara White'
H/S 50 × 75 cm (20 × 30 in)
Seedling arose at Goldbrook Plants nursery, UK and was named in honour of Barbara White, a secretary of the Hardy Plant Society for many years. The chartreuse gold, heavily textured, orbicular leaves appeal to flower arrangers. Near-white flowers. Although slow to mature eventually becomes an impressive plant. Needs dappled light to colour.

### H. 'Bennie MacRae'
H/S 60 × 75 cm (24 × 30 in)
Seedling of open-pollinated *H. plantaginea*. Lance-shaped glossy, wavy, green leaves. Fragrant lavender flowers on very tall scapes from late summer onwards. Has larger leaves than *H.* 'Honeybells' and darker coloured flowers that are sweetly scented.

### H. 'Big Daddy'*
H/S 75 × 90 cm (30 × 36 in)
Large round, puckered blue leaves that are pest-resistant. Pale lavender flowers 90 cm (3 ft) high appear in early summer. Best sited in shade but not under the drip of trees. Makes a good architectural specimen against walls, underplanted with *Pulmonaria* 'Lewis Palmer'.

### H. 'Big Mama'
H/S 90 × 100 cm (36 × 40 in)
Form of *H. sieboldiana*. Large blue-green, cupped and pointed leaves of heavy substance, with pale lavender flowers in early summer. Good background plant to other hostas, dicentras and ferns in the shade garden.

### H. 'Bill Brincka'
H/S 70 × 150 cm (28 × 60 in)
Selection of *H. opipara*. Large, bright green leaves edged with a wide margin of gold that becomes creamier as the season progresses. Scapes 75 cm (30 in) tall carry racemes of bell-shaped, light lavender flowers with darker stripes in midsummer. This form has been given a separate name as, unlike some forms, it has no virus. Looks wonderful as an accent in a green border of ferns. Very distinctive when mature.

**H. 'Black Hills'**
H/S 75 × 125 cm (30 × 50 in)
Deep green, puckered, heavy textured leaves. Lilac flowers in midsummer on scapes just above the foliage mound. One of the darkest green hostas available, but not well known.

**H. 'Blond Elf'**
H/S 20 × 60 cm (8 × 24 in)
Small gold, wavy-edged lanceolate leaves make a wide-spreading low mound. Lavender flowers in midsummer. Best in dappled light as an edger or in an alpine bed.

**H. 'Blue Angel'** *
H/S 1 × 1.2 m (40 × 48 in)
Form of *H. sieboldiana*. Very large, glaucous bluish leaves make this a very impressive landscape hosta and it is certainly worth waiting for this to grow to maturity. Tall, dense clusters of lilac-white flowers are long lasting. Underplant with *H.* 'Wide Brim' for a dramatic focal point or with *Tiarella cordifolia* for a more subtle woodland scheme. Best in shade. Once established is surprisingly tolerant of a dry situation and because the leaves are not puckered but point downwards they do not collect debris from trees.

**H. 'Blue Belle'**
H/S 25 × 50 cm (10 × 20 in)
Tardiana group TF 2 × 22. Bluish leaves, attractive mauve-lilac flowers well above the foliage mound. Very similar to *H.* 'Blue Cadet'. Good edging plant in shade.

**H. 'Blue Blush'**
H/S 20 × 45 cm (3 × 18 in)
Tardiana group TF 3 × 1. Excellent blue foliage, mainly lanceolate leaves with lilac flowers just above the foliage mound in midsummer. Slow to establish but an excellent smaller growing hosta suitable for edging in shade. Considered by some to be the bluest of this group. Grow with *Dicentra formosa* 'Stuart Boothman' and *Lamium maculatum* 'Beacon's Silver'.

**H. 'Blue Boy'**
H/S 30 × 50 cm (12 × 20 in)
Probably a *H. nakaiana* seedling. Small, wavy, glaucous blue-green leaves and pale lavender flowers. Lovely with dicentras or underneath *Cornus alba* 'Aurea' in association with *Molinia caerulea* 'Variegata'.

**H. 'Blue Cadet'**
H/S 38 × 55 cm (15 × 22 in)
Blue-green, heart-shaped leaves form a dense rounded mound. Dark lavender flowers in midsummer. Excellent edger in dappled shade.

**H. 'Blue Danube'**
H/S 25 × 50 cm (10 × 20 in)
Tardiana group TF 2 × 24. Very blue, slightly rounded leaves with pale lavender flowers with a darker but still pale stripe, slightly above the foliage mound in early summer. One of the first of this group to flower. A very pretty plant for edging a shady walk or in association with *Carex comans*.

**H. 'Blue Dimples'**
H/S 30 × 60 cm (12 × 24 in)
Tardiana group TF 2 × 8. Thick blue leaves of heavy substance with dimples on mature plants. Pale lavender flowers in midsummer. Partial to deep shade.

**H. 'Blue Moon'** *
H/S 10 × 30 cm (4 × 12 in)
Tardiana group TF 2 × 2. Small neat, rounded but flattish grey-blue leaves. Dense clusters of bluish-mauve flowers appear in midsummer just above the foliage mound. Slow. The foliage colour is intensified

61

Three very new hostas for accents among the blues. Left to right at the front: 'Goldbrook Glimmer', 'Snow Cap' and 'Pizzazz' with *Pulmonaria mollis* 'Royal Blue' and ferns.

in shade. Not vigorous and probably rare as most plants in commerce are probably in fact *H*. 'Dorset Blue' which is very similar but a much stronger-growing variety.

### *H*. 'Blue Skies'

H/S 20 × 40 cm (8 × 16 in)

Tardiana group TF 2 × 6. Roundish, pointed, blue leaves which grow fairly flat to the ground. Hyacinth-like pale lavender flowers in late summer. Best in shade. Has given rise to an all-green sport, *H*. 'Emerald Skies', with shiny emerald green foliage which is very slow.

### *H*. 'Blue Umbrellas'

H/S 90 × 100 cm (36 × 40 in)

Form of *H. sieboldiana*. Very large, bold blue-green leaves of heavy substance. Pale lavender flowers above the foliage mound in early summer. Although this will tolerate sun, it is far more impressive in dappled shade as a background plant to *Dicentra spectabilis* and *H*. 'Pearl Lake'.

### H. 'Blue Wedgwood'*

H/S 25×55 cm (10×22 in)
Tardiana group TF2×9. Lovely wedge-shaped, heavily seersuckered blue leaves. Takes a number of years to develop adult foliage. Often muddled with H. 'Blue Dimples' when juvenile. Lavender flowers in midsummer. Good planted with pale pink astilbes.

### H. 'Bold Ribbons'

H/S 25×60 cm (10×24in)
Green lance-shaped leaves with a creamy yellow edge that fades to creamy white. Tall violet flowers in midsummer. Makes good ground cover as is stoloniferous. Needs plain neighbours as the foliage is striking. Very similar are H. 'Neat Splash Rim' and H. 'Yellow Splash Rim', the stable forms of H. 'Neat Splash' and H. 'Yellow Splash'. All are popular with flower arrangers and easy to grow.

### H. 'Bold Ruffles'*

H/S 60×90 cm (24×36 in)
Large blue-grey ruffled leaves. Pale lavender flowers in midsummer. Needs to be grown in good soil in part or full shade. Not good as a container plant but suitable for flower arrangers.

### H. 'Bright Glow'

H/S 38×55 cm (15×22 in)
Tardiana type. Thick, textured, heart-shaped leaves change to gold. White flowers in early summer. Needs some sun to colour but not hot and dry. Slow.

### H. 'Bright Lights'

H/S 30×50 cm (12×20 in)
Bright gold-centred leaves with blue-green margins. Probably from H. tokudama 'Flavo-circinalis' but with reversed colouring. Light lavender flowers in midsummer. Slow. Best in the dappled light and makes a striking mound. One for the flower arrangers. Use as the highlight plant among blue hostas and gold sedges.

### H. 'Brim Cup'*

H/S 30×38 cm (12×15 in)
The slightly cupped and puckered green leaves have a wide creamy yellow margin that fades to white. Lavender flowers on 45 cm (18 in) scapes in midsummer. This will become popular. Best in shade or dappled light and looks delightful with Athyrium filix-femina 'Minutissimum' and small white astilbes.

### H. 'Buckshaw Blue'

H/S 35×60 cm (14×24 in)
Probably a H. tokudama seedling. Very blue cupped foliage of heavy substance. Greyish white flowers 45 cm (18 in) high appear in summer. Slow to mature and best in shade. Looks good with pink or blue hardy geraniums.

### H. 'Candy Hearts'

H/S 38×55 cm (15×22 in)
Seedling of H. nakaiana. Heart-shaped green leaves, 45 cm (18 cm) bell-shaped lavender flowers in midsummer. Two recent sports of this are H. 'Amber Maiden', which has a chartreuse edge deepening to yellow during the season, and H. 'Heartsong' with a white edge and probably smaller growing.

### H. 'Carrie Ann'

H/S 8×20 cm (3×8 in)
Small wavy green leaves have a creamy white margin. Delightful white flowers on 50 cm (20 in) scapes in late summer. Suitable for the shady rock garden with Mitella caulescens and tiny ferns.

### H. 'Celebration'

H/S 25×45 cm (10×18 in)
Small cream-centred, green lanceolate leaves. Lavender flowers in summer. Striking red seed pods. Must have part shade and needs care as slugs love it. Best grown in a pot as it is not a good garden plant, but the leaves are much loved by flower arrangers.

63

### H. 'Chartreuse Wiggles'
H/S 8×25 cm (3×10 in)
Narrow, ruffled, lance-shaped leaves of chartreuse yellow. Lavender flowers in late summer. This is an interesting little hosta that needs care in early years and is probably best grown on a raised bed in dappled shade. Stoloniferous.

### H. 'Chinese Sunrise'
H/S 38×70 cm (15×28 in)
Form of *H. lancifolia*. Narrow, lance-shaped, glossy chartreuse gold leaves with a green margin. Colour fades to all green in the summer. Stoloniferous and vigorous. Abundant dark lavender flowers in late summer. Associates well with *Hakonechloa macra* 'Alboaurea', *H.* 'Inaho' and dark green filigree ferns.

### H. 'Christmas Tree'*
H/S 45×90 cm (18×36 in)
A *H.* 'Frances Williams' cross. Large, heavily corrugated green leaves with a creamy white edge. Light lavender flowers from midsummer onwards with very leafy scapes that give the impression of a Christmas tree. Looks super all season and even the flower stems decorated with black seed pods should appeal to the flower arranger. For a dramatic group grow with *Veratrum nigrum*, *Salix elaeagnos angustifolia*, ferns and *Ophiopogon planiscapus nigrescens* in light shade.

### H. clausa normalis
H/S 20×60 cm (8×24 in)
Shiny dark green leaves with striking purple funnel-shaped flowers on 60 cm (24 in) scapes in midsummer. Useful ground cover as it is stoloniferous and the flowers are very attractive. Like nearly all green hostas a very underrated plant.

### H. 'Colossal'
H/S 90×100 cm (36×40 in)
An enormous mound of large green leaves with pale lavender flowers in midsummer. Plain green hostas are very useful as green mounds are restful. Underplant with *Pachysandra terminalis* 'Variegata' for complete ground cover.

### H. crispula
H/S 60×90 cm (24×36 in)
Large heart-shaped, dark green, wavy leaves with an irregular white margin. Tall trumpet-shaped pale mauve flowers in midsummer. Spectacular when well-grown but needs careful siting in dappled shade, out of the winds and danger from early frosts. Looks lovely with Solomon's seal and blue flowers.

### H. 'Daybreak'
H/S 50×75 cm (20×30 in)
Dense clump of shiny deep gold foliage. Leaves are of a good texture. Lavender blue flowers on 70 cm (28 in) scapes. Not well known but highly thought of in USA. Vigorous. Best in dappled light for leaf colour. For a striking group underplant with a lily-of-the-valley such as *Convallaria majalis* 'Lineata'.

### H. decorata
H/S 30×75 cm (12×30 in)
Medium-sized broadly oval green leaf with a white margin. The blunt rounded end distinguishes this from *H. undulata* 'Albo-marginata' ('Thomas Hogg') with which it is confused. Scapes 60 cm (24 in) tall with narrow bell-shaped, dark violet flowers in midsummer. Rarely planted today as usually not very vigorous but if happy in cool woodland soil it will make wide spreading mats as it is stoloniferous. *H.* 'Betsy King' is an all-green seedling with a very free-flowering habit.

### H. 'Dorset Blue'
H/S 20×45 cm (8×18 in)
Tardiana group TF 2×4. Small, very blue, slightly

cupped leaves with greyish lavender flowers in midsummer just above the foliage mound. One of the best of the smaller blues. Lovely in dappled shade as an edger or in an alpine bed with small geraniums such as *Geranium renardii*.

### *H.* 'Duchess'
H/S 13×25 cm (5×10 in)
Sport of *H. nakaiana* seedling. Small mound of dark green, lanceolate leaves edged creamy white. Scapes 45 cm (18 in) tall with medium purple flowers in midsummer. Suitable for tiny gardens and alpine beds. Dappled shade.

### *H.* 'Elfin Power'
H/S 20×38 cm (8×15 in)
Narrow lanceolate mid-green leaves with a white margin. Racemes of lavender flowers 60 cm (24 in) tall in late summer. Very pretty. *H.* 'Pixie Power' has a small green leaf with a white middle and only grows 10 cm (4 in) high. Both are slow and need some shade.

### *H.* 'Emily Dickinson'
H/S 50×75 cm (20×30 in)
Medium green leaf with irregular cream margin. Many fragrant bright lavender flowers on 70 cm (28 in) stems in midsummer. Will become popular when it ceases to be so expensive.

### *H. fluctuans* 'Variegated'*
H/S 90×100 cm (36×40 in)
Large upright, vase-shaped mound of green centred, heavy-textured leaves edged in creamy gold and topped by 1.5 m (5 ft) of pale lavender flowers in midsummer. This is slow to mature but when it does is spectacular. A very choice, as yet expensive, variety that should be in every garden. It makes a striking focal point among ferns and is better used as a specimen plant with contrasting foliage in a shady spot. The Japanese use it as a container plant.

### *H. fortunei*
H/S 60×90 cm (24×36 in)
A group of hostas that are not species but for convenience retain their name. Good foliage plants with heart-shaped leaves that make medium-large mounds with generally mauve-violet flowers well above the foliage in late summer. Emerge late so are rarely damaged by frosts. Make good container plants. Name now usually applied to a plain green-leaved plant although not technically correct.

### *H. fortunei* 'Albo-marginata' ('Marginato-albo')
H/S 55×80 cm (22×32 in)
Darkish green leaves with a white back are edged with an irregular white margin that is variable in the same plant and from season to season. When at its best is superb but often disappoints. Must have moist shade.

### *H. fortunei* 'Albo-picta'
H/S 55×90 cm (22×36 in)
In spring the leaves are creamy yellow with a green margin but they fade to dull green as the season advances. This is accelerated in very warm weather. Trumpet-shaped pale mauve flowers in midsummer. *H.* 'Chelsea Babe' looks like a smaller version, so named because it is at its best in late May in Britain, at the time of the Chelsea Flower Show. Probably of mixed parentage and not very vigorous. *H.* 'Phyllis Campbell' looks like a more vigorous *H. fortunei* 'Albo-picta', with leaves of thicker texture that fade later. All need partial shade.

### *H. fortunei* 'Aurea'
H/S 40×75 cm (16×30 in)
Medium-sized soft yellow leaves that fade to green. Pale purple flowers 60 cm (24 in) high in midsummer. Very attractive used as underplanting for shrubs and especially useful where a gold theme is required in early summer but not later. Two improved forms of

**Young plants of** *H.* **'Regal Splendor' (cream edge) and** *H.* **'Hadspen Blue' with** *Astilbe simplicifolia* **'Sprite',** *Acer negundo* **'Flamingo' and** *Rubus thibetanus* **'Silver Fern'.**

this are *H.* 'Gold Haze' and *H.* 'Gold Leaf'. The first is much larger and more vigorous than the type and forms a cascading mound which is very impressive in the early garden. *H.* 'Gold Leaf' has a sheen to the leaf. Both fade to green later in the season.

**H. fortunei 'Aureo-marginata'\***
H/S 55 × 90 cm (22 × 36 in)
Light yellow edge to mid-green leaf. Violet trumpet-shaped flowers rise to 90 cm (3 ft) in midsummer. Makes an excellent, vigorous mound especially effective planted with *Ligularia przewalskii* 'The Rocket', *Iris pseudacorus* 'Variegata' and *Matteuccia struthiopteris* (ostrich feather fern) in a moist border where it will take a fair amount of sun. Excellent for flower arrangers and it also makes a good container plant.

**H. fortunei 'Hyacinthina'**
H/S 60 × 90 cm (24 × 36 in)
Slightly rugose grey-green leaves with fine white line on the edge. Good funnel-shaped violet flowers well above the foliage mound in midsummer. An invalu-

able plant for mass planting and as a foil to hotter colours. *H. fortunei* 'Hyacinthina Variegata' has a wider creamy margin to the leaf that fades as the season advances.

### H. 'Fragrant Bouquet'
H/S 45×65 cm (18×26 in)
Dense mound of apple green leaves edged creamy yellow, with very large, fragrant whitish flowers in summer on 90 cm (3 ft) scapes. This is still very expensive but will become popular as the flowers are superb. It is reputed to be sun-tolerant and pest-resistant. Lovely with ferns and green and yellow variegated grasses and for picking.

**H. 'Mildred Seaver', a relatively new variety, planted with *Polystichum braunii*, a dark green glossy fern that emphasizes the wide creamy band of the hosta leaf.**

### H. 'Fragrant Gold'
H/S 48×65 cm (17×26 in)
Seedling of *H.* 'Sum and Substance'. Medium-sized, heavily textured leaves in chartreuse gold that tolerate sun. 75 cm (30 in) tall fragrant bluish trumpet-shaped flowers with very leafy scapes which appear in late summer.

**H. 'Francee'***

H/S 55×90 cm (22×36 in)

A *H. fortunei* form. Excellent white-edged heart-shaped leaves of a rich green. Pale lavender flowers on 75 cm (30 in) scapes. One of the best in the garden and in a container. Associates beautifully with *Aruncus aethusifolius*, *Geranium sanguineum album*, ferns and taller astilbes, and can make an impressive feature in a group of white and green plants. Invaluable. Emerges late with very attractive young shoots and is rarely damaged by late frosts. Rapid grower. Other similar hostas are *H.* 'North Hills' and *H.* 'Carol' both with white edges.

**H. 'Frances Williams'***

H/S 75×100 cm (30×40 in)

Superb sport of *H. sieboldiana* 'Elegans'. Round, puckered, heavily textured blue-green leaves with a wide margin of muted yellow. Near-white flowers from early summer. Underplant with smaller blue hostas such as *H.* 'Halcyon' and *H.* 'Blue Wedgwood', or with *Dicentra formosa* 'Langtrees'. If grown in too much sun the leaf margin scorches but if given a moist spot and dappled shade can become one of the most impressive hostas. *H.* 'Samurai' is very similar but is faster growing and stands more sun. Some forms appear better than others but it could be in time that all will grow as well; divisions from older clumps appear superior to those from more juvenile plants or from tissue culture.

**H. 'Fresh'**

H/S 20×50 cm (8×20 in)

Gold, undulating, lance-shaped leaves with a creamy white rim. Lavender flowers in midsummer. Needs shade to dappled light and makes an interesting edging plant or could be used in a rock garden as an effective contrast to mossy saxifrages and other alpines.

**H. 'Fringe Benefit'**

H/S 60×90 cm (24×36 in)

Good, textured heart-shaped green leaves, medium to large with a wide creamy white edge. Lavender flowers in early summer. A good increaser that appears more resistant to slugs than some and useful for planting large areas. Will grow in fairly sunny spots but the foliage is certainly more attractive in some shade. An easy, adaptable hosta that can be used in many ways. Grow with *Arum italicum* 'Pictum' and *Polygonatum × hybridum*.

**H. 'Frosted Jade'**

H/S 80×100 cm (32×40 in)

Very large mound of frosted grey-green leaves with a white edge. Pale lavender flowers in midsummer. Grow in dappled shade with *Cornus alba* 'Elegantissima' and *Brunnera macrophylla*.

**H. 'Geisha'**

H/S 35×45 cm (14×18 in)

Yellow-green, glossy leaves margined with darker green that are slightly ruffled and with a good texture. Twisted, upright habit makes this a very distinctive hosta. Light purple flowers from midsummer onwards. A desirable plant with a future. Group with other green-gold hostas such as *H.* 'Spritzer', *H.* 'Inaho' and *H.* 'Chinese Sunrise', ferns and yellow grasses.

**H. 'George Smith'**

H/S 90×100 cm (36×40 in)

The first of the *H. sieboldiana* 'Elegans' sports with a gold centre and blue margin to be registered. It arose in the garden of George Smith, the well-known flower arranger, and should become available in the future. Superb foliage at its best in dappled shade. White flowers in early summer just above the foliage. *H.* 'Borwick Beauty' and *H.* 'Color Glory' are similar, if not in fact the same, and only time will tell if they should all be called *H.* 'George Smith'. Invaluable for the flower arranger. Use as specimen hosta with plainer neighbours.

### *H.* 'Ginko Craig' *
H/S 25×45 cm (10×18 cm)
Lance-shaped, white-edged leaves with attractive tall purple flowers in late summer. Fast grower, useful as an edging plant and to underplant larger white-edged hostas in a border with some shade. Grows well in a pot.

### *H.* 'Gloriosa'
H/S 45×60 cm (18×24 in)
Form of *H. fortunei*. Thin white edge to cupped, dark green leaf. Mauve flowers in midsummer. This is not easy to grow well but when it does is very distinctive and refined. Avoid tree drip but needs some shade and good cultivation.

### *H.* 'Goldbrook' *
H/S 55×100 cm (22×40 in)
Form of *H. fortunei*. Dense, cascading mound of green leaves with a broad creamy yellow edge that can extend into the leaf giving a marbled effect. Edge fades to creamy white. Pale lavender flowers on 70 cm (28 in) scapes in midsummer. Makes a very impressive container plant and an excellent leaf for the flower arranger. Associate with *Pachysandra terminalis* 'Green Carpet' and *Anemone* × *hybrida* 'Alba'. *H.* 'Spinners' is similar but larger and emerges later in the spring.

### *H.* 'Goldbrook Gold'
H/S 60×75 cm (24×30 in)
Seedling of open-pollinated *H. sieboldiana*. Heavily textured heart-shaped gold leaves with a white back. Will stand some sun and although slow is worth waiting for. Far superior to *H.* 'Golden Sunburst' that scorches badly if not grown in shade.

### *H.* 'Goldbrook Grace'
H/S 15×25 cm (6×10 in)
Sport of *H.* 'Golden Prayers' with an irregular green rim to gold leaf that fades to a beige-green with a creamier centre as the season advances. Pale lavender flowers that just top the mound appear through the summer. Appears vigorous and associates well with *H.* 'Zounds' in a dappled shady position. Also suitable for a rock garden.

### *H.* 'Gold Edger'
H/S 30×45 cm (12×18 in)
Small heart-shaped, chartreuse gold leaves. Many pale lavender flowers in midsummer. A rapid grower that needs some sun to colour. Useful edging hosta. *H.* 'Birchwood Parky's Gold' is similar but less sun-tolerant (although it will not colour in deep shade), with a thinner leaf texture. Sometimes called *H.* 'Golden Nakaiana' which is not a valid name. Both are vigorous, attractive hostas for ground cover.

### *H.* 'Gold Regal'
H/S 60×90 cm (24×36 in)
Medium to large chartreuse gold leaves of upright habit. Tall scapes with good bell-shaped lavender flowers in midsummer. When young a rather ungainly plant but makes a good garden plant with leaves that are thick enough that they are not often damaged and will stand some sun as long as conditions are moist. Will not colour in shade. Needs to be underplanted and not used as a specimen or as a container plant.

### *H.* 'Gold Standard' *
H/S 65×100 cm (26×40 in)
Sport of *H. fortunei*. The heart-shaped leaves emerge green but gradually change to gold edged with green. Pale lavender flowers in midsummer. If well grown and sited this is one of the best of the more recent hostas. It needs dappled light; too much sun and it

69

**H. 'Krossa Regal' growing with H. montana 'Aureo-marginata' in Longwood Gardens, USA. Excellent hostas for pots and for flower arrangers.**

*H.* 'Shade Fanfare' a reliable cultivar, photographed in David
**Foreman's garden,** UK.

whitens, not enough and the gold does not develop. Superb in the garden and container, a flower arrangers' delight. Use as the highlight plant in a green and gold grouping. H. 'Richland Gold' is an all-gold sport, similar in habit but the foliage is pale yellow-green. One for dappled shade.

### H. 'Golden Bullion'*
H/S 30×45 cm (12×18 cm)
All-gold sport of H. tokudama 'Flavo-circinalis'. Chartreuse yellow cupped leaves, slightly pointed. Pale lavender flowers just above the foliage mound. As yet fairly new but highly rated in USA. Appears to grow better than H. 'Golden Medallion'.

### H. 'Golden Medallion'
H/S 38×60 cm (15×24 in)
All-gold sport of H. todudama 'Aureo-nebulosa' and H. tokudama. Heavily seersuckered, cupped gold leaves with racemes of near-white flowers in early summer. Pest-resistant but very slow. Does not grow well in a container. Many of the plants sold under this name are H. 'Golden Sunburst', a much larger and faster-growing hosta.

### H. 'Golden Prayers'*
H/S 35×60 cm (14×24 in)
Small to medium golden leaves which are slightly puckered when mature. Pale lavender flowers in early summer and often repeat blooms. Best in partial shade as it colours well, but if no sunlight will fade to chartreuse. Looks effective in groups underplanting other hostas of a similar colour scheme. A good pot plant and popular with flower arrangers for smaller arrangements. H. 'Little Aurora' is very similar but slightly smaller.

### H. 'Golden Sculpture'*
H/S 75×100 cm (30×40 in)
Broad, chartreuse gold leaves, of a good substance that are tolerant of some sun as long as not hot and dry. Makes a large, very impressive mound. Pest-resistant. Near-white trumpet-shaped flowers on 90 cm (3 ft) stems. Use as a focal point underplanted with smaller gold hostas, low-growing white astilbes, yellow day lilies and ferns. Excellent garden and flower arranging plant.

### H. 'Golden Sunburst'
H/S 75×100 cm (30×40 in)
The all-gold sports of H. 'Frances Williams', whether occurring naturally or in tissue culture. Large gold leaves that burn in sun and must have dappled light; in full shade tends to fade to green. Whitish flowers in early summer.

### H. 'Golden Tiara'*
H/S 30×50 cm (12×20 in)
Sport of H. nakaiana. Compact, heart-shaped green leaves edged gold with 60 cm (24 in) purple flowers in midsummer. Vigorous, attractive smaller hosta very suitable for the front of the border underplanted with Chrysogonum virginianum. Has given rise to a number of sports, some naturally and some in tissue culture which now form the Tiara Series. The following are of interest and some have great potential for the garden or a container. H. 'Diamond Tiara' has a green leaf with a creamy margin. H. 'Emerald Tiara' is the reverse colour pattern of H. 'Golden Tiara' with a gold centre and green rim. Appears vigorous. H. 'Golden Scepter' is the all-gold version which needs some shade, very bright early in the season but has a rather thin leaf. H. 'Jade Scepter' is chartreuse green, vigorous, and it should appeal to flower arrangers. Grow under Polygonatum falcatum 'Variegatum'. H. 'Platinum Tiara' has a gold leaf with a white margin. Although slow initially this makes an impressive small plant but needs some care and dappled shade. Highly thought of in USA.

**H. 'Goldsmith'**
H/S 50×75 cm (20×30 in)
One of Eric Smith's gold hostas with *H. fortunei* 'Aurea' in its parentage. Early gold foliage that holds most of the season topped by leafy scapes with lavender flowers in midsummer. Upright habit and excellent grower. This was originally given to Jerry Webb labelled 'Goldsmith', but was then thought to be *H.* 'Granary Gold', but as a published description of another similar plant with this name exists, the laws of nomenclature mean that the original name stands. Has probably been distributed as *H.* 'Golden Age' and *H.* 'Gold Haze', which fades to green far earlier in the season. *H.* 'Granary Gold' is one of Eric Smith's best gold hostas, with large gold leaves that fade to creamy green towards the end of summer.

**H. 'Great Expectations'***
H/S 55×85 cm (22×34 in)
Sport of *H. sieboldiana* 'Elegans' that arose in the garden of John Bond, the keeper of the Savill Gardens in England, and although it is the same sport as *H.* 'George Smith' it appears different. Green-blue leaves with a gold centre. White blooms from early summer on 82 cm (33 in) scapes. Destined to be the hosta of the nineties. Even a young plant looks distinctive. Plant with *H.* 'Halcyon' and golden grasses.

**H. 'Green Fountain'***
H/S 90×115 cm (36×45 in)
Seedling from *H. kikutii*. Lustrous cascading green mound with leaning scapes of pale lilac flowers from midsummer through to autumn. A very distinctive and excellent green hosta that grows vigorously. The reddish tinge of the petioles is enhanced by planting with the fern *Dryopteris erythrosora*, which unfurls with coppery fronds. Excellent habit for a container and popular with flower arrangers.

**H. 'Green Piecrust'***
H/S 70×90 cm (28×36 in)
Large wavy-edged dark green leaves suggesting a piecrust. Pale lavender flowers in early summer. Would look effective in dappled shade underplanted with epimediums.

**H. 'Green Sheen'***
H/S 70×100 cm (28×40 in)
Good textured, large, pale green leaves with a sheen. Tall stems of pale lavender flowers in late summer. Although green a distinctive, refined plant that makes a very large mound and would be effective pale contrast against *Polystichum braunii* in a green border with *Helleborus corsicus* and *Euphorbia amygdalioides robbiae*.

**H. 'Ground Master'**
H/S 25×55 cm (10×22 in)
Undulating lance-shaped, matt green leaf with creamy edge. Tall attractive purple flowers in late summer. Vigorous ground cover and for edging in shade or dappled light. *H.* 'Resonance' is very similar, especially when juvenile. Effective planted under *H. ventricosa* 'Variegata' in a hosta border.

**H. 'Ground Sulphur'**
H/S 13×20 cm (5×8 in)
Small lanceolate gold leaves with racemes of pale lavender blooms on 20 cm (8 in) scapes in midsummer. Good grower that appears to stand some sun. One for the alpine bed or the edge of a small bed.

**H. 'Hadspen Blue'**
H/S 30×60 cm (12×24 in)
Tardiana group TF 2×7. Medium-sized, glaucous blue, thick leaves. Scape purple-dotted at the base with lavender flowers just above the foliage mound in midsummer. Pest-resistant. Slow to mature but when grown in partial shade will eventually be one of the

73

*H.* 'Sum and Substance' growing in a pot at Goldbrook Plants,
one of the best hostas for resistance to slug and snail
damage. Excellent large leaves of chartreuse gold.

*H.* 'Frances Williams' beginning in part to sport to gold.
When this division is removed it becomes *H.* 'Golden
Sunburst', the name given to the sport.

bluest hostas in the garden. Lovely grown with *Dicentra* 'Pearl Drops'.

### H. 'Hadspen Heron'
H/S 23×55 cm (9×22 in)
Tardiana group TF 2×10. Small, narrow, glaucous blue-green leaf. Short scape with racemes of pale lavender flowers in midsummer. Emerges early and can be frost damaged. Looks better if divided regularly as is rather untidy when allowed to become a large specimen.

### H. 'Halcyon' *
H/S 38×70 cm (15×28 in)
Tardiana group TF 1×7. Very blue, heart-shaped leaves which are even deeper blue in shade. Good lilac-blue flowers on purplish scapes in midsummer. One of the best of the Tardiana group, holding its colour for most of the season. Invaluable in the shade garden and excellent ground cover under shrubs; especially effective with silvery foliage and under shrub roses. One of the few blue hostas that grows well in a pot to maturity. Has given rise to sports, one of which is *H.* 'Goldbrook Glimmer'. This has blue leaves with a cloudy lighter middle, a very unusual colour effect which will be popular with flower arrangers.

### H. 'Harmony'
H/S 18×40 cm (7×16 in)
Tardiana group TF 2×3. Similar in leaf shape to *H.* 'Hadspen Heron' but with purple-dotted scapes and purple flowers that are the darkest of the group.

### H. 'Holly's Honey'
H/S 45×60 cm (18×24 in)
Shiny dark green, very ruffled leaves similar to *H. ventricosa*. Very tall purple flowers in midsummer. Slow to establish but a very distinct green hosta. Will be popular with flower arrangers when more readily available.

### H. 'Honeybells'
H/S 75×120 cm (30×48 in)
Hybrid of *H. plantaginea*. Fresh green, undulating leaves with racemes of fragrant, palest lilac flowers in late summer. Very vigorous and useful for ground cover. Stands more sun than most but not hot and dry.

### H. 'Hydon Sunset'
H/S 23×45 cm (9×18 in)
Seedling of *H.* 'Wogon Gold' and *H. gracillima*. Small leaves, gold on emergence which gradually fade to a duller shade. Smooth scapes 30 cm (12 in) tall with deep purple flowers in midsummer. Needs dappled light for best leaf colour as it easily scorches in too much sun. Excellent edger or for a rock garden. *H.* 'Dawn' ('Sunset') is similar although of a different lineage, the gold holding longer, and with fewer veins in the leaf. The base of the scape is slightly ridged, suggesting the possible influence of *H. venusta*. The flowers are slightly paler and more bell-shaped.

   *H.* 'Dawn' has been distributed as *H.* 'Sunset' but this was not a registered name and as it is so easily mixed up with *H.* 'Hydon Sunset', the British Hosta and Hemerocallis Society have decided to register it as *H.* 'Dawn' to differentiate it more clearly. *H.* 'Dawn' is also muddled up in the trade with *H.* 'Wogon Gold' ('Wogon Giboshi'), a poor grower which has more elongated yellow leaves, smooth scapes and flowers with yellow anthers (*H.* 'Dawn' has bluish anthers). *H.* 'Dawn' has recently given rise to a green-rimmed sport called *H.* 'Green with Envy' which should make a very attractive addition to beds planted with small hostas and shade-loving alpines.

### H. hypoleuca
H/S 45×90 cm (18×36 in)
Pale green oval leaves with a pronounced white back. Scapes are leaning with trumpet-shaped pale mauve-violet flowers in late summer. Very slow. Needs shade

but stands dryish soils. A recently introduced plant that is very similar is called *H.* 'Maekawa' which forms a symmetrical cascading mound with plenty of lavender flowers just above the foliage in midsummer. Seems more vigorous.

### *H.* 'Inaho'
H/S 25 × 55 cm (10 × 22 in)

A *H. lancifolia* form that has masqueraded under many names, including *H. tardiva* and *H. sieboldii* 'Inaho'. Very similar in colour to *H.* 'Chinese Sunrise' but much smaller. Leaves streaked green and gold, with 45 cm (18 in), slightly red-spotted scapes carrying racemes of purple flowers with bluish anthers. Very slow initially but makes a very attractive small mound when mature. Partial sun.

### *H.* 'Invincible'*
H/S 30 × 60 cm (12 × 24 in)

Undulating, glossy green leaves that are slug-resistant. Racemes of fragrant light lavender flowers in late summer on 50 cm (20 in) scapes. This is an excellent hosta that deserves to be more widely grown. The leaves are very handsome and distinctive. A lovely subject for the white and green garden and one of the best green leaves for flower arranging. Can make an impressive clump in a container and although it will grow in some sun looks better in dappled light. Very vigorous.

### *H.* 'Iona'
H/S 50 × 70 cm (20 × 28 in)

Sport of *H. fortunei*. Greyish cast to the green leaf with a good creamy white margin that holds all season. Plant with *Liriope muscari*. A similar hosta is *H.* 'Sundance', which is the variegated form of *H. fortunei* 'Aoki' but with the creamy margin rather narrow on juvenile plants but increasing in width with age.

### *H.* 'Iron Gate Glamour'
H/S 70 × 75 cm (28 × 30 in)

Medium to large leaves are green edged with creamy white. Scapes 90 cm (3 ft) tall with large fragrant lavender flowers in late summer. One of the more recent scented hostas that will become popular. The flowers are pale enough to be used in a white garden that uses pale flowers to enhance the effect. Could be planted with *H.* 'Invincible' and *H.* 'So Sweet' to make a fragrant group that all flower together.

### *H.* 'Janet'
H/S 38 × 60 cm (15 × 24 in)

Chartreuse yellow to white leaves with a green edge of a thin texture. Lavender flowers in midsummer. Not the easiest of hostas to grow as it must have dappled shade but popular with flower arrangers and probably best grown in a pot. Similar in appearance to the much more vigorous *H.* 'Gold Standard'.

### *H.* 'June'*
H/S 25 × 50 cm (10 × 20 in)

A very recent sport of *H.* 'Halcyon', found in tissue culture by Neoplants. The glaucous gold leaf has a narrow green-blue edge. It is very striking although slow to grow initially. One to use as a specimen in dappled light and will be sought after by flower arrangers once it becomes more widely available. Associate with ferns and gold grasses.

### *H. kikutii*
H/S 40 × 60 cm (16 × 24 in)

Slender green leaves with an arching habit. Slightly leaning scapes have reddish petioles with 60 cm (24 in) stems of lavender flowers in early autumn. There are a number of variable forms from the wild and these are being given cultivar names in USA. Elegant foil for variegated hostas and the fluffy flowers of *Smilacina racemosa*.

77

**H. 'June', a superb new sport that arose in tissue culture from H. 'Halcyon'.**

### H. kikutii 'Pruinose'*

H/S 30×50 cm (12×20 in)

The long, very narrow green leaves, reminiscent of *H. longissima*, have a heavy substance and a white back. Scapes to 45 cm (18 in) have a cluster of near-white lavender-tipped flowers in late summer and early autumn. A distinctive, very attractive, slow-growing plant that should be planted where its subtle effect can be appreciated. Should appeal to flower arrangers.

### H. 'Krossa Regal'*

H/S 75×100 cm (30×40 in)

Related to *H. nigrescens*. Large, glaucous, blue-grey leaves of a heavy substance that become more green as the season advances. Distinctive, attractive vase-shaped mound. Spires up to 1.5 m (5 ft) of bell-shaped lilac flowers in midsummer. Excellent growth habit, pest-resistant and superb as landscape or container plant. Bloom on the leaf lasts longer in some shade. Effective with *Hakonechloa macra* 'Alboaurea'.

### H. lancifolia

H/S 45×75 cm (18×30 in)

Narrow, lanceolate, shiny green leaves form a dense

arching mound. Many racemes of trumpet-shaped deep violet flowers with lilac-blue anthers from late summer through to autumn. The colour of the anthers distinguishes this from *H. sieboldii* which has yellow anthers. Excellent for ground cover and edging. There are some smaller forms in cultivation and *H.* 'Change of Tradition' and *H.* 'New Tradition' are recent variegated sports.

## *H.* 'Leather Sheen'
H/S 35×60 cm (14×24 in)
Dark green, leathery but glossy leaves. Scapes to 75 cm (30 in) with pale lavender flowers in midsummer. A useful foil to brasher plants.

**H. 'Brim Cup', a young plant of an excellent new smaller-growing hosta, in association with *Clematis jouiana* 'Praecox'.**

## *H.* 'Lemon Lime'
H/S 15×45 cm (6×18 in)
Small chartreuse gold, wavy leaves with no purple spots at base of petioles, which distinguishes it from *H.* 'Hydon Sunset', *H.* 'Dawn' ('Sunset') and *H.* 'Wogon Gold', although similar in appearance. Lavender flowers 25 cm (10 in) high from midsummer onwards. A small vigorous hosta for dappled shade.

79

**H. 'Little Blue'\***
H/S 32 × 45 cm (14 × 18 in)
Seedling of *H. ventricosa*. Not small and not blue! Glossy dark green foliage with tall purple flowers in midsummer. Much smaller than parent. Attractive green mound.

**H. 'Little White Lines'**
H/S 20 × 45 cm (8 × 18 in)
Sport of a *H. venusta* seedling. Small mid-green leaves edged with white. Scapes 50 cm (20 in) tall with purple flowers in midsummer. Seems vigorous.

**H. longipes latifolia hypoglauca 'Hachijo Urajiro'**
H/S 30 × 70 cm (12 × 28 in)
Superb shiny green leaf of a good substance with a white back. One of the many in this complex and they are closely related to *H. kikutii*. Characterized by leaning scapes which are sometimes nearly horizontal. This rare form has very distinctive foliage but is slow growing with 75 cm (30 in) long slightly leaning scapes.

**H. longissima**
H/S 25 × 50 cm (10 × 20 in)
Very long, narrow, dull green leaves of a slightly leathery texture. Strong scapes 55 cm (22 in) tall with reddish purple funnel-shaped flowers with blue-purple anthers in late summer. The flowers of *H. sieboldii*, which is often mistaken for *H. longissima*, have yellow anthers. I have a form which has much shorter petioles and flowers that do not have the reddish tinge. This could be *H. longissima brevifolia* or just another variant from the wild. Many new forms exist, some variegated, and are being registered with cultivar names. Prefers a damp spot, not too shady and should be placed so that the long narrow leaf is appreciated.

**H. 'Love Pat'\***
H/S 45 × 90 cm (18 × 36 in)

Seedling of *H. tokudama* that is larger than the species. Very beautiful cupped, glaucous blue leaves topped with near-white flowers in early summer. A superb newer hosta which although slow is worth the wait and is different from *H.* 'Buckshaw Blue', probably also a *H. tokudama* seedling. Associate with low-growing shade-loving plants such as *Lamium maculatum* 'White Nancy' so that the foliage mound can be appreciated, against a backdrop of *Elaeagnus angustifolia* 'Caspica' for a blue-silver group. Best not planted under trees as the leaves will collect all the detritus.

**H. 'Midas Touch'\***
H/S 50 × 65 cm (20 × 26 in)
Heavy textured gold, dimpled and cupped leaves with a sheen. Pale lavender flowers 50 cm (20 in) tall in midsummer. Very slow. Needs some sun to colour and in cool climates will grow in full sun. Grow with *Molinia caerulea* 'Variegata', *Cornus alba* 'Aurea' and *Iris sibirica* in moist soil.

**H. 'Mildred Seaver'\***
H/S 40 × 60 cm (16 × 24 in)
Good rounded green leaves of medium size with a wide creamy yellow margin which becomes white. Many scapes of pale lavender flowers in midsummer. Appears vigorous. Best in part shade as highlight to a green border. Like so many hostas looks lovely with green ferns such as *Polystichum setiferum* 'Herrenhausen'.

**H. minor\***
H/S 15 × 45 cm (6 × 18 in)
Small, dark green, wavy-edged leaves with 45 cm (18 in) ridged scapes of attractive mauve funnel-shaped flowers in midsummer. Larger than the very similar *H. venusta*. Needs some shade to grow well and when happy makes quite rapid mounds for a small hosta.

*H. minor* 'Alba' is an incorrect name often given to *H. sieboldii* 'Alba'.

### *H. montana*
H/S 100×100 cm (40×40 in)
Large oval, glossy, dark green leaves topped by tall very pale violet funnel-shaped flowers in midsummer. There are many forms of *H. montana* so this description can only be a generalization; some have darker flowers. All are vigorous, large and often superb foliage plants, and have been much used in the raising of a number of hybrids. Many newer forms are being collected in Japan and some have already found their way into specialists' gardens. I do not believe this is the same as *H. elata*, which I feel is probably a hybrid related to *H. fortunei* which it resembles. This is a foliage plant *par excellence* and, like most green hostas, is rarely planted.

### *H. montana* 'Aureo-marginata'*
H/S 70×90 cm (28×36 in)
Huge, pointed green leaves with a wide yellow margin. Much taller near-white flowers in midsummer. Superb but very slow to establish and as it is the first hosta to emerge is often frost damaged. If carefully sited or grown in a large container protected from early frosts it is one of the most spectacular foliage plants for the gardener and the flower arranger. A white-edged sport of this is called *H.* 'Mountain Snow', and as it also has near-white flowers it could have a future within the white garden, but it is as yet very new and expensive. Grow either hosta with *Dicentra spectabilis* 'Alba' and *Primula denticulata* 'Alba' for a late spring group. The all-gold sport *H.* 'Emma Foster' is very slow and of a weak constitution.

### *H.* 'Moon Glow'*
H/S 40×60 cm (16×24 in)
Seedling of *H.* 'August Moon' with good textured gold leaves edged in white. Mature leaves become cupped and dimpled, the young ones being smooth. Near-white flowers in midsummer. Considered one of the best of this type; vigorous. The white rim is emphasized if contrasted with ferns or could be planted with gold hostas and *Lysimachia nummularia* 'Aurea'. The all-gold sport is called *H.* 'Harvest Glow'.

### *H.* 'Moonlight'*
H/S 50×70 cm (20×28 in)
Sport of *H.* 'Gold Standard'. One of the best of the white-edged gold types. Must have some sun to colour but if too hot will scorch. A striking hosta when well grown; looks good underplanted with small gold hostas with a dark green background.

### *H. nakaiana*
H/S 25×60 cm (10×24 in)
Smallish mound of deep green foliage with purple flowers on ridged scapes in midsummer. Very floriferous. The dimensions given are only a guide to size as many forms exist. Has given rise to many hybrids and seedlings that have been named, such as *H.* 'Bouquet', *H.* 'Candy Hearts', *H.* 'Happy Hearts', *H.* 'Marquis', *H.* 'Pearl Lake' and *H.* 'Valentine Lace', and these make very attractive smaller hostas with excellent flowers.

### *H.* 'Nicola'
H/S 40×75 cm (16×30 in)
Tardiana group. The only named green-leaved hosta in the group. Good dark green, matt leaves with many stems of pinkish flowers in mid to late summer. Very vigorous and is particularly effective with pale pink astilbes underplanting *Acer negundo* 'Flamingo'.

### *H. nigrescens*
H/S 70×90 cm (28×36 in)
Oval, slightly cupped, glaucous leaves are grey-blue

**A large planting of *H. fluctuans* 'Variegated' in Longwood Gardens, USA.**

*H.* 'Francee', in David Foreman's garden, UK. One of the best
hostas for gardens and pots.

on emergence and greener later. Distinctive, large vase-shaped clump with the leaves having very long stems. Pale lavender flowers in midsummer reach to 1.5 m (5 ft). *H.* 'Krossa Regal' arose from this species.

### *H.* 'Northern Halo'
H/S 70×90 cm (28×36 in)
Tissue culture sport of *H. sieboldiana* 'Elegans'. Bluish corrugated leaves edged white. Near-white flowers in early summer. Most of the *H.* 'Northern Halo' in commerce are of a very cupped form with a narrow white edge and this is inferior to the wide-edged type which was given an award in USA. Expect to find the better form in the future in specialist nurseries. *H.* 'Northern Lights' has a cream-white central blade to the glaucous blue-green leaf. It is very slow and has a tendency to revert.

### *H.* 'On Stage'
H/S 35×60 cm (14×24 in)
Form of *H. montana*. The creamy white leaf is edged with two tones of green with some streaks from the margin into the centre. Blooms in late summer with racemes of lavender flowers. Emerges later than *H. montana* 'Aureo-marginata' and appears reasonably vigorous for a medio-variegated type.

### *H.* 'Osprey'
H/S 23×50 cm (9×20 in)
Tardiana group TF 2×14. Bluish cupped leaves of a thick texture. Good white flowers in midsummer. This is the only white-flowering hosta in the Tardiana group, all the others have some colour in the blooms. Useful for the white garden and very attractive in flower.

### *H.* 'Pastures New'
H/S 30×75 cm (12×30 in)
A *H. nakaiana* cross. Bright grey-green, heart-shaped leaves make a very dense, rapid-growing mound. Many pale lavender flowers are held well above the foliage mound. There seem to be two forms of this in cultivation, one much greener than the other and possibly the better plant. Perhaps this should become *H.* 'Green Pastures' to differentiate it. Flowers slightly later with shorter scapes. Superb planted in a container.

### *H.* 'Pearl Lake'
H/S 38×90 cm (15×36 in)
Dense mound of heart-shaped, green-grey foliage. Abundant lavender flowers on 80 cm (32 in) purplish stems from early summer onwards. A delightful hosta whether planted in the garden or in a container. Vigorous. Very useful as an edger in pink, blue and white colour borders.

### *H.* 'Piedmont Gold'
H/S 50×90 cm (20×36 in)
Large crinkle-edged gold leaves. Mature plants have an attractive habit. Pale lavender or near-white flowers on scapes just above the leaf mound in early to midsummer. Needs partial shade as it will become papery in too much sun. Colours well in dappled light. When well grown one of the best of the larger golds. A recent sport with a white margin to the gold leaves is *H.* 'Evening Magic', which will probably not grow quite so large.

### *H.* 'Pizzazz'
H/S 50×75 cm (20×30 in)
Very heavy, textured, heart-shaped blue-green leaves with a variable margin of creamy yellow. Many racemes of pale lavender flowers in mid to late summer. Best in shade or dappled light. One to look out for as it appears distinct. Will need careful placing, probably with blues and golds. Good with *Carex* 'Frosted Curls'.

**H. plantaginea**

H/S 60 × 100 cm (24 × 40 in)

Light green, oval, glossy leaves with scapes of very fragrant tubular trumpet-shaped white flowers 10–15 cm (4–6 in) long in autumn. Must have a sunny, moist site to flower. Can be grown in a large container in a fairly sunny spot. It has given rise to a number of forms and sports, the latest of which are as yet not readily available: H. 'Aphrodite' has double flowers, H. 'Chelsea Ore' a mainly gold leaf with a green rim and in cooler climates needs to be grown in a pot. H. 'White Shoulders' has a narrow white edge to the green leaf, and H. 'Venus' has more petals in the flowers than H. 'Aphrodite'.

**H. pycnophylla**

H/S 30 × 70 cm (12 × 28 in)

Species that is rare in gardens but very useful for hybridizing. Pale grey-green, wavy leaves with a pronounced white back. Leaning, slightly purple-dotted flowering stem with pale mauve trumpet-shaped blooms. Slow to establish and best with some shade. Seems to grow well in a pot. Handsome.

**H. 'Regal Splendor'** *

H/S 75 × 100 cm (30 × 40 in)

Tissue culture sport of H. 'Krossa Regal'. Slow in early years but eventually an excellent large, vase-shaped specimen with leaves that are greyish blue with a good cream margin. Tall light lavender flowers. A very distinctive newer hosta. Plant with lower-growing blue hostas and Dicentra 'Pearl Drops'.

**H. 'Reversed'** *

H/S 35 × 65 cm (14 × 26 in)

Blue-green foliage with large creamy centre. Attractive flowers. Needs some shade and time to build up vigour. Makes a good container plant and repays feeding and care. Excellent for the flower arranger. A very

lovely hosta when well grown and one that is best watered underneath. Group with ferns.

**H. rohdeifolia**

H/S 30 × 45 cm (12 × 18 in)

(H. rohdeifolia 'Aureo-marginata', formerly called H. helonioides 'Albo-picta'.) Lance-shaped green leaf, edged yellow fading to white. Purplish flowers in mid-summer well above the foliage mound. H. helonioides 'Albo-picta' is similar but the edge is white on unfurling and not yellow.

**H. 'Royal Standard'**

H/S 60 × 120 cm (24 × 48 in)

A hybrid from H. plantaginea. Fairly large bright green leaves offset the scented, trumpet-shaped white flowers which appear on 90 cm (3 ft) scapes in late summer. As long as the soil is moist it will be happy in all but the hottest sun. Excellent for the white garden and for ground cover as it grows rapidly. Some double flowering forms have been discovered; expect these to be named shortly.

**H. 'Royalty'**

H/S 25 × 35 cm (10 × 14 in)

The small gold leaves are pointed with dark purple flowers in late summer. Striking and quite vigorous.

**H. rupifraga**

H/S 20 × 60 cm (8 × 24 in)

Distinctive, medium-sized, heart-shaped leaves are a glossy pale green, very thick and leathery with undulations. Attractive pale purple, bell-shaped flowers from early autumn onwards. Forms vary slightly from the wild. Excellent hosta; true forms are rarely available.

**H. 'Saishu Jima'**

H/S 8 × 38 cm (3 × 15 in)

Form of H. sieboldii. Small, green, very narrow leaves

85

*H.* 'Iona' growing in the garden of Jackie Rowan in Ampfield, Hampshire, UK. Looks good all season.

*H.* 'Royal Standard', a reliable white-flowering scented
hosta.

with ruffles; 25 cm (10 in) pale purple flowers in late summer. Suitable for alpine beds and as a small edger. A very similar but slightly larger hosta is *H*. 'Haku-jima'.

### *H.* 'Sea Dream'
H/S 60 × 70 cm (20 × 28 in)
Leaves are bright gold with a white margin. Tall lavender flowers in midsummer. Must have some shade. Like all white-edged golds, looks best with golds, whites and greens.

### *H.* 'Sea Drift' *
H/S 60 × 90 cm (24 × 36 in)
Good-textured pie-crusted green leaves that appeal to flower arrangers. Tall scapes, to 90 cm (3 ft), with lavender-pink flowers in midsummer. Slow to establish and not suitable for a pot.

### *H.* 'Sea Gold Star' *
H/S 50 × 75 cm (20 × 30 in)
Dimpled, very heavy textured bright gold leaves with 90 cm (3 ft) near-white flowers in midsummer. Very slow to become established and needs four or five years before it starts to reveal its potential. Some sun to colour but not the midday sun. Superb foliage when mature.

### *H.* 'Sea Lotus Leaf' *
H/S 45 × 60 cm (18 × 24 in)
Glossy dark blue-green rounded leaves that are so cupped that the water collects in each leaf. Very pale lavender to near-white bell-shaped flowers in midsummer just above the leaf mound. Slow but distinctive foliage plant. Needs to be sited away from tree drip.

### *H.* 'Sea Monster'
H/S 65 × 100 cm (26 × 40 in)
Corrugated green leaves of a good substance that make a large mound. Near-white blooms in early summer.

### *H.* 'Sea Octopus'
H/S 23 × 55 cm (9 × 22 in)
Narrow green leaves with undulating margins. Scapes 80 cm (32 in) high have purple flowers in early autumn. Vigorous smaller hosta suitable for edging and as a foil to variegated hostas with similar leaf shape such as *H. sieboldii*.

### *H.* 'Shade Fanfare' *
H/S 45 × 60 cm (18 × 24 in)
In the early season the green leaf has a wide creamy margin but as the season advances more yellow tones develop if the plant is in some sun but not if grown in shade. Stems 60 cm (24 in) tall of lavender flowers in midsummer. Vigorous, easy cultivar already very popular with gardeners and flower arrangers. Grow with *Miscanthus sinensis* 'Zebrinus' for an intriguing contrast of texture, form and variegation in a place shaded from the hottest sun of the day. Looks good with *Digitalis ambigua*, *Helleborus corsicus* and erythroniums in a shady green and cream scheme.

### *H.* 'Shining Tot'
H/S 5 × 20 cm (2 × 8 in)
Tiny, shiny, deep green leaves of a good substance. One of the smallest hostas. Light blue trumpet-shaped flowers on 13 cm (5 in) arching scapes in summer. Best in partial shade although will tolerate sun in all but the hottest places. A delightful little plant that is a good increaser but needs to be seen close up on a raised bed.

### *H. sieboldiana* 'Elegans' *
H/S 90 × 125 cm (36 × 50 in)
The best known of the many *H. sieboldiana* forms. Very large, heart-shaped, cupped and puckered bluish leaves that are pest-resistant. Trumpet-shaped

lavender-white flowers just above the foliage mound in early summer. Best in partial shade as the bloom on the leaf is retained for longer but remarkably effective in a moist spot even in some sun. One of the most popular hostas and extremely useful in many situations in the garden. A slightly smaller cultivar is *H.* 'Helen Doriot' which has similar coloured flowers. One with whiter flowers is called *H.* 'Blue Seer' which, although slow, is a very impressive plant in a shady spot and suitable for the white garden. There are many named selections; all are good garden plants.

### *H. sieboldii*
H/S 30 × 60 cm (12 × 24 in)
Often called *H. albomarginata* which is incorrect. Lance-shaped, matt green leaves irregularly edged white. Trumpet-shaped violet flowers with yellow anthers in late summer. Quickly makes dense clumps and is very useful for edging in partial shade. There are many forms and named seedlings which have been selected for improved foliage or flowers but generally they are not as vigorous as the type. The best known are *H.* 'Louisa' and *H.* 'Emerald Isle', both with white flowers and green leaves edged white.

### *H. sieboldii* 'Alba'
H/S 13 × 30 cm (5 × 12 in)
Often erroneously called *H. minor* 'Alba'. Small green lanceolate leaves with tallish white flowers from mid-summer to early autumn. Not strong growing. *H.* 'Bianca', *H.* 'Snowflakes' and *H.* 'Weihenstephan' are named selections with larger white flowers and a more vigorous habit.

### *H. sieboldii* 'Kabitan'
H/S 25 × 45 cm (10 × 18 in)
Small, lance-shaped, thin textured, ruffled yellow leaves with a green margin. Tallish trumpet-shaped deep purple flowers in midsummer. When well grown very distinctive but must have some shade as it will scorch in sun. Seems a much better plant in USA than in Britain. Best grown in pot to establish.

### *H. sieboldii* 'Silver Kabitan'
H/S 20 × 38 cm (8 × 15 in)
Also erroneously known as *H.* 'Haku Chu Han'. Small lanceolate white leaves have a wide green margin. Purplish flowers well above the leaf mound in mid-summer. Very slow to grow and best in a pot in partial shade until established. When well grown is a delight-ful little hosta. *H.* 'Squiggles' appears similar but with a larger white centre to the green leaf and lovely white flowers on pale cream scapes 30 cm (12 in) high. Probably best grown in a pot in partial shade.

### *H.* 'Silver Lance'
H/S 30 × 50 cm (12 × 20 in)
Very long, narrow, dark green leaves with a narrow white margin. Makes a slightly cascading mound. Racemes of deep lavender flowers 60 cm (24 in) tall from late summer through to autumn. Elegant smaller hosta that needs careful placing to be appreciated.

### *H.* 'Snow Cap'*
H/S 40 × 60 cm (16 × 24 in)
Blue leaves have a wide creamy white edge and are of good substance. Whitish flowers. Will need to grow in shade for best colour. Gives a lovely accent with blue-foliaged dicentras and smaller blue hostas and will appeal to flower arrangers.

### *H.* 'Snowden'*
H/S 90 × 100 cm (36 × 40 in)
Raised by Eric Smith from *H. sieboldiana* and *H. fortunei* 'Aurea'. Large glaucous grey-blue leaves gradually change to grey-green. When happy makes a large mound. Many scapes with bell-shaped white flowers in midsummer. Slow to start but given good cultural conditions, dappled shade and plenty of

89

*H.* 'Zounds', an excellent gold in association with *Molinia caerulea*, *Cornus alba* 'Aurea' and *H.* 'Frances Williams' in the distance.

*H.* 'Sea Drift', a piecrust hosta in Longwood Gardens, USA.

moisture this is a spectacular plant for the garden and flower arranger. I have found it makes a superb container plant and is ideal for the white garden underplanted with white hardy geraniums or *Pulmonaria* 'Sissinghurst White'.

### H. 'So Sweet'*
H/S 35×55 cm (14×22 in)
Glossy green leaves with variable creamy white margin which begins creamy yellow. Fragrant white flowers on 60 cm (24 in) scapes, the buds faintly tipped with lavender in late summer. This is a lovely variety, great in the white garden and for flower arranging. One of the new hostas that is distinctive and very pretty. Plant with *Aruncus aethusifolius*, small ferns and white violets in shade or dappled light.

### H. 'Spritzer'*
H/S 45×35 cm (18×14 in)
Lanceolate leaves are two tones of green with a yellow to cream centre. It grows upright and arches over with the same type of habit as *H.* 'Green Fountain', which is one of its parents. White flowers tinged bluish purple on 75 cm (30 in) scapes from midsummer onwards. Very elegant in dappled light against *Cornus alba* 'Aurea' and *Hakonechloa macra* 'Alboaurea' underplanted with *Lysimachia nummularia* 'Aurea'. Relatively pest-resistant and will stand more sun than most; best in dappled light.

### H. 'Stiletto'
H/S 15×20 cm (6×8 in)
Undulating, very narrow lance-shaped leaves are green with a narrow white rim. Scapes 30 cm (12 in) tall with lavender flowers in late summer. Interesting but as yet little-known hosta.

### H. 'Sugar and Cream'*
H/S 60×100 cm (24×40 in)
A tissue culture sport of *H.* 'Honeybells'. A far superior plant with a cream edge to the green leaf. Pale lilac-white fragrant flowers in summer. This has vigour, a good habit and is very easy to mix with other foliage plants. It makes an elegant container plant but needs a large pot.

### H. 'Sum and Substance'
H/S 75×120 cm (30×48 in)
Huge chartreuse gold, thick, glossy leaves of a heavy substance. Very impressive and nearly slug-proof. Tall lavender flowers in late summer. Looks good underplanted with small gold hostas or used as an architectural specimen among lower-growing foliage plants. Needs some sun to colour and as long as it is not too dry will stand nearly full sun. One of the largest-leaved hostas and one of the most spectacular.

### H. 'Summer Fragrance'
H/S 60×90 cm (24×36 in)
Seedling of *H. plantaginea* (crossed with an unknown hosta). Cream-white margin to a slightly wavy green leaf. Tall scapes with large, beautiful, scented bluish flowers in late summer. Best in shade or dappled light. Good grower. Place in the garden where the fragrance will be appreciated.

### H. 'Sun Power'
H/S 60×90 cm (24×36 in)
Large, slightly twisted, golden ruffled leaves with an upright habit. Pale lavender flowers in midsummer, 90 cm (3 ft) high. Needs dappled light to colour and takes time to make an impressive specimen.

### H. 'Tall Boy'
H/S 50×90 cm (20×36 in)
Hybrid of *H. rectifolia*. Leaves green and relatively close to the ground. Not particularly good foliage but has a superb flowering display with very tall scapes of deep purplish blue flowers for many weeks in summer. Spectacular when used *en masse* for ground cover.

### H. tardiflora *
H/S 25×60 cm (10×24 in)
Lance-shaped, dark green, lustrous leaves with a heavy substance. Lavender-purple, trumpet-shaped flowers on red stems just above the foliage in early autumn. Excellent for the front of the border and very underrated.

### H. 'Tiny Tears'
H/S 8×15 cm (3×6 in)
Seedling of H. venusta. Tiny green leaves form a very small mound for the rock grden in partial shade. Purple flowers in midsummer. H. 'Thumb Nail' is similar but even smaller with light blue trumpet flowers on a 25 cm (10 in) scape.

### H. tokudama *
H/S 35×90 cm (14×36 in)
Heavily textured, cupped and puckered blue leaves. Trumpet-shaped greyish white flowers in midsummer just above the foliage mound. Very slow but distinctive hosta that prefers shade (not under trees) and useful in the white garden.

### H. tokudama 'Aureo-nebulosa' *
H/S 30×55 cm (12×22 in)
Leaves have an irregular cloudy yellow centre with a bluish margin. Leaf colour is variable and some forms are far better than others. Scapes 60 cm (2 ft) tall have clusters of whitish blooms from early to midsummer. Eye-catching variety very popular with flower arrangers although very slow to increase. H. 'Goldbrook Gift' is a sport with a bluish leaf and a yellow margin narrower than H. tokudama 'Flavo-circinalis'. H. 'Winning Edge' is a selfed H. tokudama 'Aureo-nebulosa' with a wide cream edge to green-blue centre.

### H. tokudama 'Flavo-circinalis' *
H/S 45×75 cm (18×30 in)
Heart-shaped blue leaves with a wide creamy yellow margin, more pointed than H. tokudama. Looks like a small H. 'Frances Williams' but has a pale lavender flower with darker stripes slightly later and the leaves are not as cupped when mature. Superb but slow.

### H. undulata 'Albo-marginata' *
H/S 55×90 cm (22×36 in)
Commonly known as H. 'Thomas Hogg'. Wavy, white-edged green leaves with rather flat petioles. Often muddled with H. crispula which has more undulate leaves and petioles that are narrow and grooved. Pale purple flowers on 90 cm (3 ft) scapes in early summer. Rapid developer and grows nearly anywhere. Excellent under trees and as a container plant. Plant with Solomon's seal, Geranium phaeum album and pulmonaria.

### H. undulata 'Erromena'
H/S 50×75 cm (20×30 in)
Mid-green, wavy, tapering leaves with 90 cm (3 ft) attractive pale mauve flowers in early summer. Multiplies well and makes good ground cover.

### H. undulata 'Univittata' *
H/S 38×70 cm (15×28 in)
Wavy, oval green leaf with a central cream blade. Violet flowers in early summer. Reasonably vigorous and very distinctive in summer. Reliable under trees. As the foliage is so distinct, needs careful placing or can look fussy. Good with green hostas and with the soft shield fern, Polystichum setiferum. H. undulata undulata has a very wide cream centre to the leaf and is not very vigorous. There are many named forms but those with very narrow medio-variegation often revert to green as they are unstable.

### H. 'Vanilla Cream'
H/S 13×25 cm (5×10 in)
Small lemon-green leaves of heavy substance, with slightly reddish scapes 30 cm (12 in) tall carrying

93

lavender flowers in midsummer. Slow growing and suitable for alpine beds in dappled light.

### H. ventricosa *
H/S 50×90 cm (20×36 in)
Heart-shaped, slightly wavy, dark green glossy leaves. Good 90 cm (3ft), deep purple bell-shaped flowers in late summer. Excellent green mound that is very effective under variegated shrubs such as *Elaeagnus ebbingei* 'Limelight'. *H. ventricosa* 'Aureo-maculata' has a central gold splash to the green leaf which fades later. Not very vigorous and smaller growing.

### H. ventricosa 'Variegata' *
H/S 50×90 cm (20×36 in)
(Registered in USA as *H. ventricosa* 'Aureo-margin-ata'.) The dark green leaves have a striking creamy yellow edge that becomes whiter as the season advances. Excellent racemes of deep purple flowers in late summer. Although slow initially, when mature it is one of the most spectacular of the variegated hostas.

### H. venusta
H/S 8×25 cm (3×10 in)
Small heart-shaped, darkish green leaves. Many funnel-shaped lavender-violet flowers on 25 cm (10 in) ridged scapes in midsummer. Delightful, vigorous little hosta that is very easy to grow in partial shade. Has given rise to many named seedlings such as *H.* 'Tiny Tears', *H.* 'Thumb Nail' with lilac flowers, and *H.* 'Po Po' which has a more rounded leaf. Very ruffled *H. venusta* seedlings and crosses are being selected for naming.

### H. venusta 'Variegated'
H/S 8×15 cm (3×6 in)
Probably a hybrid as the scapes are not ridged. The tiny leaves have two tones of green with creamy centres. Lavender flowers on very pale scapes often with a green streak appear in midsummer well above the leaf mound. Best grown in a pot until established although for such a small plant is relatively vigorous. Lovely with the filigree foliage of tiny ferns and *Aruncus aethusifolius*.

### H. 'Vera Verde'
H/S 15×38 cm (6×15 in)
Formerly called *H. gracillima* 'Variegated'. Small lance-shaped matt green leaves, edged white. Lavender flowers in midsummer. Stoloniferous. Useful edger for borders and rock gardens in all but full sun.

### H. 'Wide Brim' *
H/S 45×90 cm (18×36 in)
Blue-green leaves have a very wide creamy gold band that fades to cream as the season advances. The edge gets wider with age until it is more than half the leaf. Attractive lavender flowers in midsummer. Best in shade or dappled light. Excellent cultivar.

### H. 'Yellow River'
H/S 45×60 cm (18×24 in)
Pointed, heart-shaped, slightly wavy, dark green leaf with a good yellow margin. Lavender flowers in midsummer. Looks good with *Alchemilla mollis* and *Asarum europaeum*.

### H. 'Zounds' *
H/S 55×70 cm (22×28 in)
Form of *H. sieboldiana*. Large, rugose gold leaves are puckered and develop a metallic sheen with age; a fine specimen plant for light shade. Pale lavender flowers 75 cm (30 in) high in early summer. Slow. *H.* 'Dick Ward' has a green rim to the gold leaf.

Right: *H.* '**Silver Lance**'

# Ornamental Grasses, Bamboos, Rushes & Sedges

## Nigel J Taylor

***Agropyron magellanicum* is of lax habit and has a
subtle bluish tinge.**

# The Truth About Grasses

There is a wry smile on the face of the visitor to the flower show as she contemplates the display of ornamental grasses, carefully arranged in their pots on the stand. She was heading for the fuchsias when a chance sideways glance checked her progress towards those enticingly bright colours. Intrigued, she approaches the display, but is clearly hesitant about coming too close. Slowly she starts to circle the stand, though keeping at a safe distance.

The exhibitor has noticed the lady, and observes her cautious approach. He has seen the same thing many times before. He watches as she is drawn, almost involuntarily it seems, around the stand, still wary, but now venturing closer, clearly attracted, even if reluctantly, by what she beholds. She completes her tour. Now, with a knowing expression on her face, she approaches the perpetrator of this display. He knows just what is coming: 'Quite nice, aren't they?' she comments, studiedly understating her true impressions, and then, in a tone that might equally as well have been directed at an importer of cute, but rabies-carrying puppies, 'But, of course, you can't let them loose in the garden!'

This oft-repeated experience characterizes the foremost cause of prejudice against the grasses as garden-worthy plants. 'Grass gets everywhere', our sceptic reasons and, when you think about it, there is no doubting the truth of that statement. Grass *does* get everywhere – or almost – often reaching (to borrow a phrase) the parts that other plants cannot reach! The grasses, along with the sedges and rushes, some 14,500 species, are among the most successful plant types in the world, and are surely the most evident. Recall the last time you took a summer walk in the country. You may have noticed many flowers in the hedgerows, clothing the banks and roadside verges, but you can surely not have failed to observe that these were in the minority compared with the abundance of narrow leaf blades and airy or plume-like flower heads of the grass family. Meadows are a delight at certain times of the year when they are studded with the bright colours of a great variety of wild flowers. But what is the background against which these gems are displayed? And what remains when the flowers are spent, if it is not a veritable carpet of wild grasses? Woodland edge, forest glades, moorland, coastal sand dunes, ponds, lakes and their margins, indeed every ecological ingredient of our varied landscape boasts its own grasses and grass-like plants, and almost invariably they constitute the predominant vegetation. Prairie, plain and steppe afford vistas of little else but grasses. The vast areas of land that man has cultivated he has put down to grasses more than to any other crops. Corn, rice and maize, to name but three staples, are grasses, and among their further diverse types are numerous basic foods for both man and animal, besides others which are utilized commercially in a multiplicity of ways. When it comes to our sports fields, parks and, of course, gardens there is no more versatile, practical, relatively easily maintained – and pleasing – surface than the grass sward.

Yes, there is no denying the fact – grass does get everywhere! The question is, should we allow this truth to deter us from introducing grasses into the garden for any purpose other than as a lawn? Before answering this question let us allow our contender to voice a further doubt that is worrying her: 'Grasses are . . . ' she hesitates, ' . . . well, different, aren't they? I just wouldn't know where to start with them. Where do I put them? What do they like?'

The suspicion that the grasses and grass-like plants are 'different' is botanically true in quite a number of rather technical respects, but the cause of the trouble for the average gardener seems simply to be the visual perception that they have neither 'ordinary' leaves nor 'normal' flowers. Strangely, this superficial dissimilarity somehow appears to separate them by light years from the traditionally available range of familiar, 'ordinary' plants. Quite unaccountably it seems to remove them from the realm of reason which normally moves us unquestioningly to apply basic principles in our cultivation of all other commonly accepted, though still widely differing, plant types.

If either, or both, of these considerations have inhibited you from using ornamental grasses in your garden, please reflect for a moment on this reassuring statement of fact: from a gardening point of view perennial grasses may be equated exactly and absolutely with any other perennial garden plant. A like correlation may be made between annual grasses and any other annual garden plant. This basic premise immediately brings the grasses down to a level at which we can feel entirely comfortable with them, because the only difference *in gardening practice* between them and our 'normal' garden favourites is a visual one – and that is a positive blessing because, as we shall see, it gives us unique features that we may exploit to our benefit. A further happy implication is that there is a grass, just as there is a herbaceous perennial, for every spot. Indeed there are conditions where a grass is the only plant that will suit. Whatever the nature of your garden then, there will certainly be a good choice of grasses and grass-like plants from which to select that will be perfectly content with whatever you have to offer.

In the hope that at least some of the aura of mystery that often seems to shroud the subject has been dispelled, let us return to the first objection – that grasses get everywhere. Agreeing that they certainly appear to do so, our still decidedly dubious friend has an idea as to why that is the case. 'Don't they seed themselves prolifically?' she asks. 'After all, half of the weed problem in my borders is grass seedlings.'

Indeed, there are some prolific self-seeders. Many of these, however, are among the wild rather than the cultivated grasses. Even so, there are one or two ornamental species and varieties with similar reproductive habits. But then are there not other hardy perennials in our gardens whose seedlings we seem to find everywhere, and are constantly removing? If that really annoys us we throw the plant out, or perhaps avoid it in the first place. However, more than likely it makes a contribution to our planting scheme that we appreciate, and we are prepared either to tolerate its little excesses or to remove its seed heads before any damage is done. Such free self-seeders are in a tiny minority and, please note, this fact is as true of the grasses as it is of their fellow hardy perennial companions.

'Fair enough,' the visitor is gradually coming round, but she hasn't finished yet. 'I can grasp the idea that they are just like ordinary perennials but, even if they don't seed themselves everywhere, surely they run around and swamp everything within sight.' Again, yes, just a very few do. But again, so do some of the other plants in our gardens. That may well be the very reason for our planting them. We need some plants that will perform thus. We used them in full awareness of their habit of growth, and because they would do just what we wanted them to – that was to cover the ground. Nothing else would have done the job. We place them deliberately where they will fulfil their role and avoid planting them where they would overrun

99

other treasures. We acknowledge their rampant nature and if they are a little over-exuberant we restrain them once or twice a year by removing the bits that have exceeded their bounds. Again though, let it be emphasized, the number of grasses that are of running habit is very small. By far the majority, as with other hardy perennials, are clump forming.

The lady smiles, thanks the exhibitor for his patient explanation and reassurance, pays for a catalogue with the promise that she might just try a grass or two, and proceeds once more in the direction of the fuchsias. The diversion, she feels, was not a waste of time.

## Some basic botanical information

The purpose of this section is to consider the garden uses of the grasses, bamboos (essentially woody-stemmed grasses), sedges and rushes. Technical descriptions of the botanical differences within these families, and between them and other plant groups are available in other works, and only the briefest consideration seems appropriate here.

The visible parts of the plant are the stems, leaves and flowers. In the true grasses, including bamboos (Gramineae), and sedges (Cyperaceae) the stems are called culms. If you can lay your hands on a bamboo cane in the garden shed a quick look at it will reveal the three basic features which are, with very few exceptions, common to the whole Gramineae family: the culms are cylindrical, they have swollen joints called nodes, and they are hollow (except at the nodes). The sedges are different, and may therefore be readily distinguished, in that the culms are triangular in cross-section, they have no nodes, and are pith-filled, therefore solid. The rushes (Juncaceae) are generally cylindrical like the grasses but, in common with the sedges, are solid and nodeless.

The leaves are, of course, characteristic, being narrow and linear (though surprisingly broad in some cases). The rushes and sedges share an arrangement where the leaves progress in three ranks up the shoots, whereas in grasses they alternate in two opposite ranks up the culms.

So far as foliage is concerned we do find grassy and sword-like leaves in quite a number of other plants, but an examination of the flowers of the grasses reveals that they are in a world of their own – a world, not of brightly coloured invitations to buzzing bees to alight and unwittingly collect and deposit the pollen that will ensure the successful production of seed, but of wind pollination where minute pollen grains in their inconceivable millions are wafted between neighbouring or more widely separated plants. Whilst hay fever sufferers may have good reason to rue this phenomenon it none the less allows for a quite distinctive assortment of flower heads of unrivalled grace and subtlety. The true flowers are quite tiny and only in the case of the rushes do they in any way resemble 'normal' flowers. Usually a number of these tiny flowers combine in what is termed a spikelet, and in turn the full complement of spikelets constitutes the flower head, or inflorescence. There are three modes of arrangement of the spikelets which contribute to the appearance of the flower head, each with its descriptive term (Fig. 1): a spike is an inflorescence whose spikelets attach directly to its main stem (axis) without stalks. They will usually, therefore, be fairly tight and narrow. Sometimes the spikelets grow on short stalks, themselves attached to the axis. This is a

**The dense hairs of *Alopecurus lanatus* give it a silvery effect. Chippings around the crown discourage rotting in winter wet.**

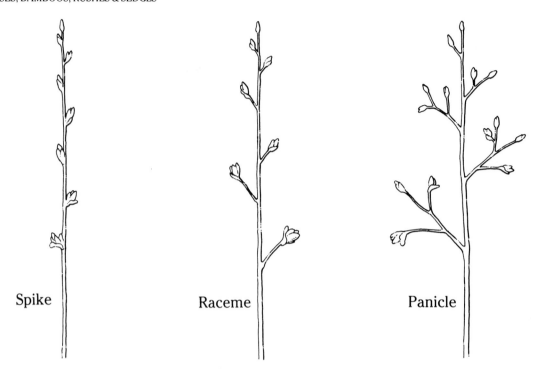

Spike       Raceme       Panicle

**Fig. 1 The three main types of inflorescence.**

raceme and will again tend to be quite narrow. The glorious plumes and open heads of many of the grasses are called panicles, where the spikelets are carried on stalks which themselves are on branches from the main stem.

As far as their aesthetic contribution to the garden is concerned grasses, bamboos, sedges and rushes all feature the characteristic, essentially erect or arching form.

The true grasses offer the greatest wealth of diverse floral beauty. There are tremendous variations in plant size and form, and in foliage size, arrangement and texture. Foliage colour is generally green (sometimes evergreen), with a small number of yellows, blues and reddish purples, and variegated forms are well represented.

The bamboos offer nothing from a floral point of view, and foliage colour is limited to shades of green although they do include some fine variegated forms and are almost invariably evergreen. They range in size from small, though often with extensive ground-covering capacity (i.e. invasive!), to very tall and almost tree-like, with a superlative grace of form.

For a kaleidoscope of fascinating foliage colours, often evergreen, the sedges are surely unrivalled, and this more than compensates for generally insignificant flower spikes and, with exceptions, limited ranges of form and size.

The rushes, including woodrushes, offer just one or two exciting, and two or three interesting forms, the remainder featuring only modest attractions, but being useful in more extreme conditions of wet or dry.

# Why Grow Grasses?

So far we have endeavoured to allay any immediate fears, and we have at least considered why, to use a double negative, you shouldn't *not* plant grasses! But you may feel that you are quite happy with your garden as it is, using, as you are, an already good variety of plant types. Why bother with having to get to know yet another group with its quirks and idiosyncrasies? Is the choice not already overwhelming without introducing more elements? Let us embark upon the positive aspects of the matter; in other words, why grasses are a must for the garden.

As gardeners desirous of using our plants much as an artist would his paints, we have available to us a varied and extensive palette of different plant types: trees, shrubs, conifers, heathers, alpines, ferns, herbaceous perennials, aquatics – and grasses. Each group is distinctive, unique in certain respects. Each offers its own peculiar features, contributing characteristics with which it alone has been endowed by the great Creator, and which no other group can anywhere near duplicate. In achieving maximum interest in our planting surely we should be actively seeking to include respresentatives of each group, each bestowing its own singular traits, thus availing ourselves of a little bit of everything that the wonderful plant world has to offer. Conversely, there would seem to be little point in depriving ourselves of something that could only enhance the overall effect. Now when it comes to the grasses we have a group of plants which is so individual, so distinct in more than one respect, that it absolutely cannot be excluded – it just must be represented somewhere. Just what is it, then, about the grasses that makes them so worthy of inclusion in the garden?

## Form

First and foremost consider their form – simple and vertically linear. There is nothing fussy about any of the grasses and they are, in consequence, intrinsically restful. Their ubiquitous distribution throughout the earth's ecosystems means that, when introduced into the garden, they inevitably bring with them something of the ethos of their natural habitat. The impact is both visual and auditory, especially in the case of the medium and larger grasses, evoking the sights and sounds of wide open spaces, a mysterious synthesis of the wild and the serene. Meadows and barley fields are conjured up, rippling and gently swishing in the breeze; the vast panorama of American prairie grasses constantly in motion like rolling ocean waves; or, in a different setting, the rustling of reed beds on wide, wild, windswept marshes. Surely no other representatives of the plant world can so easily distil the very essence of those parts of our earth that are the furthest removed from the troubles and cares with which mankind seems to have burdened himself. How refreshing, then, to be able to indulge in a little romantic relief simply by stepping out into one's garden.

There are a number of plants with more or less linear leaves, but the great majority of plants' leaves are very definitely broad and rounded in general outline. Likewise the overall shape of practically all other types of plant is decidedly rounded. They sit so densely solid, stolid, immovable – unless a real wind gets hold of them. By contrast, observe the grasses – always the first in motion in the slightest breeze. The repetition of line and curve affords a total change of texture, an important ingredient in the recipe for

103

successful planting. They stand almost alone in giving a marvellous vertical lift, an essentially upward thrust that is so refreshingly different that it offers a wonderful contrast to our other plants. That contrast must be exploited. In current parlance they are the yuppies of the plant world – upwardly mobile in a way few other plants are.

## Foliage colour

What a wonderful gift colour vision is. We could get by in monochrome (remember black and white television?), but colour immeasurably enriches life's experiences, and it seems to be the factor that makes the most immediate impression on our senses. There is no end to the array of bright colours in the plant world, largely represented in their flowers. A group of plants that is rarely anything more than subtle through virtually its entire range is therefore of great value, again by way of contrast. That group is, of course, the grasses, and it is foliage rather than flower colour to which we are here referring. Very few strong colours are reckoned among their number. *Carex elata* 'Aurea' (Bowles' golden sedge) and the bamboo *Pleioblastus viridistriatus* are a strong yellow; *Milium effusum* 'Aureum' (Bowles' golden grass) only slightly less so; *Uncinia rubra* is a rich foxy red-brown; *Imperata cylindrica* 'Rubra' a startling blood red, and the more strongly white-variegated varieties are certainly bright. Possibly the almost electric blue *Agropyron magellanicum* could be included too. But such are exceptions and are few and far between.

The point must now quickly be made that subtlety should not be confused with dullness. In fact the range of hues to be discovered among the grasses is nothing short of exciting. We have just mentioned the brighter yellows, reds, browns and blues, and the white-variegated forms. There are also yellow, cream and tri-coloured (i.e. white, pink and green) variegations, generally in the form of longitudinal stripes, but with yellow or cream cross-banding in a handful of intriguing cases. The sedges contribute some further marvellous colours, several of them quite unmatched by any other plants: silvery and whitish greens, pale and deeper olives sometimes overlaid with bronze to orange overtones, grey- and chocolate-browns through to red- and rich orange-browns, and even maroon. There are two or three variegated rushes; most are green, but there is one, the woodrush *Luzula ulophylla*, whose hairy backing to concave leaves gives a very silvery effect. Back with the grasses there is a woolly silver (*Alopecurus lanatus*), beautiful silvery blues, powder blues, purplish blues, grey-blues; blue-greens, grey-greens and mid-greens; yellows, ochres and fresh yellow-greens; deep reddish and bronzy purples and the strong red of *Imperata* just mentioned. Here, then, is a second factor which we may advantageously turn to our account: an incredible palette, predominantly subtle, a marvellous addition, and foil, to the standard plant colour range.

## Flower power

A third invaluable contribution by the grasses to the garden scene is furnished by their flower and seed heads. While retaining the vital reproductive organs of all plants they bear absolutely no resemblance to 'ordinary' flowers, as commented earlier. Adjectives such as airy, open, graceful, fluffy, lacy, shimmering,

**Alopecurus pratensis 'Aureovariegatus' with the shrub Physocarpus opulifolius 'Dart's Gold' and Acaena inermis 'Copper Carpet': totally different leaf forms in a pleasing association.**

feathery, diaphanous, wispy and silky, and nouns like plumes, spikes, sprays, clouds, and even caterpillars, shuttlecocks and bottle-brushes could rarely be applied to 'normal' flowers. One can appreciate, then, how the word texture may frequently be appropriate with reference to the flowers of grasses, whereas it is scarcely applicable otherwise in floral terms. Yes, they are different. Now, difference means contrast, and contrast is the breath of life to the garden.

Perhaps the best known among the inflorescences (flower heads) of the grasses are the glorious shaggy plumes of the better forms of pampas grass. But there is tremendous variation, ranging from short stubby spikes to the most delicate, light and airy open panicles. The individual spikelets also manifest great variety, some resembling the tiniest beads, others larger, like those of the quaking grasses (*Briza* spp.), heart-shaped and nodding, dancing in the slightest breath of wind. (Indeed the response of their flower heads to the wind is one of the most appealing characteristics of the grasses as a family.) Many feature hairs or bristles to a greater or lesser degree, such as the pampas grass just referred to, or the cotton grasses (*Eriophorum* spp.). Cultivated barley and members of the *Stipa* family are further examples. In all cases the colouring is subdued but, none the less, as with the foliage, manifests a fascinating diversity, including quiet shades of green, yellow, blue, violet, purple, brown etc. The close and comparative examination of the inflorescences of several different grasses is a delightful exercise. Generally speaking, while there are some decorative seed heads among other 'ordinary' flowering plants, many lose their appeal totally at this stage, whereas the grasses tend to hold their attractive appearance for a longer duration, right through the whole flowering and seed-forming process.

# Ease of cultivation

Always a factor to consider when selecting plants is ease, or otherwise, of cultivation, and this must rank as a further plus in our contemplation of the merits of the grasses. Remember that they may be regarded simply as straightforward perennials or annuals. The vast majority of such plants are perfectly happy in, or at the very least will uncomplainingly tolerate, most average garden soils and situations. A few will sulk if it is too dry or too wet, too sunny or too shady, too cold, too hot, or too windy. The same is true of grasses. In general they are obligingly long suffering and only too anxious to please. The range of conditions that some grasses will tolerate is actually quite incredible. Some that are normally associated with average soil conditions will actually grow in a garden pool. Others that grow naturally in water show no signs of resentment at being planted in average soil in good light. At the other extreme are those whose native habitat is sun-baked and dry, and yet which will likewise accept not unduly free-draining soil in good light with good grace. Perhaps the point that is being made is that if you have 'average soil and good light' there is not much you cannot get away with. And if you are prepared either to improve the drainage or to add moisture-retentive organic matter as appropriate to a particular species, most of the remainder may be accommodated quite happily. The odd few that might let you know if you offend them by siting them incorrectly are mentioned in the Plant Directory (see pages 140–184).

# Using Grasses in the Garden

## Broad principles of contrast and colour

The word contrast has appeared several times already with the implication that it is a feature of no little significance in garden planning. Indeed we could perhaps go so far as to say that in devising our planting schemes contrast is the single most important factor for which we should be striving. Above all else it breathes life into a scene. It creates interest.

In the many different types of plant available to us we have all the ingredients of an interesting scene. The more of those different types of which we avail ourselves the more life we inject. You, as the gardener, face the challenge of arranging the material at your disposal in the most aesthetically pleasing manner possible. This challenge is at once both daunting and exhilarating, one with which you will most likely always find yourself grappling in the search for total satisfaction with the result that you have produced. Thankfully there is great scope for contrast using any of the following factors, either alone or, much more likely, in combination.

1. COLOUR  Put a blue-leaved plant against a yellow one and you have contrast.
2. TONE  Plant dark green leaves next to paler green and again you have contrast, or, associating the same dark green with silver would give a double, and therefore stronger and more lively contrast – of colour and of tone (lightness/darkness).
3. FORM  Place erect against prostrate – another contrast – or dome-shaped with arching.
4. HABIT  Clump-formers contrast with carpeters.

5. HEIGHT  Contrast low with tall. Among the grasses there are miniatures for rock gardens or sinks, with bamboos many metres high at the other extreme.
6. FOLIAGE  Apart from colour and tone a wealth of possible contrasts are available, even among the largely linear grasses: narrow with broader, shiny with matt, smooth with hairy, large with small, long with short.
7. FLOWERS  Again contrasts galore are available, in shape, size, colour etc. However, remember that flowers are generally a decidedly more temporary feature and that other forms of contrast should be sought for the rest of the year. Where the distinctive inflorescences of the grasses are concerned we may enjoy the contrast between long and short, or between those which are tight, dense or narrow, and the more open, broad and airy examples.
8. DECIDUOUS/EVERGREEN  Do not forget that in winter the contrast between evergreen and deciduous or herbaceous plants will be appreciated, and the former should be borne very much in mind when devising planting schemes.
9. MASS  The relative number of two or more types of plant in itself provides contrast, besides balance. For example, several low rounded plants may be nicely balanced by just one contrasting vertical grass.

These nine sections embrace many times that number of contrasting permutations, and there is tremendous scope for ingenuity. Indeed it would be a fair-sized garden that was large enough to accommodate anywhere near the full range of possibilities.

The point made in section 9 is an important one. We will usually wish to avoid a too-busy, fussy effect. A

degree of restfulness is what most of us cherish in a garden, and to that end some repetition, some continuity, is appropriate. Actually the grass lawn serves that purpose quite admirably. It is intrinsically simple, a flat monotypic, monochromatic surface – the perfectly serene foil for the animation of the border. But a similar effect may be achieved within the border itself by planting several of the same, or similar plants together. This is no doubt why we are usually exhorted to plant in groups of three, five or seven (which in itself is intriguing, the uneven numbers indicating, as they seem to, our innate antipathy towards the symmetrical and formal when dealing with the things of nature). Having attained the required serenity, some kind of balance must now be sought to avoid monotony – hence, in the example above, the one vertical accent complementing the repose of the adjoining group. An area of more gently coloured plants may need balancing with one smaller splash of brightness. The reverse is also true. Any patch of vivid colour will benefit from the tranquillity of a larger balancing area of quieter hues. Each enhances the other, as well as the scene as a whole.

Reference has already been made twice to colour: first with regard to the range available among the grasses, and second as a source of contrast. To develop the subject a little further, contrast is not the only use to which we can put colour. We can contemplate and enjoy a colour quite alone and in its own right, usually when observing a plant at close quarters without reference to its neighbours. The moment we step back a bit though, and the neighbours assert themselves, we start to see colours in relation to one another. The

**The flower heads of the annual *Briza maxima* are attractive in the border or cut for indoor decoration. It is planted here with the golden hop, *Humulus lupulus* 'Aureus'.**

colour associations will then make an impression on our visual senses in one of three ways: they will either harmonize, contrast or clash. We are interested in the first two, and will probably want to avoid the third! It is actually quite difficult to concoct a clash, indeed it is virtually impossible to do so when using grasses. The danger is greater with stronger flower colours – pink with orange, for example.

The word harmony, normally implying the happy blending of any two or more factors, is rather more limited in discussing colour, signifying not just a combination of any two colours which look well together, but rather the association of closely related colours only. Using the colour circle (Fig. 2) you will observe the three primary colours and their three intermediaries. Harmony is the result of the juxtaposition

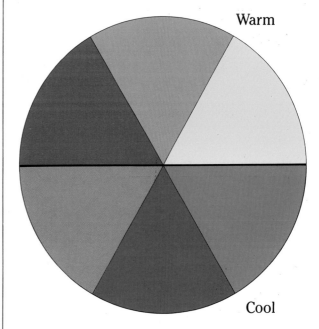

**Fig. 2 The Colour Circle.**

of any two adjoining colours. Contrasting colours are any that are not immediate neighbours to each other. (A further factor is introduced by the dark line which divides the warm colours from the cold.) Both harmonious and contrasting associations are satisfying to the eye. They differ in that harmonies are generally easier on the eye and therefore restful, whilst contrasts make a more forceful statement.

We also talked of balance – several restful shapes balanced by one vertical one. The principle of balance applies equally to the use of colour. The most satisfying planting is probably achieved by a basically harmonious arrangement, punctuated by a limited number of contrasts. These will bring that necessary sparkle to what could become a rather flat scheme, but should not be so numerous as to detract from the overall serenity of the panorama.

Yet another factor plays its part inasmuch as, in our painting with plants, colours vary not only in hue but also in lightness and darkness. We can have two colours which harmonize, but because one is light and the other dark we have a contrast of tone – say pale yellow with dark green. So our harmonies and contrasts may be of colour or tone, or both. It will be recognized that the possible permutations of tone, form, habit, height, leaf character, season of interest, limitations as to soil or situation etc. are boundless and there is no end to the scope for creativity, experiment, reassessment and rearrangement.

# Grass borders for foliage effect

We will imagine that what you have read thus far has so enthused you that you have decided to set aside a border or part of the garden exclusively for grasses. Actually this represents a swing to the other extreme wherein we are severely limiting our palette. How-

ever, experimenting with a restricted palette can be an interesting exercise for an artist, and the same is true for the gardener. Besides, if we are especially interested in a group of plants why should we not devote an area to them? There are alpine fanatics, rose or chrysanthemum fanatics, heather and conifer fanatics, even (with due respect to them) vegetable fanatics – and their gardens reflect their passion. We grass enthusiasts (graminophiles?) need not be outdone. Yet we must recognize that we are presenting ourselves with a real challenge. We want our border to be, not just a collection of grasses, but a lively, interesting entity. Yes, we are back with contrast, and yet we have drastically limited the scope for that contrast. We have no deep purple, no silver, few really dark tones, and somewhat limited variety in leaf shape – certainly nothing rounded. We must therefore exploit to the fullest such contrast as is available. Select contrasting tones and colours, leaf and flower forms, and height, form and habit. Successful grass gardens can be achieved. The recent garden festivals at Stoke and Glasgow in the U.K. both featured examples, the one at the latter, in 1988, attracting particular comment.

Now, at last, let's get down to some real planting! We will assume that we have the luxury of an empty border in a position in good light with reasonable soil, already dug over and with some organic matter incorporated, just waiting for some plants.

The following scheme would suit a border of some 2 m (6½ ft) by 15 m (50 ft) and, in its entirety, would make a magnificent planting of grasses, illustrating the whole gamut of possible colour and shape variations. However, a border this size devoted to grasses would not be suited to every garden – or gardener – and so it is divided into three sections, each with its own harmonizing colour schemes (Figs. 3–5). Of course any of the associations could be used, right down to just two or three of the varieties suggested.

## RED, YELLOW AND OLIVE HUES

Colourwise we will start with the yellows and yellow variegations, reds, olives, and greens which are on the yellow side rather than the blue. It is usually best to select the larger specimen-type plants first. (At this point I must mention that there are a number of grasses whose form dictates that they be used in this fashion – that is, as single specimens standing free from the nudging attention of any immediate neighbours which would only blur their individuality. Those which display a strongly symmetrical shape, hemispherical like *Helictotrichon sempervirens*, or erect and outward arching like *Carex buchananii*, can only be fully appreciated in isolation. Underplanting is quite permissible so long as it remains strictly round the feet of the specimen.) There is a choice of yellow variegated specimen grasses; we will employ two in this section of the border, and will aim for a contrast of form between them. *Phragmites australis* 'Variegatus' and *Miscanthus sinensis* 'Zebrinus' are both nicely erect plants, so one of those will suit us. If we choose the former we must be alert to its wandering habits, especially if the soil is at all damp, and either contain it or be prepared to remove growth that exceeds its allotted limits. We can next choose between two grasses of arching shape to contrast with the vertical nature of the miscanthus or phragmites. Either *Spartina pectinata* 'Aureamarginata' or *Cortaderia selloana* 'Gold Band', the golden variegated pampas grass, will be fine. The above caution with regard to the phragmites may be echoed in the case of the spartina, although it is more controllable, and in an especially cold region the pampas grass may need some winter protection, particularly while it is young. Both offer good flower heads as a bonus. Between these two we will use the shorter *Miscanthus sinensis purpurascens* whose leaves will become an increasingly strong reddish purple as the summer advances.

There are three fine yellow colours to come next, used in bold patches in front of and adjacent to these taller plants. Bowles' golden grass, *Milium effusum* 'Aureum', is virtually evergreen, and golden yellow in all its parts including the open flower panicles and the stems on which they are held. The bamboo, *Pleioblastus viridistriatus*, will attain 1 m (3 ft) or so, but not so much when the recommended spring cut-back is given to maintain the wonderful quality of the bright yellow-striped leaves. *Carex elata* 'Aurea' is Bowles' golden sedge, certainly the strongest yellow of all the grass-like plants. Between these last two is the tussock grass, *Chionochloa rubra*, a tuft of arching narrow foliage of a unique colour, a sort of orange ochre, grey-blue within the inrolled leaves, more brassy in winter. It is intriguing close up but nothing very special from a distance except when associated with bright yellow, when it really comes into its own. The rich red-browns of *Uncinia rubra* and *Uncinia uncinata* would look splendid in the foreground here, although they might not survive in colder areas without protection.

*Carex kaloides* and *Schoenus pauciflorus* are sedges of pale orange-brown and maroon respectively, both fairly erect, the former with flat leaves, the latter more needle-like. In absolute contrast to the schoenus is the beautiful, low-growing *Hakonechloa macra* 'Aureola' with soft lax leaves of yellow and green overlaying one another as the clump gently spreads. A reddish flush usually suffuses the leaves as autumn arrives. Between the two strong yellows of milium and pleioblastus is the dramatic rich red of the Japanese blood grass, *Imperata cylindrica* 'Rubra'. The amount of red increases as the summer progresses and, especially in the grouping here suggested, the effect is positively stunning. *Carex dipsacea* is a rich olive, almost bronzy in full sun, and with narrow arching leaves. It will stand out nicely in front of the yellow bamboo. It adjoins a front-of-border carpet of the

111

useful foxtail grass, *Alopecurus pratensis* 'Aureo-variegatus'. Clip this one back in early summer before it flowers and it will remain low, dense and bright. To the right of the sedge is space for a form of the wood-rush, *Luzula sylvatica* 'Hohe Tatra'. In all its varieties the woodrush is a valuable evergreen, holding its own in most situations including those which are often a problem, such as dry shade. This variety produces broad, rich green leaves during the summer which are pleasing enough, but it is in the winter that it really comes up trumps, transforming itself into a mound of strong, shiny yellow, a constantly glowing treat through the bleaker months of the year. *Carex testacea* forms arching tufts of a paler olive than *C. dipsacea*, with bright orange overtones in full sun, and looks good against yellow. Its neighbour is a fairly recent variety of the native wavy hair grass, *Deschampsia flexuosa* 'Tatra Gold', quite delightful in flower, although it is the lovely clean, brightest yellow-green of the narrow leaves that is the main attraction of this cultivar. Sadly, though, if you garden on shallow chalk, this is one of the few grasses that will not be happy with you. Against this I have chosen another fine variety of the woodrush, *Luzula sylvatica* 'Marginata', a smart plant with a narrow cream margin to the deep green leaves. The palm branch sedge, *Carex muskingumensis*, with bright, fresh green leaves completes this group. If your soil is on the damper side of average there are no plants included here that would complain – in fact several of them would be that much happier.

**Harmonizing colours, contrasting leaf shapes: the sedges *Carex dipsacea* (left) and *C. morrowii* 'Fisher's Form' (right) with *Tolmiea menziesii* 'Taff's Gold' (centre) and *Lonicera nitida* 'Baggesen's Gold'.**

## BLUE, GREEN AND CREAM HUES

We proceed now to a more relaxed scheme and, leaving the yellow end of the spectrum we move to the mid- and blue-greens and to cream and white variegation which gives the added sparkle that is always welcome.

Two more varieties of the stately miscanthus family are the specimen plants in this section. *Miscanthus sinensis* 'Silver Feather' is the taller: erect and then arching, with drooping leaves, and with fine autumn inflorescences. *M.s.* 'Gracillimus' is less erect, and with very narrow grey-green, white mid-ribbed leaves, curled at the tips. An alternative in this position (except in colder areas) would be the white-variegated pampas grass, *Cortaderia selloana* 'Silver Stripe'. *Carex pendula* makes quite an impression with shiny rich green, arching leaves and long flowering culms with drooping heads. You may have seen it growing wild in damp woodland. Three markedly variegated forms appear next, all with foliage to about the 60 cm (2 ft) mark, and all of which are of spreading habit and will therefore need watching. (Additionally they will all grow in damp soil if required, the second and third even in water.) *Carex riparia* 'Variegata' can look almost white, with just a narrow green edge; *Phalaris arundinacea* 'Feesey's Form' is broader leaved and even whiter; and *Glyceria maxima* 'Variegata' is of essentially cream appearance, being only narrowly green-striped. The new growth is pleasingly pink-flushed. Each of these will create bright pools between the miscanthus specimens. The middle rank plants start with the snowy woodrush, *Luzula nivea*, so named on account of its white flower heads. The evergreen leaves are dark green and hairy-edged. *Carex oshimensis* 'Variegata' makes evergreen clumps of neatly green and white striped leaves. *Stipa gigantea* is a fairly low plant but sends up marvellous open plumes to 2 m (6 ft) or so. Broad leaves are the valuable

113

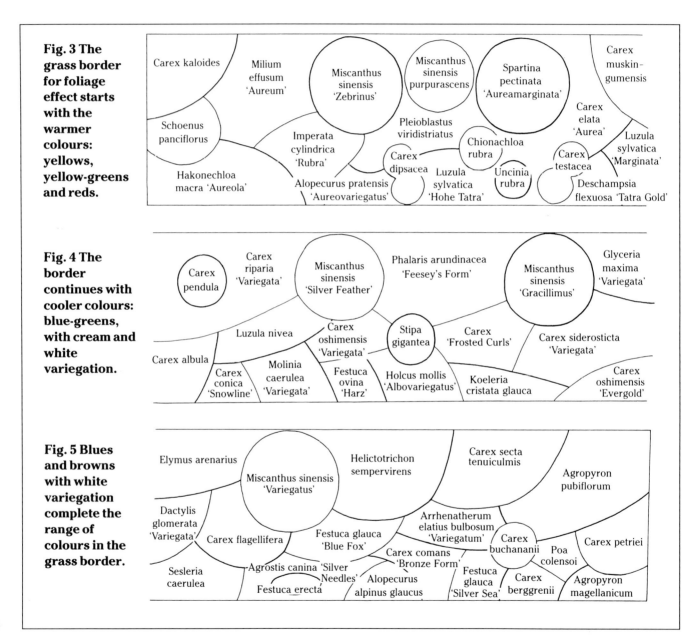

**Fig. 3 The grass border for foliage effect starts with the warmer colours: yellows, yellow-greens and reds.**

**Fig. 4 The border continues with cooler colours: blue-greens, with cream and white variegation.**

**Fig. 5 Blues and browns with white variegation complete the range of colours in the grass border.**

feature of the next sedge, *Carex siderosticta* 'Varie-gata'. They may exceed 2.5 m (1 in) in width, and have white stripes. In this plan they are deliberately used against the almost hair-like tresses of *Carex* 'Frosted Curls'. The colour in this variety is a silvery green. Other suggestions for this spot would be the pale grey-green *Sesleria nitida* or the blue-green quaking grass, *Briza media*. The colour of *Carex albula* is an unusual whitish green and its narrow but tough leaves form a symmetrical mop-head. *Carex conica* 'Snowline' is a charming little plant, neat, evergreen, and with a narrow white margin. It is used here at the front of the border, but it would also be at home in a rock garden, sink, or even in a pot on a well-lit window sill indoors.

*Molinia caerulea* 'Variegata' is a beauty. Fairly erect, it makes a tight, well-behaved clump with cream stripes to the blades. The flowers often show touches of purple and are held on cream stems. It will show up well placed in front of the darker green snowy wood-rush. It will also contrast nicely with the blue-green, purple tipped tussocks of *Festuca glauca* 'Harz'. The next plant is the mat-forming *Holcus mollis* 'Albo-variegatus' with soft, short leaves edged white. An alternative would be *Agrostis canina* 'Silver Needles' whose name aptly describes its narrowest of white-edged blades. *Koeleria cristata glauca* makes tidy blue-green mounds topped with pleasing flower heads. To round off this section we have another ever-green sedge, *Carex oshimensis* 'Evergold'. This is a particularly attractive variety with long narrow leaves arching out to form a low mound, and displaying a prominent creamy yellow median stripe. (This plant, too, will grow indoors in good light.)

## BLUES AND BROWNS WITH WHITE VARIEGATION

The progression of colours moves on finally to the fas-cinating combination of blues and browns, with the additional crispness of white variegation. Assuming that this is a continuous border, the creams of the last section are matched with blues in this one – again a lovely association. *Miscanthus sinensis* 'Variegatus' is the specimen here, the best of the taller variegated grasses, surging upwards before cascading out. As an alternative on a slightly smaller scale we could select the new *Calamagrostis arundinacea* 'Overdam'. This has white-variegated leaves, usually pink-flushed, and delightful feathery flower heads, purplish becoming greyish pink and reaching 1.2 m (4 ft). *Elymus arenarius* is robust and vigorous and will need restraining, but it is a splendid grey-blue with stiff blue flower heads turning buff. The other taller specimen is *Carex buchananii*, with narrow red-brown foliage rising erectly to about 75 cm ($2\frac{1}{2}$ ft) and curling at the tips. Differing shades of brown are contributed by *Carex flagellifera*, a flat mid-brown, *Carex secta tenuiculmis*, slightly larger and a deep warm brown, the grey-brown *Carex comans* 'Bronze Form', and *Carex petriei*, erect and curly-topped like *Carex buchananii* but shorter and with wider blades of pinky brown. Quite different is the tiny *Carex berggrenii*, whose 5 cm (2 in) blunt leaves are a metallic grey-brown. Among these the blues are interspersed. *Helic-totrichon sempervirens* is a fine steely blue forming a hemisphere of stiff leaves. The marvellous silvery blue of *Agropyron pubiflorum* is the most showy of all. It forms fairly erect clumps which spread only gently, retains its colour (though somewhat more green) through the winter, and seems just as good in shade. Coming down in height to about 25 cm (10 in) we have the narrow in-rolled leaves of *Poa colensoi*, which are of a good blue and again manage to maintain a good appearance right through winter. Of similar height and making a tight clump of pale blue is *Festuca glauca* 'Blue Fox', while *Festuca glauca* 'Silver Sea' is more compact and of a more silvery blue. The nature of *Festuca erecta* is given away by its name. This

115

Falkland Islander makes a low vertical accent of a subtle leaden blue, and in our scheme stands out of a carpet of *Agrostis canina* 'Silver Needles' mentioned earlier. *Alopecurus alpinus glaucus* features unusual colouring in that the silvery blue is often distinctly purplish. Two patches of cleanest white variegation are provided by *Dactylis glomerata* 'Variegata' and *Arrhenatherum elatius bulbosum* 'Variegatum'. The leaves of *Sesleria caerulea*, the blue moor grass, are held in a somewhat horizontal plane and form a very dense clump. The upper surface is blue, the undersides dark green, and a pleasing feature of the plant is its very early purple flower. Possibly the most brilliant pale blue leaves of any garden plant are displayed by *Agropyron magellanicum*. It is really startling and provides a fitting finale to our grass border.

# Grass borders for flower effect

The wonderful range of foliage colour among the grasses and their lengthy period of interest mean that a border planted along the lines just discussed, including as it does a significant number of evergreens, will offer something to enjoy the year round, and the many differing flower heads will come and go as a bonus. An area given over primarily to floral effect is a different story, as any cultivator of the more traditional herbaceous border will know. The glory of summer may have as its price a decidedly uninspiring winter aspect. But what choice is there? The plants which sport those incredible extravaganzas of colour, so carefully selected and astutely juxtaposed for maximum summer impact, are rarely renowned for any great contribution outside that season. Thankfully the grasses are more obliging. For a start, as observed earlier, the period of interest of the inflorescences of the grasses is, more often than not, far longer, as

flower heads mature to seed heads with little, if any, diminution of appeal. It is therefore no difficult task to achieve a progressive overlap of floral interest. Secondly the stems and foliage of many of the grasses fade most gracefully and may readily be left standing through the autumn and winter. The obligatory cutback of the herbaceous border to forestall the untidy mess that would inevitably follow instantly creates a yawning void where we have become accustomed to bulk and form. If we have made use of grasses those factors may be retained and enjoyed, along with the accompanying rustling sound effects. When it finally becomes necessary to cut them down in late winter the anticipation of spring and imminent regrowth is perfectly adequate to tide one over a brief period of bareness.

A current trend in North America is to use grasses in a way that recalls the heady days of the pioneering spirit, in creating 'prairie gardens'. In its simplest and therefore perhaps most evocative form this involves the mass planting of just one type of grass. The resulting sea of waving flower heads is a joy to behold. Extending the range to two or three, or at most four species adds variety to the scene. Now this idea assumes that a fair amount of space is available, and probably in an informal, even wild, setting, and most of us are not favoured with such suitable expanses. However, the principle of this concept is one that is wholly applicable to far more restricted settings. So, where it is the effect of the flower heads that is to be the main feature try this suggestion: use just two, three or four species, and fill the available space with these.

Here is one grouping (Fig. 6) that would provide interest from mid summer right into winter – and

**The glorious colouring of *Carex elata* 'Aurea' is a spectacular feature in this yellow and green scheme.**

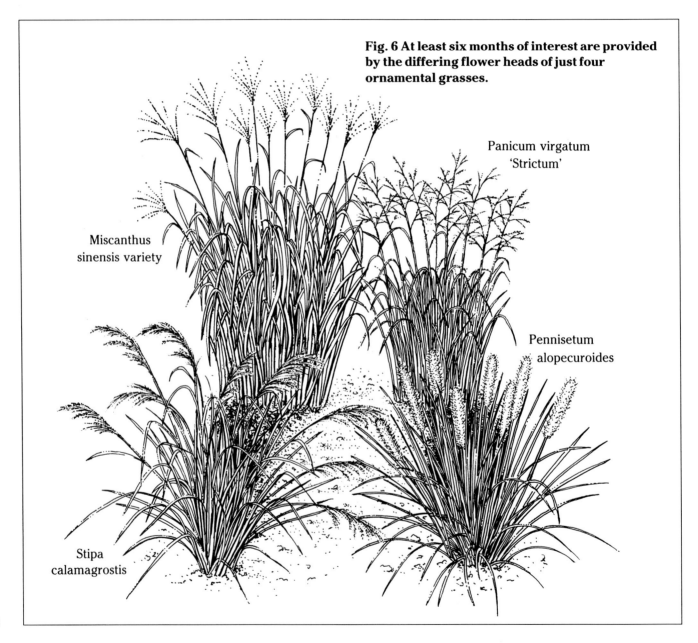

**Fig. 6 At least six months of interest are provided by the differing flower heads of just four ornamental grasses.**

Panicum virgatum 'Strictum'

Miscanthus sinensis variety

Pennisetum alopecuroides

Stipa calamagrostis

that's quite something. An area just 2 m (6½ ft) square would accommodate one plant of each of the four types suggested, two behind and two in front. At the back use any *Miscanthus sinensis* variety, except perhaps *M.s.* 'Variegatus', *purpurascens* and 'Gracillimus' which are not always reliably free-flowering, especially after a poor summer. Most varieties come into flower only in early autumn, although some, like 'Kleine Fontane' are much earlier. There are also variations in plant size ('Gracillimus' types are usually smaller), openness of the flower head (widest in 'Silberspinne') and flower colour – some, such as 'Kascade', 'Graziella', 'Malepartus' and 'Rotsilber' manifesting striking glistening red colouring, especially in the earlier stages of flowering.

Next to the finger-like miscanthus plumes, the airy, wide-open heads of *Panicum virgatum* 'Strictum' will create a pleasing contrast. They will appear at about the same time, starting tight but soon opening right out and, like miscanthus, will stand into the winter months. A fine autumn show of bright yellow leaves will add to the display, unless you select as an alternative one of the purplish-red varieties, whose leaves become progressively deeper in colour, and with chestnut brown flowers and seed heads.

Coming forward to the spot in front of the miscanthus we can find a home for one of the longest flowering of the grasses, *Stipa calamagrostis*. Once the flowers have made their initial appearance in early summer they just keep coming, right through until the autumn, and then stand well into winter. Furthermore they are a delight to behold – long, loose, feathery panicles, glinting with silver at first. This, and a pennisetum, our other foreground grass, are more arching in habit and will hide any tendency of the two varieties behind to look a little bare from the knees down. We could use *Pennisetum alopecuroides* in one of its selected forms, or *P. orientale*. These bear attractive

bottle-brush or caterpillar flowers in profusion from late summer. They will, however, need some winter protection in colder areas.

An alternative combination (Fig. 7), with a similar long period of interest, could comprise varieties of *Calamagrostis* × *acutiflora*, *Molinia caerulea* and *Deschampsia caespitosa*. The calamagrostis is a grass of bolt upright habit and appears in the varieties 'Stricta' and 'Karl Foerster', with long, narrow, feathery inflorescences. This may be placed back left, flanked by a *Molinia caerulea arundinacea* form such as 'Karl Foerster' (a second reference to this worthy gentleman prompts a mention of his leading role in raising ornamental grasses and selecting many of the fine forms available to us today), or 'Windspeil', bearing graceful open flower heads.

The foreground feature in this group is *Deschampsia caespitosa*, the beautiful native tufted hair grass. The evergreen basal leaf clump is dwarfed from mid summer onwards by a hazy cloud of delicate flowers which progress through seed-bearing and remain into winter. Variations in flower colour are reflected in several varietal names, 'Bronzeschleier', 'Goldgehaenge' and others. If one plant were placed centrally in this arrangement room would be left either side which might well be occupied by the perennial quaking grass, *Briza media*, or its annual counterparts, *B. maxima* and *B. minor*, each with pendant trembling lockets in various sizes. Seeds of these latter two, scattered in spring will quickly produce flowering plants, as would those of the charming little hare's tail, *Lagurus ovatus*, with fluffy fat spikes.

There are a number of annual grasses which, like their popular bedding counterparts in a dazzling array of multifloriferous and grandifloriferous varieties, put in a really hard summer's work. They are easily raised from seed and should certainly not be forgotten as an alternative when there are spaces to be filled.

Other associations may be worked out following the basic idea of using flower heads which contrast as starkly as you wish. If more space is available try to resist the temptation to add a plethora of further types. The subtlety of these inflorescences allows for, perhaps even calls for, the multiple planting of each different type, and especially of the smaller ones. In restricted areas the same strategy can be adopted on a reduced scale using grasses of correspondingly smaller stature.

# Mix-and-match planting

If we are to be perfectly realistic we must acknowledge that most of us are unlikely to devote large areas of our gardens solely to grasses, much as we might like them. In practice the suggested grass border for foliage effect, while demonstrating both the feasibility of such a concept and a logical way of progressing through the colour range, is more likely to be referred to for ideas on small-scale associations, perhaps just two, three or four grasses in a group. The point has been constantly reiterated that the best effect will be achieved by drawing from as many of the available plant types as possible. Without doubt the grasses are shown off to their best advantage in the company of the more traditional rounder-leaved plants. The converse must also be true. This would seem to lead us to the conclusion that we can plant our grasses with any and all other types of plant, virtually indiscriminately, and be assured of success. Believe it or not there is much truth in this. I have often made the comment in response to requests for suggestions on

**The evergreen sedge *Carex flagellifera* is planted here with a hosta, nicely demonstrating that blue and brown are good companions.**

livening up a part of the garden that 'isn't quite right', 'Plant a grass or two' and it invariably works wonders, at least from the point of view of form and texture.

However, by adopting a more considered approach we can expect even better results. For a start, there is one group of plants that will do no favours to grasses, nor receive any in return, and that is those with similarly linear or sword-like leaves – crocosmias, irises, kniphofias, hemerocallis and the like. Secondly, form and texture are only part of the story, and not usually the most important part. The earlier comment that colour is the factor that normally makes the first and greatest impression on our senses is worth repeating here. So colour, along with the closely related tone, will be the first consideration in the suggestions that follow, with form and texture as close runners-up.

Here are some colour-coordinated schemes in the mix-and-match style which draw on a variety of plant types, but in each of which a significant contribution is made by the grasses. Once again, just a small segment of one of the plans may provide inspiration for a gap that needs filling.

FIGURE 8: PURPLE, PINK, SILVER, BLUE AND WHITE-VARIEGATED

This scheme employs colours that are not well represented among the grasses, i.e. silver, deep purple and pink. Blue and white-variegated grasses are added in a mutually flattering association. There is barely a hint of green to be seen.

1 *Elaeagnus commutata*.
  Large silver shrub.
2 *Acer negundo* 'Flamingo'.
  Beautiful pink- and white-variegated large shrub or small tree.
3 *Cotinus coggygria* 'Royal Purple'.
  The best rich purple large shrub.

121

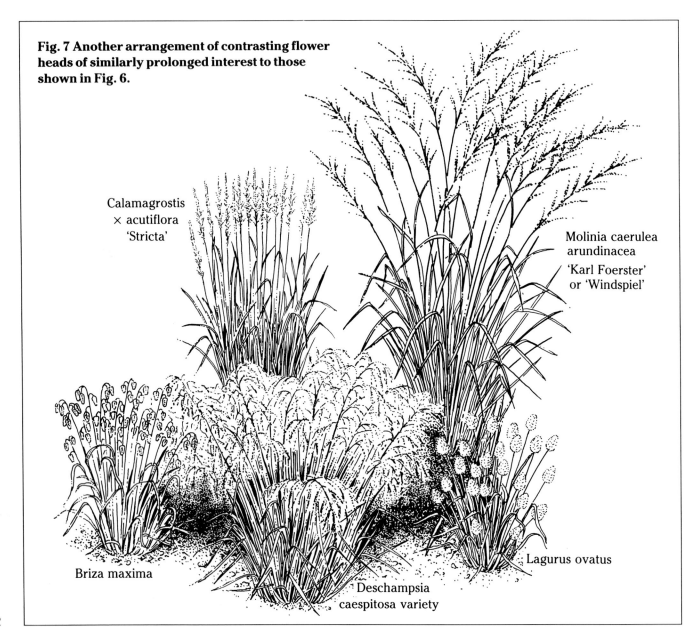

**Fig. 7 Another arrangement of contrasting flower heads of similarly prolonged interest to those shown in Fig. 6.**

Calamagrostis × acutiflora 'Stricta'

Molinia caerulea arundinacea 'Karl Foerster' or 'Windspiel'

Briza maxima

Deschampsia caespitosa variety

Lagurus ovatus

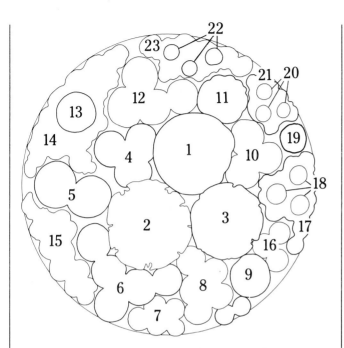

**Fig. 8 Purple, pink, silver, blue and white-variegated.**

4 *Elymus arenarius*.
Erect medium grey-blue grass.
5 *Euphorbia dulcis* 'Chameleon'.
Splendid new low euphorbia with deep purple leaves and flowers.
6 *Artemisia ludoviciana latiloba*.
Upright very silver perennial.
7 *Sedum* 'Vera Jameson'.
Greyish-purple round leaves. Rose red flowers.
8 *Agropyron pubiflorum*.
Erect silvery blue grass.
9 *Spiraea* × *vanhouttei* 'Pink Ice'.
New low shrub. Delicate pink new leaves, becoming cream then white-variegated. White flowers.

10 *Calamagrostis arundinacea* 'Overdam'.
New white-variegated, purple-flushed erect grass. Purplish, then greyish pink flower heads.
11 *Ruta graveolens* 'Jackman's Blue'.
Low evergreen mound of blue divided foliage.
12 *Phalaris arundinacea* 'Tricolor'.
White-variegated grass with good reddish purple flush.
13 *Helictotrichon sempervirens*.
Steely blue evergreen grass. Graceful flower heads.
14 *Stachys byzantina* 'Silver Carpet'.
Non-flowering woolly leaved silver carpeter.
15 *Agropyron magellanicum*.
Intense pale blue-leaved grass.
16 *Agrostis canina* 'Silver Needles'.
Prostrate white-variegated grass. Purplish flowers.
17 *Ajuga reptans* 'Burgundy Glow'.
Magenta, cream and grey-green carpeter. Blue flowers. Interplanted with *Alopecurus alpinus*. Low, silvery purple-blue grass.
18 *Arrhenatherum elatius bulbosum* 'Variegatum'.
Cleanly white-striped grass.
19 *Hebe* 'Wingletye' or *Hebe pinguifolia* 'Pagei'.
Low bluish evergreen shrubs.
20 *Festuca glauca* 'Blue Fox' or *Poa colensoi*.
Short blue grasses.
21 *Artemisia stelleriana prostrata*.
Silvery white carpeter.
22 *Festuca erecta*.
Stiffly straight-leaved blue-green grass.
23 *Holcus mollis* 'Albovariegatus'.
White-variegated carpeting grass.

## FIGURE 9: MID- TO YELLOW-GREEN, OLIVE, YELLOW AND YELLOW-VARIEGATED

Always a fresh and cheerful mix, this scheme includes a preponderance of fairly intense colours. Cream

123

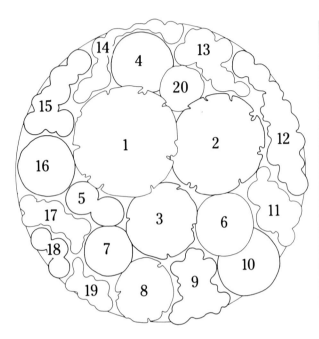

**Fig. 9 Mid- to yellow-green, olive, yellow and yellow-variegated.**

variegation may be added, being considerably softer. Some find the dramatic contrast of purple a welcome inclusion – for many it is just too extreme. Yellow, cream and white flowers would add further interest.

1 *Elaeagnus pungens* 'Maculata'.
Yellow-variegated evergreen shrub.
2 *Sambucus racemosa* 'Plumosa Aurea' or 'Sutherland Gold'.
Splendid yellow cut-leaved shrub.
3 *Lonicera nitida* 'Baggesen's Gold'.
Evergreen shrub with tiny gold leaves.
4 *Spartina pectinata* 'Aureamarginata'.
Yellow-margined arching grass.
5 *Lysimachia ciliata*.

Perennial with brown new leaves and pale yellow flowers.
6 *Miscanthus sinensis* 'Zebrinus'.
Stately grass with yellow cross-banded leaves.
7 *Chionochloa rubra*.
Evergreen arching grass with unusual brassy leaves.
8 *Choisya ternata* 'Sundance'.
Bright yellow evergreen shrub.
9 *Carex testacea*.
Orange-over-olive leaves. Evergreen sedge.
10 *Juniperus communis* 'Depressa Aurea'.
Prostrate conifer. Yellow in summer, bronze in winter.
11 *Carex dipsacea*.
Leaves bronze over deep olive. Evergreen sedge.
12 *Carex fortunei* 'Fisher's Form'.
Evergreen sedge with cream-edged leaves.
13 *Carex muskingumensis*.
Fresh green-leaved sedge.
14 *Carex elata* 'Aurea'.
Bowles' golden sedge, very bright. Or *Milium effusum* 'Aureum', Bowles' golden grass.
15 *Alopecurus pratensis* 'Aureovariegatus', or *Hakonechloa macra* 'Aureola'.
Bright yellow-variegated grasses.
16 *Deschampsia caespitosa* 'Goldgehaenge'.
Grass with haze of golden flowers over green leaves.
17 *Lamium maculatum* 'Cannon's Gold'.
Dead nettle with all-yellow leaves.
18 *Carex umbrosa* 'The Beatles'.
Neat, low sedge.

**Another evergreen sedge, *Carex oshimensis* 'Evergold' contrasts superbly with the broad, dark leaves of *Ajuga reptans* 'Braunherz'.**

19 *Hedera helix* 'Angularis Aurea'.
   Ivy with bright yellow young leaves.
20 *Foeniculum vulgare purpureum*.
   Bronze fennel. Bronze-black leaves. Yellow flowers.

## FIGURE 10: GREY- AND BLUE-GREEN, BLUE, SILVER, WHITE- AND CREAM-VARIEGATED

It is important to keep to the blue side of mid-green and exclude any hint of yellow. The inclusion of cream variegation may seem a contradiction, but it is actually a most effective addition. This is an essentially pale-toned scheme, which could be used in light shade if necessary.

**Fig. 10 Grey- and blue-green, blue, silver, white and cream-variegated.**

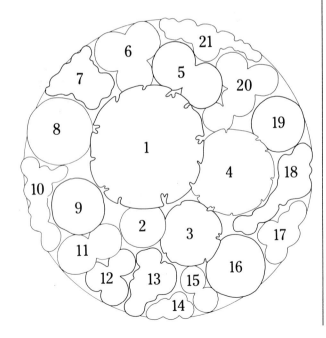

1 *Cornus alba* 'Elegantissima'.
   White-variegated shrub.
2 *Juniperus scopulorum* 'Skyrocket'.
   Tall narrow grey-green conifer.
3 *Miscanthus sinensis* 'Variegatus'.
   Handsome grass with striking white variegation.
4 *Olearia macrodonta*.
   New Zealand holly, evergreen olive-grey leaves.
5 *Hebe carnosula*.
   Small blue evergreen leaves. White flowers.
6 *Tanacetum densum amani*.
   Low evergreen mound of deeply cut silver leaves.
7 *Carex conica* 'Snowline'.
   Neat low evergreen sedge. Deep green leaves with white margins.
8 *Dorycnium hirsutum*.
   Soft grey-green leaves. Pinky white flowers.
9 *Stipa calamagrostis*.
   Attractive free-flowering grass.
10 *Festuca glauca* 'Harz'.
   Blue-green grass with purple tips.
11 *Phalaris arundinacea* 'Feesey's Form'.
   Grass with strongly white-variegated leaves.
12 *Hosta* 'Halcyon'.
   Good blue heart-shaped leaves.
13 *Molinia caerulea* 'Variegata'.
   Neat cream-variegated grass.
14 *Carex atrata*.
   Grey-green leaved sedge.
15 *Artemisia pontica*.
   Perennial with soft feathery grey-green leaves.
16 *Cotoneaster horizontalis* 'Variegatus'.
   Herringbone cotoneaster with small white-edged leaves.
17 *Carex oshimensis* 'Evergold'.
   Evergreen sedge with broad central cream stripe.
18 *Agropyron pubiflorum*.
   Erect silvery blue grass.

19 *Helichrysum serotinum.*
Curry plant. Intensely silver low shrub. Cream buds. Remove yellow flowers as they open.
20 *Glyceria maxima* 'Variegata' or *Phalaris arundinacea* 'Luteopicta'.
Cream-variegated grasses.
21 *Koeleria cristata glauca.*
Blue-grey leaves. Nice grassy flower heads.

## FIGURE 11: YELLOW, BROWN, ORANGE AND RED

A planting scheme exclusively of these colours gives a most vivid, almost fiery colour scheme, strengthened still further with bright yellow or red flowers if desired. Botanical purples may be added and some unusual effects may be achieved when these are used next to browns.

1 *Berberis thunbergii* 'Gold Ring'.
Reddish-leaved shrub with narrow gold margin.
2 *Foeniculum vulgare purpureum.*
Fennel with bronze-black leaves. Yellow flowers.
3 *Choisya ternata* 'Sundance' or *Ilex crenata* 'Golden Gem'.
Evergreen shiny yellow-leaved shrubs.
4 *Thuya occidentalis* 'Rheingold'.
Orange conifer.
5 *Milium effusum* 'Aureum'.
Yellow grass.
6 *Carex flagellifera.*
Brown mop-headed evergreen sedge.
7 *Carex elata* 'Aurea'.
Bright yellow-leaved sedge.
8 *Carex buchananii.*
Foxy-brown evergreen sedge.
9 *Juniperus communis* 'Depressa Aurea'.
Prostrate conifer, yellow in summer, bronze in winter.
10 *Acorus gramineus* 'Ogon'.
Evergreen fans of bright yellow grass-like leaves.

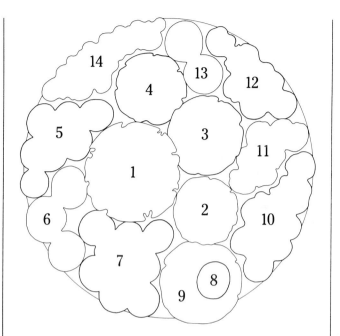

**Fig. 11 Yellow, brown, orange and red.**

11 *Lychnis* × *arkwrightii.*
Very dark purplish leaves. Vermilion flowers.
12 *Alopecurus pratensis* 'Aureovariegatus' or *Hakonechloa macra* 'Aureola'.
Bright yellow-variegated grasses.
13 *Carex secta tenuiculmis.*
Deep warm brown evergreen sedge.
14 *Acaena inermis* 'Copper Carpet'.
Bronze cut-leaved evergreen ground cover.

## FIGURE 12: YELLOW, BLUE AND SILVER

This colour scheme is pretty if perhaps somewhat bland inasmuch as there is a virtual equality of light value. We are therefore deprived of the contrast of light and dark which add sparkle and crispness to the scene. However it is still very pleasing.

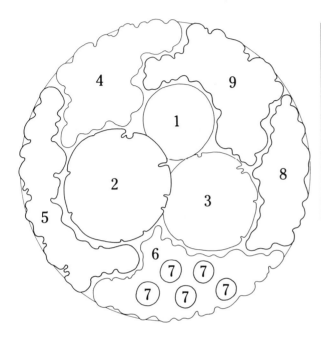

**Fig. 12 Yellow, blue and silver.**

1 *Chamaecyparis lawsoniana* 'Pembury Blue'.
   Good blue pyramidal conifer.
2 *Senecio* 'Sunshine'.
   Silver-grey evergreen shrub. Yellow flowers.
3 *Lonicera nitida* 'Baggesen's Gold'.
   Evergreen shrub with tiny yellow leaves.
4 *Carex elata* 'Aurea'.
   Bright yellow sedge.
5 *Agropyron magellanicum*.
   Intense pale blue-leaved grass.
6 *Artemisia stelleriana prostrata*.
   Silver-white carpeter.
7 *Festuca glauca* 'Blue Fox' or *Poa colensoi*.
   Short blue tufted grasses. Evergreen.
8 *Agropyron pubiflorum*.
   Erect silvery blue grass.

9 *Artemisia ludoviciana latiloba*.
   Upright very silver perennial.

## FIGURE 13: BLUE, BROWN AND SILVER

Another wonderful combination, for which we are heavily dependent on grasses.

1 *Artemisia stelleriana prostrata*.
   Silver-white carpeter.
2 *Alopecurus alpinus glaucus*.
   Low, silvery purple-blue grass.
3 *Cerastium tomentosum columnae*.
   Compact form of the silver-leaved, white-flowering snow-in-summer.
4 *Carex buchananii*.
   Foxy-brown evergreen sedge.
5 *Hebe pinguifolia* 'Pagei'.
   Low blue-grey evergreen shrub. White flowers.
6 *Agropyron magellanicum*.
   Intense pale blue-leaved grass.
7 *Chamaecyparis lawsoniana* 'Blue Surprise' or 'Van Pelt's Blue'.
   Grey-blue conifers with a hint of purple in winter.
8 *Santolina chamaecyparissus*.
   Cotton lavender. Evergreen silver leaves.
9 *Carex comans* 'Bronze Form'.
   Fine-leaved, mop-headed, evergreen brown sedge.
10 *Festuca glauca* 'Blue Fox'.
   Short blue tufted grass. Evergreen.
11 *Acaena inermis* 'Copper Carpet'.
   Bronze cut-leaved ground cover.
12 *Carex berggrenii*.
   Dwarf grey-brown sedge.

**The broad leaved *Carex siderosticta* 'Variegata' is the centrepiece of this semi-shady planting. It also looks good in a pot.**

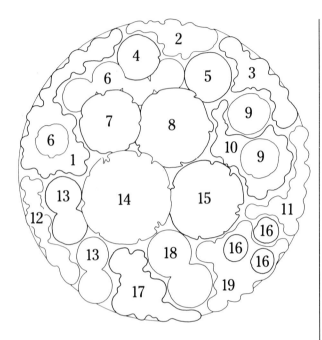

**Fig. 13 Blue, brown and silver.**

13 *Agropyron pubiflorum.*
Erect silver-blue grass.
14 *Weigela florida* 'Foliis Purpureis'.
Unusual brown-leaved shrub, dusky pink flowers.
15 *Ruta graveolens* 'Jackman's Blue'.
Low evergreen mound of blue divided foliage.
16 *Carex petriei.*
Small, curly-topped, pinky-brown evergreen sedge.
17 *Stachys byzantina* 'Silver Carpet'.
Non-flowering woolly-leaved silver carpeter.
18 *Artemisia ludoviciana latiloba.*
Upright very silver perennial.
19 *Festuca glauca* 'Silver Sea'.
Small tufted silver-blue grass.

# 'Grasses and ground cover' borders

This idea is a compromise between the all-grass and 'mix-and-match' suggestions. It gives the pre-eminence to grasses which many enthusiasts may desire, but still retains the facility for using colours, shapes and textures which are complementary and additional to those of the grasses. My somewhat arbitrary rule is that with grasses up to about 60 cm (2 ft) in height the surrounding ground cover plants should not exceed 10 cm (4 in); with grasses between 60 cm (2 ft) and 1.2 m (4 ft) the maximum ground cover height should be around 20–25 cm (8–10 in); and nothing in excess of 45 cm (18 in) should be planted with grasses over 1.2 m (4 ft). Some of these useful plants, many evergreen, are listed below.

GROUND COVER PLANTS UP TO 10 cm (4 in):

*Acaena*, in variety
*Achillea*, in variety
*Ajuga*, in variety
*Antennaria dioica*
*Artemisia stelleriana prostrata*
*Cerastium tomentosum columnae*
*Cotula potentilloides*
*Fragaria* × *ananassa* 'Variegata'
*Glechoma hederacea* 'Variegata'
*Hedera*, in variety
*Lamium*, in variety
*Lysimachia nummularia* 'Aurea'
*Parthenocissus henryana*
*Sagina subulata* 'Aurea'
*Sedum*, in variety
*Thymus*, in variety
*Trifolium repens* 'Quadrifolium Purpurascens'
*Vinca minor* varieties
*Waldsteinia ternata*

**Fig. 14 In a shady spot the association of *Melica nutans* and *Lamium maculatum* 'Aureum' offers harmonious colours and contrasting leaf form and texture. The melica is shiny and green whilst the heart-shaped leaves of the lamium are matt yellow.**

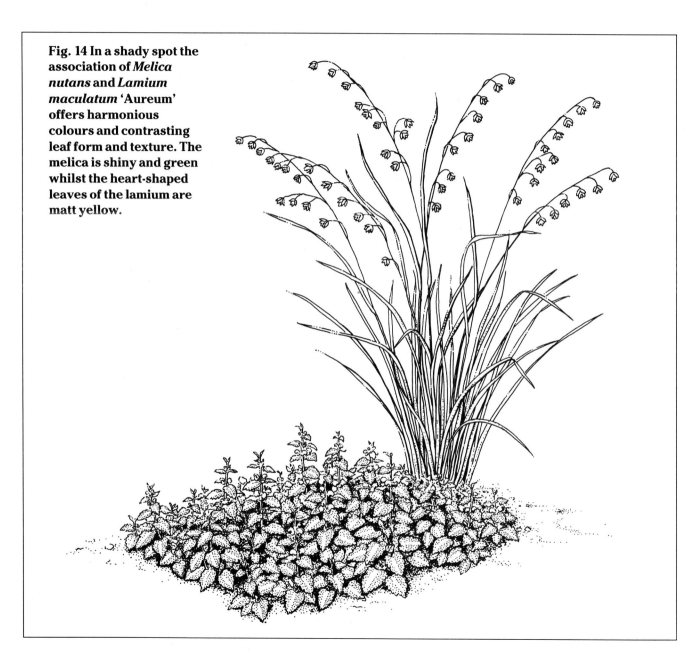

GROUND COVER PLANTS 10–25 cm (4–10 in):

*Aegopodium podagraria* 'Variegata'
*Bergenia*, in variety
*Euphorbia myrsinites*
*Hebe*, in variety
*Hosta*, in variety
*Houttuynia cordata* 'Chameleon'
*Juniperus*, in variety
*Ophiopogon planiscapus* 'Nigrescens'
*Pachysandra terminalis*
*Ranunculus repens* 'Joe's Golden'
*Sedum*, in variety
*Stachys byzantinum* 'Silver Carpet'
*Symphytum* 'Goldsmith'
*Tolmeia menziesii* 'Taff's Gold'
*Vinca major* varieties

GROUND COVER PLANTS 25–45 cm (10–18 in):

*Artemisia*, in variety
*Cotoneaster horizontalis* 'Variegatus'
*Euonymus fortunei* varieties
*Euphorbia dulcis* 'Chameleon'
*Hebe*, in variety
*Heuchera micrantha* 'Palace Purple'
*Rubus idaeus* 'Aureus'

# Shingle, rock and paved gardens

We have so far discussed only the interrelationship of plant material and have discovered numerous possibilities for pleasing associations. When we embark on a consideration of the materials with which we surround our plants we enter a whole new realm of contrast: that between those living, moving plants, ever-changing through the transient phases of growth and development, and inanimate materials, natural or manufactured, solid, consistent, unyielding. We can cover the surface with shingle or pebbles. We can assemble arrangements of rocks, larger stones or boulders. We may introduce either stepping stones or a continuous path through the planting, with a further choice of natural stone or the straight lines, rectangles and precise circles of man-made slabs. Round wooden stepping stones and log-roll edging are also available.

Furthermore, many of these items may be obtained in a choice of colours and tones, offering further possibilities of harmony and/or contrast with each other and with our grasses. For example, the warm creamy buffs of Cotswold and similar stone combine delightfully with the blue and brown grasses. Given a piece of virgin ground and a free choice as to how to use it I would go for a 'grasses and ground cover' planting in a rock, shingle and natural paving setting.

It is important to remember when gardening in this style that the additional features are there to be seen as part of the overall scheme, so we are not looking for total ground coverage as we might be ordinarily. Unplanted areas should be allowed for with the planting arranged in carefully orchestrated, probably irregular, groups and masses.

For a virtually maintenance-free garden lay medium- to heavy-gauge polythene over the soil and pierce holes in it for planting. Then spread shingle over the entire surface. You will need to bear in mind that creeping plants will not be able to spread (should you want them to) unless you progressively cut away the polythene from around them.

**A close-up of the glorious plumes of *Cortaderia selloana*.**

## GRASSES FOR HOT, SUNNY SPOTS

Whether or not the 'greenhouse effect' will give us hotter, drier summers remains to be seen. However, some soils are very light and free-draining, and just a few days of sunshine will leave them parched. The situation can be improved by incorporating plenty of organic material into the soil at planting time, and by mulching, but here are some grasses that will tolerate such conditions, once established:

*Agropyron magellanicum*
*Alopecurus alpinus glaucus*
*Alopecurus lanatus*
*Corynephorus canescens*
*Elymus arenarius*
*Eragrostis curvula*
*Festuca* – all blue-leaved types
*Festuca mairei*
*Helictotrichon sempervirens*
*Koeleria cristata glauca*
*Lagurus ovatus*
*Pennisetum* species
*Poa colensoi*
*Poa labillardieri*
*Poa buchananii*

## GRASSES FOR SHADE AND WOODLAND

There is a grass for every conceivable situation, and the woodlands and glades of the temperate regions of the world are well-endowed in this respect. Although most of them will grow quite satisfactorily in more open conditions, and most of those whose natural habitat is open and sunny are not in the least troubled by light shade, it is good to know that there are a number of grasses that we can draw from when it comes to rather darker situations. Grasses happy in shade include:

*Agrostis canina* 'Silver Needles'
*Aira elegantissima*
*Bromus ramosus*
*Carex conica* 'Snowline'
*Carex fraserii*
*Carex grayi*
*Carex morrowii* varieties
*Carex oshimensis* varieties
*Carex pendula*
*Carex plantaginea*
*Carex saxatilis* 'Variegata'
*Carex siderosticta* 'Variegata'
*Carex umbrosa* 'The Beatles'
*Chasmanthium latifolium*
*Chusquea couleou*
*Deschampsia caespitosa* and varieties
*Deschampsia flexuosa*
*Holcus mollis* 'Albovariegatus'
*Luzula* species and varieties
*Melica nutans*
*Melica uniflora* 'Variegata'
*Milium effusum* 'Aureum'
*Pleioblastus* – several species
*Poa chaixii*
*Sasa veitchii*

## GRASSES FOR WET SOILS, BOG GARDENS AND WATER

The tolerance that some of the grasses show to a diverse range of conditions is no better demonstrated than by some of those mentioned here, which will grow in ordinary, even rather dry soils but also with their feet in water. The following plants will all tolerate wet soil, and those marked with an asterisk will grow in water:

*Arundo donax**
*Carex elata* 'Aurea'**
*Carex grayi**

**Fig. 15** *Achnatherum brachytrichum* features attractive purplish-grey flower heads on erect culms. The small leaves of *Cotoneaster horizontalis* 'Variegatus' are an interesting feature around the base of the grass.

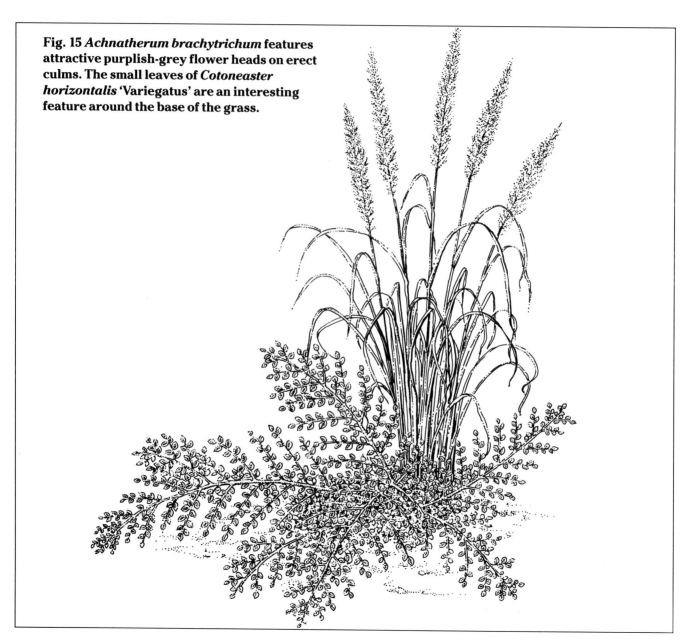

*Carex riparia* 'Variegata'
*Carex trifida*
*Cyperus* species*
*Eriophorum angustifolium* *
*Glyceria maxima* 'Variegata'*
*Juncus effusus* and varieties*
*Molinia caerulea* and varieties
*Phalaris arundinacea* varieties*
*Phragmites australis* and varieties*
*Scirpus lacustris* 'Albescens'*
*Scirpus lacustris tabernaemontani* 'Zebrinus'*
*Spartina pectinata* 'Aureamarginata'
*Typha* species and varieties*

GRASSES IN POTS AND TUBS

Certain grasses are well suited to growing this way, notably those of arching growth or of hemispherical shape which manifest a degree of symmetry. The classic grass for pot culture is undoubtedly *Hakonechloa macra* 'Aureola'. *Carex siderosticta* 'Variegata' is also good, as are the taller *Carex buchananii* and *Chionochloa rubra*. The evergreen dome of *Helictotrichon sempervirens* is another candidate. Note any particular cultural requirements of the plants concerned, and water assiduously.

# Coloured lawns?

If common grasses can be sown, or laid as turf, and maintained as a lawn the question must be put: What about a coloured or variegated lawn? Well, it is theoretically possible. Probably the best ornamental grass

**Cortaderia selloana 'Gold Band' in the grass border at the Royal Horticultural Society's garden at Wisley, Surrey. The blue *Elymus arenarius* is behind.**

for this purpose would be *Agrostis canina* 'Silver Needles' which would give an interesting whitish effect and could be mown as normal once well established. Other candidates which could be cut with the mower blades set high would be *Holcus mollis* 'Albovariegatus' and *Alopecurus pratensis* 'Aureovariegatus'. Other small grasses such as the blue festucas could be close-planted and trimmed over with shears, but would not take too kindly to being walked on regularly. There are drawbacks, however. Every seed that lands on your 'lawn' is going to develop into a green-leaved grass or weed – and will stand out like a sore thumb, unless you are prepared for some diligent hand-weeding. May I suggest that this fascinating idea be implemented in small areas only, that can easily be given the attention they will need, not as true lawns for walking on, but perhaps to create pleasing geometrical patterns using several varieties adjoining each other. Alternatively squares, rectangles, T- or L-shapes etc. could be formed within areas of paving slabs and filled with a single type of grass.

# Grasses for indoor arrangements

It should not be forgotten that the grasses are a major source of valuable material for cutting for fresh or dried arrangements and many respond well to dyeing. Books on the subject will give details relevant to particular species, but as a general rule flower heads need to be cut well before maturity to lessen the risk of shattering.

# Cultivation and Propagation

## Choosing your grasses

Preliminary to cultivation and propagation is the purchase of plants. There is considerable confusion over the correct naming of some of the grasses and, particularly, the sedges. While it is good to see more grasses appearing in garden centres I am appalled at the lack of attention to this important matter. If you want to be fairly sure of getting the plants you particularly want it is far safer to go to a specialist nursery.

Whatever the source, if you are buying on the spot rather than ordering by post (which will often be the only way of acquiring many less common varieties) be sure that the plant is well established in its pot. It is the responsibility of the nurseryman to care for the plant until that point is reached, and it will then have the best chance of growing away happily.

## Tidying up

The grasses as a group are no more difficult to cultivate than any other group of plants. Some species have particular needs and these should be noted when purchasing and planting. Spring and summer planting especially should be followed by conscientious attention to watering until the plant is established. Subsequent care more or less parallels that for most herbaceous perennials. If they are evergreen the leaves may suffer some winter damage, particularly at the tips. Such damage should be removed in the spring, but do not trim away more than is necessary for a tidy appearance. Through the course of the year a certain amount of dead foliage may become apparent, and often this can be removed by running the fingers, or even a comb, through the plant. In other cases it may be necessary to take the scissors to them and simply cut away what is obviously dead material.

With herbaceous grasses you have a choice: if you like the look of the withered foliage, stems and flower heads, leave them standing until late winter and then cut them to the ground. Don't delay any longer or you may damage the emerging leaves which will then have flat rather than pointed tips! If they are untidy in the autumn, and will clearly do nothing to enhance the winter garden, cut them right back straight away. One or two varieties become untidy around the middle of the summer or lose the brightness of their variegation and, as with some other perennial plants, these can be cut back for a second flush of attractive growth. Some forms of *Phalaris arundinacea* are examples of this.

## Coping with invasive species

It is worth giving a little thought to those grasses which are invasive spreaders, inasmuch as several of them are most desirable plants which one may be loathe to exclude from the garden. Apart from this latter course it seems to me that one has three options.

First, they can be grown in pots or tubs. They are ideal candidates for this type of culture because they will fill out their containers quite rapidly. Watering must never be neglected, and feeding during the growing season will help. If necessary they can be split and started again every two or three years.

A second possibility is to surround the plant with material that will physically restrict its spread. A plastic bucket with the bottom cut out is often suggested, and will be fine for small to medium grasses. A plastic dustbin treated the same way and cut in half would give two reasonably sized barriers. Again it will be beneficial to lift the plant and divide and replant it at intervals as it may die out in the middle. Larger and stronger grasses are best restrained with concrete, to a depth of at least 45 cm (1½ ft). This could be cast *in situ*, or paving slabs could be arranged vertically in the ground, or one might be able to obtain sections of large-diameter concrete pipework. None of these are particularly straightforward options, and in appropriate circumstances mowing round clumps of such grasses will be equally effective.

The third choice is a simple one: acknowledge the threat when you first put the plant in, allot it a realistic area into which to spread, and then take your spade to it regularly, cutting it back to well within this area. In practice, one inspection when new growth has appeared in spring and another in mid to late summer will be the most that is required. I know of no grass that will put up much resistance to a sharp spade at such regular intervals. This controlled approach effectively eliminates any potential threat. After all, when you think about it, it is the established, out of control clump which always causes the real headache.

# Pests and diseases

Pests and diseases are rare. Occasional greenfly or blackfly attacks may be dealt with using any of the appropriate products available. Just two or three grasses may be seen to be developing rust on the leaves in summer, especially if you live in an area where cereal crops are grown. Early treatment with Dithane 945 (produced by PBI), following the manu-facturer's recommendations closely, should solve the problem and prevent spread.

# Propagating grasses

Propagation by division is possible with all the grasses and, apart from a tiny minority where cuttings are an alternative, is the only method in the case of the many cultivars. So far as the species are concerned seed will give larger numbers without disturbing the plant itself. The collecting of seed may be carried out when the flower head turns brown, first checking that the individual seeds come away readily. This may usually be done either by pulling at the hairlike awns or by gently rubbing the head between fingers and thumb where awns are absent. Store the seed in an envelope in a cool, dry place until required.

Seeds of hardy annuals may be sown in spring direct into prepared soil where they are to grow. Autumn sowing of many of them will produce more robust plants the following year, often flowering earlier. Half-hardy annuals and perennials should be sown and pricked out in warmth in early spring, hardened off and planted out after frosts, or sown direct into the ground in late spring. Hardy perennials can be sown in pots or trays in spring, preferably with some protection, pricked out and planted in their growing positions when large enough.

Division is simply a matter of lifting the grass and prising the crown apart. The more robust grasses may call for the use of secateurs, a spade or the traditional two forks back to back. Usually several small plants may be obtained by this method. The divisions should be replanted and watered regularly until established. The safest time to carry out division is from when the plants start into growth in spring until mid summer. Winter division will usually result in dead plants.

139

# Plant Directory

The following list gives basic details of a significant proportion of the grasses that are available to gardeners. As well as the botanical name and plant family the dimensions of each plant are given. '*L*' indicates the height and then spread of the leaves, '*Fl*' the flowering height. To ascertain the planting distance between two plants add together the figures given for their spread and divide by two. Unless otherwise stated it may be assumed that the plant is perennial and herbaceous, i.e. dying back in winter.

## ACHNATHERUM

***Achnatherum brachytrichum***    Gramineae
*L* 60 × 60 cm (2 × 2 ft)    *Fl* 1.2 m (4 ft)
Green leaves, slightly bronze-flushed when young, emerge early, forming a loose drooping clump. Long, narrow, slightly open feathery heads of greyish pink adorn the plant in late summer and autumn. A striking feature in the middle of the border between shrubs. Most soils in sun or light shade.

## AGROPYRON

***Agropyron magellanicum***    Gramineae
*L* 15 × 30 cm (6 × 12 in)    *Fl* 15 cm (6 in)
Leaves, culms and flower spikes all boast the brightest pale blue colour, and are all decidedly lax. Use for foreground planting, perhaps as a carpet around the erect reddish brown *Carex buchananii* and backed by a silver shrub. Evergreen, but less blue in winter. Average to dry soil in sun.

***Agropyron pubiflorum***    Gramineae
*L* 50 × 30 cm (20 × 12 in)    *Fl* 75 cm (2½ ft)
An erect, slowly expanding clump of lovely pale silvery blue, looking good with brown sedges, with purple-leaved plants such as the new *Euphorbia dulcis* 'Chameleon', or with pink-flushed variegated plants like *Spiraea × vanhouttei* 'Pink Ice'. Add silver for a finishing touch. Inflorescence in early to mid summer of no great significance. Leaves greener in winter. Most soils which are not too heavy, in sun or moderate shade.

## AGROSTIS

***Agrostis canina*** 'Silver Needles'    Gramineae
*L* 8 × 30 cm (3 × 12 in)    *Fl* 20 cm (8 in)
Discovered as a chance seedling in a London garden by John Fielding who brought me a plant, and I suggested the name 'Silver Needles' as appropriately describing its narrowest of blades, each cleanly white-margined. A delightful little grass, essentially horizontal in habit, spreading gently by overground runners, forming a carpet, though never a nuisance. Use to surround erect deeper green grasses. Good in small pots, also for variegated lawns, planted 20 cm (8 in) apart. Flowers are a delight, airy clouds of

**It would be difficult to devise a more dramatic contrast than that between *Glyceria maxima* 'Variegata' and *Ligularia dentata* 'Othello' – both best in damp soil.**

glistening purple – but best removed before seeding. Most soils (except the driest) in sun or moderate shade.

### Agrostis nebulosa   Gramineae
*L* 20 × 30 cm (8 × 12 in)   *Fl* 35 cm (14 in)
Cloud bent grass. Annual. Good for drying, attractive in the border. Well justifies its common name, producing veritable clouds of small spikelets in delicate open heads floating over smaller clumps of foliage. Sow seeds *in situ* in spring or autumn to flower in mid to late summer. Average to good soil in sun.

## AIRA

### Aira elegantissima   Gramineae
*L* 15 × 20 cm (6 × 8 in)   *Fl* 30 cm (12 in)
Hair grass. Another annual, named after its very fine leaves. If anything more dainty than *Agrostis nebulosa* (above), with tiny silvery spikelets in loose, airy panicles in early summer. A popular grass for drying. Sow seeds where they are to grow in ordinary to light soil in sun or part shade.

## ALOPECURUS

### Alopecurus alpinus glaucus   Gramineae
*L* 15 × 30 cm (6 × 12 in)   *Fl* 25 cm (10 in)
Blue foxtail grass. I find myself increasingly fond of this little grass. Silvery overtones to subtle grey-blue to purple leaves. Gentle spreader, not a nuisance, forming very loose clumps – a few leaves here, a tuft there – hence ideal for intermingling with other carpeters, such as the magenta and cream *Ajuga reptans* 'Burgundy Glow', or any of the prostrate silvers. Stubby purplish flower spikes in spring. Average to light soil in sun.

### Alopecurus lanatus   Gramineae
*L* 8 × 12 cm (3 × 5 in)   *Fl* 15 cm (6 in)
Silver foxtail grass. A little gem with thickly woolly leaves appearing silvery over grey. Hardy but dislikes winter wet so some care is required. Alpine house cultivation would be ideal; otherwise protect with the traditional overhead pane of glass, or simply surround with a good layer of grit in a quick-draining soil in full sun. Suitable for sinks. Small fat flower heads in spring.

### Alopecurus pratensis 'Aureovariegatus'
Gramineae
*L* 40 × 30 cm (16 × 12 in)   *Fl* 70 cm (28 in)
Golden foxtail grass. Slowly spreading clump of marvellous yellow leaves, narrowly striped green, forming a bright patch at the front of the border. Trim once or twice in summer to keep it low (if desired). Cylindrical flower spikes, early summer. Average to good soil in sun or light shade. Use as a carpet round brown or olive sedges, or with any yellow-green or yellow-variegated shrub. The ground-hugging *Acaena inermis* 'Copper Carpet' is another splendid companion.

## ANDROPOGON

### Andropogon scoparius   Gramineae
*L* 90 × 45 cm (3 × 1½ ft)   *Fl* 1 m (3¼ ft)
Little blue stem. A grass of the North American plains, grown for its progressively changing foliage colour. Emerging in spring a pale grey green, it develops through purple in late summer to splendid foxy red tones in autumn. Erect growing, tight clump, topped in autumn by wispy inflorescences. Apparently hardy, but dislikes waterlogging in winter, and should therefore be planted in good but well-drained soil in sun.

**Fig. 16 The white-striped *Arrhenatherum elatius bulbosum* 'Variegatum' stands out of a carpet of the deep blackish-purple foliage of *Trifolium repens* 'Quadrifolium Purpurascens'.**

## ARRHENATHERUM

***Arrhenatherum elatius bulbosum* 'Variegatum'** Gramineae

*L* 30 × 30 cm (1 × 1 ft)    *Fl* 45 cm (18 in)

Variegated bulbous oat grass, or onion couch. Possesses the strange characteristic of forming small bulbs at the base of the stems. Pure white-striped and margined grey-green leaves, very clean-looking. Narrow panicles in summer. Cut back for a second flush when foliage deteriorates after mid summer. Good in groups, or as specimens in a carpet of darker tones. Avoid the driest soils. Sun or part shade.

## ARUNDO

***Arundo donax*** Gramineae

*L* 4 × 1.5 m (13 × 5 ft)    *Fl* 4.5 m (15 ft)

Giant reed. From southern Europe, so requires a warm spot, in good to moist soil. Long grey-green leaves splay out from the stems, alternating in decidedly regular fashion. Use at the back of a large border or as a specimen, preferably cutting the stems right down each winter. Large late autumn flower heads not usually produced in cooler climates. Good examples may be seen in Britain at the Royal Horticultural Society's gardens at Wisley, Surrey.

***A.d* 'Variegata'**   Surely one of the most striking of all the grasses, with broad creamy white margins and stripes. It is also decidedly tender, requiring virtually frost-free conditions. Try planting it in a pool with several inches of water above the crown. A shorter plant than the all-green species, to about 1.8 m (6 ft).

***Arundo pliniana*** is of similar height, with short stiff leaves coming quickly to a point, giving a rather spiky appearance.

## AVENA

***Avena sterilis***   Gramineae

*L* 60 × 60 cm (2 × 2 ft)    *Fl* 1 m (3¼ ft)

Animated oat. Popular annual for the garden or indoor decoration, fresh, dried or dyed. Loose heads of nodding bristled spikelets, green becoming papery. Sow seeds *in situ* in spring or autumn. Any soil in sun.

## BOTHRIOCHLOA

***Bothriochloa caucasica***   Gramineae

*L* 40 × 60 cm (16 × 24 in)    *Fl* 75 cm (2½ ft)

Beard grass. Features reddish purple inflorescences in late summer, with arching foliage also turning reddish towards the autumn. Flower heads comprise multiple

143

*Hakonechloa macra* 'Aureola' is a choice grass for good soil,
here seen in a classic association with the broad leaves
of a blue hosta.

145

A telling contrast of colour, tone and form, with *Holcus mollis* 'Albovariegatus' and the purplish, ribbed leaves of *Plantago major* 'Rubrifolia'.

spikes arising from the stem in quite erect fashion like a small miscanthus. Average soil in a sunny, sheltered spot. Protect in extreme cold, or save the seed and sow *in situ* in spring.

## BOUTELOUA

**Bouteloua gracilis**   Gramineae
L 25 × 30 cm (10 × 12 in)    Fl 50 cm (20 in)
Mosquito grass or signal-arm grass. Appropriately descriptive common names refer to the flowering head, the rachis (main stalk) of which is held almost horizontally to the upright culm, and from which hang the densely packed brownish-purple spikelets and their dangling florets – a distinctive and most intriguing arrangement. Flowers through the summer. Dense clumps of narrow green leaves. Grasses of the open prairies of the Americas, requiring well-drained soil in sun.
**Bouteloua curtipendula** is larger and with erectly held inflorescences.

## BRIZA

The botanical names of the three quaking grasses to consider progress not only alphabetically but in descending order of the size of the dangling spikelets, of value in the garden as they tremble and dance in the wind, and when cut as valuable contributors to dried flower arrangements.

**Briza maxima**   Gramineae
L 40 × 30 cm (16 × 12 in)    Fl 60 cm (2 ft)
The largest of the *Briza* family is an annual with light green, rather oblong spikelets in late spring and through the summer.

**Briza media**   Gramineae
L 40 × 30 cm (16 × 12 in)    Fl 60 cm (2 ft)
Perennial species. Heart-shaped purplish spikelets,

early to late summer, above a dense clump of somewhat blue-green leaves. Good soil in sun or part shade.

**Briza minor**   Gramineae
L 30 × 25 cm (12 × 10 in)    Fl 45 cm (1½ ft)
Lesser quaking grass. Smaller in all its parts but bearing a greater number of spikelets over a long period.

## BROMUS

**Bromus brizaeformis**   Gramineae
L 50 × 30 cm (20 × 12 in)    Fl 75 cm (2½ ft)
Large heads of gracefully drooping spikelets similar to those of *Briza maxima* but longer and more pointed. May be picked and dried. Annual. Sow spring or autumn in any soil in sun or part shade, to flower throughout the summer.

**Bromus macrostachys** var. **lanuginosus**
Gramineae
L 25 × 20 cm (10 × 8 in)    Fl 50 cm (20 in)
The effect is almost woolly – quite different from the other species described here – with whitish heads of compact spikelets arising from a tight clump. Annual. Sow spring or autumn where it is to flower. Sun or part shade.

**Bromus madritensis**   Gramineae
L 30 × 25 cm (12 × 10 in)    Fl 60 cm (2 ft)
Compact brome. Long bristly spikes with strong reddish purple colouring in early summer. Annual. Sow spring or autumn in ordinary soil in sun or part shade.

**Bromus ramosus**   Gramineae
L 45 × 30 cm (1½ × 1 ft)    Fl 1 m (3¼ ft)
Wood or hairy brome. Perennial British native for more shady areas or, given good soil, in sun. Graceful in flower with open branched heads of drooping spikelets, narrow, bristled, and of rather wispy effect, mid and late summer.

## CALAMOGROSTIS

### Calamogrostis × acutiflora 'Karl Foerster'
Gramineae
L 100×45 cm (3¼×1½ ft)    Fl 1.5 m (5 ft)
Strongly vertical form, culms thrusting skywards topped by long, narrow, but slightly open, pinkish brown flower heads which remain well into the winter. Most soils, sun to part shade. Clump forming.

### Calamogrostis arundinacea 'Overdam'
Gramineae
L 60×45 cm (2×1½ ft)    Fl 1.2 m (4 ft)
A most exciting recent introduction, this variegated grass is invaluable for the middle of the border. Leaves emerge with yellow margins and stripes, but before long, as they arch out from the rising culms, the yellow gives way to white with a pink flush, overlaid with a silky sheen. Flower heads in mid to late summer are purplish becoming greyish pink. Loose clump, gently spreading but not invasive. Average soil in sun or part shade.

## CAREX

### Carex albula    Cyperaceae
L 20×40 cm (8×16 in)    Fl 20 cm (8 in)
The first of some 35 members of this major family of sedges that we shall be considering is typical of several, mainly from New Zealand, which form a dense tuft of narrow evergreen leaves, starting erect, but soon lengthening and arching outwards in symmetrical fashion to produce a mop-head, or 'pudding-basin' hairstyle effect. I notice when exhibiting these species that there seems to be an irresistible urge to touch them and run one's fingers through their long tresses. They all need planting with a little space around them so that their form is not lost. Most are in distinctive colours, C. albula being on the smaller side and with unusual whitish green colouring, excellent in lighter-toned plantings. Insignificant flower spikes, of similar colour, produced mostly within the foliage. Easy in most soils in sun or light shade. Could be confused with C. comans or C. 'Frosted Curls'.

### Carex atrata    Cyperaceae
L 15×30 cm (6×12 in)    Fl 30 cm (12 in)
Jet sedge. Quite an unusual colour for this family, rather glaucous blue-green. Leaves fairly broad, keeled, and tapering to a point. Rhizomatous, forming a slowly spreading clump, for the front of the border. Flower spikes oval, almost black. Any soil in sun or part shade.

### Carex berggrenii    Cyperaceae
L 5×15 cm (2×6 in)    Fl 5 cm (2 in)
Interesting dwarf sedge, forming loose, slowly spreading clumps. Leaves a most unusual grey- to reddish brown with a metallic sheen, blunt-ended. Small brown flower spikes in mid summer. Good to moist soil in sun. Don't allow it to be swamped by neighbouring plants. There are also forms with grey-green leaves, both of normal width and much narrower.

### Carex buchananii    Cyperaceae
L 75×60 cm (2½×2 ft)    Fl 75 cm (2½ ft)
One of several brown-leaved species whose names have become dreadfully confused in the trade. Actually quite distinctive, essentially erect form, arching outwards to produce a vase shape. Taller than the others with decidedly curled leaf tips. Narrow but extremely tough leaves, rich reddish brown, often with orange flecks. Brown flowering spikes through the summer on stems which may exceed 1 m (3¼ ft), curving back down to the ground. Easily grown in most soils in sun. Usually hardy but will require protection in extreme cold. Ideal for use as a vertical accent with lower-growing yellow-leaved plants.

147

**Carex comans**   Cyperaceae
L 45 × 90 cm (1½ × 3 ft)   Fl 45 cm (1½ ft)
A mop-headed sedge, larger than *C. albula* with very narrow pale green leaves. Mid summer flower spikes mostly hidden within the foliage. Most soils in sun. Evergreen.
**C.c. 'Bronze Form'** Of identical size and habit but pale warm brown in colour. Unusually effective with silver-leaved plants and the blue grasses.

**Carex conica 'Snowline'**   Cyperaceae
L 12 × 15 cm (5 × 6 in)   Fl 15 cm (6 in)
Neat and pleasing, if not especially showy, forming a low arching tuft. Narrow white margins to deep green leaves. Small flower spikes in early summer. Good soil in sun or shade. Protect in extreme cold. Evergreen.

**Carex dipsacea**   Cyperaceae
L 38 × 75 cm (1¼ × 2½ ft)   Fl 60 cm (2 ft)
An arching, clump-forming sedge of quite unusual colouring. Evergreen leaves deep olive green, overlaid with a bronzy glaze. Small black flower spikes in summer. Good soil in sun or shade, but note that the bronze colouring will be lost in insufficient light Use in association with yellow and yellow-variegated plants.

**Carex elata 'Aurea'**   Cyperaceae
L 70 × 45 cm (2¼ × 1½ ft)   Fl 75 cm (2½ ft)
Bowles' golden sedge. Strongest yellow colouring of all the grass-like plants, with only narrow green margins and presenting a truly magnificent spectacle. Mr Bowles must have whooped with delight when he first came across this plant in the Norfolk Broads! Upper, male spikes brown, lower ones green, like fat caterpillars. Needs good to wet soil in sun. Would form a startling partnership with the Japanese blood grass, *Imperata cylindrica* 'Rubra'.

**Carex firma 'Variegata'**   Cyperaceae
L 8 × 10 cm (3 × 4 in)   Fl 10 cm (4 in)

A real dwarf, ideal for a sink or trough, or for a place in the rock garden free from the interference of neighbouring plants. Short, very stiff leaves quickly narrow to a point, shiny dark green with bold and clearly defined creamy yellow margins. Small dark brown flower spikes. Grow in limy soil, incorporating both grit and organic matter, in full sun.

**Carex flagellifera**   Cyperaceae
L 45 × 90 cm (1½ × 3 ft)   Fl 45 cm (1½ ft)
Another brown species which is frequently misnamed. Similar habit to *C. comans* 'Bronze Form', tufted, with arching leaves forming a mop-head, but the leaves broader, and of a warm, much redder brown, almost gingery. Avoid the driest soils, otherwise easy in a sunny position. Plant either with silvers and yellows or silvers and blues.

**Carex fraseri**   Cyperaceae
L 15 × 38 cm (6 × 15 in)   Fl 30 cm (12 in)
A distinctive sedge requiring moisture-retentive lime-free soil in shade. Small, round, bright white flowers appear in spring as the broad leaves unfurl.

**Carex 'Frosted Curls'**   Cyperaceae
L 60 × 45 cm (2 × 1½ ft)   Fl 60 cm (2 ft)
Similar in style to *C. albula* and *C. comans*, with narrow, pale green leaves giving a shiny, silvery effect, but much more erect, with curling tips. Pale green flower spikes inconspicuous within the foliage. Most soils in sun or part shade.

**Carex grayi**   Cyperaceae
L 60 × 45 cm (2 × 1½ ft)   Fl 60 cm (2 ft)
Mace sedge. Fascinating pale green seed heads,

**An association of strong colours: the grass is *Imperata cylindrica* 'Rubra', with *Houttuynia cordata* 'Chameleon' and a yellow carpet of *Lysimachia nummularia* 'Aurea'.**

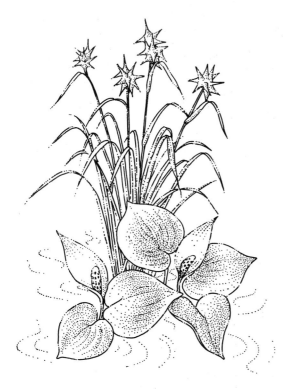

**Fig. 17 Interesting plant associations are possible in the garden pool. Here *Carex grayi* with its curious seed heads contrasts with the broad leaves and spathes of *Calla palustris*, the bog arum.**

knobbly and globe-shaped, a novel addition to cut flower arrangements. These develop through the summer above fairly broad, erect clumps of fresh green leaves which retain their colour well into the autumn. Grow in good soil in semi-shady border, or in water, or anything in between.

***Carex kaloides*** Cyperaceae
*L* 50 × 20 cm (20 × 8 in)   *Fl* 50 cm (20 in)
Shiny leaves vary between ochre and pale orange-

brown, fairly stiff and held upright, best displayed with yellows, interesting with blues. Pale brown inflorescences thin and insignificant. Good soil in sun.

***Carex morrowii* 'Fisher's Form'** Cyperaceae
*L* 40 × 30 cm (16 × 12 in)   *Fl* 45 cm (1½ ft)
Particularly showy evergreen sedge. Broad, stiff leaves conspicuously margined and striped with cream. Flowering spikes pale green, appearing in spring. Good soil in sun or shade.
***C.m* 'Variegata'** The greeny white stripes not very prominent but the plant as a whole makes a good feature with evergreen leaves of a particularly rich green. Flowers and growing preferences as above.

***Carex muskingumensis*** Cyperaceae
*L* 75 × 45 cm (2½ × 1½ ft)   *Fl* 75 cm (2½ ft)
Palm branch sedge. Cheerfully fresh green leaves differing from those of most of the sedges in that they arise from the erect culms rather than from the crown of the plant, the topmost group resembling palm branches. Forms gradually spreading clumps. Golden brown spikes in early summer of no great interest. Try using this carex with golden-leaved shrubs and perennials, especially hostas, in good soil in sun or part shade. The variety **'Wachtposten'** has yellow-green leaves.

***Carex ornithopoda* 'Variegata'** Cyperaceae
*L* 15 × 25 cm (6 × 10 in)   *Fl* 20 cm (8 in)
A neat low tuft of green leaves with a central white stripe, for the front of the border, or the rock garden, in most soils in sun or part shade.

***Carex oshimensis* 'Evergold'** Cyperaceae
*L* 25 × 38 cm (10 × 15 in)   *Fl* 30 cm (1 ft)
Deservedly one of the best known sedges. A low mound of long, arching, evergreen leaves, deep green with a broad central stripe of creamy yellow. In full sun this latter colour predominates, whereas in shade

the contrast between this and the green is more evident. Brown flowering spikes through spring. Good soil in sun or moderate shade, or even indoors as a pot plant in good light.
*C.o.* **'Variegata'** has a white central stripe.

***Carex pendula*** Cyperaceae
*L* 60 × 120 cm (2 × 4 ft)    *Fl* 1.2 m (4 ft)
Drooping sedge. Terminal flowering spikes hang from long arching stems in early summer. Broad, keeled leaves, shiny green, blue underneath. Needs some space around it. Best in good soil in informal areas in part shade.

***Carex petriei*** Cyperaceae
*L* 25 × 15 cm (10 × 6 in)    *Fl* 25 cm (10 in)
Like a small *C. buchananii*, with narrow, erect leaves, curled at the tips, but the colour is different – pale pinky brown. A good short vertical accent plant amongst prostrate silvers and blues. Most soils in sun.

***Carex pilulifera*** **'Tinney's Princess'** Cyperaceae
*L* 10 × 15 cm (4 × 6 in)    *Fl* 15 cm (6 in)
A delightful form of a small British native, the pill sedge. Similar effect to that of the better known *C. oshimensis* 'Evergold', but in a far more delicate mode, with essentially creamy yellow leaves narrowly green-margined. Small flowers held above the neat mound of foliage in late spring and early summer. Any lime-free soil in sun or shade. Small enough for a sink or trough, or delightful at the border front or in the rock garden.

***Carex plantaginea*** Cyperaceae
*L* 15 × 30 cm (6 × 12 in)    *Fl* 20 cm (8 in)
Plantain-leaved sedge. A North American native. Broad, somewhat ribbed leaves up to 2.5 cm (1 in) in width, flushed reddish at the base. Yellow-brown flower spikes in spring. A plant for good soil in cooler situations in part or full shade.

***Carex riparia*** **'Variegata'** Cyperaceae
*L* 45 × 30 cm (1½ × 1 ft)    *Fl* 60 cm (2 ft)
One of the few sedges that could be called invasive, especially in moist conditions, but a most striking plant, especially in spring and early summer, with long, narrow leaves of pure white usually only narrowly margined with green. Flowering spikes, too, are quite smart, blackish, in late spring and early summer. Good to moist soil in sun or part shade.

***Carex saxatilis*** **'Ski Run'** Cyperaceae
*L* 10 × 15 cm (4 × 6 in)    *Fl* 10 cm (4 in)
An interesting small sedge with somewhat contorted leaves striped with white, and gradually forming a low carpet. Good to damp soil in some shade.

***Carex secta*** Cyperaceae
*L* 45 × 75 cm (1½ × 2½ ft)    *Fl* 45 cm (1½ ft)
An arching clump of narrow, evergreen leaves, splendid bright green, excellent with yellows. Tiny spikelets alternate up the flowering culms in early to mid summer. Good to moist soil in sun.
*C.s. tenuiculmis* A recently available form with glowing, deep warm brown foliage.

***Carex siderosticta*** **'Variegata'** Cyperaceae
*L* 25 × 40 cm (10 × 16 in)    *Fl* 30 cm (1 ft)
A handsome, slowly spreading clump of broad, overlapping leaves, up to 2.5 cm (1 in) in width, white-margined and striped, and with a reddish flush at the base. Narrow flowering spikes in spring. Requires good soil in sun or, preferably, part shade.

***Carex testacea*** Cyperaceae
*L* 50 × 75 cm (20 × 30 in)    *Fl* 50 cm (20 in)
An eyecatching evergreen sedge from New Zealand. Might be confused with *C. dipsacea* but has narrower, longer leaves, paler olive, the upper parts which receive full light being orange. Flowering spikes differ, too, in being pale brown rather than black. Excellent

151

*Lamarckia aurea* is an annual grass with intriguing
downswept flower spikes.

**The evergreen woodrush *Luzula sylvatica* 'Marginata'
softens the lines of the brick wall.**

in company with yellows. Good to moist soil – in sun for the best colour.

### Carex trifida   Cyperaceae
L 90 × 75 cm (3 × 2½ ft)    Fl 1.2 m (4 ft)

A robust sedge forming an erect clump of broad, grey-green evergreen leaves. The flowering culms hold multiple large brown spikes above the foliage from early to mid summer. A handsome plant for good soil through to boggy conditions.

### Carex umbrosa 'The Beatles'   Cyperaceae
L 10 × 20 cm (4 × 8 in)    Fl 15 cm (6 in)

Imagine the heads of John, Paul, George and Ringo with hair dyed green and you have a fair impression of this small sedge! Gently spreading clump of narrow leaves topped by brown spikelets in spring. Happy in most soils in sun or shade, this neat plant is ideal for underplanting shrubs.

### Carex uncifolia   Cyperaceae
L 8 × 12 in (3 × 5 in)    Fl 5 cm (2 in)

Dwarf sedge with narrow, curved leaves forming a dense tuft. Plants raised from seed may vary in their unusual colouring between reddish bronze and a paler pinkish bronze. Small flowering spikes hidden within the foliage. Good soil in a sink, rockery or at the front of the border with small blue grasses and creeping silver-leaved plants.


## CHASMANTHIUM

### Chasmanthium latifolium   Gramineae
L 100 × 45 cm (3¼ × 1½ ft)    Fl 1.2 m (4 ft)

Spangle grass. Interesting features are the 2 cm (¾ in) broad leaves (hence *latifolium*) splaying out from the culms, and the large ironed-flat spikelets which hang gracefully in open panicles. Full sun, so long as the soil is not too poor, through to moderate shade.

## CHIONOCHLOA

### Chionochloa conspicua   Gramineae
L 1 × 1 m (3¼ × 3¼ ft)    Fl 1.8 m (6 ft)

Chionochloas are the tussock grasses from New Zealand, all featuring dense clumps of arching foliage. This and the next species are the most ornamental

**Fig. 18 The subtle colouring of *Chionochloa rubra* is best displayed against bright yellow, here represented in the foliage of the evergreen shrub *Choisya ternata* 'Sundance'. *Hedera helix* 'Angularis Aurea' creeps around its feet.**

overall, reminiscent of the pampas grass but with more open, lax feathery plumes of creamy white, flowering early, from mid summer onwards. Good soil in sun, some shelter. Protect in extreme cold. Excellent dried.

***Chionochloa flavescens***   Gramineae
*L* 75 × 90 cm (2½ × 3 ft)    *Fl* 1.5 m (5 ft)
Similarly ornamental, generally smaller than *C. conspicua*, leaves unusual brownish green. The large, pale, airy panicles appear even earlier, from late spring in a good year, and remain right through until the autumn. Fine addition to dried arrangements. Similar cultural requirements to previous species.

***Chionochloa rubra***   Gramineae
*L* 75 × 60 cm (2½ × 2 ft)    *Fl* 75 cm (2½ ft)
Superficially drab, but closer inspection reveals subtle colouring: ochre upper surfaces to the narrow evergreen leaves, grey-blue undersides, and brassy tips. With its outward-arching form it requires a specimen position, and should be planted with bright yellows. Sparse mid summer flowers borne just above the clump. Average to moist soils in sun.

## CHUSQUEA
***Chusquea couleou***   Gramineae (Bambuseae)
*L* 3.6 × 1.5 m (12 × 15 ft)
A tall Chilean bamboo with thick, solid culms of greenish yellow. The short leaves on densely clustered branches are an attractive feature, especially at the point when these are combined with the current year's shoots ready to burst from their protective white sheaths. These taller, clump-forming bamboos may be used as foreground or lawn specimens, much as a large shrub or small tree might be, or among lower shrubs at the back of a border. Good soil in sun or shade.

## COIX
***Coix lacryma-jobi***   Gramineae
*L* 75 × 45 cm (2½ × 1½ ft)    *Fl* 75 cm (2½ ft)
Job's tears. Annual. The strange seed cases, hard, oval, pearly grey, may be removed when mature, dried and strung as beads. Leaves broad with a notably pale central vein. Treat as a half-hardy annual, sowing seed under glass in early spring and planting out after frosts in good soil in sun.

## CORTADERIA
***Cortaderia fulvida***   Gramineae
*L* 1.2 × 2 m (4 × 6½ ft)    *Fl* 2 m (6½ ft)
Our look at the genus which includes the pampas grass starts with two earlier flowering relatives from New Zealand. This is the least hardy, and if grown away from milder areas should be protected through really cold spells. Evergreen foliage makes a tidy, tight clump. Flower heads appear from early summer, not nearly so full or shaggy as a pampas, but no less pleasing, and hanging slightly to one side. Colour pinkish cream, becoming ivory. Free-draining soil in sun.

***Cortaderia richardii***   Gramineae
*L* 1.5 × 1.8 m (5 × 6 ft)    *Fl* 2.5 m (8 ft)
Toe-toe. On a larger scale, with flower heads more substantial than those of *C. fulvida*, whiter in colour, and carried on arching culms which reach way beyond the limits of the foliage beneath, requiring a space some 4–5 m (13–16 ft) in diameter. Well-drained soil in sun.

***Cortaderia selloana***   Gramineae
*L* 1.5 × 2 m (5 × 6 ft)    *Fl* 3 m (10 ft)
The familiar pampas grass, much used, sometimes unwisely so, in small suburban gardens, without due consideration to its ultimate size. Large, dense tussock of sharp-edged leaves topped by shaggy plumes in late summer and autumn, requiring considerable space in

***Melica uniflora*** **with its graceful beadlike flowers is planted
here with a fern in a shady setting which both prefer.**

**Yellow and blue are cheerful companions. *Milium effusum*
'Aureum' grows here in partial shade with self-sown
forget-me-nots.**

which to be appreciated, but unrivalled when such space is available. Choose named varieties as seed-raised plants may bear disappointing flower heads. Dried heads are popular, but do pick them young for the best results. Well-drained soil in an open position. A cut-back in spring every two or three years will maintain a tidy appearance. Protect newly planted specimens from extreme cold in their first winter.

**C.s. 'Gold Band'** Smaller, with 1.5 m (5 ft) plumes over 1 × 1.5 m (3¼ × 5 ft) foliage. Increasingly effective as the summer progresses, with broadly yellow-margined leaves becoming steadily richer in colour. A splendid feature in the autumn garden.

**C.s. 'Monstrosa'** The largest variety, with enormous open, shaggy plumes to 2.7 m (9 ft) just above the 2 m (6½ ft) foliage clump.

**C.s. 'Pumila'** The best green-leaved pampas grass for the smaller garden. Flower heads more erect, almost cigar-shaped, and produced in abundance, 1.8 m (6 ft) over 1 m (3¼ ft) foliage.

**C.s. 'Rendatleri'** Carries large plumes of purplish pink to 3 m (10 ft).

**C.s. 'Rosea'** Features a distinct pink flush to the silvery plumes. Overall a little smaller, to 2.5 m (8 ft).

**C.s. 'Silver Stripe'** A white-margined cultivar which, like 'Gold Band', gets better as the weeks go by. Not quite so hardy as most, nor offering such an impressive floral display, but still an exciting feature plant. 1.8 m (6 ft) flowers over 1 m (3¾ ft) foliage.

**C.s. 'Sunningdale Silver'** Among the larger forms, this variety has no rivals when it comes to the quality of its 2.7 m (9 ft) flower heads, which are a joy to contemplate. Open, feathery and glistening creamy white, borne on sturdy, erect culms over 1.5 m (5 ft) foliage.

## CORYNEPHORUS

**Corynephorus canescens** Gramineae
L 10 × 15 cm (4 × 6 in)    Fl 25 cm (10 in)

Grey hair grass. A plant of poor, thin soils. Dense tufts of stiff, narrow leaves, blue-grey with a hint of purple and reddish at the base. Small heads of reddish spike-lets with unusual club-shaped bristles in mid summer. Sun.

## CYPERUS

**Cyperus eragrostis** Cyperaceae
L 60 × 30 cm (2 × 1 ft)    Fl 75 cm (2½ ft)
From South America and related to the papyrus of warmer climes. Normally hardy. May be grown in the pond or in the border in good to wet soil but may require protection if extreme cold threatens. All parts of the plant are a fresh, bright green, including the attractive flowering spikelets borne in umbels from mid summer to early autumn, and which may be used to good effect in floral decoration. Easily raised from seed.

**Cyperus longus** Cyperaceae
L 100 × 60 cm (3¼ × 2 ft)    Fl 1 m (3¼ ft)
Galingale. Long, corrugated leaves of the shiniest mid-green. Pendulous, branched flowering heads carried on arching stems, bearing reddish brown spikelets, an asset to late summer flower arrangements. A rapid spreader in proportion to the dampness of the environment, and will grow in water. Will need containing in confined quarters.

## DACTYLIS

**Dactylis glomerata 'Variegata'** Gramineae
L 45 × 45 cm (1½ × 1½ ft)    Fl 75 cm (2½ ft)
Showy white-striped form of the British native cocks-foot. Dense arching clumps. One-sided panicles divided into groups of densely clustered green spike-lets. Remove before seeds drop. Ordinary soil in sun or part shade.

## DESCHAMPSIA

***Deschampsia caespitosa*** Gramineae
$L 50 \times 50$ cm $(20 \times 20$ in$)$  $Fl$ 1.2 m (4 ft)
Tufted hair grass. Undoubtedly one of the most graceful wild grasses. Clouds of hazy flower heads on erect stems through the summer months in a variety of tints and varying heights as reflected in the selected forms which follow. These stand well into the winter and are fine subjects for picking and drying. Leaves in a dense evergreen clumps. Tolerant of a range of conditions from ordinary to damp soil, and sun to part-shade. Use in woodland or natural gardens, or in the border for contrast standing above lower plants or between shrubs.
***D.c.*** **'Bronzeschleier' ('Bronze Veil')**  The bronze veil forms as the silvery green flowers mature.
***D.c.*** **'Goldgehaenge' ('Golden Showers')**  Golden yellow flowers appear a little later on 1 m (3¼ ft) stems.
***D.c.*** **'Goldschleier' ('Golden Veil')**  Bright golden yellow flower heads rise to about 1.2 m (4 ft).
***D.c.*** **'Goldtau' ('Golden Dew')**  A more compact form, with flower heads to about 75 cm (2½ ft) over 40 cm (16 in) foliage, with later flowers maturing to warm gold.
***D.c.*** *vivipara*  Sometimes offered with the variety name 'Fairy's Joke' attached. Something of an oddity, the joke being that as the 'flowers' develop you realize that they aren't flowers at all, but tiny plantlets which, as they steadily enlarge, gradually weigh the culms down until, from an erect 75 cm (2½ ft) start, they touch the ground, sometimes rooting at the point of contact. Such a form is technically described as viviparous.

***Deschampsia flexuosa***  Gramineae
$L 15 \times 20$ cm $(6 \times 8$ in$)$  $Fl$ 45 cm (1½ ft)
Wavy hair grass. Also grows wild in Britain, in similar conditions to its larger relative, and is tolerant of even more shade. Prefers acid soils, so not suitable for chalk. A smaller grass, leaves very narrow, bright mid-green. The flowers are a graceful delight, purplish and glistening with silver as they react to the gentlest breeze, narrow at first, subsequently opening out. For the front of the border, or in woodland settings.
***D.f.*** **'Tatra Gold'**  A lovely variety with absolutely the freshest and cleanest bright green yellow leaves imaginable. A little less yellow as the season advances, or if grown in too shady a spot.

## ELYMUS

***Elymus arenarius***  Gramineae
$L 60 \times 60$ cm $(2 \times 2$ ft$)$  $Fl$ 1.5 m (5 ft)
Invasive, especially in dry soils, but none the less a fine grass. Grey-blue leaves and stiff stems bearing long wheat-like heads in summer. Effective with purples and silvers, for example *Cotinus coggygria* 'Royal Purple' and *Senecio* 'Sunshine', or with pink-flowered grasses such as *Pennisetum orientale* and *P. villosum.* Average to light soil in sun.

## ERAGROSTIS

***Eragrostis curvula***  Gramineae
$L 75 \times 60$ cm $(2½ \times 2$ ft$)$  $Fl$ 90 cm (3 ft)
African, or weeping love grass. Needs a warm sunny spot and a specimen position with space around it so that the arching form of both the narrow foliage and the long, open panicles of tiny spikelets, oddly coloured dark greyish, may be fully appreciated. Flowering period, late summer to early autumn. Protect from extreme cold.

## ERIOPHORUM

***Eriophorum angustifolium***  Cyperaceae
$L 30 \times 30$ cm $(1 \times 1$ ft$)$  $Fl$ 45 cm (1½ ft)
Cotton grass. Grown for the cotton wool effect of the mass of soft hairs attached to the multiple seed heads.

**Fig. 19 *Elymus arenarius* can be invasive, but its pale blue leaves and thrusting flower heads make it a splendid companion to larger shrubs, such as *Acer negundo* 'Flamingo' with its pink, white and green foliage. *Stachys lanata* 'Silver Carpet' provides appropriate ground cover.**

Flowers late spring to early summer. Normally used as a marginal plant in ornamental pools, but will also grow in damp soil – but watch its creeping roots.

***Eriophorum vaginatum*** Gramineae
*L* 30 × 15 cm (12 × 6 in)    *Fl* 45 cm (1½ ft)
Hare's tail. Flower heads slightly smaller than those of *E. angustifolium*, and borne singly, in mid to late spring. Clump forming rather than running. Ordinary to damp soil will suffice.

## FESTUCA

***Festuca amethystina*** Gramineae
*L* 25 × 25 cm (10 × 10 in)    *Fl* 45 cm (1½ ft)
*F. glauca* and its varieties, discussed shortly, are the best known fescues or blue grasses. This species is similar but a little larger with pale grey-blue foliage, and flowering heads opening to a branched panicle in late spring and early summer. Well-drained soil in full sun.

***Festuca erecta*** Gramineae
*L* 30 × 20 cm (12 × 8 in)    *Fl* 40 cm (16 in)
A grass of upright habit from the Falkland Islands. Narrow leaves rise stiffly like needles from a tight clump. The subtle leaden blue looks good standing out of a silver or white-variegated carpet. Late spring to early summer flowers are a typical, gradually opening small panicle. Average to dry soils in full sun.

***Festuca eskia*** Gramineae
*L* 8 × 15 cm (3 × 6 in)    *Fl* 15 cm (6 in)
A soft little grass forming rich green, gently spreading mounds. More carpet-like if clipped back at regular intervals. Flowers, early to mid summer, green, turning brown. Average soil in sun. Fun with the cheerful hummocks of *Thymus* 'Archer's Gold'.

***Festuca filiformis*** Gramineae
*L* 30 × 30 cm (1 ft × 1 ft)    *Fl* 30 cm (1 ft)
Somewhat similar to *F. eskia* but on a decidedly larger scale.

***Miscanthus sinensis* 'Silver Feather' features in a pleasant autumn scene.**

160

***Festuca glacialis***   Gramineae
*L* 5 × 10 cm (2 × 4 in)     *Fl* 13 cm (5 in)
A tiny, dense mound of very narrow whitish blue-green leaves. Violet spikelets, mid to late summer. Well-drained soil in full sun.

***Festuca glauca* 'Azurit'**   Gramineae
*L* 20 × 15 cm (8 × 6 in)     *Fl* 35 cm (14 in)
All of the *F. glauca* varieties are useful for edging or as foreground groups, either massed or spaced as small specimens, interplanted with prostrate silvers. Best foliage colour is maintained by dividing the clumps every two to three years. Small, open flower heads appear in early summer. 'Azurit' is taller than most, and an excellent blue.

***F.g.* 'Blaufuchs' ('Blue Fox') and *F.g.* 'Blauglut' ('Blue Glow')**   Both good blue selections, 15 cm (6 in) high.
***F.g. coxii***   Another good blue, but rarely flowers, if you should find that an advantage.
***F.g.* 'Harz'**   This gives an altogether different effect, with blue-green leaves tipped purple and greyish purple flower heads 15 cm (6 in) high.
***F.g.* 'Meerblau' ('Ocean Blue')**   Features blue-green foliage, to a similar height as *F.g.* 'Harz'.
***F.g.* 'Minima'**   There is some doubt as to whether this tiny grass is a festuca at all. Wiry little leaves, 5 × 10 cm (2 × 4 in), of very pale blue. An ideal candidate for a sunny sink or trough.
***F.g.* 'Seeigel' ('Sea Urchin')**   Green hair-fine leaves.

***F.g.* 'Silbersee' ('Silver Sea')** Makes a neat, tight little mound to a maximum of 12 cm (5 in), selected both for its dwarfness and its pale silvery blue colouring.

***Festuca mairei*** Gramineae
*L* 60 × 60 cm (2 × 2 ft)    *Fl* 1 m (3¼ ft)
Maire's fescue. From a different mould altogether. Longer leaves, shiny grey-green, almost silvery. Spring flower heads, thin and nothing special. If planting in groups, separate the individual specimens, and surround them perhaps with the white-variegated holcus. Average soil in sun.

***Festuca paniculata*** Gramineae
*L* 40 × 40 cm (16 × 16 in)    *Fl* 1 m (3¼ ft)
Broader leaved than any of the other fescues described here, smooth, mid-green, paler on the

**Fig. 20 In a sunny, well-drained position the rigid, silvery blue, pointed leaves of *Festuca punctoria* contrast beautifully with the pink and white variegation and pale pink flowers of *Sedum spurium* 'Variegatum'.**

reverse. Tidy inflorescence of quite large spikelets. Most soils in sun or light shade.

***Festuca punctoria*** Gramineae
*L* 15 × 30 cm (6 × 12 in)    *Fl* 30 cm (1 ft)
Porcupine grass. Rigid, sharply pointed leaves, a fine silvery blue. As the leaves lengthen they tend to splay out leaving the centre bare and rather unsightly. Lifting and replanting a little deeper in early summer will keep it neat. A sunny, well-drained spot is important.

***Festuca vivipara*** Gramineae
*L* 15 × 30 cm (6 × 12 in)    *Fl* 35 cm (14 in)
Another of those oddities which surprise you by producing tiny plantlets instead of true flowers. Intriguing, certainly, and worthy of garden space as a conversation piece at least. Hair-fine, somewhat grey-green leaves. Each plantlet is carried on a short reddish stalk.

## GLYCERIA

***Glyceria maxima* 'Variegata'** Gramineae
*L* 60 × 45 cm (2 × 1½ ft)    *Fl* 90 cm (3 ft)
Marvellous cream foliage, only narrowly green-striped and with a pink flush upon emerging in spring. Spread will be determined significantly by soil conditions. Grown literally in water, or in wet ground it may be invasive, but in ordinary border conditions it is more restrained. Open, yellow-green flowering panicles. Cream and blue mix beautifully, so try with the prostrate conifer *Juniperus squamata* 'Blue Carpet', or with blue hostas or hebes.

## HAKONECHLOA

***Hakonechloa macra* 'Aureola'** Gramineae
*L* 20 × 40 cm (8 × 16 in)    *Fl* 25 cm (10 in)
A choice grass which requires good soil in sun or part shade. A slow starter but gradually forms a mound of

arching, overlapping leaves, bright yellow with rich green stripes, often with a reddish flush towards the autumn. Insignificant flowers, late summer. Makes a classic combination with *Hosta* 'Halcyon'.

## HELICTOTRICHON

***Helictotrichon sempervirens*** Gramineae
*L* 45×75 cm (1½×2½ ft)    *Fl* 1.2 m (4 ft)
A fine evergreen grass for a sunny position in ordinary to light soil. Steely grey-blue leaves from a tight central clump form a hemisphere of some 38 cm (15 in) radius. Graceful nodding flower heads on arching stems, spring and early summer. Give it a specimen position among low silvers, purples and pinks.

## HOLCUS

***Holcus mollis*** 'Albovariegatus'    Gramineae
*L* 15×40 cm (6×16 in)    *Fl* 30 cm (1 ft)
Excellent carpeting grass of bright creamy white effect, with only a narrow central green stripe. Plant under darker upright grasses, or allow to intermingle with the purple-leaved clover, *Trifolium repens* 'Quadrifolium Purpurascens', for an interesting effect. Pale green inflorescences during the summer are not abundant and are best removed before seeding. Average soils in sun or moderate shade.

## HORDEUM

***Hordeum jubatum*** Gramineae
*L* 50×30 cm (20×12 in)    *Fl* 75 cm (2½ ft)
Foxtail barley. Highly decorative in the garden or for drying and dyeing. A host of long bristles (awns) arises from the nodding flower spike in early and mid summer, pale green with a hint of red, turning buff. Cut back if untidy in late summer. Best treated as an annual sown direct into the soil in sun in spring or autumn.

## HYSTRIX

***Hystrix patula*** Gramineae
*L* 90×45 cm (3×1½ ft)    *Fl* 1.2 m (4 ft)
Bottle brush grass. Aptly named, as the Latin generic name, *Hystrix*, means porcupine. Upright culms from a loose clump of broad green leaves. Long, narrow, erect heads of awned (bristled), regularly spaced spikelets are held initially at an angle, then at right angles to the stem. The individual spikelets are green, sometimes pink-tinged, appearing around mid summer and remaining of interest into the autumn. Good for cutting and drying. Ordinary soil in sun or part shade.

## IMPERATA

***Imperata cylindrica*** 'Rubra'    Gramineae
*L* 35×20 cm (14×8 in)
Japanese blood grass. Mid-green leaves, appearing quite late, quickly become blood red at the tips. By autumn the whole plant is aglow – quite astonishing! Prefers good soil which does not dry out and a little shade. Not reliably hardy in extreme cold so be prepared to give protective covering. Christopher Lloyd suggests planting with the black-leaved *Ophiopogon planiscapus* 'Nigrescens'. I would add some bright yellow.

## INDOCALAMUS

***Indocalamus tessellatus*** Gramineae
(Bambuseae)
*L* 1.5×1.8 m (5×6 ft)
A bamboo grown for its enormous shiny leaves achieving a length of almost 60 cm (2 ft) and 10 cm (4 in) wide, weighing down the slender green culms, and bestowing a luxuriant effect. A stand of this will be impressive but invasive.

163

**Evening sunlight filters through the tall *Miscanthus sinensis* 'Variegatus', *Cotinus coggygria* 'Royal Purple' and a foreground clump of *Artemisia* 'Powis Castle'.**

The charming *Molinia caerulea* 'Variegata' brightens a border in dappled shade.

## JUNCUS

***Juncus concinnus***   Juncaceae
*L* 25 × 15 cm (10 × 6 in)   *Fl* 30 cm (1 ft)
An interesting rush from Pakistan with erect cylindrical leaves, deep red at the base and nodes, and rather scabious-like, creamy white flower heads. Moist soil in sun.

***Juncus decipiens* 'Curly Wurly'**   Juncaceae
*L* 10 × 30 cm (4 × 12 in)   *Fl* 10 cm (4 in)
A much more refined plant in every way than the more familiar corkscrew rush (below). Narrow, cylindrical leaves like coils of the green plastic-coated wire used in the garden. Small brown flower heads in summer. Good to damp soil in sun or part shade.

***Juncus effusus* 'Spiralis'**   Juncaceae
*L* 45 × 90 cm (1½ × 3 ft)   *Fl* 45 cm (1½ ft)
Corkscrew rush. The common name is precisely descriptive of the strange mode of growth. The spiralled, cylindrical, shiny green leaves either lie flat on the ground or grow more erect. Pale brown flower heads through the summer. May be grown in damp soil or in water, in sun or part shade.

***Juncus inflexus* 'Afro'**   Juncaceae
*L* 45 × 90 cm (1½ × 3 ft)   *Fl* 45 cm (1½ ft)
If you have neither damp soil nor water but have a hankering for a corkscrew rush choose this variety, with blue-green leaves, which will grow in ordinary soil in sun or part shade. Again, pale brown flower heads in summer.

***Juncus xiphioides***   Juncaceae
*L* 30 × 30 cm (1 × 1 ft)   *Fl* 40 cm (16 in)
Couldn't be more different to the foregoing. Erect, iris-like leaves, one margin of which appears papery and colourless, giving the impression of variegation. Pale, flat flower heads from early summer turn a rich reddish colour as the seeds ripen. Forms a loose, spreading clump. Good to moist soil or plant actually in water.

## KOELERIA

***Koeleria cristata glauca***   Gramineae
*L* 15 × 15 cm (6 × 6 in)   *Fl* 35 cm (14 in)
Crested hair grass. Of similar stature to the blue fescues but with broader, grey-green leaves and more showy inflorescences – a longer, dense panicle (in early to mid summer) of shiny spikelets arranged in noticeably regular fashion up the flowering stem. Plant at the front of the border, singly or in groups, perhaps with white-variegated plants. A chalk lover but will grow happily in most soils in sun.
   ***Koeleria vallesiana*** is a very similar plant, confined in Great Britain to limestone hills in Somerset.

## LAGURUS

***Lagurus ovatus***   Gramineae
*L* 30 × 30 (1 × 1 ft)   *Fl* 50 cm (20 in)
Hare's tail. Easily grown annual, much used for dried arrangements and dyes well. Its soft, hairy, dense heads, oval-shaped and palest green, becoming creamy white in colour, are also of value in the garden. Sow seed in the chosen spot in spring. Average to light soil in sun.
***L.o. nanus*** is a delightful miniature form.

## LUZULA

***Luzula alopecurus***   Juncaceae
*L* 15 × 15 cm (6 × 6 in)   *Fl* 30 cm (1 ft)
A species of woodrush with the emerging brown flower heads enveloped in cocoon-like silky hairs.

***Luzula × borrerii* 'Botany Bay'**   Juncaceae
*L* 15 × 15 cm (6 × 6 in)   *Fl* 25 cm (10 in)
New leaves in spring are striped white and sometimes

pink-flushed, a somewhat fleeting phenomenon, often requiring close inspection to be observed at all. The effect is enhanced in shade. The older leaves are a quietly pleasing pale matt green. Typical heads of brown flowers in summer. Damp or dry soil in shade.

### *Luzula nivea*   Juncaceae
$L\,30 \times 25\,cm\,(12 \times 10\,in)$   $Fl\,50\,cm\,(20\,in)$

Snowy woodrush. Distinctive, shiny white, compact flowering heads well above the dense clump of deep green evergreen leaves endowed with numerous marginal hairs. A pleasant antidote to brighter colours in sun or shade.

### *Luzula pumila*   Juncaceae
$L\,5 \times 8\,cm\,(2 \times 3\,in)$   $Fl\,12\,cm\,(5\,in)$

A tight little mound of narrow, rather stiff leaves, ideal for a sink or trough, or for small pockets in the rock garden. Small brown flower heads in early summer.

### *Luzula sylvatica forma*   Juncaceae
$L\,35 \times 30\,cm\,(14 \times 12\,in)$   $Fl\,60\,cm\,(2\,in)$

This is an interesting form with new shoots almost white, gradually turning green. All these varieties of the greater woodrush are valuable evergreens, providing the densest of slowly spreading ground cover in sun or, perhaps more usefully, in shade, damp or dry. They are broad leaved, slightly hairy at the margins and bear open heads of chestnut brown flowers in mid to late spring.

**L.s. 'Hohe Tatra'** Sometimes distributed as *L.s.* 'Aurea', this is of very recent introduction and is surely set to be a winner. Brightest yellow winter colour of any of the plants considered in this book, broad leaves contributing to the considerable impact. As the new growth emerges the colouring moves through lime-yellow to fresh yellow-green during the summer, before returning to its brightest best in winter cold.

**L.s. 'Marginata'** The most commonly encountered variety and an excellent plant. Shiny rich green leaves have neat, narrow, cream margins.

**L.s. 'Select'** A new, larger and more robust form, with foliage to about $60\,cm\,(2\,ft)$.

**L.s. 'Tauernpass'** By contrast, a lower-growing variety with slightly broader leaves, reaching only $25\,cm\,(10\,in)$.

### *Luzula ulophylla*   Juncaceae
$L\,10 \times 12\,cm\,(4 \times 5\,in)$   $Fl\,15\,cm\,(6\,in)$

Recently introduced to a wider market from New Zealand seed by Graham Hutchins. Most interesting species, with very dark green leaves so V-shaped in section that the abundant silver hairs on the reverse are a prominent feature, giving a splendid silvery effect. The very tight clump sends up flowering stems in early summer topped by a single black spike.

## MELICA

### *Melica altissima* 'Atropurpurea'   Gramineae
$L\,90 \times 45\,cm\,(3 \times 1\frac{1}{2}\,ft)$   $Fl\,1.2\,m\,(4\,ft)$

Each spikelet, hanging from the stem at a 45-degree angle, is purple in colour, turning paler as the seed heads mature. Avoid the heaviest soils, otherwise easy in sun or part shade. This, and **M.a. 'Alba'** with almost white spikelets, can be of rather untidy habit but are worth growing for their flower heads.

### *Melica nutans*   Gramineae
$L\,30 \times 30\,cm\,(12 \times 12\,in)$   $Fl\,45\,cm\,(1\frac{1}{2}\,ft)$

Nodding or mountain melick. Loose clump of fresh green leaves. Flower heads, late spring and through the summer, hanging as a graceful one-sided panicle of sparse, small, oval-shaped spikelets. Most at home in part shade but full sun is acceptable in good soil.

### *Melica uniflora* 'Variegata'   Gramineae
$L\,20 \times 30\,cm\,(8 \times 12\,in)$   $Fl\,25\,cm\,(10\,in)$

A lovely variety of the wood melick with centrally

167

**Although not always hardy *Pennisetum villosum* is well worth raising from seed for its fluffy late summer flower heads.**

*Phalaris arundinacea* 'Feesey's Form' is a less commonly
encountered variety of the familiar gardener's garters,
with a white central stripe.

white-striped leaves often flushed purple. Lower section of the culms purplish. Good soil in some shade. Plant in groups for best impact. Small dark, beadlike spikelets resemble blackfly on first appearing!
**M.u. var. albida** Bears small white flowers on erect, branched stems over fresh green leaves in late spring and early summer.

### MILIUM

**Milium effusum 'Aureum'**  Gramineae
L 30 × 20 cm (12 × 8 in)    Fl 60 cm (2 ft)
Bowles' golden grass. An excellent lightener of part-shaded spots. Every part of this plant is bright yellow: the broad, soft, somewhat floppy leaves, the flowering stems, and the open panicle of tiny spikelets on hair-fine branches in early summer. Slightly more green as the season progresses or in too much shade. Average to good soil in semi-shade. When well suited will self-seed happily. Splendid between green or yellow-variegated shrubs.

### MISCANTHUS

**Miscanthus floridulus**  Gramineae
L 2.7 × 1.5 m (9 × 5 ft)    Fl 3 m (10 ft)
Apparently this is the correct name for the grass that has been distributed for years as M. sacchariflorus, which is shorter, earlier flowering, and possibly less hardy. To what extent M. sacchariflorus is grown at all in our cooler climate it will be interesting to ascertain.
Strong grower, forming erect, slowly spreading clumps. Broad grey-green leaves, 75 cm (2½ ft) in length, with a silvery midrib, arch outwards from the upward thrusting culms. Whitish flower panicles rarely produced except in warmer areas. Use as an isolated specimen or accent plant, as a background plant to lower planting, or as a screen which will reach its full height only in late summer. The dead foliage

rustles and flutters but is best cut back by early winter or it will be scattered around the garden by winter winds. Tolerant of most soil conditions, in sun or part shade, but will reward planting in good soil.

**Miscanthus sinensis**  Gramineae
L 1.8 × 1.5 m (6 × 5 ft)    Fl 2.1 m (7 ft)
To date at least 40 forms and cultivars of this wonderfully stately plant have become available, and as there are some quite small varieties this is surely one grass that no garden should be without. Easy-going as to requirements and, while doing best in good moisture-retentive soil, will not object to anything from light to heavy soil in sun or light shade. Erect habit of growth with long leaves cascading from stout culms. One or two forms do not flower regularly, but most do, appearing between mid summer and mid autumn and lasting through the winter. The panicles are roughly fan-shaped with multiple finger-like spikes, shining, silvery pinkish to reddish brown. Selected forms have whiter or redder colouring. Best planted in some isolation or with only low-growing plants around them so that their architectural qualities may be fully appreciated. Flowering stems may be cut and dried for indoor decoration.
**M.s. 'Cabaret'**  A wonderful new variegated form with green margins and stripes to a white leaf.
**M.s. 'Flamingo'**  Pale purplish pink flowers appear in late summer, 1.8 m (6 ft) tall, over 1.2 m (4 ft) foliage.
**M.s. 'Goldfeder'**  This has yellow margins to the leaves.
**M.s. 'Goliath'**  A strong grower with larger flower heads in early autumn, 2.5 m (8 ft).
**M.s. 'Gracillimus'**  Maiden grass. Does not regularly produce flowers in cooler climates, but it has a pleasing form with very narrow arching leaves in a dense, compact clump providing interest right through the winter. 1.2 m (4 ft) foliage.

**M.s. 'Graziella'** An excellent narrow-leaved variety, similar to 'Gracillimus', but a good flowerer, pale, silvery panicles appearing in late summer, reaching 1.8 m (6 ft).

**M.s. 'Kascade'** Wide-open, lax panicles, rich deep red at first, and reaches 2.1 m (7 ft).

**M.s. 'Kleine Fontane'** A smaller variety with long, narrow leaves and pinkish flower heads, quite early, from mid to late summer onwards, 1.5 m (5 ft) over 1 m ($3\frac{1}{4}$ ft) foliage.

**M.s. 'Malapartus'** The broad leaves attain a purplish flush by autumn. The flowers, to 1.6 m ($5\frac{1}{2}$ ft), opening purple-red, become silver from late summer.

**M.s. 'Morning Light'** This has very narrow foliage to 1.2 m (4 ft), each leaf having a thin white marginal stripe in addition to the silvery midrib.

**M.s. 'Nippon'** With its 90 cm (3 ft) clump of narrow leaves, this is an excellent variety for the smaller garden. Early autumn flower heads to 1.2 m (4 ft) open a good red.

**M.s. 'Punktchen'** This variety is similar to 'Strictus', with creamy-yellow cross-banding. It reaches 1.5 m (5 ft).

**M.s. purpurascens** Flowers, when they do appear, which is not regularly, reaches 1.2 m (4 ft) in mid autumn, but this form compensates with foliage colour – a deep purplish flush becomes apparent in the summer, the normally silver median stripe being pink, and intensifies to bright brown and reddish tones. The foliage is 75 cm ($2\frac{1}{2}$ ft) high.

**M.s. 'Rotsilber'** Prominent central silvery stripe to the narrow leaves. Good red flower heads, especially on opening out in early autumn, 1.5 m (5 ft) over 1 m ($3\frac{1}{4}$ ft) foliage.

**M.s. 'Silberfeder' ('Silver Feather')** Similar to the species in size, it develops excellent silvery flower heads in early autumn, becoming pale pinkish brown, and lasting well into the winter.

**M.s. 'Silberspinne'** Forms an erect 1 m ($3\frac{1}{4}$ ft) clump of narrow leaves, with 1.2 m (4 ft) panicles of long, open, spidery fingers from early autumn, reddish at first, becoming silvery.

**M.s. 'Sirene'** Another tallish variety, the 1.8 m (6 ft) flower heads opening rich red-brown in early autumn.

**M.s. 'Strictus'** One of the few grasses with transverse yellow bars across the leaves, appearing from mid summer on. Pinky brown flower heads rise to 1.8 m (6 ft) in the autumn. Of particularly erect and narrow habit.

**M.s. 'Variegatus'** A truly stately variegated grass – a veritable fountain of markedly white-striped leaves. Use as a stunning contrast to purple-leaved and dark green shrubs, or as a harmonizing tone but sharply contrasting form in paler planting schemes. Not reliably free-flowering, but when they do appear in mid autumn the panicles are pinkish, to 1.8 m (6 ft) over 1.5 m (5 ft) foliage.

**M.s. 'Zebrinus'** With similar transverse banding to M.s. 'Strictus' but is of more spreading habit. The two varieties are probably totally confused in the trade.

**Miscanthus tinctoria 'Nana Variegata'**
Gramineae
L 38 × 45 cm (15 × 18 in)    Fl 75 cm ($2\frac{1}{2}$ ft)
Here is a super little plant which should soon be getting around in the trade. The smallest of the family, small enough for the tiniest garden. Forms a loose, spreading clump of fresh, yellow-green leaves with narrow white stripes. Pale brownish flower heads in early autumn. Good soil in sun or part shade.

**Miscanthus yakushimensis**    Gramineae
L 75 × 45 cm ($2\frac{1}{2}$ × $1\frac{1}{2}$ ft)    Fl 1.2 m (4 ft)
We conclude this splendid genus with another dwarf species, much like a small M. sinensis but with pale leaves, and pale pinky brown flowers with fewer, long, slender fingers.

171

## MOLINIA

### Molinia caerulea 'Heidebraut' ('Heather Bride')
Gramineae

$L$ 60 × 40 cm (24 × 16 in)    $Fl$ 1.2 m (4 ft)

The purple moor grass is another species which has benefited from the careful selection of distinctive varieties by German nurserymen. In the wild it grows in areas of damp, acidic moorland but, in fact, is quite at home in most average to moist soils in sun or part shade. This variety has yellowish stems and inflorescences with glistening spikelets and seed heads.

*M.c.* **'Moorhexe' ('Bog Witch')** Less tall, with foliage to about 35 cm (14 in), of rigidly erect form. Tight, almost needle-like, dark flower heads stand to attention in late summer, reaching 75 cm (2½ ft). The upright growth of this form suits it admirably for use as a vertical specimen among lower, light-toned plants.

*M.c.* **'Variegata'** Neat and attractive in every respect. From a compact 35 cm (14 in) clump arise leaves of cream with pale green stripes which remain attractive long after they have faded to a pale buff colour in the autumn. Creamy yellow stems bear nicely contrasting purplish spikelets rising to about 60 cm (2 ft) in late summer. Avoid the hottest spots and plant with any blue to grey-green foliage.

### Molinia caerulea arundinacea 'Bergfreund'
Gramineae

$L$ 75 × 60 cm (2½ × 2 ft)    $Fl$ 1.6 m (5½ ft)

The English translation of the varietal name is 'Mountain's Friend'. This and the following are varieties of a taller-growing subspecies, and make quite imposing plants for many weeks after the inflorescences appear in late summer. The foliage in this form provides marvellous golden yellow autumn colour and the small spikelets give a particularly delicate effect.

*M.c.a.* **'Karl Foerster'** Fairly erect and with open, airy, purple flower heads to about 1.8 m (6 ft).

*M.c.a.* **'Skyracer'** Features the tallest flower heads of all, reaching some 2.2 m (7½ ft).

*M.c.a.* **'Windspiel' ('Windplay')** The 2 m (6½ ft) yellowish inflorescences are more substantial, and have larger spikelets. The name is indicative of its graceful swaying in the breeze.

*M.c.a.* **'Zuneigung' ('Affection')** Of similar height; it derives its name from the habit of its culms of entwining and disengaging in the wind – apparently reminiscent of an amorous couple!

## MUHLEMBERGIA

### Muhlembergia japonica 'Cream Delight'
Gramineae

$L$ 20 × 90 cm (8 × 36 in)    $Fl$ 20 cm (8 in)

Brought to me by two Japanese variegated plant enthusiasts, the naming to be confirmed. A lovely plant, creamy white margined and striped, purplish at the nodes, and of distinctive habit: the culms are initially erect, but as they lengthen soon become prostrate, splaying out to fill a circle of some 90 cm (3 ft) diameter. Flower heads at the ends of these stems, dense clusters of silver and purple spikelets, in late summer. Proving thoroughly hardy. Good soil in sun or part shade.

## PANICUM

### Panicum clandestinum    Gramineae
$L$ 50 × 25 cm (20 × 10 in)    $Fl$ 75 cm (2½ ft)

Deer tongue grass. Will require protection in winter away from warm areas or micro-climates. Interesting leaves, in excess of 2.5 cm (1 in) wide but only 17 cm (7 in) long, with rounded, hairy base clasping the stems. Flower heads late summer and early autumn, typically diffuse and airy. Good soil in sun.

### Panicum miliaceum　Gramineae
*L* 80 × 35 cm (32 × 14 in)　*Fl* 1 m (3¼ ft)

An important food plant in many parts of the world, millet may be grown in the garden, and its culms, with their dense flopping inflorescences, cut for fresh or dried arrangements. Sow seed in spring in good soil in sun. **P.m. 'Violaceum'** has purple flower heads.

### Panicum virgatum 'Haense Herms'　Gramineae
*L* 60 × 30 cm (2 × 1 ft)　*Fl* 90 cm (3 ft)

Switch grass offers two good features in all its cultivars – a positively vertical line, and late summer to autumn flower heads which, although large, are comprised of such tiny spikelets, so well spaced, that they give a wonderfully hazy effect. This and the varieties **'Rehbraun'**, **'Rotstrahlbusch'** and **'Rubrum'** all feature reddish brown foliage during the course of the season, intensifying in the autumn. Any soil that is not too heavy, in sun or light shade.

**P.v. 'Strictum'**　A narrowly erect form growing to about 1.4 m (4½ ft) in flower, with green leaves becoming bright golden yellow in autumn, then fading paler. May be enjoyed until late winter before cutting back.

## PENNISETUM

### Pennisetum alopecuroides　Gramineae
*L* 90 × 75 cm (3 × 2½ ft)　*Fl* 1 m (3¼ ft)

Swamp foxtail or fountain grass. The pennisetums as a genus generally feature bristly flowers resembling hairy caterpillars or bottle brushes. *P. alopecuroides* grows in dense clumps of bright green, narrow, arching leaves. In late summer and early autumn the long spikes appear, varying from a bluish purple to pale pinkish brown with, for the brief duration of their

**The wonderful bright colouring of the bamboo *Pleioblastus viridistriatus*.**

appearance, bright orange-red stamens. Good soil in full sun. Protect from extreme cold.

**P.a. 'Hameln'** A low-growing form, to about 50 cm (20 in), and flowers earlier.

**P.a. 'Woodside'** A free-flowering, colourful form.

**Pennisetum macrourum** Gramineae
L 100 × 75 cm (3¼ × 2½ ft)   Fl 1.5 m (5 ft)
Normally hardy, this is a taller species from southern Africa with narrow, 30 cm (1 ft), cylindrical spikes in late summer, green becoming pale brown. Decorative in the garden and for flower arrangements. Well-drained soil in sun.

**Pennisetum orientale** Gramineae
L 30 × 45 cm (1 × 1½ in)   Fl 45 cm (1½ ft)
One of the best grasses for floral effect, and for its long period of interest, but requiring winter protection in colder areas – or it may be raised from seed sown in spring under glass. The grey-brown leaves form a dense clump surmounted by numerous pinkish bottle brushes, long and feathery, from mid summer on into the autumn. Sunny, well-drained soil.

**Pennisetum setaceum** Gramineae
L 45 × 60 cm (1½ × 2 ft)   Fl 75 cm (1½ in)
Not very hardy and best grown as an annual in most areas, starting the seed off under glass in spring. Graceful, arching habit. Long, pink, feathery spikes over a long period from mid summer to early autumn. Ordinary soil in sun or part shade.

**Pennisetum villosum** Gramineae
L 45 × 60 cm (1½ × 2 ft)   Fl 60 cm (2 ft)
Feather top. Best grown as an annual from seed sown under glass in spring, as it is not always hardy. The plump, feathery flower heads, slightly pinkish in colour, are borne in late summer and early autumn, and are useful for cutting, drying and dyeing. Good soil in sun or part shade.

## PHALARIS

**Phalaris arundinacea 'Feesey's Form'**
Gramineae
L 75 × 60 cm (2½ × 2 ft)   Fl 1.2 cm (4 ft)
It is another variety of *P. arundinacea* (see 'Picta', below) which affords most gardeners their introduction to ornamental grasses. The experience is almost invariably an unhappy one, as they battle with its invasive nature. The woman in Chapter 1 was undoubtedly a case in point! However, these are all strikingly handsome plants and eminently worthy of use in the right place. Use among established shrubs or where cover is needed. If they lose some brightness around mid summer cut them back to about 20 cm (8 in) for a second flush of growth. Will tolerate dry soils or, at the other extreme, will grow in water, in sun or shade.

'Feesey's Form' is the best and least commonly seen variety. Wonderful white effect, with only narrow green margins and stripes. A little less tall and vigorous than the other forms.

**P.a. luteopicta** Another most attractive form with pale creamy yellow stripes. Benefits from a mid summer cut-back. Flower heads 1.2 m (4 ft) tall in mid summer over 75 cm (2½ ft) foliage.

**P.a. 'Picta'** Already mentioned, this is a markedly white-striped form, and is fast-spreading.

**P.a. 'Tricolor'** The white margins and stripes manifest a pronounced purplish pink flush, maintained throughout the season, especially in sun.

**Phalaris canariensis** Gramineae
L 60 × 30 cm (2 × 1 ft)   Fl 75 cm (2½ ft)
Canary grass. Used for dried flower arrangements and for bird seed. Dense, short, fat, pale green heads from early summer to early autumn. Annual, grown from seed sown in spring where it is to flower. Any average soil in sun or part shade.

## PHLEUM

***Phleum pratense***   Gramineae
*L* 90 × 60 cm (3 × 2 ft)   *Fl* 1.2 m (4 ft)
Timothy grass, cat's tail. Native British grass which may be grown in the garden for its long, narrow, cylindrical flower spikes which can be cut for fresh or dried arrangements, or for dyeing. Most soils in sun or part shade.

## PHRAGMITES

***Phragmites australis giganteus***   Gramineae
*L* 3 × 1 m (10 × 3¼ ft)   *Fl* 3.5 m (12 ft)
This form is even taller than the British native Norfolk reed, vigorous, indeed invasive, and should be contained if planted anywhere other than where its rapid spread is really desired, such as in lakeside settings. Warm locations are preferred, or submerged in water.
***P.a.* 'Variegatus'**   The best taller yellow-variegated grass, 1.4 m (4½ ft) with richly coloured stripes – but invasive, so will need containing or watching closely. Doesn't have to be grown in water – good soil is perfectly adequate. Splendid shaggy purple flower heads 1.5 m (5 ft) high in late summer. A form with creamy white variegation is also sometimes seen under the same name. Infinitely better is a newer variety called 'Karka' which is shorter and with far more conspicuous creamy white stripes.

## PHYLLOSTACHYS

***Phyllostachys aurea***   Gramineae (Bambuseae)
*L* 3.6 × 2 m (12 × 6½ ft)
This bamboo does not really live up to the promise of its botanical name, the culms never being more than yellowish green. That said, the plant itself is always pleasing and displays the odd characteristic of increasingly swollen and distorted lower nodes. For much

brighter yellow culms look for the variety called 'Holochrysa'. Best in sun. Moderate spreader.

***Phyllostachys nigra***   Gramineae (Bambuseae)
*L* 4 × 2 m (13 × 6½ ft)
Black bamboo. Thick canes become shiny black in their third season. The abundant foliage and arching nature of the moderately spreading canes add grace. Sun or part shade.

## PLEIOBLASTUS

***Pleioblastus humilis pumilis***   Gramineae (Bambuseae)
*L* 1 × 1 m (3¼ × 3¼ ft)
A short but invasive bamboo with bright green leaves and very slender culms. Grow it in sun or shade, either contained, or where it can be mown around, or where it really doesn't matter if it spreads as dense, low cover. Bamboos such as this are useful in that, once established, they will colonize difficult spots such as dry shade under trees.

***Pleioblastus pygmaeus***   Gramineae (Bambuseae)
*L* 20 × 75 cm (8 × 30 in)
A real dwarf, but a real spreader. With its small leaves it is by no means unattractive and there are situations where its invasive nature may be appreciated, but a physical barrier will usually be necessary in smaller settings. Sun or shade.

***Pleioblastus variegatus***   Gramineae (Bambuseae)
*L* 100 × 45 cm (3¼ × 1½ ft)
Striking creamy white variegation. Only a moderate spreader, forming dense clumps of erect, very slender culms. Excellent in good soil in sun or part shade, between or against darker-leaved shrubs to emphasize its variegated leaves.

**The withdrawal of pigment from the leaf margins of the bamboo *Sasa veitchii* gives the impression of variegation.**

**The arching leaves of *Spartina pectinata* 'Aureamarginata' demonstrate a grace of form.**

***Pleioblastus viridistriatus*** Gramineae
(Bambuseae)
*L* 100 × 45 cm (3¼ × 1½ ft)
A magnificently bright bamboo, leaves predominantly yellow with variable stripes. Best colouring in sun and in good soil. In a sheltered spot where the foliage suffers little winter damage the plant may be left to increase gradually in height, but the best policy is to cut it down to the ground in early spring for an annual flush of fresh new growth.

## POA

***Poa acicularifolia*** Gramineae
*L* 4 × 15 cm (1½ × 6 in)    *Fl* 10 cm (4 in)
A fascinating little mat-forming grass. Tiny leaf blades alternating up the short erect stems are surprisingly stiff and quite prickly. Rather sparse flower heads on delicate wiry stems in late spring. For lighter soils in sun.

***Poa buchananii*** Gramineae
*L* 10 × 15 cm (4 × 6 in)    *Fl* 20 cm (8 in)
Another small, distinctive grass, forming tight clumps of deep grey-blue, purple-tinged leaves which are flat to slightly boat-shaped, fairly stiff and held in a more or less horizontal plane. Flower spikes emerge in early summer in a colour exactly matching that of the leaves, becoming olive-grey. Well drained soil in sun.

***Poa chaixii*** Gramineae
*L* 38 × 38 cm (15 × 15 in)    *Fl* 90 cm (3 ft)
Broad-leaved meadow grass. Useful, robust plant with broad, shiny evergreen leaves of rich green, making a solid clump. Numerous flowering stems bear clouds of purplish spikelets in late spring and early summer, standing erect, well above the foliage. A splendid grass for shade, although it will happily tolerate full sun so long as the soil is not too dry.

***Poa colensoi*** Gramineae
*L* 20 × 20 cm (8 × 8 in)    *Fl* 40 cm (16 in)
In considerable contrast, this hardy New Zealand meadow grass is very narrow-leaved, cylindrical and of excellent blue, not unlike the better varieties of *Festuca glauca*, but perhaps a richer colour. Evergreen. Summer flowers.

***Poa × jemtlandica*** Gramineae
*L* 10 × 15 cm (4 × 6 in)    *Fl* 25 cm (10 in)
When I obtained this grass it was described simply as 'a rare hybrid in the wild, collected Ben Nevis'. I was surprised at flowering time in early summer to discover that this is another viviparous grass, bearing tiny red-based plantlets on amazingly tough stems in the place of true flowers and seed. Forms a small mound of grey-green foliage. Average soil in sun.

***Poa labillardieri*** Gramineae
*L* 60 × 90 cm (2 × 3 ft)    *Fl* 90 cm (3 ft)
Narrow, blue-grey evergreen leaves arch upwards and outwards from a central clump. For a specimen position, preferably with adjacent silver foliage. Summer inflorescence rather open and sparse. From Australia and New Zealand, it needs a sunny, well-drained spot, and may not be hardy in cold climates.

## POLYPOGON

***Polypogon monspeliensis*** Gramineae
*L* 50 × 35 cm (20 × 14 in)    *Fl* 75 cm (2½ ft)
Annual beard grass. Many dense, cylindrical, silky flower spikes up to 15 cm (6 in) long are produced throughout the summer months. Sow *in situ* in late spring in ordinary to good soil in sun.

## PSEUDOSASA

***Pseudosasa japonica*** Gramineae (Bambuseae)
*L* 4 × 2 m (13 × 6½ ft)

178

A very plain bamboo, adequate for screening but generally best avoided in favour of any of the more ornamental species.

## RHYNCHELYTRUM

**Rhynchelytrum repens**   Gramineae
L 30 × 60 cm (1 × 2 ft)    Fl 60 cm (2 ft)
Ruby, or Natal grass. Open heads of small, fluffy rosy red or pinkish flowers on a plant of rather lax habit. Sow seed under glass in spring or give winter protection to this rather tender perennial. Good soil in a sunny, sheltered spot. May be dried and dyed.

## SACCHARUM

**Saccharum ravennae**   Gramineae
L 90 × 90 cm (3 × 3 ft)    Fl 1.8 m (6 ft)
Ravenna grass. Preferred in colder zones of the United States to the pampas grass, the situation seems to be reversed in Great Britain, where it is hardy only in warmer localities. Narrow, grey-green arching foliage colours well in the autumn. Flowering plumes in late summer and early autumn, much narrower and more open than those of the pampas grass, one-sided, and silvery to purplish-grey in colour. Good, well-drained soil in sun.

## SASA

**Sasa veitchii**   Gramineae (Bambuseae)
L 1.2 × 1.2 m (4 × 4 ft)
An invasive, broad-leaved bamboo featuring pale edges to the leaves. This is due to a withdrawal of colour from the current year's foliage later in the season, rather than being a true variegation, although this is the overall effect. Grows in sun or shade. See under *Pleioblastus humilis pumilis* and *P. pygmaeus* for comments on the use of invasive bamboos.

## SCHOENUS

**Schoenus pauciflorus**   Cyperaceae
L 25 × 30 cm (10 × 12 in)
A useful sedge featuring rare dark tones. Dense tuft of straight, narrowly cylindrical leaves, green only at the base, thereafter a really deep brownish maroon – a colour which stands out well against pale shingle or chippings, or an underplanting of low, light-toned foliage. The sparse flowers are barely apparent at the tips of the culms. Any soil in sun.

## SCIRPUS

**Scirpus lacustris 'Albescens'**   Cyperaceae
L 120 × 45 cm (4 × 1½ ft)    Fl 1.2 m (4 ft)
This form of the bulrush gives an interesting effect to the larger pool, with tall, narrow, cylindrical stems rising erect and virtually leafless from the water, white to all intents and purposes, though actually narrowly green-striped. Branched flower head of reddish brown spikelets. Plant up to 15 cm (6 in) below the surface of the water.

**Scirpus lacustris tabernaemontani 'Zebrinus'**
Cyperaceae
L 100 × 45 cm (3¼ × 1½ ft)    Fl 90 cm (3 ft)
Transversely banded leaves, creamy white alternating with grey-green. A most showy effect. Similar treatment to the previous variety.

## SESLERIA

**Sesleria caerulea**   Gramineae
L 15 × 25 cm (6 × 10 in)    Fl 25 cm (10 in)
Blue moor grass. Grows wild in northern parts of Britain, and is well worth cultivating in the garden. Very dense tuft. Leaves a good grey-blue above and shiny dark green beneath, carried in a horizontal fashion which results in the blue predominating. The

**The feathery heads of *Stipa calamagrostis* appear from mid
summer right into the autumn.**

The showy glistening flower heads of *Stipa gigantea* are
here picked out by the sun against a background clump
of *Miscanthus floridulus*.

flower heads, appearing quite early, around mid spring, are short and rounded, violet to silver-grey. Medium to light soils in sun or part shade.

***Sesleria heufleriana*** Gramineae
*L* 35 × 45 cm (14 × 18 in)   *Fl* 60 cm (2 ft)
Fresh green leaves are topped by narrow purplish spikes throughout the summer.

***Sesleria nitida*** Gramineae
*L* 30 × 40 cm (12 × 16 in)   *Fl* 50 cm (20 in)
Not exciting, but certainly pleasing. Leaves long, very smooth, pale grey-green, each terminating in a tiny spike. Narrow, cigar-shaped flower spikes in late spring also pale greyish. Any average soil in sun or part shade. Excellent in paler schemes with silver and white variegation.

## SETARIA

***Setaria italica*** Gramineae
*L* 60 × 30 cm (2 × 1 ft)   *Fl* 60 cm (2 ft)
Foxtail millet. Popular seed for cage birds, and much used for cutting and drying. Long, heavy flower heads in late summer and early autumn. Annual. Sow seed in spring where it is to flower.

***Setaria lutescens*** Gramineae
*L* 60 × 30 cm (2 × 1 ft)   *Fl* 60 cm (2 ft)
Yellow bristle grass. Grey-green foliage, and yellow or reddish bristly spikes, densely clustered along the stem. Annual. Treat as above.

## SHIBATAEA

***Shibataea kumasasa*** Gramineae (Bambuseae)
*L* 1.2 × 1 m (4 × 3¼ ft)
A neat bamboo of only slowly spreading habit, with very slender culms arising earlier in the year than most. Sun or shade.

## SINARUNDINARIA

***Sinarundinaria murielae*** Gramineae (Bambuseae)
*L* 4 × 2 m (13 × 6½ ft)
A most graceful specimen bamboo for good to slightly damp soil, preferably with some shelter. Almost tree-like in shape, with initially erect culms becoming arching, almost sagging, and well clothed with narrow, 12 cm (5 in) long leaves.

***Sinarundinaria nitida*** Gramineae (Bambuseae)
*L* 4 × 2 m (13 × 6½ ft)
Not dissimilar to the above but with smaller, less bright green leaves, giving an even more delicate effect. The culms are dark purplish. In both species the current year's culms shoot up, quite straight, to 2–3 m (6½–10 ft), not branching at all until the second season. Both may also be used for screening, planted 1.5 m (5 ft) apart.

## SORGHASTRUM

***Sorghastrum avenaceum*** Gramineae
*L* 75 × 45 cm (2½ × 1½ ft)   *Fl* 1.2 m (4 ft)
Will need some protection in cold areas but well worth growing for its leaves which are greyish, sometimes yellowish green, purple-flushed on hairy purple culms, and for its mid to late summer flower heads. These are quite dense panicles of shiny reddish spikelets with yellow stamens. Prefers fertile, well-drained soil in sun.

## SORGHUM

***Sorghum halepense*** Gramineae
*L* 120 × 60 cm (4 × 2 ft)   *Fl* 1.8 m (6 ft)
A robust grass of spreading habit for a sunny position in fertile soil, and requiring protection away from mild localities. Open purplish flower heads.

## SPARTINA

### *Spartina pectinata* 'Aureamarginata'
Gramineae
*L* 120×90 cm (4×3 ft)   *Fl* 1.5 m (5 ft)
Long, ribbon-like leaves arching out and downwards, yellow-green with a yellow marginal band. Forms loose, spreading, but not uncontrollable clumps, especially in wet soils. The specific epithet *pectinata* describes the comb-like nature of the early autumn flowers, although the 'teeth' are held at an angle. Greenish with purple stamens, they make an unusual addition to dried flower arrangements.

## SPODIOPOGON

### *Spodiopogon sibiricum*   Gramineae
*L* 90×40 cm (36×16 in)   *Fl* 1.5 m (5 ft)
Rarely encountered, but grown for its open, tapering, reddish panicles, the white hairy spikelets borne on ascending branches from mid to late summer. Broad, fresh green leaves, again tapering, held horizontally to the erect culms, and developing purplish autumn colouring. Forms moderately spreading clumps in good soil in sun or part shade.

## STENOTAPHRUM

### *Stenotaphrum secundatum* 'Variegatum'
Gramineae
*L* 10×30 cm (4×12 in)   *Fl* 15 cm (6 in)
Intriguing and striking, but frost-tender, requiring heated greenhouse or conservatory protection to survive our colder winters. Can be used in pots or in summer bedding schemes. Water well. Short, broad leaves, strongly cream-striped, arise from the smooth, almost rigid, stems which creep along the ground. The peculiar inflorescences are produced in late summer.

## STIPA

### *Stipa arundinacea*   Gramineae
*L* 45×90 cm (1½×3 ft)   *Fl* 45 cm (1½ ft)
Pheasant grass. Open, airy panicles of shining brown spikelets on very drooping stems. Tight clumps of shiny evergreen leaves, becoming increasingly bronzed as they mature, and acquiring orange and red streaks from late summer and through the winter. Sunny position in good, even heavy soil. Generally hardy except in cold northern areas, but even if the plant is killed seedlings will usually appear.
**S.a. 'Autumn Tints'** and **'Golden Hue'**   Selected by Graham Hutchins as being particularly good colour forms, the former for its reddish brown colouring and the latter for its pale yellow-green leaves – quite different.

### *Stipa calamagrostis*   Gramineae
*L* 75×120 cm (2½×4 ft)   *Fl* 1.2 m (4 ft)
Valued for its long flowering period, from early summer into the autumn. The feathery panicles on arching culms which are reddish at the base, may reach 25 cm (10 in) in length, waving gracefully in the breeze. Leaves, in a dense clump, are bluish green. Easy to grow in most soils in sun.

### *Stipa gigantea*   Gramineae
*L* 75×120 cm (2½×4 ft)   *Fl* 2 m (6½ ft)
A glorious specimen plant with erect culms bearing enormous open, oat-like heads of bristled spikelets, around mid summer, over a dense clump of narrow, evergreen foliage. Both culms and flower heads attain a glowing golden hue as they mature. Looks good against a background of darker-leaved plants, but don't crowd it. Average to light soil in sun.

### *Stipa pennata*   Gramineae
*L* 45×35 cm (18×14 in)   *Fl* 75 cm (2½ ft)
This species, too, features attractive flower heads but

183

in a totally different idiom. Though each head bears only a few spikelets it is bestowed with delicate substance by the feathery awns which may reach 25 cm (10 in) in length. Flowers mid to late summer over a tight clump of mildly arching foliage. Ordinary to light soil in sun.

**Stipa tenuissima**   Gramineae
L 50 × 30 cm (20 × 12 in)   Fl 60 cm (2 ft)
The narrowest of yellow-green foliage grows in particularly erect fashion, topped in mid summer by drooping flower heads of pure gossamer – surely among the most delicate of all grassy inflorescences, resembling billowing clouds when planted in a group, or rolling ocean waves. Ordinary soil in sun.

**S. tenacissima** is of no ornamental interest.

## TYPHA

**Typha angustifolia**   Typhaceae
L 90 × 60 cm (3 × 2 ft)   Fl 1.5 m (5 ft)
Lesser reed mace. Not strictly within the limits of this book, but near enough to warrant inclusion. These are for planting in water or very wet soil. The familiar poker heads, the female spikes, which appear below the smaller, short lived, terminal male spike, are popular for use in dried arrangements. Reddish brown pokers in late summer borne on stiff stems above narrow green leaves. More restrained than the next species but still too vigorous for anything smaller than a large pool. Plant to a depth up to 15 cm (6 in).

**Typha latifolia**   Typhaceae
L 1.5 × 1 m (5 × 3 ft)   Fl 2.5 m (8 ft)

Great reed mace. Too big and aggressive for the average garden pool, best used for lakeside planting. Leaves broad, grey-green. Dark brown pokers can be up to 30 cm (1 ft) in length, on strong, absolutely erect stems, in late summer.

**T.l. 'Variegata'**   A splendid new variety, strikingly white-striped. Probably somewhat less vigorous than the type, but still invasive.

**Typha minima**   Typhaceae
L 45 × 20 cm (18 × 18 in)   Fl 75 cm (2½ ft)
More refined in all respects. Narrow, grassy leaves. Flowering stems carry shorter, more rounded heads of reddish brown. Plant in wet soil or in the pool to a depth of 10 cm (4 in). Spreads controllably.

## ZEA

**Zea mays**   Gramineae
L To 150 × 45 cm (5 × 1½ ft)
Maize, Indian corn. Important, widespread food crop. Some highly ornamental forms may be used in the border, as 'dot' plants in summer bedding, or in pots in the greenhouse. Various strains are available, green and white, or with additional yellow and pink, as in **'Harlequin'** and **'Quadricolor'**, or with white, yellow, orange, red, blue or brown kernels, e.g. **'Amoro'** and **'Multicolor'**. Half-hardy annual. Sow seeds early in the year in warmth, planting out after frosts in good soil, keeping well watered. The multi-fingered flower heads at the top are male, the lower, female inflorescences develop into the edible cobs.

**Agrostis canina 'Silver Needles'**.

# Hardy Ferns

## Michael Jefferson-Brown

**Moisture-loving neighbours with the soft shield fern, *Polystichum setiferum*, including hostas, arums and *Rheum palmatum*.**

# Introducing Ferns

Ferns are among the world's oldest living things, they dominated the planet's vegetation through the Carboniferous period, well over 200 million years ago, when they would have been growing with huge mosses and horsetails that could have been thirty metres – a hundred feet high!

Ferns remain an important part of our vegetation. Their diversity and intricate designs have given botanists lots of scope for debate; they generally agree that there are around 10,500 species arranged in some 240 genera. Little wonder there are several views of their botanical arrangement. While there are some exceptional annual species, most are long-lived perennials that have their roots well dug into the soil. A few send slender scrambling stems up trees or rocks to become climbers. Quite a number grow as epiphytes, plants perching on trees and rooting into the plant debris lodged in nooks on the branches, but these are more numerous in humid tropical forests. Others are adapted to life on rockfaces; there are a handful of attractive small species such as wall rue and the rusty-back fern that were originally rock-dwellers but have jumped gratefully on to man-made walls, often forming considerable colonies.

Sizes range from the wall rue, *Asplenium rutamuraria*, which usually only reaches a height of about 5–6 cm (2–3 in), to the tree ferns found in New Zealand and elsewhere, the largest of which can have trunks over 10 m (30 ft) high. The size of ferns in a cool temperate climate varies hugely according to their habitat. The widespread male ferns, *Dryopteris filixmas*, may be scarcely 60 cm (2 ft) in one site but up to 1.5 m (5 ft) in another. Fronds of the royal fern, *Osmunda regalis*, are capable of growing as long as 3.5 m (12 ft) in an ideal habitat, though in less wet and luxuriant places they may measure only 60 cm (2 ft).

## Habits of growth

Many ferns are definitely deciduous, the fronds rusting and collapsing with the frosts of autumn. Hillsides of bracken, *Pteidium aquilinum*, turn from the fresh green of unfurling fronds to the rich mature colour of summer and then to the golds and fawn buffs of autumn followed by deeper rusty shades. Some ferns try for evergreen status and will make it in milder winters, though fading and becoming sensibly deciduous in harder times; other species are steadfastly evergreen.

The leaf surfaces, the fronds, may be uncut, botanically 'entire', like the hart's tongue fern, *Asplenium scolopendrium*, that can carpet the ground of moist woods and copses, or can be so intricately cut as to rival filigree lacework.

While all species increase from dust-like spores released from the fruiting organs located on the underside of adult fronds, a number of kinds augment this method by sending out stoloniferous shoots below ground, each of which will start a new plant. Others will produce small plantlets on some of the fronds, with these either rooting if in contact with the soil and then becoming independent, or, when mature, dropping away from the frond and then rooting into the soil to start a new plant.

Ferns are widely distributed throughout the world. Some remain almost identical throughout their distribution, but others are more volatile and will mutate to produce many variations, some remarkably dissimilar to the parent species. The soft shield fern, *Polystichum setiferum*, for example, has had over 300 mutant forms named, some of these being very desirable and sought-after cultivars.

# Culture in the past

The hey-day of fern culture was in the Victorian age, when it was not unusual for the whole family to set out on fern forays, digging up interesting specimens from the countryside and bringing them back to grow in their gardens. Even the most modest mutation was likely to be seized upon as a find and the specimen dug up and transported back home to be planted up outside in the fernery. Such behaviour would be regarded now as criminally vandalous, and rightly so. There are plenty of fern specialists who propagate from nursery stock, and plants are easily raised from spores collected in the wild without damaging growing plants.

The next step for the Victorians would have been to confer a name on the find. The genus and species having been determined, further descriptive Latin names were tacked on until some poor plants were saddled with names five or six words long – almost a descriptive sentence.

The inclination of some ferns to spawn mutations freely meant that at the height of the fern cult some species had over 300 cultivars listed under their specific name. There are still considerable numbers of cultivars available but the lists do not approach these phrenetic lengths. Nowadays names tend to be shorter; generic and specific names may be followed by a varietal name and if necessary by a form name, this last being in English and often being the name of the person distinguishing the form.

As pollution in the cities and towns got worse, many ferns suffered badly and enthusiasts began to grow their specimens in cool conditions under glass. Ferneries so created were a feature of many houses in Victorian times and such culture was popular till the outbreak of the First World War. At that time some of the stately gardens had very large collections both outside and under glass. The vastly changed economic conditions that emerged after the First World War caused upheavals in gardens as elsewhere. Most collections suffered and very many were either lost or very severely restricted.

Today several factors have combined to encourage a renaissance of interest in ferns. First, air pollution has been much improved; ferns, with their ability to act as monitors of bad air pollution, will now grow happily once more in areas where they have not been seen for decades. Most ferns enjoy at least some shade and as modern housing and building is getting more cramped the extra proportion of shade does provide suitable living quarters that other plants may find difficult.

However, the most important factor in this renewed interest is the realization of the beauty of these plants. They are some of the loveliest of living things. Also they seem to bring with them a sense of unusual atmosphere, perhaps something unavoidable with such age-old plants, lending a garden or a part of it a feeling of peace and timelessness almost impossible to achieve with other plants.

The garden designer must have ferns. In shade, by water, under trees, between shrubs, in the rock garden or miniature plantings ferns are invaluable.

Overleaf:
**Dryopteris filix-mas 'Grandiceps'. A crested form of the strong male fern. 'Grandiceps' is a name covering a series of plants of this type.**

189

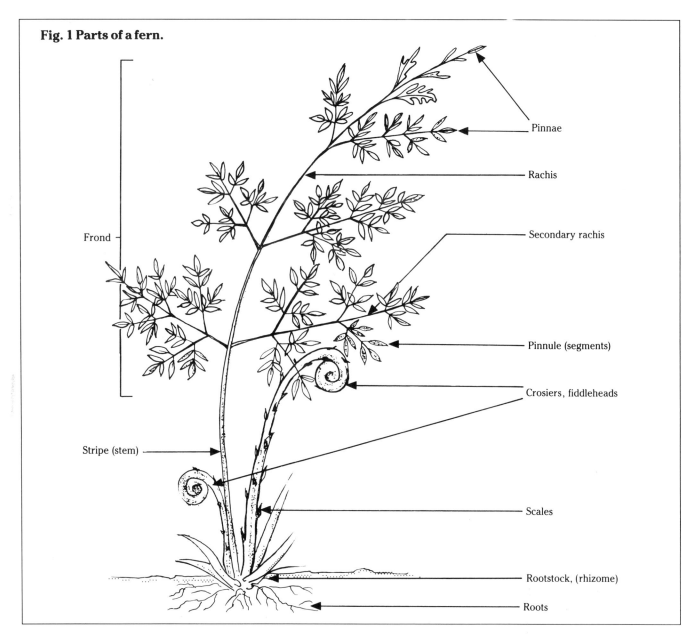

**Fig. 1 Parts of a fern.**

Frond

Pinnae

Rachis

Secondary rachis

Pinnule (segments)

Crosiers, fiddleheads

Stripe (stem)

Scales

Rootstock, (rhizome)

Roots

191

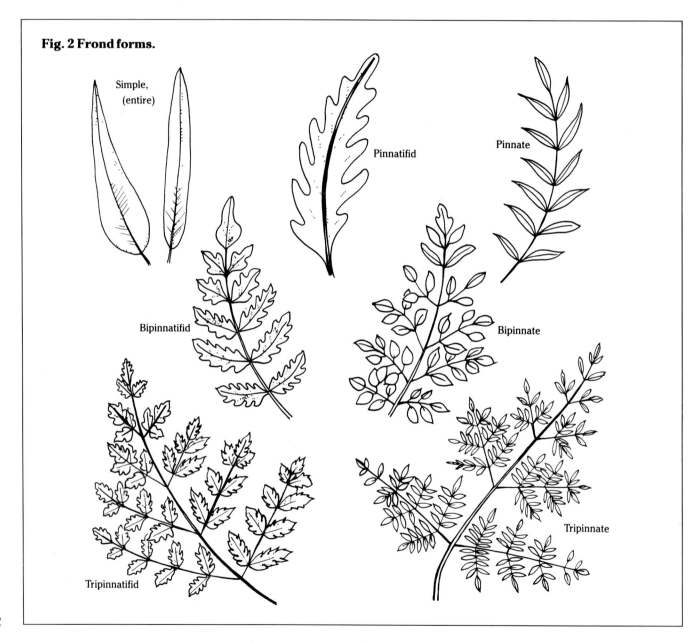

**Fig. 2 Frond forms.**

Simple, (entire)

Pinnatifid

Pinnate

Bipinnatifid

Bipinnate

Tripinnatifid

Tripinnate

# Their working parts

Gardeners used to the normal run of plants can find ferns just a little strange. They organize their lives differently from most garden plants. Without loading the text with abstruse botanical terms it makes sense to describe briefly some of the parts of the plants and the way they work (Fig. 1). This can be important to make sure cultural methods are sensible.

FRONDS

These may be whole, expressed botanically as 'simple' or 'entire', like those of the hart's tongue fern, or they may be divided like those of bracken (Fig. 2). The blade of the frond can extend almost to soil level as in the lady fern or be borne aloft by a stem or stripe, as in bracken.

Fronds of a plant may all look alike whether they are sterile ones, or are fertile with spore-carrying 'sori' on the underside, but in some species such as the ostrich feather fern, (*Matteuccia struthiopteris*), sterile and fertile fronds are completely dissimilar (Fig. 3).

FROND DIVISION

Specific descriptive words are used to describe the complexity of the division of fern fronds. These sound a lot more complicated than they are, and the following can be referred to until one is certain of their meaning.

**Pinnatifid** Frond blade is lobed like an oak leaf, but the lobes do not reach down to the midrib (rachis).

**Pinnate** Front blade is divided into segments (pinnae), the division reaching down to the rachis.

**Fig. 3 Dimorphic fern, *Blechnum*, sterile and fertile fronds.**

193

Familiar examples are the ash and rowan leaf.

From these the complexity increases by there being further stages in the division. Each of the first set of segments can be further divided to give twice-divided fronds:

**Bipinnatifid** The rachis supports a series of pinnae which are lobed but not divided down to the secondary rachis.

**Bipinnate** In fronds that are twice-pinnate the rachis supports a series of pinnae, each of which is divided down to the secondary rachis. These ultimate segments are called pinnules.

Further divisions take the blade division from double to three, four or even five times. Obviously the greater the division the more intricate the appearance and often the greater the beauty. Some of the most popular and pleasing of ferns have their blades three times divided: *tripinnatifid* (each of the secondary divided segments are now lobed) and *tripinnate* (the secondary segments are divided down to the tertiary rachis, giving now quite small segments or pinnules). These divisions may also be described as two, three, four etc. times pinnate.

## SORI AND SPORES

Sori are the fruiting bodies found on the underside of fertile fronds. They vary in shape and arrangement, a most important diagnostic feature. The sori are made up of clusters of capsules, known as sporangia, which contain the spores by which ferns increase (Fig. 4). They act in a distinctly different way from seeds.

**Grasses and ferns in a Worcestershire garden. In the foreground is a *Polystichum setiferum* form and also featured is a male fern.**

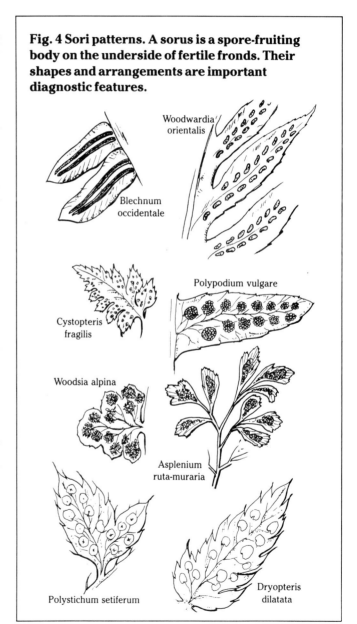

**Fig. 4 Sori patterns. A sorus is a spore-fruiting body on the underside of fertile fronds. Their shapes and arrangements are important diagnostic features.**

Woodwardia orientalis

Blechnum occidentale

Polypodium vulgare

Cystopteris fragilis

Woodsia alpina

Asplenium ruta-muraria

Polystichum setiferum

Dryopteris dilatata

Ferns are produced in a two-generation process. The spore, unlike a seed, has no embryo – that is, a plant-in-waiting genetically programmed from its parents. If a spore lands on a suitable surface it germinates to form a flat green cell mass called a prothallus. This has fine hair-roots holding it to the soil surface but cannot itself grow into a fern proper. The scaly flat prothallus will produce organs of two kinds, male and female. The male organ, the antheridium, releases a host of minute bodies, antherozoids, which, like animal sperm, are mobile. Tails lash these bodies through films of moisture towards the female organ, the archegonium, within the centre of which there is a free germ or egg-cell with which the antherozoids can combine and begin to produce the first small frond. At this time the first-generation part of the fern cycle, the flat prothallus, wastes away (Fig. 14).

## ROOTSTOCKS

The rootstocks are the vital centres of the fern plant as they contain the growing point of the plant, the meristem. They differ in form between genera and species. Many remain as compact tufts, but others creep at soil level or just below. The extent of this creeping is from a gentle expansion of the tuft to a widespread colonizing effort. While they may all be correctly termed rhizomes, it is convenient to call the compact tufted examples rootstocks and the creeping ones rhizomes. Rhizomes may or may not branch as they expand.

Roots of ferns are fine and normally much branched. They work in the upper layers of the soil, not normally going to any great depth. Usually they react badly to their root system being disturbed.

# Ferns as Foliage Plants

In the ornamental garden ferns stand or fall as foliage plants; they have no flowers. The regal fern, *Osmunda regalis*, is sometimes called 'the flowering fern' but this is a nonsense name. It is the pinnae at the top of the upright fertile fronds densely covered with brown fruiting bodies that might just be likened to the flowering heads of an astilbe or some vigorous dock species! One has the feeling that a flowering part on a fern would be a total irrelevance, as it can be with some more orthodox plants used almost exclusively for their foliage beauty.

There are places in most gardens where it is not only possible to plant a wide selection of ferns but highly desirable because they are going to give a better return than other types of plant in the same site. Damp and shade that are anathema to many plants will suit ferns literally down to the ground. The point will not be laboured here as a chapter is devoted to the creation of a fernery, and the pros and cons together with the practical details will be explored there.

The beauty and diversity of ferns is quickly realized but is always worthy of closer attention. Aesthetically they must have a lot to contribute in most gardens. Their utility is multi-faceted and, an important point, many will grow where little else will flourish. There are types to suit most situations. There is a large number of small hardy ones whose diminutive stature and neat pleasing appearance makes them ideal companions for alpine plants, whether they be grown in a traditional rock garden, in rock beds or, indeed, in containers. Here, as elsewhere, the character of ferns is a pleasing contrast to other plants.

With the limited space of many modern gardens, every square inch has to pay the maximum rent in beauty and integrated design value. Here perhaps is the role that is waiting to be explored most popularly by the ferns. While they have a wonderful aloofness, a feeling of timelessness or almost of a parallel creation, the plants will and do associate very effectively with a wide variety of plants and may well be the first choice of companions when planting mixed beds, whether they be herbaceous, bulbous or shrubby. Needless to say, their value in light woodland is impossible to exaggerate – the raising of the ambience is dramatic. On the 'tingle factor' scale we must reach the upper levels, and the dullest person will feel the thrill.

In the herbaceous border the cool colouring, the classic design forms and their very sense of stillness makes them perfect foils to the extrovert flowering plants. The flowers are highlighted, warring colours are separated and the ferns will look tailored and distinguished when earlier herbaceous plants begin to fade away and look tired.

The habits and forms of ferns contrast completely to those of shrubs and so interact with them to provide a very dynamic picture. The varying sizes of ferns means that there are plenty to choose from, to work into the front of a shrubbery or any position further back.

The periods of the year when most ferns are at their best coincide almost exactly with the times when householders and gardeners are most likely to be out and about in the garden either working or taking their leisure. As spring warms up the majority of ferns move into more lively action and begin to unfurl new fronds, always a most exciting procedure to watch. By the end of the spring when summer weather should be arriving the ferns should be fully reclothed and looking perfect. There are small evergreen kinds that look quite reasonable through the winter – the spleenwort, *Asplenium trichomanes*, for example, which looks well either growing on a wall, in a pathway or in among small rock garden plants. However, a few months of hard weather can play havoc with some kinds that will remain pleasingly dressed and fully evergreen in milder winter and areas. The hart's tongue fern in its several forms will often look respectable and attractive in the difficult months before the late spring when glossy shining new fronds appear. These types can be planted in places more obvious in the winter months. Also outstanding as an all-weather evergreen is the common polypody, *Polypodium vulgare*, which gains its new foliage in the summer and looks fresh and lively through the winter. Particularly attractive are the forms with more intricate fronds, the cultivar *P.v.* 'Cambricum' and *P.v.* 'Cornubiense'.

## Design

One works in a garden to maximize the beauty of the whole as well as of all its parts. Design is at the heart of the matter. The planting may be very naturalistic, but what may look like a happy accident is usually the result of sensitive thinking. Of course every gardener will admit that some of the happiest things that happen are really accidents. We accept the bonus with thanks and learn from them. How one tackles these matters are practical details that will be taken up in the next chapter. Here some suggested ground rules may help.

**In the shade of a tall north-facing wall is *Dryopteris affinis* 'Grandiceps Askew', a distinct scaly male fern living with the contrasting *Helleborus argutifolius*.**

The 'rules' are prefaced by the caveat that none of the rules are absolutes, they can be broken but their breaking is likely to be successful only when special circumstances obtain or special physical conditions have been reordered. Some of the rules may seem totally obvious, but when in haste can be overlooked.

Practical advice on preparing suitable sites, general maintenance and preferences of individual types are given in later chapters, but always bear in mind that a fern, like any other plant, should only be planted in a position where it may reasonably be expected to flourish.

Size of fern should be appropriate to the site and the companion plants. Small kinds should not be dominated by vigorous large neighbours who will inevitably force them into a subordinate position where they may eventually be swamped and killed.

The 'rule of three' states that three plants of a cultivar or a species planted in sensible proximity will be more effective than three times the effect of one plant. There is a magic factor in the equation. There may be good reasons for planting only one specimen; in limited spaces the planting of three royal ferns could be foolhardy. But where space allows, the overall design effect of three plants is, importantly, more than a collection of different singletons. Apart from the aesthetics of the matter, there is the psychological factor of a number of plants of a cultivar or species growing together suggesting that they are happy, that they have formed a colony and are increasing. The onlooker absorbs this, even if subconsciously.

Returning to visual effects, gardeners soon realize that it is a lot easier to create a pleasing design when, instead of a staccato effect of a series of single different plants, one can create varying planted shapes of plants interlocking with each other. It may well be that dissimilar larger plants and shrubs can be planted singly, their size alone helping to avoid a spotty effect.

**Fig. 5 Crested fern, *Dryopteris affinis* 'Cristata The King'. Pinnae and terminal crests.**

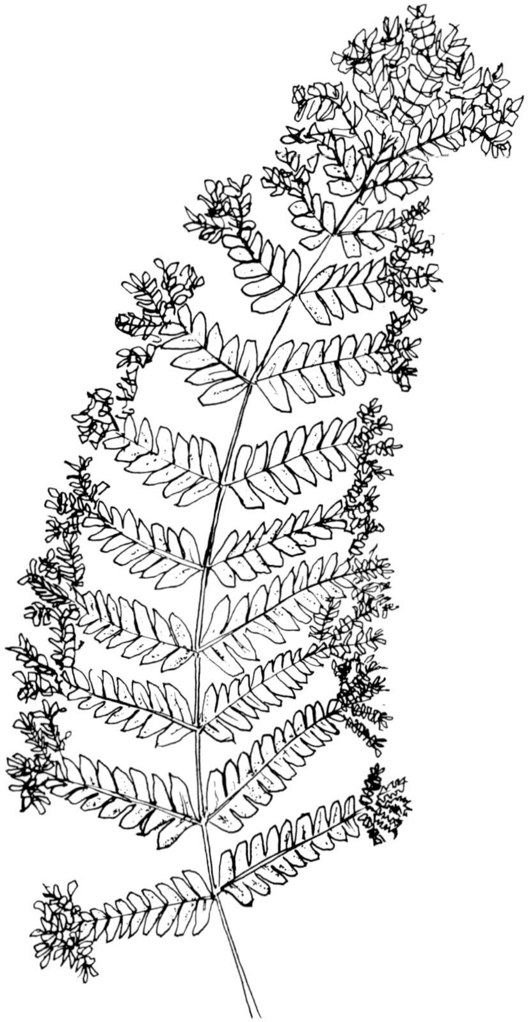

**Fig. 6 Cross-like doubled pinnae formation of *Athyrium filix-femina* 'Victoriae'.**

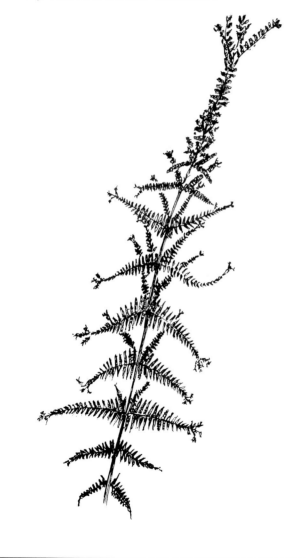

But even so the background provided by drifts of plants like ferns between these shrubs or larger plants cannot help but make a more satisfying overall picture. A sense of unity is created.

The importance of contrast as a guiding principle in garden design is perhaps more relevant when the concern is with foliage and is therefore a leading consideration when planting ferns. Often the first concern of gardeners when thinking, even haphazardly, of design factors is to worry about colour. Harmony and contrast of colour is of course important, but flowers are not all, even in the herbaceous border. They come and go, but the foliage is present, if not all the time, then for a greater part of the year. It would not be wrong to start one's thinking in all garden design with foliage. This, combined with the form and habit of plants, will be the backbone of design plans.

Either planted in an area dignified with the status of a fernery or mixed with other types of plants, the ferns are going to be most effective where the individual characteristics of one kind contrast with those of another. The lacy intricacy of fronds that are three, four or five times pinnate will be enhanced by the puritan austerity of some plain dealers like the hart's tongues. The upright stance of many such as the ostrich fern against the horizontal patterns of *Polystichum setiferum* adds point and lustre to both. Another example of contrasting types that can highlight each other would be the very stylized dark-fronded *Adiantum pedatum* with upright, dark, thin stems and more or less horizontal, evenly divided frond blades and the soft shield fern or *Dryopteris erythrosorus* with their triangular paler green fronds reaching outwards from a basal rootstock.

Texture is also a factor. Some ferns are glossy highly polished artifacts, others are almost velvety. Many mutant forms have the fronds decorated with ruffled edges; others go to the extent of ending their fronds with crests like some fancy type of fowl. Very ornate ones can make their fronds highly textured with ruffles and crested parts not only at the end of each frond but all down each side of them (Figs. 5 & 6). A vigorous dressy example can be cited from the many male fern mutants: *Dryopteris filix-mas* 'Grandiceps Wills' quickly makes a multi-crowned plant with fronds having neatly crested pinnae and substantial terminal crests. Quite extraordinary is the tatting fern, *Athyrium filix-femina* 'Frizelliae', with very narrow fronds having pinnae almost rolled up into little balls or beads along each side of the rachis (midrib). There are many variants of the tatting fern; in *A.f-f.* 'Frizelliae Capitatum' the terminal crests are much branched, a most unusual design.

And of course there is colour. There are many greens from pale golden greens to apple shades and dark, almost blue-greens. Some have their young foliage flushed with red, orange and bronzes, and a few will keep at least a portion of this colouring through life – one of the most popular is *Dryopteris erythrosorus* with well-cut triangular fronds a polished coppery pink when young. The colours hold until the frond becomes fully mature, by which time there are likely to be new young fronds with this attractive colouring. In other types the blade colour contrasts tellingly with the rachis stem colour: *Dryopteris wallichiana* has fresh fronds of lime green highlighted by the black rachis.

The role that ferns are called on to play in garden design will vary. They may well take on the lead part. Some of the larger ones, like the royal fern or the broad buckler fern, *Dryopteris dilatata*, are capable in the right site of producing fronds up to 1.5 m (5 ft) long and will have no difficulty in dominating the stage. They can be grandly theatrical. Others can be just as tellingly effective but manage it best by a corps de ballet triumph: the ostrich feather fern, *Matteuccia struthiopteris*, planted in a suitable spot, will quickly grow into a colony to create a wonderful ensemble.

**The form of fern fronds can be highlighted by rocks or more rigid pieces of garden infrastructure such as these steps. The design contrast is always effective.**

# Using Ferns in the Garden

Ferns belong to the long still early morning of the world. They are not of the hustle and bustle of modern times and the often rapidly changing régimes of twentieth-century gardens, and they are all the better for it. They can give to our plantings a sense of living timelessness and design devoid of any possible charge of egotistical self-importance – something that one can imagine of the bedding salvias, many strutting hybrid roses, the extrovert spring forsythias and the summer armies of geraniums in Ruritanian dress uniforms. I am not anti-flower; having spent almost my entire working life breeding them I could not be. But, and it is a monumental 'but', we ought to start in our garden designing by considering the leaves of the garden rather than the flowers of whatever field.

Ferns will associate well with almost all types of plant, their party manners are immaculate. Dignity and decorum are all. Never themselves in their cups, they will bring sobriety and distinction to more flamboyant extrovert neighbours. They are the garden's most diplomatic of plants. And now, having said that they will mix with all types, one can qualify this by saying that they do seem to be especially effective with certain genera and species of plants, an affinity obviously not based on blood relationships but on aesthetic ones and such practical matters as enjoying similar growing conditions (Fig. 7).

## Suitable sites

### WATERSIDE AND WET AREAS

Water is a magic element in garden design. To combine it with the beauty of ferns is big magic. Not all ferns will be happy with their roots in very wet soil but the royal fern is never more at home than growing by the waterside. Here is a plant in its element. If you have the space, planting *Osmunda regalis* by the side of either a formal or an informal pool can be one of the best bits of gardening you will ever do.

*Osmunda regalis* is a prima donna. It seems always more than life size! At all times it is an arresting plant. In spring there are no other plants so excitingly dramatic as the new stems reach up and the magnificent crosiers unfurl. Young fronds are a vivid sea green that becomes a richer deeper colour in maturity. The orange-brown young stalk becomes green, a contrast to the distinct upright fertile fronds, warm rusty brown flower-like spikes owing much of their colour to the fruiting organs. With the severer cold weather of autumn the fronds all turn colour and rust away, but even in the first half of winter the pile of dead foliage is impressive. The species and its cultivars will all be happy planted by the side of still or running water and can luxuriate in such sites so as to produce fronds which can measure over 3 m (10 ft) long and 1 m (3 ft) wide.

**Fig. 7 Planting diagram, suggesting different types of planting sites.**
1. *Dryopteris filix-mas*  2. *D.f-m.*'Cristata'
3. *Matteuccia struthiopteris*  4. *Asplenium scolopendrium*  5. *A. trichomanes*
6. *A. ceterach*  7. *Adiantum pedatum*
8. *Dryopteris dilatata*  9. *Polypodium vulgare*
10. *Osmunda regalis*  11. *Athyrium filix-femina*.

If space precludes such generous gestures, and one should remember that over the years a plant can develop several crowns so that the basic rootstock can form a very large tussock, then one should look to the buckler ferns, *Dryopteris dilatata* in particular.

The broad buckler fern, *Dryopteris dilatata*, is one of the most attractive of hardy species with much divided fronds. In the wild it is usually found close to water, perhaps by streams, by ponds, or in moist woods. It loves to run its roots through deep leaf mould. The size of the fronds depends on the age of the plant and the type of habitat. The species can be found low down or quite high up hillsides, but the higher specimens are likely to be much dwarfer and restricted in size than in the lush lowland spots. The usual 30–60 cm (1–2 ft) fronds can be four to five times longer in encouraging conditions. At this optimum size they go some way to approaching the proportions of the royal fern. It is a species that has produced several interesting forms, usually much smaller than the type but just as fond of a good watering hole.

Both the royal fern and the broad buckler fern are perhaps at their best close to water in an informal arrangement. They can be impressive in the civilization of formal surroundings but it seems a little unfair to try to have such marvellous plants tamed like tigers in a compound.

Other ferns worth considering for a moist spot include relations of the broad buckler fern. The hay-scented buckler fern, *Dryopteris aemula*, is a fine kind

**Forms of the common polypody, *Polypodium vulgare*; here *P.v.* 'Cambricum' and others shown as colonizing ferns making very pleasing ground cover. To rear is a tree fern, *Dicksonia antarctica*, probably the hardiest of the tree ferns but requiring protection in hard winter weather.**

with neatly cut fronds found growing wild in warm shady wooded areas, often by a stream or within the spray of a waterfall. *Thelypteris palustris* (syn. *D. thelypteris*) is commonly known as the marsh buckler fern and will flourish in really boggy peaty soils.

The influence of microclimate is well demonstrated by the hart's tongue fern, *Asplenium scolopendrium*, which in moist spots can produce very long 'tongues'. The hart's tongue fern can colonize old wells and here, with the moisture and wind-sheltered environment the fronds can be 60 or even 90 cm (2–3 ft) long, two or three times their norm. Plants that have succeeded in growing in drier spots like walls or dry hedgerows can be very stunted and on occasion may have fronds only 8–10 cm (3–4 in) long. Again in areas of high rainfall or shaded moist woodland banks plants may have most of their fronds hanging downwards, with always a few upright ones for balance – an impressive picture. Performances in such natural sites suggest how these plants may be used in the garden. The hart's tongue is certainly one that will be delightful in a cool moist sheltered spot, but can look tired and second-rate in a dry spot where it can be battered and bruised by wind. There are a lot of welcome mutants of the type plant.

The lady fern, *Athyrium filix-femina* in its variety of delightful forms, is at its best in moister spots but does not require visible water.

The many forms of the scaly male fern, *Dryopteris affinis* (*D. pseudomas*) are among those that like a moist soil but also require good drainage to do well. *D.a.* 'Cristata The King' is one of the joys of the fern family, certainly one of the best of hardy kinds, but many of these *D. affinis* cultivars are exceptionally fine and easy types.

In this moist environment, hostas can grow hand-in-hand or leaf by frond with ferns in most welcome patterns of beauty. Many ferns will be happy with just

207

those soil conditions and sites that are chosen to persuade hostas to perform at their best. Moisture rather than drought rules in places where some shade at least is allowed rather than the unrelenting baking of the sun. Broad, undivided patterns of leaves arranged in an informal bouquet, often crowded and close to the ground, make the hostas one of our leading foliage plants. Distinct from ferns, they have some of their classical feeling, but they have leaves of different texture and form that provide contrast but not in too glaring a manner. Even the variegation that many cultivars engage in is managed without too extrovert and carnival a spirit, a sartorial adventure of dignified distinction. Such refined use of colour is effective in the hostas alone, but is given extra point against the ferns which, with very rare exceptions, do not adopt any form of variegation.

## WOODLAND

Ferns are possessed of a magical aura. But this is not something they hug to themselves; they quickly create an atmosphere all around and nowhere is this more telling than in light woodland. Here one enters a new world, it envelops one; above and all around the vegetation dominates, and the right ferns planted here can be really bewitching. They may grow to their optimum size and beauty, undisturbed by either over-enthusiastic gardeners hoeing the soil and destroying shallow roots or by less kindly aspects of the weather. Partial shade will be welcomed, but so too will the shelter from wind which can be one of the main hazards of some of the most intricate and splendid cultivars. Nor need one have acres of woodland to manage this woodland atmosphere. A group of three trees suitably planted around will create the magic, and where space is at a real premium a solitary tree with shrubs can be effective.

A very telling picture can be created by inter-planting some of the evergreen polypody ferns, *Polypodium vulgare* forms, with the autumn-flowering hardy cyclamen, *C. hederifolium* and especially the vivid white form. The bright clean shining green of the ferns and the magic lantern flowers of the cyclamens is a refreshing and bright contrast of colour and form. A collection of snowdrops growing alongside both deciduous and evergreen ferns provides an equally appealing combination, the snowdrop foliage disappearing as the deciduous ferns unfurl their new fronds. Hart's tongue ferns and snowdrops complement each other delightfully. Later bluebells can be in bloom as the earlier deciduous ferns have freshly broken into growth and so together engage in a piece of ever-fresh garden theatre. Even the simple picture of evergreen ferns holding their bright green fronds proudly among the rusted fallen leaves of autumn is always an attractive picture, natural and uncontrived and all the better for being so.

## DRY AREAS

There is a number of small species that are found growing on walls, sometimes where it is difficult to see how roots can penetrate apparently perfectly sound cement mortar. In stone walls with older and crumbling mortar, or where the absence of mortar is made good by a little soil and detritus, some of these little plants can form substantial colonies. Their homes must at times be exceedingly arid and the plants hard-pressed to survive despite long-ranging roots. The very pleasing rusty-back fern, *Asplenium ceterach* (*Ceterach officinarum*), is very drought resistant (Fig. 8). The fronds curl up into what looks like a dried wasted piece of material at times, but with a shower of rain they unfurl apparently undamaged and ready to carry on growing. Plants may spread happily but will rarely be more than 5–10 cm (2–4 in) high.

Other wall dwellers include the pretty little common

or maidenhair spleenwort, *Asplenium trichomanes*, the usual form of which will relish the lime it finds in old mortar, but there is a look-alike subspecies that is a lime-hater (Fig. 9). While it is fun to have these little plants growing on walls, they can also be grown in rock beds or sink gardens. The tiny dark wall spleen-wort, *Asplenium ruta-muraria*, is more difficult away from walls; it may well be best to resist any attempt to grow this anywhere else. Other spleenworts can be relied on to manage in very dry spots and can be useful in rock gardens or rock beds. The black spleen-wort, *Asplenium adiantum-nigrum*, is a popular neat plant usually under 30 cm (1 ft) high and with dark, neatly divided fronds which are polished and of very thick texture.

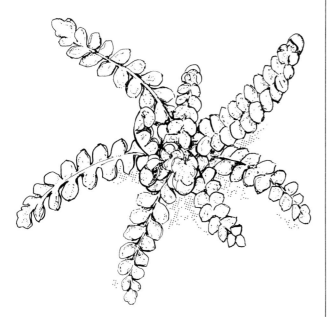

**Fig. 8 *Asplenium ceterach*, the rusty-back fern.**

**Fig. 9 *Asplenium trichomanes*, the maidenhair spleenwort.**

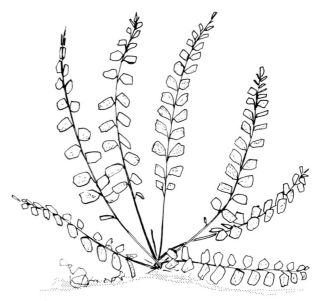

## SPECIMEN FERNS

Often ferns can make a dramatic point planted as single specimens alone on the stage or accompanied by very demure or low-growing planting such as creeping Jenny or, in drier situations, thymes and harebells. There will be no dispute about who is playing the star role. A waterside clump of the royal fern, *Osmunda regalis*, or the broad buckler fern, *Dryopteris dilatata*, will need no help to make a really fine solo effect.

209

The male fern, *Dryopteris filix-mas*, is a robust plant with many very good variants. These will all do well in semi-shaded situations and will manage very nicely in neutral or acid soils. Of many fine cultivars, *D.f-m.* 'Cristata Martindale' is a strong grower with each frond decorated with ornate crests at the ends of the fronds and at the end of each of the pinnae.

A relative to the last is the scaly male fern, *Dryopteris affinis* (*D. pseudomas*), described as 'scaly' because of the covering of coppery scales that decorate the new fronds in the spring. Of many variants one has been long known as the king fern. This is *D.a.* 'Cristata The King', a fertile kind of which the best forms are perhaps 1 m (3 ft) high with widely spreading fronds heavily crested at the end of each pinna and at the apex of each frond.

The soft shield fern, *Polystichum setiferum*, is a popular kind for planting in prominent positions as its light green, very intricately cut fronds are a delight as the orange crosiers unfurl or in full soft velvety maturity. In drier situations the plants will perhaps not reach over a pleasing 60 cm (2 ft) while being of basically horizontal design, but good forms grown in moist sheltered spots can be majestic at 1.5 m (5 ft). As it is likely to produce lots of small plantlets from the rachis, a single specimen can soon become a clump or a colony. But if a single clump is what one wants, it is no great hardship to remove the smaller offspring to other welcoming sites.

On a smaller scale one can make good use of a plant like the hart's tongue fern, *Asplenium scolopendrium*, in cool moist spots. It can be a very effective solitary specimen plant, quite quickly forming a large clump. It is a very accommodating plant, either as the type or one of its cultivars, as it can often be poked into corners where little else would flourish and provide punctuation along a path or at the base of a wall.

In light woodland very many ferns can be used in solitary splendour (Fig. 10). The shelter from wind will enable some of the more intricate lacy-fronded types such as some of the lady ferns (*Athyrium filix-femina* 'Victoriae' is a good example) to develop their full potential and make a splendid plant perhaps 1 m (3 ft) high and as much across.

## COLONIZING FERNS

Mention has been made above of the colonizing propensity of the soft shield fern, *Polystichum setiferum*. If space allows a colony of these, perhaps five or more plants can look very distinctive. Grown in numbers the characteristics of the fern are emphasized. Perhaps the best known colonizer is the very popular shuttlecock or ostrich feather fern, *Matteuccia struthiopteris*. This is another plant that will adapt its size to its conditions, upright fronds reaching some 40–50 cm (16–20 in) in spartan areas, but with plenty of moisture can reach 1–1.5 m (3–5 ft). Wherever they are placed they are likely to send out plenty of creeping black rooting rhizomes. Along these at intervals they produce new clusters of fronds to start fresh independent plants. This robust species is at its best in moist acid soils, and at its most prolific in loamy conditions. Anyone with the space will allow it quite a bit of freedom but there may come a time, fairly soon, when the hoe is brought into play to ensure a sensible limit to its territorial ambitions. It is a species which has contentedly naturalized outside its native habitats and in places it has made itself at home with very impressive stands by pools and lakes.

*Blechnum spicant* is commonly called the ladder fern because of the regular rung-like disposition of the undivided pinnae. It is a native British plant that can be

**North wall site with hart's tongue fern, *Asplenium scolopendrium*, happy in the company of ivies.**

**Fig. 10 Plant associations: birches, rhodo-dendrons, dogwood, hostas, pulmonarias with ferns.**

found growing on shady moist rocky spots or on the floor of woods. In cultivation it soon makes a wide clump. It is, of course, very hardy, and so too is *Adiantum venustrum* from parts of the Himalayas and Canada. Its triangular to ovate fronds measure 15–30 cm (6–12 in) long and start bright apple green but become bluey green with maturity.

While a number of species such as the shuttlecock fern will quickly cover a wide area of ground if given half a chance, most are more circumspect, even among those that like to form colonies. *Adiantum pedatum* is such a one and perhaps would be among the first ten to be recommended to a beginner. It is certainly a distinct kind. Its creeping rhizomes steadily extend the size of the clump. Producing lots of rigidly upright purple black stems it arranges its fronds almost horizontally some 30 cm (12 in) or so from the ground. The stems are as thin as threads but very strong. The fronds have lots of evenly sized oblong pinnules like fan blades, arranged apparently on some subtle aerodynamic principle. The blade of each of these horizontal fronds is about 10 cm (4 in) long. Plants develop as dense ground cover in the humus and moisture they relish.

## ADAPTABLE FERNS

The male fern, *Dryopteris filix-mas*, is probably one of the most widespread of fern species, being found throughout the whole of Europe including Britain, in Central and North America as well as in Asia. It is undemanding in its requirements, growing wild in our woodlands, lanes, hedgerows and open heathland. In any of these places it will manage on really very poor dry tack. This is one of the species that has given rise to many named cultivars which all have the same strong constitution and can exist nicely where other kinds might falter. While the type is a strong, large extrovert, many of the mutant cultivars are much smaller and can be incorporated into planting designs where the type would be much too much of a good thing.

Another very widely distributed fern is the common polypody, *Polypodium vulgare*, which does best in humus-rich soils that are very well drained. In the wild it can be found around the bases of trees like oaks, even climbing up moister boles by way of fissures in the bark. It can run over the stones or bricks of old walls and perhaps cover them completely if there has been a layer of detritus or moss laid down for the creeping rootstocks to make their way through. It is found quite frequently in hedgerows that have been unmolested by sprayers and tidy-minded gardeners. Some of the mutant kinds are very interesting and attractive; they are adaptable and have even been used in hanging baskets.

If one grows some of the lady ferns, *Athyrium filix-femina*, near the male ferns, the idea of gender difference becomes clear: the lady fern forms are somewhat lighter and more delicately graceful than the male ferns, and the light airy effect is exaggerated in some cultivars such as *A.f-f.* 'Victoriae', with long narrow fronds in some cases over 1 m (3 ft) long and with very narrow pinnae precisely paired to make crosses. Pinnae and fronds are ended with tasselled crests. It is a fertile kind so it makes sense to pick out a good example of 'Victoriae' and then perhaps to plant in a group or groups of three.

## FERNS IN MIXED COMMUNITIES

There may be sites in the garden that seem so suited to fern culture that one quickly succumbs to the idea of planting up a collection of ferns – and indeed the next chapter is devoted to the creation of a fernery. But most gardeners, while perhaps admitting special favourites, are likely to be interested in a wide range of plants and will want to create a garden landscape

213

that looks well at all times of the year and is very varied. Ferns are ideal plants in mixed communities, they obviously usually grow in mixed vegetation in the wild. Expanses of unaccompanied bracken are the exception to the usual disposition of ferns to work with all sorts of plants and perhaps to benefit from the activities of these other characters. The shade afforded by some will help, the shelter from wind will aid others, the leafy detritus that turns to leaf mould will help most. Ferns in their turn can help their neighbours.

Part of the garden stage is swept bare for winter but becomes lively before spring arrives, and through the early months of the gardener's year is decorated by a succession of bulbous plants. Snowdrops and winter aconites are accompanied or rapidly followed by early crocuses, scillas, chionodoxas, muscari, small tulips and early daffodils. It is a bit of stage craft repeatedly performed in our gardens, but is always fresh and exciting. The foliage of these smaller bulbs is no great eyesore as it is dying down, but neither is it a matter of any very great beauty. If ferns occupy the same ground they will come into active growth just after the bulbs have finished and take a more commanding presence on the stage as the bulbs' foliage wastes away. Almost nothing could be more neatly arranged.

Ferny blades of many types can contrast well with the foliage, form and flowers of herbaceous and shrubby plants; they can also maintain a sense of decorum when some colourful floral exhibitionists are perhaps at war with their pigments. The ferns provide a buffer zone between the colours and of course have a timeless feeling of order and design that adds gravitas to the whole and will certainly be more lasting than the passing *joie de vivre* of plants with seasonal floral displays. The corner of a bed or border can be made dramatic by the planting of a strong-growing fern such as one of the interesting male ferns able to stand up like Horatio at the bridge and let no one pass without stopping to admire. You might try the very strong *Dryopteris filix-mas* 'Grandiceps Wills', standing some 60 cm (2 ft) or more tall with bold fronds decorated with crested pinnae and large terminal extravaganzas, hugely decorative flourishes in the form of crests. A single plant will soon be a bustling scrum of crowns.

Some good border plants are not outstanding foliage plants: alliums, while respectable in youth will often allow their foliage to become tired with burnt-off ends before the flowers have begun to open. The ferns cast an attractive veil over such wayward behaviour.

The bare ground below a specimen tree can be transformed by a colony of *Polypodium vulgare* 'Cambricum' or 'Cornubiense'. A moist spot can be given over to the hart's tongue fern, not a single specimen but some dozens, with groups of the very interesting mutant forms.

In semi-shade drifts of lady ferns will look wonderful for months and quite often throughout the year. They can be made to look even more exciting by sub-letting some of their ground space to groups of lilies. You could try *L. martagon* on any soils including limy ones. These same soils could support the wonderful yellow *L. szovitsianum* or the later flowering orange *L. henryi*. The stylized foliage of *L. pardalinum*, the leopard lily, produced in whorls at intervals up the stems will, with the nodding brilliant red and golden spotted flowers, make a notable contrast to the delicacy of the ferns. Many other lilies will enter into a marriage of convenience with ferns, benefiting from the cool shade round their roots that a colony of ferns will provide.

**Popular soft shield fern, *Polystichum setiferum*, looking well contrasted to formal pathway and falling greenery of winter-flowering jasmine, *Jasminum nudiflorum*.**

Where labour saving is an element in the gardening equation, ferns can hold their own with the best. A mixed planting of shrubs and ferns makes sense and magic. Rhododendrons look extremely well-matched with ferns growing among them, the somewhat heavy foliage being lightened by the ferns' lighter touch.

## FERNS IN CONTAINERS

This section is not concerned with ferns grown under glass or inside, whether or not they are hardy, but outside ferns can be grown in pots and other containers. This gives us the advantage of mobility. The ferns may be brought into prominence when they are at their most interesting and attractive; deciduous ones can be moved off-stage through the winter. One method of using potted ferns where space is very limited is to sink the whole pot into the garden for the summer, perhaps following a sunken potful of tulips or daffodils that has passed out of blooming.

As ferns are not happy to have their roots disturbed or to dry out it follows that, within reason, the bigger the pot they are housed in the happier they are likely to be. They will need repotting at intervals, the more vigorous ones perhaps annually. To minimize the effect of root disturbance the best time to do the job is in spring or early summer when they are ready to grow vigorously. Pots can become a mass of roots quite quickly. Some indication of their activity can be gauged by the fact that some indoor ferns need repotting every six months.

Almost any of the hardy ferns will grow well in pots using suitable compost and provided they are shaded and not allowed to dry out. While a fern in full growth can be brought into a prominent position on the patio for special occasions, if this is a sunny or windswept spot, the pot should be moved back into a more sheltered spot after its outing. Drying and battering wind is one of the main dangers to many ferns.

Under glass many ferns can be grown in hanging baskets, and some of the hardy kinds can be used in the same way outside, provided again that they are not placed in a wind tunnel and are carefully managed. Certainly they make a change from lobelia, petunias and fuchsias, although it is perfectly possible to have such colourful plants, especially trailing kinds, alongside the ferns.

# Creating a Fernery

Ferneries are not quite the current 'in' thing, but they could be one of the garden fashions of the nineties. There is no doubt about the increasing interest in the plants; books and articles abound and more and more nurserymen and garden centres are beginning to list at least a few of the numerous kinds. Whether this renaissance will lead to the creation of ferneries is perhaps a debatable point; I feel that it is likely for several reasons.

These reasons can be simply listed. Ferns are beautiful. There is a wide choice of kinds that are easy to grow. They will virtually manage themselves and can be grown in many sites that are not all that attractive to many other plants. Damp and shaded or semi-shaded areas that are very suitable for ferns are likely to be more plentiful as houses and other buildings take up a greater proportion of living space. The plants do not necessarily need very deep soils; they are basically surface-rooting, relying on a considerable number of roots working on an egalitarian basis – they have no equivalent of the tap root or the main roots of most flowering plants.

Should a portion of ground be designated 'the fernery' and devoted more or less exclusively to these plants, what might the drawbacks be? It would be less than honest to suggest that all ferns are equally interesting and attractive every month of the year. The majority of hardy kinds are deciduous, some more so than others. There are evergreen ones, but even these are probably at their most lively when the new fronds are unfurling or have just spread themselves out through the spring and early summer. So the impact of a fernery is lessened in winter. But I am not convinced that the lesser winter appeal is a huge handicap. Less time is spent out in the garden during the winter and much can be done to make the fernery pleasing in these months without resorting to planting it with a plethora of plastic gnomes!

## The concept

The idea is a simple one. A fernery is an area devoted to the culture of ferns. There may or may not be other plants present, but any strangers will play a very secondary role. In gardening terms it is often a convenience as well as a visually effective plan to mass forces, to bring together collections of plants of a genera or family within sections of the garden. The rose garden is the most popular example, but irises, peonies, heathers and many other plants can be similarly honoured. There is, however, a difference of quality. Ferns have an age-long history and have their own rules of growth, propagation and leaf structure. They are set apart from the rest of vegetative creation in rather a similar way to that of the fauna and flora of Australasia, which might belong to another planet so different is it from the rest of the world's living things. There is enormous appeal in creating a small garden populated solely by these curiosities of the plant world.

## Making a hardy fernery

There may be many attitudes towards this venture. Size will depend on inclination and available suitable space. A very pleasing collection can be housed on normal flat ground but a sloping area allows greater scope for the display of the plants and the matching of sites to species. There is much to be said in favour of the traditional plan for a fernery and this is now detailed.

## SITE

The ideal site will be moist and cool. It will be protected from strong sunlight and from the damaging effects of blustery winds. An area shaded by buildings or tall deciduous trees may meet the shade and shelter requirements. The lie of the land will vary but one which does not receive direct sunlight will prove excellent, being also an aspect not favoured by most other types of plants.

In the siting and layout of the fernery top priority should be to provide a series of microclimates that will suit a whole series of different ferns. What none of them wants is searing winds; the ravine should be a place of calm not a wind-funnel. Shelter from buildings, from trees and from clumps of shrubs will all help, and any winding 'valleys' built into the form of the structure will be beneficial. The careful siting of clumps of larger and more robust ferns where they will help temper the wind to the shorn lambs, and provide a peaceful haven for more delicate cultivars.

## FORMATION

The design of the fernery is going to involve to a greater or lesser degree the reshaping of the plot as it has been inherited from Nature, the last owners or the builders. The form of the ground and rock cover will then be further exploited by the sensitive planting of the ferns themselves and possibly some associated non-fern plants.

**One of the bolder ferns, like this male fern, can be used as strong punctuation in a border, perhaps as here on the corner where it also helps to soften a hard border outline.**

**Fig. 11 Fernery construction. Effort is made to create shaded and moist planting sites.**

If it is possible to create the effect of a mini-ravine this will have many benefits. The drainage is likely to be easily managed, but with very much moister conditions towards the bottom, so that species with differing moisture requirements can be sensibly stationed. The steep slopes will also make it very much easier to examine and enjoy the ferns once they are established, as many will be closer to eye level – a consideration that all will appreciate and certainly those of more mature years (Fig. 11).

The ravine effect can be achieved by exaggerating any natural changes of soil level by manual effort or by hiring a calfdozer to push and manipulate the soil until you have the contours that please. Rocks can be an integral part of the design and if laid out well will give pleasure even in the winter when there will be less to be contributed by the collection of ferns. The basic rules of rock garden construction should be observed so that there is not the constant irritation of some ridiculous contradiction in the strata of rocks laid. The stumps of felled trees are often utilized to provide shelter and suitable microclimates for some ferns. They are likely to become covered with a selection of mosses that will look well – and could provide a further field for study!

Even a small valley, ravine or bankside will look more natural if the lines are curving rather than straight, so that the eye is led forward to the partially or completely hidden section beyond. Where space allows the pathway may divide so that there are two valleys.

PATHS

Along the bottom of our ravines will be the pathway along which we and our admiring visitors will travel. The lower ground will attract maximum moisture and is where rain will collect, so that the path needs to take account of this and allow for very good drainage. If the path is made of stone or paving stones it should be borne in mind that the conditions are likely to encourage the growth of algae and mosses and so create a surface that, when moist, can be treacherous underfoot. We do not want to create a hazard to life and limb. If stones are securely mounted on a good depth of clean gravel and their edges are proud of the surrounding gravel or soil one should be safe. Alternatively the path may be made of some suitable gravel laid over a clean-draining hardcore base.

# Planting

While any landmoving operations may take place any time that suits, the planting up of the fernery is likely to be more successful in getting the plants established more quickly if undertaken either in early autumn or spring. In a mild winter it may well be possible to continue planting some of the stronger kinds quite late in the season. Where there is any doubt, and certainly where the fernery is in a rather open, exposed site or in a cold area, it may be wiser to choose spring as the main planting time, when most ferns will be becoming much more active in their roots prior to unfurling new fronds.

The majority of ferns will manage in a fairly wide variety of soils, not hugely objecting to a range of soil structures or a fairly wide band of pH levels, but most probably do best in slightly acid soils of an open loam enlivened with leaf mould. Further advice on preparing the soil is given on pages 230–232.

DISPOSITION OF FERNS

First an elementary word of warning. Ferns sold by specialists, garden centres and other outlets will usually be young plants looking very sweet and small in modestly sized pots. Because these young plants

221

look just like miniature adults, they may give a false impression of the dimensions of the plant in maturity. One can even find the royal fern, *Osmunda regalis*, looking demure in a 8 cm (3 in) pot, giving no indication of the possible 1–2 m (3–6 ft) height and greater spread that it can soon achieve. Responsible dealers will have some indication of mature sizes on labels or display cards, but we have all heard of baby alligators being sold as pets, or tiny puppies that have grown to difficult dimensions. It can happen with ferns if we are not careful.

While there are a lot of small ferns that can be planted quite close together, many of the medium and larger ones are going to need plenty of room; they will look far better with some air space around each specimen rather than crowded like travellers in the rush hour.

We have the terrain in front of us, we have a selection of ferns to be planted. We act as generals disposing our forces to the best effect, taking account of soil conditions, of aspect, of the ultimate sizes of the specimens and of their colours, forms and characters.

Perhaps first of the considerations when sorting out the plants is to achieve a balance of deciduous and evergreen kinds so that no area becomes devoid of growing interest for the winter months – or at least to ensure that the most obvious and most important sites are well-furnished with interest throughout the year (Figs. 12 & 13).

There can be quite dramatic differences of texture and of colour. The hard polished surfaces of the hart's tongue are totally distinct from the soft velvety feel

**Pond surrounded with moisture-loving plants, ferns, blue *Iris sibirica* and yellow *Iris pseudacorus*, trollius and astilbes. The silver-leaved tree is the useful willow-leaved pear, *Pyrus salicifolia*.**

and look of some of the cultivars of the soft shield fern, *Polystichum setiferum*.

In colour there are interesting changes through the life of many species. New young foliage may be very much brighter and lighter than adult foliage. One of the most attractively coloured is *Dryopteris erythrosorus*, with young fronds a shining copper-tinted pink or pale orange. As it continues to produce fresh fronds for a considerable part of the year there are usually the younger flushed fronds contrasting to the more sober older ones. The new fronds of *Dryopteris wallichiana* are almost golden, a colour made even more eye-catching by the dark, near-black rachis. In contrast, *Adiantum venustrum* can look blue-rinsed in maturity. *Athyrium nipponicum pictum* has burgundy coloured rachis and pinnae midribs, while the pinnae are grey merging to green at the edges, and even the standard male fern is really a light green in some forms but notably darker in others, like *Dryopteris filix-mas* 'Depauperata' with narrow pinnae and fronds a dark polished colour.

To contrast the colours will be almost as important as displaying the varying growth habits of associated kinds. Size and solidity of one kind can be emphasized by the petite growth and delicacy of neighbours. Some, like many *Polystichum setiferum* forms, have spreading, intricate fronds at low angles close to the horizontal, while the ostrich feather fern, *Matteuccia struthiopteris*, is upright, imitating its other common name of shuttlecock fern. Many start displaying the blades of their fronds close to the base of the rootstock; others, like *Adiantum pedatum*, have their fronds held aloft by erect stems and the larger-scale *Dryopteris dilatata* will start its wide triangular fronds well clear of its rootstock.

Allow for the colonizing abilities of some, and the increasing clump size of others. Larger kinds will contrast with ground-cover, creeping kinds like the

223

Fig. 12 Wet and waterside plant associations. Hostas, ligularias, reeds, grasses, calthas, irises with ferns: 1. *Dryopteris dilatata* 2. *D. filix-mas* 3. *Asplenium scolopendrium* 4. *Polystichum setiferum* 5. *Osmunda regalis.*

Fig. 13 Plant associations: conifers, rhododendrons, Virginia creeper, hostas, bergenias etc. 1. *Matteuccia struthiopteris* 2. *Dryopteris filix-mas* 'Cristata' 3. *Polystichum setiferum* 4. *Dryopteris dilatata* 5. *Athyrium filix-femina*.

attractive *Blechnum penna-marina*, which in friable moist shady spots will spread very swiftly and make a dense pattern of neat narrow fronds. Although this enjoys a moist spot it is one of the kinds that can stand up to a large ration of sunshine.

The overall unity of feeling of ferns means that it is difficult to make real blunders in contrasting their characters, but, while the overall principle of design is governed by the need to make the most of each specimen by contrasting it with dissimilar kinds, one does not want to end with a spotty effect even in a modestly sized planting. Much can be done to avoid this by planting some of the small or medium ones in groups of three or five. This helps to give a more cohesive feel to the whole and certainly does not preclude us from having single specimens both large and small. One or two strong ferns may be placed in rather more prominent exposed positions, sentinels guarding the whole area.

A smallish fernery may not allow the indulgence of planting a shrub or two or perhaps introducing a few of the smaller lilies. One can make much of the inviolated purity of the planting, but where space permits I am not so sure that an odd shrub and stray clump of flowering plants does not somehow emphasize the fern-ness of the ferns!

SELECTING THE FERNS

The choice is very wide, but in the end the final selection is going to depend on such practical factors as available space and soil conditions together with personal preferences. Each enthusiast may have a different set of plants in his or her collection but if

**In a shaded border a number of ferns can look well much of the year and be interplanted with bulbs such as snowdrops, small daffodils and early herbaceous flowers such as hellebores.**

called on for a restricted list it is likely that there will be a common core. The Plant Directory (pages 244–272) describes briefly many of the available hardy ferns, but here are some kinds, grouped by height, that could be useful in various ways. But first a list that could make a good starter collection.

**Top ten**

*Adiantum pedatum*   American maidenhair
*Asplenium scolopendrium*   hart's tongue
*Athyrium filix-femina* 'Victoriae'   lady fern form
*Dryopteris affinis* 'Cristata The King'   scaly male fern form
*Dryopteris erythrosorus*   autumn fern
*Dryopteris filix-mas* 'Cristata Martindale'   male fern form
*Matteuccia struthiopteris*   ostrich feather fern
*Osmunda regalis*   royal fern (or, less huge but still impressive, any good form of *Dryopteris dilatata*)
*Polystichum setiferum* 'Divisilobum Iveryanum'   soft shield fern form
*Polystichum setiferum* 'Pulcherrimum Bevis'   soft shield fern form

**Dwarf ferns:** 8–30 cm (3–12 in) high

*Asplenium adiantum-nigrum*   black spleenwort
*Asplenium ceterach*   rusty-back fern
*Asplenium ruta-muraria*   wall rue
*Asplenium scolopendrium* 'Marginata Irregulare'   hart's tongue form
*Asplenium trichomanes*   maidenhair spleenwort
*Asplenium viride*   green-ribbed spleenwort
*Athyrium filix-femina* 'Congestum Minus'   (and other dwarf forms of lady fern)

*Blechnum penna-marina*   alpine water fern
*Gymocarpium dryopteris plumosum*   oak fern form
*Polypodium vulgare* 'Cornubiense'   common polypody form
*Polystichum setiferum* 'Congestum'   (and other dwarf forms of soft shield fern)
*Polystichum tsus-simense*
*Woodsia obtusa*
*Woodwardia radicans* 'Angustifolia'

**Medium ferns:** 30–60 cm (12–24 in) high

*Adiantum pedatum*   American maidenhair
*Asplenium scolopendrium* forms   hart's tongue
*Athyrium filix-femina* in many forms   lady fern
*Dryopteris erythrosorus*   autumn fern
*Dryopteris filix-mas* in many forms   male fern
*Dryopteris marginalis*   marginal shield fern
*Onoclea sensibilis*   sensitive fern
*Polypodium vulgare* and forms   common polypody
*Polystichum acrostichoides*   Christmas fern
*Polystichum aculeatum* forms   prickly shield fern
*Polystichum setiferum* in many forms   soft shield fern
*Woodwardia radicans*

**Larger ferns:** over 60 cm (24 in)

*Athyrium felix-femina* in many forms   lady fern
*Blechnum tabulare*
*Dryopteris filix-mas* in many forms   male fern
*Dryopteris goldieana*
*Dryopteris wallichiana*
*Matteuccia struthiopteris*   ostrich fern
*Osmunda regalis*   royal fern
*Osmunda spectabilis*
*Polystichum aculeatum*   prickly shield fern

# Growing Hardy Ferns

## What ferns like

Some mention has been made of the conditions ferns enjoy. Requirements vary but there are several common factors.

Above all others, there is one thing that ferns need. This is a stable root environment. They are shallow-rooting plants and resent their roots being disturbed, so extensive hoeing around them is bad policy. Whilst some strong species can be lifted and pulled apart into several pieces as a sensible method of propagation, to many kinds overcoming this cavalier treatment will take a long time to accomplish, and to some this rough division will be instant death.

Whilst there are kinds that grow in the most exposed places, on the whole ferns enjoy a degree of protection from high winds. Certainly the larger kinds with delicate fronds can be spoilt by being continually buffeted by wind. Some ferns protect themselves a little from excessive transpiration by curling up their fronds, but this does give them a pinched look – rather like holiday-makers shrouded with rainwear in poor weather.

To look their best they also need space. Young ferns can look charming even as small plants as sold by nurserymen, but make sure that you leave enough for the established mature plant to spread its fronds without hindrance. A crowded fern can look miserable in the same way that a cat caught in a rainstorm looks a travesty of its normal elegant self. They are certainly companionable plants that look better for the contrast of differing neighbours, but do not crowd them.

Dislikes may be similarly listed and cultivars will have graduated responses to these.

Enemy number one is strong sunlight. Even an hour or so of hot sunshine can hurt more delicate kinds by scorching fronds and creating bleached patches or causing new growth to shrivel. Such damage can be aggravated by attendant factors like drying winds, lack of humidity and lack of soil moisture.

Wind can be a major problem, blowing the fronds back and forth and causing them to be bruised or broken. Even a steady breeze can reduce the humidity and dry out the fronds, especially the vulnerable younger ones. The wind-tunnel effect that can occur between buildings can rule out what might be otherwise a good site.

Some ferns are well adapted to survive dry spells but dryness at the roots is death to many and to others will cause discomfort, seen in the unhappy, shrunken appearance of the fronds.

Very cold weather coming as an unexpected spell during growing periods will stop growth and adversely affect some less robust kinds. Frost will stop active growth at the end of the season, but a severe one after growth has got under way in the spring can turn new fronds black and require the plants to make a fresh start. Mild frosts at this time may well be survived without damage if the plants have some shelter from the neighbouring buildings or shrubs and trees. Some species that can achieve evergreen status in mild winters will quickly become deciduous if harder conditions arrive.

As a general rule, then, ferns like shade, humidity, shelter from wind, constant fresh, non-stagnant soil moisture, open soil structure with adequate oxygen, free soil drainage and a high humus content in the top-soil. Each species or cultivar may be more or less tolerant of different levels of these factors, especially sunlight, moisture and wind. In the individual descriptions in the Plant Directory (pages 244–272) note is made of these requirements.

## Preparing the soil

Although one or two ferns, such as the pretty parsley fern, *Cryptogramma crispa*, inhabit screes, this is an unusual habitat for a fern, as it is so poorly provided with the humus that most demand. As ferns like to have a well-aerated soil it follows that very heavy clays are also bad news. The structure of heavy clays will be improved by the particle-flocking action stimulated by dressings of lime. Organic matter will help to make all soils more lively and the beneficial effects of earthworms make their significant contribution. Heavy clays often suffer from having thin topsoil so that all that can be done to build this up to combat clay's compacting inclination will be to the good. Deep digging will improve structure and drainage especially if straw, bracken waste minus the roots, and almost any form of organic material is dug in. Builders' rubble put well down is not harmful.

Pure sands are as unfriendly – they tend to dry out quickly and have little or no humus. Like heavy soils, light sands can be much improved by cultivation, especially by incorporating lots of humus as well-rotted compost, grass cuttings, leaf mould or shredded organic matter. Open soil is going to dry out on the surface quickly, so a mulch of leaves, shredded bark or other humus-rich detritus will keep the surface-rooting ferns cool and moist.

**A community of ferns including hart's tongue, *Asplenium scolopendrium*, and *Adiantum pedatum* growing with lily of the valley.**

While ferns enjoy moisture, they mostly hate stagnant water. If your proposed site is likely to hold water for long periods it would be advisable to lay drainage pipes down to take away the excess to some lower point or into a drainage system. In the previous chapter it was suggested that a ravine-type contour would be suitable for a fernery; this may entail excavating soil and this could be used to build up levels around and so improve drainage. Paths at the bottom of such 'ravines' can be laid on a generous depth of drainage material and further improve the ferny environment.

As the soil down below is not going to be explored much by the fern roots, its management should be such as to support a healthy top spit. The top 15–25 cm (6–10 in) of soil can be concentrated upon and a generous allowance of compost made up of approximately 2 parts good loam or rottted turf, 1 part leaf mould and 1 part grit or coarse sand (clean of clay particles) would be beneficial. Repeated mulching of the surface will quickly encourage the soil bacteria and earthworms to increase their numbers and activity. The mulches will have the effect of giving the topsoil a better structure, one that will retain moisture better and usually add to the acidity content.

As a generalization ferns grow well on neutral or slightly acid soils. While at first this may seem to preclude their culture in chalky areas it is not necessarily so. There are many acid-loving plants to be found growing in chalklands, where the important topsoil has been turned acid and its acidity maintained by the continued dropping of tree leaves. There are also some ferns that are positive lime lovers. Some of the more notable ones are listed. (Not all of these species are readily available, but should be obtainable from specialist nurseries. Details of the more common species are given in the Plant Directory on pages 244–272.)

## Lime lovers

*Adiantum reniforme*
*Asplenium adiantum-nigrum*
*Asplenium ceterach*
*Asplenium fontanum*
*Asplenium resiliens*
*Asplenium rhizophyllum*
*Asplenium ruta-muraria*
*Asplenium scolopendrium*
*Asplenium trichomanes*
*Asplenium viride*
*Cryptogramma crispa*
*Cyrtomium falcatum*
*Cystopteris bulbifera*
*Cystopteris fragilis*
*Dryopteris ludoviciana*
*Gymnocarpium robertianum*
*Matteuccia struthiopteris*
*Pellaea atropurpurea*
*Polypodium australe*
*Polypodium vulgare*
*Polystichum aculeatum*

# Planting and choosing plants

Probably the best times for planting will be early autumn, allowing plenty of time for the plants to get rooted into the surrounding soil before winter, or in the spring just when the roots are becoming active. My own preference is to plant in the early spring.

Ferns are grown for sale in pots and available year round, so many of the stronger ones can be added during the growing months, from spring until the first autumn frosts.

The choice will be between young plants in 8 cm (3 in) pots and very much larger and more expensive specimens in 15- or even 20-cm (6–8 in) pots. Unless

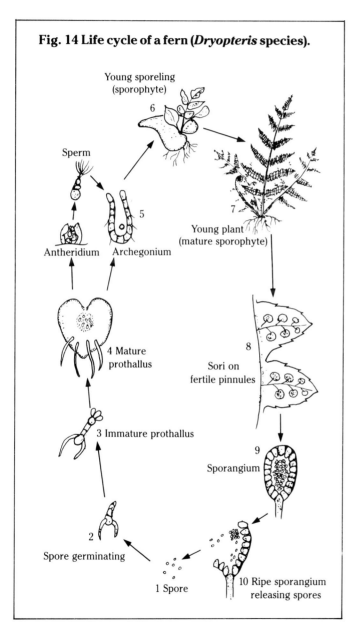

**Fig. 14 Life cycle of a fern (*Dryopteris* species).**

Young sporeling (sporophyte)
6

Sperm

5

Antheridium    Archegonium

Young plant (mature sporophyte)
7

4 Mature prothallus

8

Sori on fertile pinnules

3 Immature prothallus

9

Sporangium

2

Spore germinating

1 Spore

10 Ripe sporangium releasing spores

you have good reason to want a mature look immediately, there is little really to be gained by choosing larger plants. Try to pick out specimens that look fresh, that are growing strongly without being hopelessly potbound, and which have the character that you want.

This last point is more important with some named cultivars than others. Most ferns on offer will be clones or very uniform specimens raised from spores. Some spore-fertile kinds do vary a little, however, so it is worth trying to pick out the best-looking plants, perhaps those that show the neatest or most intricate leaf divisions. This may not always be very easy as young plants do not always reflect exactly the appearance that will be adopted by the mature plant. However, it is rather like ducks – it is difficult to find an ugly or unpleasing one!

While still not around in huge numbers, there is an increasing number of nurseries specializing in ferns now, and even your local garden centre may be beginning to stock some of the more common varieties of ferns. Specialist firms will be expert on the raising of ferns and usually give all the information that buyers need, but garden centres may not be so careful and their staff less knowledgeable.

The main point is to make sure that the ferns chosen are hardy; many attractive ferns sold in small pots are only suitable for frost-proof indoor culture. On the other hand, garden centre selections will sometimes concentrate on the male fern, *Dryopteris filix-mas* and the lady fern, *Athyrium filix-femina*; both are attractive but, being strong-growing, wild types, they may be bolder than you want. Although they will be splendid in spacious wild or larger woodland gardens, they will grow too vigorously in smaller gardens, taking up room that could be more interestingly planted with less robust forms of these and other species.

233

# Propagation

Ferns may be propagated in several ways, including by spores, plantlets, bulbils, offsets, layering or simple division.

## BY SPORES

In nature the usual method of increase is by spores, very light dust-like particles that may be dispersed in huge numbers over very wide areas. While spores are like seeds in giving rise to totally separate, distinct new individual's, they are fundamentally dissimilar as they contain only half the number of chromosomes of the parent. When they find a suitable habitat and start into growth they give rise to green film-like prothallus, a complete plant generation from which sexual parts should arise. If fertilization takes place a small plant will arise and begin to produce roots, the prothallus having shrivelled away (Fig. 14).

Spores are produced from sori to be found on the underside of fertile fronds. In some species the fertile fronds look totally different from the normal fronds. The sori are usually small raised areas, sometimes rounded but each species tends to have a distinct shape. The colour may be a rusty orange but can be brown or black. When the spores are ripe they will be released in large numbers. A small sample piece of frond can be taken from the mother plant and laid on a clean piece of paper. If left to dry a while and then tapped the frond's sori should, if the spores are ripe, release the dust-like particles very freely. Spores can be stored in clean labelled envelopes or paper packets before being sown. Spores from various species become ripe at different times. Many spores remain

***Polystichum setiferum* with companions on north-facing wall. Included in picture is the virginia creeper and winter-flowering *Viburnum tinus*.**

viable for months, a few have shorter lives, but best results are obtained from sowing fresh spores.

It is important to regard the raising of ferns from spores as a clinical procedure. There are always moss spores and other microscopic organisms present in the air, in sowing media and on pots. These have to be thwarted or they will smother the surfaces of the potted spores. The procedure is as follows:

**1**  Select a sowing medium, whichever is felt the most convenient. Commercial growers are likely to use a mix of 1 part peat and 2 parts coarse sand or grit. This should be sterilized.

**2**  Wash out pots, new ones being preferable. Use earthenware pots if they are to be placed in the oven (see 4 below).

**3**  Use grit or clean coarse sand for the bottom third or half of the pot. Then add sowing medium to within 1 cm ($\frac{1}{2}$ in) of top of pot. Shake level but do not press too hard.

**4**  Pour boiling water through a sieve over the potful until all is soaked and the sowing medium has become very hot. Alternatively the pot can be given 10 minutes in the microwave or placed for half an hour in a cool oven at 93°C (200°F).

**5**  Allow the pot to cool a little.

**6**  Lightly distribute spores over surface of growing medium. It is easier to pour them on to a sheet of paper and tap this gently, rather than sprinkling with the fingers, but they are very light, so avoid draughts and do not sneeze!

**7**  Spray with mist of previously boiled or distilled water.

**8**  Immediately seal top of pot with plastic cling-film.

**9**  Stand pot in container of clean water and cover with shading.

**10**  Keep warm. Most spores germinate most freely in the temperature bands of 24–28°C (75–85°F).

**11**  Spores may germinate after two or three weeks but may take longer. Keep the pots standing in some water and covered until you can see the first true small fronds appearing above the prothallus.

**12**  At this stage take away the plastic covering, maintain humidity, but allow small plants to become more hardened.

**13**  The usual mass of little plants can be pricked out in groups into trays or 8 cm (3 in) pots and grown on in a standard potting compost. They can be further divided as they grow. A plant that has nicely filled a 8 cm (3 in) pot will be ready to place into its garden site.

## BY DIVISION

This may seem the most obvious way to propagate ferns. With many, such as the stronger *Dryopteris* and *Athyrium* forms, this can be done relatively easily in early spring. Divided portions with good amounts of roots can be planted directly into their positions and watered in. More delicate kinds may be planted in pots where they can be more carefully tended, keeping them in a cool, moist, humid area.

All old fronds, worn or damaged rhizomes and old or fractured roots should be removed when division takes place.

Often it is easier to divide a relatively young specimen than a very long established one. It can be a mistake to be too greedy in dividing, especially one of the rarer, more important kinds. One can congratulate oneself on the number of divisions only to find that they do not survive and one may have killed an old friend. Better to take just an odd piece or so from such a specimen.

Kinds like the ostrich feather fern, *Matteuccia struthiopteris*, with many running rhizomes giving rise to new plants will be easy to propagate, but one should only remove parts of such rootstocks that have well-rooted fresh young plants. Pieces of creeping rhizome without rooted plantlets may not give rise to fresh plants.

## BY OTHER METHODS

Some ferns are so obliging as to produce a series of tiny plantlets on some of their fronds and others offer bulbils. The very attractive soft shield fern, *Polystichum setiferum*, is one which, when it has established itself, will often be prolific with embryo plants all along the frond midribs, the rachis, one at the base of each pinna. As the frond ages the bulbils grow with their own small fronds developing. In nature a proportion of these would become fresh plants as the parent frond begins to rot and be covered with humus detritus. On strong plants such as these species the process can be quickened by cutting away the whole frond when the plantlets look quite advanced and placing the frond in a tray of potting mixture. Keep relatively cool and moist until the little plants have rooted and are growing away.

Alternatively the fronds of a growing plant can be layered. Extra humus-rich soil can be worked in below a frond which is then securely pegged down. The young bulbils along the rachis soon form independent little plants.

The hart's tongue fern, *Asplenium scolopendrium*, offers an unusual method of increase (Fig. 15). It can be propagated by removing the old frond stems with swollen bases. While it is possible to use this method at any time from early spring through almost to the end of the summer, I have had most success from propagation in the spring. Even without any green blade, these swollen bases to the rachis will produce a series of little white bulbils if inserted in a mix of peat and coarse sand and kept moist and warm in a shaded position for some 5–12 weeks. The little bulbils will begin to develop roots and become independent plants. This is a particularly welcome trait for some of

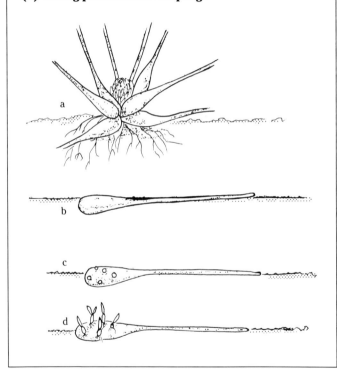

**Fig. 15 Propagation of *Asplenium scolopendrium*. (a) Remove old stems (stripes) with swollen bases, the fronds having withered. (b) Stripe laid in moist mix of sand and peat or similar material. (c) White bulbils develop after 6–12 weeks. (d) Young plantlets developing.**

the better forms of mutant kinds such as *A.s.* 'Crispum'.

Tissue culture is a possibility for those with a scientific bent but requires more equipment and resources than the average gardener possesses. Tubers are also a recognized form of increase for certain species, but not for any of the ferns normally grown for the ornamental garden.

# Round-the-Year Maintenance

The idea is simply to make the most of your ferns, to plant them in suitable positions where they will display themselves to their best advantage, and as part of the overall garden design to allow them to play their part by contributing their own beauty. We shall want to keep them growing healthily, affording us the means to increase them if we wish and to accentuate their best features, especially as they develop new fronds in the spring and early summer.

Most of the hardy ferns are remarkably easy to grow and many will survive years and even decades of neglect still looking well. Most of the routine culture matters are almost too obvious to mention, but even obvious things can get overlooked.

## Watering

A steady supply of soil moisture and a humid atmosphere is what most ferns want. Hosing down with a strong jet from a hosepipe is likely to compact the soil and splash mud over the fronds. Very much better, if the soil and plants are in danger of becoming parched, is to rely on a sufficiently long dose of a light spray to moisten thoroughly the top few inches of soil. Certain areas may be kept rather more moist by laying down trickle irrigation, a pipe with regulated nozzles that allow a constant slow dribble of water. The supply can be turned on when needed. Young, newly planted specimens and propagated pieces will need to be looked after especially carefully to prevent their roots from drying out.

Establishing a topsoil that is protected from drying out with mulches of leaf mould, shredded bark, leaves and even gravel will be the most natural and prudent way not only to keep the roots moist and cool but to insulate from possibly traumatic fluctuations of temperatures.

## Feeding

Most garden soils will contain all the nutrients that ferns need to grow, but to get them to really flourish it may be politic to feed them. Slow-release fertilizers are ideal, incorporated into the soil when planting and thereafter the natural feed from the soil and mulches can be augmented in the spring and early summer, just as ferns come into their really active period of fresh growth. No fertilizer should touch the ferns themselves.

Organic fertilizers will release their nutrients slowly over a long period; complete fertilizers like National Growmore are balanced mixes of inorganic chemicals that will be useful in complementing natural food. Such fertilizers will be particularly useful when and wherever dressings of shredded bark are applied, as uncomposted bark tends to entice the soil bacteria to work on the breaking down of their tissue, thereby leaving the soil rather thinly manned with bacteria and consequently with lower supplies of nitrogen being released.

*Osmunda regalis*, **the royal fern, in spring with crosiers unfurling; these can be 45–75 cm (18–30 in) long. Mature fronds may measure from 60 cm–1 m (2–3 ft) to a breathtaking 3–3.3 m (10–12 ft).**

# Mulching

Mulches of all sorts of organic material are just what the ferns need. Most mulches will provide balanced feeding as the material turns to humus and is incorporated into the soil. Mulches can be applied from spring onwards. Incidentally a very good one can be made out of young, shredded bracken. It is particularly rich in potassium. The old browned fronds of bracken gathered at the end of the year may give a useful physical cover but will be less nutritious. Care should be taken not to introduce rooted pieces – best to enjoy bracken in the countryside, not in the garden.

The blanket effect of mulches means that they not only feed, but will keep soils moist and cool. As they get incorporated into the topsoil they will do a lot to change the texture of the soil and keep it healthily aerated. It is difficult to exaggerate the benefits of generous mulching with materials like well-rotted compost and leaf mould. They should also help to inhibit weed growth.

# Weeding

Ferns do not like being messed about, especially around their roots. Hoeing weeds out will inevitably cut through large numbers of fern roots and considerably dent their performance. It makes sense to try to maintain a weed-free regime. Heavy mulches will make it child's play to pull out any weed that tries to associate itself with the ferns.

Obviously, any site infested with permanent or persistent weeds should be thoroughly cleaned prior to any planting. Should some really naughty weeds establish themselves among ferns and prove difficult to remove without causing severe disturbance the answer may well be to use a systemic weedkiller and to paint the weed leaves. However carefully used, a sprayer with a systemic weedkiller is likely to damage or kill the ferns as well as weeds.

# Pruning

It may sound curious to talk of pruning ferns. What is suggested is that when the new fronds are just about to be unfurled it may be sensible to remove some of the older ones that are wasting away and rotting. This is often more easily and neatly done with a sharp pair of secateurs than pulling by hand. The old frond material can be composted. During the winter the fronds may look decorative, whether evergreen or as rusted deciduous parts, and they can do some good protecting the plant, but new growths are likely to look more impressive clear of any half-dead or completely dead material. It is not a matter of being excessively tidy, merely making the most of the drama of the new growths – and you may well think that some of the bolder kinds do not need this tidying operation. However if you start pulling and pruning when the young fronds are just uncurling you are likely to break some as they are very brittle – proceed with caution!

# Thinning

Colonizing ferns such as the ostrich feather fern, *Matteuccia struthiopteris*, and the soft shield fern, *Polystichum setiferum*, can have population explosions and by becoming too crowded the full beauty of each plant can be spoilt. It makes sense to remove a number of the new plants and either start a fresh colony elsewhere, give them away to friends or help the funds of a local garden society or fund-raising event by putting them on their sales table.

# Moving

Should ferns need moving, either because a specimen has grown too large for its position or because too many have grown together, whole established plants or youngsters can be moved successfully with a little care. Both large and small plants should be watered thoroughly before being dug up. They should be moved with the least possible root disturbance. Large plants will have a mass of roots, all close to the surface but extending quite widely. Plants can be lifted by being first dug widely around and being undermined with a spade. Each plant, freed of its connection with the soil, can be lifted or slid on to a sheet of strong polythene or something similar and pulled or wheeled away to the new site. It should be replanted immediately, to the same depth as before, maybe a couple of centimetres or an inch or so deeper to allow for soil settlement. Once in their new positions, plants and the surrounding soil should be watered and the surface mulched.

# Maladies

When a fern looks unwell, check that the trouble is not simply that it is growing in an unsuitable position. Wind, strong sunlight, or too dry or alkaline a soil may be causing troubles. Root rot can be instigated by badly waterlogged soil. If such factors appear not to be at fault then it may be a matter of looking to the pests and diseases. Happily these are not too numerous for ferns – especially the outdoor hardy ones.

## PESTS

Slugs and snails may enjoy the same moist conditions as ferns, but they are unlikely to be much of a nuisance as they will probably prefer lettuces and other goodies. The same tends to apply to caterpillars and even aphids. Traditional methods of controlling all these pests should suffice. Pyrethrum and Derris dusts, used as contact sprays, will control caterpillars and aphids if an infestation occurs. Certainly aphids can sometimes be a nuisance. They will cause some distortion and even prevent new fronds from unfurling if large numbers busy themselves sucking juices from the tenderest parts. A jet of water can help wash them away but surer destruction of the pest is effected by spraying with pyrethrum or similar insecticide.

## DISEASES

These are not numerous, nor are they normally very serious in temperate parts of the world and among hardy ferns. The fungi which can attack all parts of a fern are a problem only in very warm, humid climates, and bacterial diseases are very rare.

Viruses may be suspected if there is distortion of leaf blades or stems and if fronds become patchily marked with paler colours in mosaic patterns. If a virus is suspected it would be wise to consult an expert. There is no cure for virus diseases; infected plants should be burnt.

# Seasonal diary

**Late winter**
Construction and land-shaping work (see Chapter 4) – Check slug and snail population (a continuing task)

**Early to mid-spring**
Prune old fronds – Plant new specimens – Divide those plants which need propagating – Mulch

**Late spring/early summer**
Continue mulching if not complete – Enjoy new growth

241

### High summer to early autumn
Harvest and sow ripe spores – Propagate new young stock of *Polystichum setiferum* varieties – Visit fern nurseries, exhibits and gardens to select further additions to collection

### Late summer through autumn
Grow on new young plants from spores, bulbils etc.

### Late autumn and winter
Tidy ferns of loose, slug-friendly detritus – Drop hints to friends and relations about new ferns and books you would be pleased to receive!

**Fresh fronds of *Polypodium vulgare* produced in summer now in association with the autumn hardy cyclamen, *C. hederifolium*.**

# Plant Directory

Gardeners know that botanists like playing games. It is a good day if between breakfast and suppertime some botanist somewhere has not changed the name of one or more ferns. Often this takes the form of shuttling a species back and forward between two genera, as is the case with the hart's tongue fern which never knows whether it is in bed with the *Asplenium* or *Phyllitis* family. Do not despair. I try to give the commonest synonyms, but have taken *The Encyclopaedia of Ferns* by David L. Jones as the authority to follow. If you are in difficulty you may find a current edition of *The Plant Finder* useful to establish the names currently in use in Britain for kinds offered for sale. You will find that it does not agree in all cases with the names used here, but it does give synonyms so that it is easy to track down the plant you are interested in.

Some of the information is compressed to save space and repetition. For each entry the botanical name is given first, followed by the common name (not necessarily universally used) and then an indication of natural distribution (unless a nursery-selected or raised cultivar). Also listed are:

**F** Frond length. The range of length given is due to natural variation within species but even more as a result of habitat conditions.

**acid/alkaline** Most ferns are tolerant of a range of pH values and will be very happy with neutral soil, but a preference for acid or alkaline soils is shown. Similarly, it is assumed that all ferns will flourish in moist conditions, so **dry** indicates a fern capable of growing in less moist conditions than most; **wet** a preference for extremely damp soil.

## ADIANTUM

***Adiantum pedatum***    AMERICAN MAIDENHAIR
*N. America, N. India, Japan*
**F** 30–50 cm (12–20 in); acid; deciduous
This is a variable, distinct and very attractive species which is well worth having in every collection. Creeping dark wiry rhizomes produce many erect thread-thin but strong stems, in the usual forms some 30 cm (12 in) or so high. The frond blades are displayed almost horizontally as a series of opposite fan-like oblong blades. Colour is a rich matt green. The overall blade length will be around 10 cm (4 in). It does best in cool shaded spots. Plants increase steadily in size in humus-rich soils. All forms are attractive.
***A.p.* 'Aleuticum'** A Canadian form, with frond blades usually pointing more upwards. It is much dwarfer, at only 10–15 cm (4–6 in), a hummock of pale green with a hazy bloom finish.

***Adiantum × tracyi***
*N. America*
**F** 40–60 cm (16–24 in); acid; deciduous
Pleasing cold-resistant sterile hybrid between *A. pedatum* and *A. jordanii* (the Californian maidenhair), which has appeared sporadically in the wild. Its fronds are more heavily divided than *A. pedantum*, being 2–3 pinnate.

*Adiantum venustum*   EVERGREEN MAIDENHAIR
*N. India, Canada*
**F** 25–75 cm (10–30 in); acid; evergreen
This is a reliable strong plant with wide, more or less triangular frond blades some 12–30 cm (5–12 in) long and divided 3–4 pinnate. Creeping roots will support a wide plant that is very lovely in spring with pale green crosiers and fronds, these taking on a distinct bluish shade with maturity.

## ASPLENIUM

*Asplenium adiantum-nigrum*   BLACK SPLEENWORT
*Europe inc. Britain, Africa, Asia, N. America*
**F** 12–40 cm (5–16 in); alkaline/dry; evergreen
This globe-trotting little species is often found growing on walls, often in old mortar. It is a proper miniaturized fern, with long triangular frond blades 2–3 pinnate, distinctively leathery-textured and of a well-polished dark green. It is more tolerant of sun than most and looks well in the rock or sink garden in a well-drained spot.

*Asplenium ceterach (syn. Ceterach officinarum)*
RUSTY-BACK FERN
*Europe inc. Britain, Africa, India*
**F** 5–15 cm (2–6 in); alkaline/dry; evergreen
This is another of the delightful little plants that can colonize an old wall, making free with the mortar and being able to withstand long periods of drought. It behaves rather like the so-called resurrection ferns in that the fronds can curl up and look dead but be quickly unfurled and prettily displayed with a shower of rain. Thick-textured, paired pinnae are somewhat square with the corners rounded off, their undersides thickly covered with silvery brown scales. This useful little fern can be grown in a corner of the rock garden, on walls, or in containerized miniature gardens.

*Asplenium* × *hybridum*
*Mediterranean*
**F** 5–15 cm (2–6 in); acid/dry; evergreen
A series of pinnatifid fertile hybrids between *A. ceterach* and *A. sagittatum*, a somewhat larger species.

*Asplenium ruta-muraria*   WALL RUE or WALL
SPLEENWORT
*Europe inc. Britain, Asia, N. America*
**F** 5–10 cm (2–4 in); alkaline/dry; evergreen
More often seen on walls than the rock crevices which are its natural habitat. A very dark little plant with small thick blades of a few pinnae and wiry stems. Best grown on walls, being introduced as spores or tiny plants raised from spores, as it dislikes the root disturbance likely to be encountered with pot culture.

*Asplenium scolopendrium* (syn. *Phyllitis scolopendrium*)   HART'S TONGUE
*Europe inc. Britain, Asia, N. America*
**F** 23–60 cm (9–24 in); alkaline; evergreen
The undivided fronds of this famliar wild plant are especially lovely when new, but they can maintain a very dressy appearance for months and, in a spot free of buffeting wind, can be one of the best kinds through the winter months. For this reason it is worth growing some of the better mutant forms – but do not forgo the type.
*A.s.* **'Capitatum'**   Heavy crests at the frond ends.
*A.s.* **'Crispum'**   A sterile form, with the margins beautifully crimped into a ruff. Should be in every collection.
*A.s.* **'Crispum Golden Queen'**   Distinguished by its frilled fronds and glowing golden-green colour.
*A.s.* **'Digitatum'**   Very different from the type, with very divided cristate fronds ending with wide flat crests. the whole is likened by some to the fingers of a hand.

*Adiantum pedatum*, the very distinct fern with fronds held almost horizontally on thread-like wiry stems, here in company with *Lonicera standishii* and *Cotoneaster horizontalis*.

**The silver birch has the hart's tongue fern at its base and the
male ferns as neighbours.**

**A.s. 'Laceratum'**  As its name implies, has fronds with cut margins.

**A.s. 'Marginatum'**  Distinctly narrower fronds than type, and these deeply cut.

**A.s. 'Marginatum Irregulare'**  A form in which the margins are more randomly lobed and cut.

**A.s. 'Sagittatum'**  As the name suggests, the blades are shaped like arrow heads, the bases being deeply lobed to give this effect.

***Asplenium trichomanes***  COMMON or MAIDENHAIR SPLEENWORT
*Worldwide*
F 10–40 cm (4–16 in); alkaline; evergreen
A pretty little fern to be found growing happily on walls, especially in old mortar with some lime. The largest colony I know is in such a wall facing west, but the plants will grow in any exposure. The plants make a neat rosette of many dark stemmed fronds, each carrying perhaps over thirty pairs of matched pinnae. Purple-black stems contrast with the shining bright green of the oval pinnae. There is a subspecies, *A.t.* ssp. *trichomanes* which is similar but is a lime-hater.

**A.t. 'Cristatum'**  This is a fertile form that first appeared in Britain in which each pinna is much divided into crests.

***Asplenium viride***  GREEN or GREEN-RIBBED SPLEENWORT
*Europe inc. Britain, Asia, N. America*
F 10–15 cm (4–6 in); alkaline; evergreen
Another pretty miniature, rather like the last species but more usually found on moist rock surfaces rather than walls. It differs also by having green stems, rachis, palmate veining and lightly serrated margins. These serrations are rounded and the colour is a lighter green. It grows well in a rock garden corner or in pots with some lime in the soil.

## ATHYRIUM

***Athyrium deltoidofrons***
*China, Korea, Japan*
F 25–50 cm (10–20 in); acid; deciduous
Attractive bipinnate yellow-green triangular fronds that look well against neighbouring darker kinds. Best in not too deep shade.

***Athyrium distentifolium* (syn. *A. alpestre*)** ALPINE LADY FERN
*Europe inc. Britain, Iceland, N. America*
F 25–50 cm (10–20 in); acid; deciduous
Delicately posed, erect, pale green fronds are triangular in outline, similar to the lady fern but usually smaller with proportionately broader pinnae. Creeping rhizomes can make pleasing plants with rounded rosettes of fronds.

***Athyrium filix-femina***  LADY FERN
*Europe inc. Britain, India, China, Japan, N. and S. America*
F 50–150 cm (20–60 in); acid; deciduous
This widespread popular fern grows best in deep loamy humus-rich soils in shade or semi-shade. It is one of the most lively mutators, at one time having over 300 named forms. The type is graceful, usually bipinnate, with long lacy fronds of light green, though some forms are darker.

**A.f-f. 'Congestum'**  Dwarf with well-formed narrowly pointed fronds. Around 15 cm (6 ins) high. The variety 'Congestion Minus' is a diminutive, neat fern with precise, well-cut fronds in attractive rosettes.

**A.f-f. 'Congestum Cristatum'**  Little fern with intricately cut, densely packed fronds with terminal crests.

**A.f-f. Cristatum group**  A series of fertile plants, the pinnae of which have crests displayed flat like fans all along the margins and at the end of each frond. The series is variable; it is wise to see the plant you are buying, some are considerably more ornate than others. 50–90 cm (20–36 in).

**A.f-f. 'Fieldii'** An unusual form with long narrow fronds with short pinnae arranged in pairs and so forming crosses with their opposite pairs. A curious effect on fronds that can be 90 cm (36 in) long.

**A.f-f. 'Frizelliae'** The tatting fern. The slender rachis appears to be threaded with a series of paired beads, the pinnae being reduced to flattish rich green balls. 25–50 cm (10–20 in). There are also variants, such as 'Frizelliae Capitatum' and 'Frizelliae Cristatum' where the frond ends have severally branched crests.

**A.f-f. 'Glomeratum'** A form with narrow fronds with both pinnae and ends crested.

**A.f-f. 'Minutissimum'** A very pretty light green fertile mutant, with many well-furnished long, triangular, bipinnate fronds. These may measure 12–20 cm (5–8 in) long. Clumps look very pleasing.

**A.f-f. Plumosum group** A series of plants 20–40 cm (8–16 in) tall, having light green fronds pleasingly divided perhaps three or four times pinnate. The best forms are wonderfully intricate and pure magic when grown in a sheltered shaded or semi-shaded spot. Fronds float like feathers.

**A.f-f. 'Victoriae'** Strong plant but most interestingly styled in delicate filigree parts. Fronds end in tassles and all the pinnae and their divisions are arranged in pairs at right angles to each other, forming delightfully tasselled crosses.

### *Athyrium frangulum*
*Japan*
**F** 12–40 cm (5–16 in); acid; deciduous
A pretty, lightly coloured kind with the rachis a reddish purple. Double or triple pinnate arrangement of widely triangular fronds very well displayed in a crowded arrangement. Very distinctive between rocks.

### *Athyrium niponicum pictum*   JAPANESE PAINTED FERN
*Japan, Korea, China*
**F** 40–60 cm (16–24 in); acid; deciduous
This is a lovely fern for a sheltered spot, the name gives a clue to its attraction. Like the last species this is broadly triangular with a pointed frond end. It is usually bipinnate but can be tripinnate. To get the best colouring in the young fronds the plants want to be in shade but with plenty of light, when the rachis and pinnae ribs are a rich burgundy while the soft grey green of the blade can be suffused with red and blue shades merging to green at the margins. Mature fronds are still colourful, though darker, and make patterns of colour, tone and form with the brighter colours of the younger ones.

### *Athyrium pycnocarpum*   AMERICAN GLADE FERN
*N. America*
**F** 50–120 cm (20–48 in); acid; deciduous
Wide rosettes of spreading bold fronds, light green in youth but becoming darker and turning warm buff before being discarded. Protect young growth from slugs etc.

## BLECHNUM

### *Blechnum penna-marina*   ALPINE WATER FERN
*New Zealand, Australia, S. America*
**F** 15–30 cm (6–12 in); acid/wet; evergreen
Makes a good ground-cover plant, rapidly colonizing moist open soils rich in humus. Rather like *B. spicant* but a somewhat smaller, more social spreading plant with many narrow single pinnate well-furnished fronds making dense cover. It will withstand quite a lot of sunshine provided the roots are moist. Will respond well to feeding. There is a smaller subspecies of similar character, *B.p-m* ssp. *alpina*, the pinnae neatly jostling each other along the rachis.

249

250

**Ferns happy in a garden setting. Here are male ferns,**
***Dryopteris filix-mas*, at Longstock Hampshire, UK.**

**Small pond planted around with grasses and ferns in half shade, a natural and pleasing combination that does well in even more difficult very shady areas.**

***Blechnum spicant***    HARD FERN
*Europe inc. Britain, N. America*
**F** 25–60 cm (10–24 in); acid; evergreen
Sterile fronds have an outline shaped like a spearhead, four or five times longer than broad. These spread out more or less horizontally, being neatly and singly pinnate. Pinnae are close to each other down to the rootstock. The fertile fronds are dissimilar; they are upright and have narrow well-separated pinnae looking like a sparse comb. Colour overall is a rich light green. There are a number of crested mutants and ones with pinnae variously cut.

***Blechnum vulcanicum***    WEDGE WATER FERN
*Australia, New Zealand*
**F** 12–40 cm (5–16 in); acid/wet; evergreen
Typical *Blechnum*, with singly pinnate fronds like the hard fern but with the pinnae distinctly more pointed, fertile ones being very much narrower, and all arranged with stripe (stalk) almost as long as blade on sterile fronds and possible longer on fertile ones. Needs moisture, shade and no disturbance.

**CETARACH.** See ***Asplenium cetarach***

**CRYPTOGRAMMA**

***Cryptogramma crispa***    PARSLEY FERN
*Europe, Asia Minor, Afghanistan*
**F** 5–25 cm (2–10 in); acid; deciduous
A small fern that can sometimes be found growing wild in scree conditions. Not the easiest of garden plants and any lime is poison to it. The small fronds look not unlike parsley, but only appear in early summer and die away for the winter.

**CYRTOMIUM (syn. PHANEROPHLEBIA)**

***Cyrtomium falcatum***    JAPANESE HOLLY FERN
*Japan, Korea, China*
**F** 25–50 cm (10–20 in); acid/alkaline; evergreen

**Fig. 16** ***Cyrtomium falcatum*,** **Japanese holly fern.**

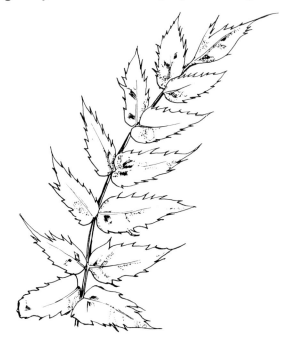

A popular kind, sensibly named as the dark green, shiny, thick-textured fronds look very much like holly leaves but with rather smaller, more numerous serrations (Fig. 16). Spreading display manner. Very adaptable as far as soils and positions are concerned and able to form very persistent, spreading colonies in healthy soils. Various forms have been selected.
***C.f.* 'Butterfield'** Looking more prickly than the species, with teeth slenderly pointed.
***C.f.* 'Mayi' ('Cristata')** Unusual, with pinnae and frond ends crested; fronds can also be divided.
***C.f.* 'Rochfordianum'** Probably the most widespread. Good dark form with well-defined holly serrations. Makes a fine cool greenhouse plant.

### Cyrtomium fortunei
*Japan, Korea, China*
**F** 20–40 cm (8–16 in); acid; evergreen and deciduous
Like *C. falcatum* but without serrations, having narrower longer pinnae and held much more upright. Shiny tough texture and rich green in colour.

### Cyrtomium lonchitoida
*Japan, Korea, China*
**F** 50–90 cm (29–36 in); acid; evergreen and deciduous
Impressive, long narrow oblong fronds with wide diamond-shaped pinnae in bright light green. It has a smoothly polished dressy appearance, with the pinnae ends curved.

## CYSTOPTERIS

### Cystopteris bulbifera  BERRY BLADDER FERN
*N. America*
**F** 30–75 cm (12–30 in); alkaline; deciduous
Bipinnate fronds tend to hang or fall from its preferred site, any semi-shaded bank or rock side with plenty of moisture and soil that is limy. Many bulbils are produced on the undersides of the fronds and these fall to the ground to form new plants.

### Cystopteris fragilis  BRITTLE BLADDER FERN
*Almost worldwide*
**F** 10–30 cm (4–12 in); deciduous
A dwarf species that is widespread on rocky mountainsides. The fragile fronds are easily broken or spoilt and perish with colder weather. It enjoys shade and moisture in rocky spot or stony soil.

## DAVALLIA

### Davallia marieseii  HARE'S FOOT FERN
*Japan, Korea*
**F** 15–30 cm (6–12 in); acid; deciduous
Unusual and popular species that is hardy in milder regions. In harder areas it makes a fine cool house plant. Has long been used as a pot plant or in hanging baskets as the furry creeping rhizomes will wander at will or can be trained. At intervals it produces very delicate lacy triangular-bladed fronds, two, three or four times pinnate. *D.m. stenolepis* is a stronger version, the scaly rhizomes being almost white.

## DRYOPTERIS

### Dryopteris aemula  HAY-SCENTED BUCKLER FERN
*Europe inc. Britain*
**F** 25–60 cm (10–24 in); acid; deciduous
A pretty fern with bi- and often partially tripinnate triangular fronds that arch outwards in a graceful manner. The common name is justified by the scent given off by a series of glands on the underside of the fronds. The stalks, approximately half the length of the fronds, shining rich green with the strong stems a purple-black contrasting with the fawn of the scales. It is found in moist, semi-shaded positions in the wild and likes similar spots in the garden.

### Dryopteris affinis (syn. D. pseudomas)
SCALY MALE FERN
*Europe inc. Britain, S. W. Asia*
**F** 50–150 cm (20–60 in); acid; deciduous
Young fronds are a yellowish green, becoming darker, as they age. Pinnate frond blades are long, relatively narrow and almost equally wide down their length. Pinnae are deeply lobed. It has given rise to some very fine garden plants.
**D.a. 'Cristata Angustata'** 40–60 cm (16–24 in). A lighter-weight appearance and not so strong as the next variety. Pinnae joined and precisely crested.
**D.a. 'Cristata The King'** 50–90 cm (20–36 in). Bold and outstandingly attractive. The parallel-sided rich green, firm-textured fronds are displayed in a very even pattern, quite upright but arching outwards and precisely and boldly crested at every pinna and frond

An effective piece of planting design with contrasting foliage
of lady fern, *Athyrium filix-femina*, broad-leaved hostas and
erect swords of iris.

255

**Collection of ferns in Shropshire garden. Forms of ground-covering *Polypodium vulgare* and an upright *Dryopteris filix-mas* are prominent.**

end. Should be in every collection. Strong plant that divides easily.

**D.a. 'Grandiceps'** With tassellated crests to frond ends.

**D.a. 'Grandiceps Askew'** 45–60 cm (18–24 in). Strong plant with notably divided and large terminal crests. Very easy and very impressive after a season or so if allowed space.

**D.a. 'Grandiceps Harvey'** 40–60 cm (16–24 in). Strong-growing kind with good terminal crests, rather narrower frond blades.

**D.a. 'Ramosissima'** 30–50 cm (12–20 in). The fronds break into many branches, each ending with large crests.

**D.a. 'Tavelii' (syn. D.a. 'Stablerii')** 45–60 cm (18–24 in). A rich, deep green, erect form with fairly narrow but well-furnished bipinnate blades, the pinnae being neatly indented and broad so that they almost overlap. The central scaly rootstock base makes a telling contrast in orange.

**Dryopteris cycadina**   SHAGGY SHIELD FERN
*India, Thailand, China, Japan*
**F** 50–90 cm (20–36 in); wet; deciduous
Can be a most impressive, distinct fern, with the stripe and underside of the rachis clothed with black scales. With stems half the length of the arching fronds the whole looks very graceful, the pinnae being from 10 cm (4 in) to possibly twice this length and deeply serrated.

**Dryopteris carthusiana**   NARROW or PRICKLY BUCKLER FERN
*Europe inc. Britain, N. America*
**F** 30–120 cm (12–48 in); acid/alkaline; evergreen and deciduous
Perhaps best left in the wild as it can spread itself around too freely. Bipinnate with fronds a broad

pointed lance shape and measuring up to 1–1.2 m (3–4 ft) long, one third of which is the stalk.

**Dryopteris clintoniana**
*N. America*
**F** 50–100 cm (20–40 in); acid/wet; evergreen
Established as a species, but thought to have arisen as a hybrid between *D. cristata* and *D. goldieana*. Can make an impressive large plant in a wet position, with spreading broad fronds either singly or doubly pinnate.

**Dryopteris cristata**   CRESTED BUCKLER or SHIELD FERN
*Europe, inc. Britain, Siberia, Japan, N. America*
**F** 50–100 cm (20–40 in); acid/wet; evergreen and deciduous
Plants grow easily in moist shady areas to form spreading rosettes of singly pinnate fronds, these contrasting with the less well-furnished upright fertile fronds.

**Dryopteris cycodina.** See **D. atrata**

**Dryopteris dilatata**   BROAD BUCKLER FERN
*Europe inc. Britain, N. & S. America, Greenland, Japan*
**F** 30–150 cm (12–60 in); acid/alkaline; deciduous
A strong-growing species particularly good in moist situations. It will grow well in soils with some lime if given a generous humus ration. It makes broad triangular fronds of rich green arranged as bi- or tripinnate blades that are widespreading and held by rich green stems. A good specimen which has got well established in deep leaf-mould may reach a very spectacular 1.2–1.5 m (4–5 ft); in less favoured spots fronds may be down to as little as 30 cm (12 in). Old plants will form a thick rootstock, sometimes like a mini-trunk.

**D.d. 'Grandiceps'** 50–90 cm (20–36 in). A mass of tassels in a thick bunch formed by crested ends of fronds, but with crests also on the flat pinnae. Impressive when settled in, perhaps beginning to come to its best in its second or third year.

**D.d. 'Lepidota'** The finely cut segments give it an airy look.

**D.d. 'Lepidota Cristata'** 30–60 cm (12–24 in). Makes the most of the finely cut appearance with crested pinnae and branching fronds.

### *Dryopteris erythrosora* AUTUMN FERN
*China, Korea, Japan*
F 20–50 cm (8–20 in); acid/alkaline; deciduous
Probably one of the kinds that should be included in the first six for a beginner. Called the autumn fern because of the beautiful colours of the young fronds, this is a species that grows well in almost any soil so long as it is well drained. While it is grown in positions from deep shade to fairly sunny, the plants are probably at their best in moist soil in semi-shade. Pointed, broad triangular fronds regularly furnished down to the base are arranged as a loose-spreading rosette. The blades are polished and when newly unfurled can be very rich shades of coppery gold, orange or red. This colouring lasts for a good number of weeks before giving way to the rich green of maturity. As plants usually continue to produce new fronds through the main growing months there is usually a pleasing medley of colours to enjoy, though the plant would still be worth growing if it were a very standard green.

### *Dryopteris filix-mas* MALE FERN
*Europe inc. Britain, Asia, N. America*
F 50–150 cm (20–60 in); acid/alkaline; deciduous
A strong-growing species, and a familiar wild fern in many areas. By no means unspectacular when growing well and shining in the fresh lighter greens of the newer fronds and the darker shades of adulthood. Fronds have pinnae from close to the rootstock and

are held at an angle not too far from the vertical so that a strong plant makes a significant impression. The orange-scaled curled crosiers unfolding is one of the ever-fresh pleasures of springtime. The type may be thought too bold or, dare one say it, too well-known for the smaller garden, but there are many delightful selections that can be really very distinct from mother! If possible see the plant you purchase so that you get a good example.

**D.f-m. 'Crispa'** Usually only about 30 cm (12 in) high. Very pleasing as a compact sturdy plant, with well-crested, tightly packed fronds.

**D.f-m. 'Crispa Cristata'** 30–40 cm (12–16 in). A good strong plant with the rich green fronds precisely crested along the pinnae ends and at the apex.

**D.f-m. 'Cristata'** 50–120 cm (20–48 in). (Be careful with the names as this is a much larger plant than the last.) Pinnae and frond ends neatly crested – almost like parsley.

**D.f-m. 'Cristata Jackson'** 60–90 cm (24–36 in). A particularly good selection with more curly crests to pinnae and frond ends.

**D.f-m. 'Cristata Martindale'** 40–45 cm (16–18 in). Exceptionally effective, with the pinnae ends very neatly crested and leading to the wide fish-tailed crested end of the frond. Strong plant.

**D.f-m. 'Depauperata'** 40–60 cm (16–24 in). Dark fronds with narrower pinnae, the segments more or less fused together. Polished appearance.

**D.f-m. 'Grandiceps Wills'** 60–90 cm (24–36 in). Grows with great vigour to make a wide plant of several crowns, each donating tall, shining green fronds boldly crested along their margins and ends.

**D.f-m. 'Mapplebeck'** 60–90 cm (24–36 in). A strong kind with wide fronds and pinnae. Pinnae finished with widely divided crests, while most fronds finish with several branches that are also crested. Each rachis is pleasingly clothed with orangey scales.

257

**Hart's tongue fern seen growing in a collection of plants as
effective for their foliage as for flowers.**

One of the attractive mutant cultivars of the evergreen hart's tongue fern, *Asplenium scolopendrium* 'Marginatum-contractum'.

***D.f-m.* 'Polydactyla'** 30–50 cm (12–20 in). Narrower, shorter fronds than type and with fussy, curly, intricate crests at pinna and frond ends.

***D.f-m.* 'Polydactyla Dadds'** 30–45 cm (12–18 in). In this clone the fronds are less crowded and the cresting flatter, more spreading and perhaps more refined.

***Dryopteris goldiana***   GIANT WOOD FERN
*N. America*
**F** 60–120 cm (24–48 in); acid; deciduous
The large fronds look well in moist shady spot. Young fronds are covered with white and fawn scales, which make it look quite distinct.

***Dryopteris marginalis***   MARGINAL SHIELD FERN
*N. America*
**F** 25–60 cm (10–24 in); acid/alkaline; deduous
Singly or doubly pinnate, with tough textured dark blue-green fronds in tufts. Grows in humus-rich shade.

***Dryopteris oreades***   MOUNTAIN MALE FERN
*Europe*
**F** 25–60 cm (10–24 in); acid/alkaline; deciduous
Singly pinnate, narrow, light green fronds in tufts. Found growing among rocks in European mountain ranges.

***Dryopteris parallelogramma.* See *D. wallichiana***

***Dryopteris phegopteris.* See *Phegopteris connectilis***

***Dryopteris pseudo-mas.* See *D. affinis***

***Dryopteris sieboldii***
*China, Japan*
**F** 15–40 cm (6–16 in); acid; deciduous
Little plant with each frond having a few large tough pinnae which droop. An unusual non-rampant character plant.

***Dryopteris thelypteris.* See *Thelypteris palustris***

***Dryopteris wallichiana* (syn. *parallelogramma*)**
*India, China, Japan, N. and C. America, Africa*
**F** 50–100 cm (20–40 in); acid/alkaline; deciduous
As it grows this species forms a tough, almost trunk-like rootstock from which a fountain of fronds appear, shining light gold and yellowy greens in their energetic spring flush, colouring that is highlighted by black rachis. Plant in loamy soil (does not mind lime) in a shady position.

## GYMNOCARPIUM

***Gymnocarpium dryopteris***   OAK FERN
*Europe inc. Britain, India, China, Japan, N. America*
**F** 15–30 cm (6–12 in); acid; evergreen and deciduous
Thin underground stems will support a clump of widely spaced fronds, their broadly triangular shape being made up by the three triangular branched blades of the fronds. The colour is pale green. There is a form called *G.d.* 'Plumosum' which is finely cut to give an even lighter, more feathery feel, the broader pinnules tending to overlap. Plants should be grown in open, humus-rich soil that does not dry out, perhaps in a shaded part of a rock bed or towards the front of the fernery.

***Gymnocarpium robertianum***   LIMESTONE OAK FERN
*Europe, N. America*
**F** 15–45 cm (6–18 in); alkaline; deciduous
Attractive small creeping fern with very pleasing tripinnate fronds sent up at intervals from the widespreading rootstock. A pretty ground-cover plant for shady spots with lime in soil.

## MATTEUCCIA

***Matteuccia orientalis***
*China, Korea, Japan*
**F** 30–90 cm (12–36 in); acid; deciduous
Similar to the next species but smaller.

**Matteuccia struthiopteris**   OSTRICH FEATHER or
SHUTTLECOCK FERN
*China, Japan, N. America, introduced (?) Europe*
**F** 50–150 cm (20–60 in); acid; deciduous
One of the easiest and most effective ferns grown in
neutral or somewhat acid soils, with some shade and
reasonable moisture. Erect fronds form a tall vase or
shuttlecock shape, the precise design of which is a
marvel as one looks down. Running rhizomes just
below the soil surface are marked at intervals by new
smaller fronds that quickly grow to mature size. If the
colony gets overcrowded some plants should be
removed. Fertile fronds may arise in the centre of the
shuttlecock; only a third of the height of the sterile
fronds, if that, they are brown and look as if made of
plastic.

## ONOCLEA

**Onoclea sensibilis**   SENSITIVE or BEAD FERN
*N. Asia, N. America*
**F** 25–60 cm (10–24 in); acid to neutral; deciduous
Singly or double pinnate, robust, low fern with
crowded triangular, light green fronds. Normal forms
are singly pinnate but with pinnae lobed to give a
pinnatifid effect. It can be made very happy by
waterside where it will run about to form considerable
colonies, the fronds often lasting quite late into the end
of the year before being seen off by hard frosts. The
fertile fronds are quite dissimilar, with spore-bearing
sporangia being formed into bunches like so many
beads or bunches of small grapes. While some have
green stems and rachis, there is a more decorative one
with red stems.

## OSMUNDA

**Osmunda banksiifolia**
*China, Japan*
**F** 25–90 cm (10–36 in); acid/wet; deciduous

Singly pinnate, light green, thin fronds have lightly
lobed segments. It likes shade, humus and acid soil
with much water.

**Osmunda japonica**
*Japan, Korea, China, N. India*
**F** 25–90 cm (10–36 in); acid/wet; deciduous
Very similar to royal fern, below, but smaller.

**Osmunda regalis**   ROYAL FERN
*Europe inc. Britain, Africa, Asia, N. and S. America*
**F** 60–180 cm (2–6 ft); acid to neutral/wet; deciduous
Probably the most imposing of the hardy ferns,
certainly the largest once established in a waterside
site. In a sheltered favourable spot a mature specimen
can produce fronds that can be between 3 and 4 m
(10–12 ft) long, with their blades 1 m (3 ft) across. In a
less favoured place the plant can still look impressive
even with fronds only 60 cm (2 ft) long.

Old established plants will form large hummocks of
woody rootstocks from which arise in spring the new
orangey stems with distinct crosiers slowly unfurling.
The stout stems are orangey brown in youth but
become yellowish later. Doubly pinnate spreading
blades are bright light green when young but become
darker with maturity. The fertile fronds are sent up
erectly and give the effect of a clustered head of some
massive dock-like flower, something that has given
rise to the false name of the flowering fern. The first
frost transforms all into a rusted mass, but the fawny
brown winter effect is not without decorative appeal.
Everyone will enjoy the royal fern, not all will have
the space to house it adequately.
**O.r. 'Cristata'.**   An unusual crested form.

**Osmunda spectabilis**
**F** 90–150 cm (36–60 in); acid/wet; deciduous.
A rather more upright grower than *O. regalis*,
sometimes reaching 1.5 cm (5 ft). Its fronds are palish
green in colour and have slender pinnae.

261

***Dryopteris dilatata***, the broad buckler fern, usually
tripinnate and very strong growing. In favourable wet sites
fronds can be 1 m (3¼ ft) long.

263

***Dryopteris filix-mas*** 'Grandiceps Askew'. A selected clone of
the 'Grandiceps' series of the male fern, particularly robust
and distinctly crested.

## PHEGOPTERIS

***Phegopteris connectilis* (syn. *Thelypteris phegopteris, Dryopteris phegopteris*)** BEECH FERN
*Europe inc. Britain, Asia, N. America*
**F** 15–45 cm (6–18 in); acid; deciduous.
With thin creeping rhizomes this species can form loose colonies in its preferred moist mountain streamside or woodland habitats. The frond stems may be twice the length of the singly or doubly pinnate fronds, and the fronds themselves are the traditional long-pointed fern triangular. A diagnostic feature is the way the lowest pair of pinnae, usually well clear of the remainder, turn or curve away from the blade, a habit not echoed by any of the other pairs.

**PHYLLITIS.** See ***Asplenium scolopendrium***

## POLYPODIUM

***Polypodium australe*** SOUTHERN POLYPODY
*Europe inc. Britain*
**F** 20–45 cm (8–18 in); acid/alkaline; evergreen and deciduous.
Singly pinnate and similar to the common polypody, *P. vulgare*, it differs in having broader blades, widest at the second, third, or fourth pair of pinnae, and usually with pinnae gently but more serrated than in the common polypody. Leaf texture is also less tough. It grows easily in semi-shade, given a loamy soil with plenty of humus. New fronds do not appear until the summer and autumn.
***P. a.* 'Cambricum'** An attractive form originally found near Powis Castle in Wales, growing on rocks in a wood, though it has been recorded at other sites in the principality. The pinnae are broader and deeply lobed and divided, tending to overlap each other.
***P. a.* 'Pulcherrimum'** In this fertile form the divisions of the pinnae usually extend right up to the midribs.

***Polypodium scouleri*** LEATHERY POLYPODY
*N. America*
**F** 20–45 cm (8–19 in); acid; deciduous.
Polished green tough blades with the divisions reaching about two-thirds the way to the midribs. This is a slow growing plant that needs good drainage, shade and to be allowed to get on in its own time.

***Polypodium vulgare*** COMMON POLYPODY
*Europe inc. Britain, Africa, China, Japan, N. America.*
**F** 10–45 cm (4–18 in); acid/alkaline; evergreen and deciduous.
Stalks are about a third of the full frond lengths and arise from creeping rhizomes. In the longer fronds the

**Fig. 17** *Polypodium vulgare*, **common polypody.**

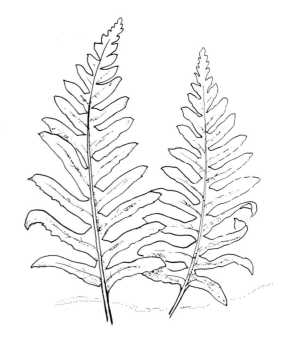

outline is of an almost parallel-sided, singly pinnate leaf a quarter wide as long, perhaps like a two-sided comb. Fronds end with a single long, blunted-ended pinna. New growth starts late in the year. While it appears to grow in a variety of soils, it certainly seems to enjoy gritty rock soils.

***P.v.* 'Bifidum'** In this form the lower pairs of pinnae are clearly lobed.

***P.v.* 'Bifidum Cristatum'** A form with pinnae lobed to more than half their depth and the fronds ending with a wide crest.

***P.v.* 'Cornubiense'** A schizophrenic fern! Apparently at random it produces three different frond forms. Firstly they are as the type, secondly ones that are filigree with divisions tri- or even quadripinnate with very thin segments, and thirdly a rather less sophisticated bolder form of this last. It makes an interesting little spreading plant to have at the front of the fernery and here you may even find a single frond trying to adopt all three forms, poor mixed-up entity!

***P.v.* 'Cristatum'** This is the standard article, but with pinnae and frond ends crested.

***P.v.* 'Interjectum'** A form with wider blades and with the basal and perhaps the next pair of pinnae turned sharply inwards.

***P.v.* 'Longicaudatum'** As type but with the terminal segment of each frond palely coloured and pulled out to a very long point.

***P.v.* 'Racemosum'** Fronds are decoratively forked.

***P.v.* 'Racemosum Hillman'** Fronds forked and sometimes crested.

## POLYSTICHUM

***Polystichum acrostichoides*** CHRISTMAS FERN
*N. America.*
**F** 25–90 cm (10–36 in); acid; evergreen and deciduous.
Attractive in a shady moist spot, especially so in the first flush of youth when the fronds are lit up with a silvery finish. Bold pinnae are rich green and singly pinnate, attractive enough to be sold sometimes as cut foliage.

***P.a.* 'Crispum'** Margins of fronds decorated in a much-curled, attractively fussy finish.

***P.a.* 'Incisum'** While singly pinnate, the pinnae are very deeply cut.

***Polystichum aculeatum*** HARD or PRICKLY SHIELD FERN
*Europe inc. Britain, N. India*
**F** 50–120 cm (20–48 in); alkaline; evergreen.
A striking plant in the wild or in the garden. Usually found in woodland or hedgerow, it forms a round clump of fronds, usually 60–90 cm (2–3 ft) long and in maturity a rich dark green. It normally manages to keep its fronds intact through the winter to make a fine contrast to the new light green, unfurling, drooping crosiers that curl over backwards, unlike the conformist majority. Singly or doubly pinnate, the tough lance-shaped pinnae are closely packed together and are deeply incised at their ends giving them a spiky or prickly appearance – hence the common names.

***P.a.* 'Acutilobum'** With narrower, very pointed pinnae.

***P.a.* 'Cambricum'** Segments are egg or sickle shaped and boldly toothed.

***P.a.* 'Pulcherrimum'** Finely drawn kind with lacy fronds with divided, fanned ends.

***P.a.* 'Pulcherrimum Gracillimum'** One of the wonders of the family, the fronds intricately divided into gossamer-thin segments that seem to float in the air. Much to be desired, but a scarce kind that is sterile.

***Polystichum andersonii*** ANDERSON'S HOLLY FERN
*N. America*
**F** 25–100 cm (10–40 in); wet; evergreen.
An attractive double pinnate species with hardy, textured holly-like fronds being unusual and generous

266

**The ostrich feather fern, *Matteuccia struthiopteris*, showing
how it can colonize a site. In a damp spot it can be one of the
easiest and most effective of deciduous ferns.**

267

*Polystichum polyblepharum* is a very hardy fern from China
and Japan, with tough, textured fronds. The adult rich green
is preceded by the very scaly new crosiers.

in ending with a useful vegetative bulbil. Easy, given moisture and shade.

### Polystichum braunii    HOLLY FERN
*Europe, China, Japan, N. America.*
**F** 25–100 cm (10–40 in); acid; evergreen and deciduous.
Another bipinnate species that mimics holly. This one is delightful in spring with the new fronds a piece of shimmering silvery magic sculpture. It likes moisture, shade and an open soil, preferably slightly acid.

### Polystichum cystostegia
*New Zealand*
**F** 10–25 cm (4–10 in); acid/alkaline; evergreen.
A little mountain fern with neat bipinnate fronds made more decorative with orangey brown scales on stems and rachides.

### Polystichum imbricans (syn. *P. munitum imbricans*)
*N. America*
**F** 25–60 cm (10–24 in); acid and alkaline; evergreen and deciduous.
Spear-shaped fronds clothed to the base with crowded overlapping pinnae in full rich green.

### Polystichum munitum    SWORD FERN
*N. America*
**F** 25–100 cm (10–40 in); acid; evergreen and deciduous.
Long, singly pinnate fronds are well-furnished to their bases and basically parallel-sided but tapering to a sword-point finish. Neatly arranged, pointed pinnae are precisely lobed. Good mid-green colour.

### Polystichum polyblepharum
*China, Korea, Japan*
**F** 50–120 cm (20–48 in); acid; evergreen and deciduous.

Easy in shade with plenty of humus when it will form a rosette of tough, shining fronds either singly or doubly pinnate. Fronds are a dark colour though young ones are paler, scaly and pleasing. Fronds may remain scaly below.

### Polystichum retroso-paleaceum
*Korea, Japan*
**F** 45–100 cm (18–40 in); acid, evergreen and deciduous.
Can make a spectacular fern in the garden or in a half-tub. A spreading rosette of bipinnate, polished, shining green frond blades with orangey rachides is made the more interesting when the new ones are covered with scales.

### Polystichum richardii
*New Zealand*
**F** 20–45 cm (8–18 in); acid/alkaline; evergreen and deciduous.
Neat round rosettes of bipinnate, robust fronds are dark green with more than a hint of blue. In shade or semi-shade in open soils it can look neat and effective, a contrast to some paler kinds or to rocks.

### Polystichum setiferum    SOFT SHIELD FERN
*Europe inc. Britain*
**F** 50–150 cm (20–60 in); acid/alkaline; evergreen and deciduous.
A height of 150 cm (5 ft) is possible but is rarely reached – in the wild 60 cm (2 ft) would be more normal and garden forms are usually less tall. The habit of the plants is spreading with elegant bi- or tripinnate long fronds reaching sideways to display the soft velvety texture, a feeling achieved by the very great number of pinnae, their veining, serration and precise positioning. The soft colouring helps the overall velvety look. In spring the new fronds are a picture as they uncurl themselves from the swathing orangey scales that will remain on the rachis and

around the rootstock. Rounded rosettes of new young plants become more complicated as the specimen ages and forms new crowns.

At all stages this is an attractive plant, the fronds often lasting through the winter looking respectable, but it may be politic to prune away some of the older more weary ones before the new flush appears. Fronds can produce a series of little bulbil plantlets along the rachides at the bases of the pinnae. As these develop, and if you wish to propagate the form, a complete frond can be removed and lowered into a tray of mixed coarse sand and clean humus, kept moist in a polythene cover and the young plants pricked out when they have rooted and started to expand their small fronds.

Over 300 forms have been named in the past.

***P.s.* 'Acutilobum'** With narrow fronds and very pointed segments. A compact kind.

***P.s.* 'Congestum'** Miniature fertile form only about 15–18 cm (6–7 in) tall. Erect fronds are bright green and thick with overlapping pinnae, looking most neat and attractive in a rock garden or wherever planted.

***P.s.* 'Divisilobum'** Gorgeous, with large fronds tri- or quadripinnate delicately cut. Curiously, those on the lower side of the pinnae are longer than those on the upper side. Young fronds as they unfurl are dressed overall with silvery white scales. The fronds reach outwards though often their tips tend to point up. Old established plants in a good spot may be a feature, measuring 1.2–1.5 m (4–5 ft) across.

***P.s.* 'Divisilobum Iveryanum'** A very classy plant some 15–45 cm (6–18 in) high. Horizontal fronds are intricately divided, with very evenly matched, spreading crests along each margin and finished with an excellent terminal one. Fanciers reckon it one of the finest.

***P.s.* 'Foliosum'** Very velvety and full with overlapping segments.

***P.s.* 'Plumosum'** 40–75 cm (16–30 in). Feathery fronds carefully cut into overlapping segments make it a quadripinnate specimen, one of the rare ones to achieve such intricacy. They look mossy soft.

***P.s.* 'Polydactylum'** Segments end with divided crests.

***P.s.* 'Pulcherrimum Bevis'** This is a much sought-after cultivar with very precisely and intricately cut fronds held firmly and as if manufactured from some strange metal. As the plant establishes itself it will expand the size of its fronds till they may be over 60 cm (2ft) long.

***P.s.* 'Rotundatum'** Unusual form in which the fronds are close to circular.

### *Polystichum tsus-simense*
*China, Korea, Japan*
**F** 15–45 cm (6–18 in); acid/alkaline; evergreen and deciduous.

A neat fern with stiff, tough-textured fronds of quite wide, rounded triangular outline, the rather broad pinnae neatly disposed. The rich dark green is suffused with a suggestion of purple when young. Makes tidy, spreading rosettes. Hardy but good in a pot as well.

## THELYPTERIS

### *Thelypteris palustris* (syn. *Dryopteris thelypteris*)  MARSH FERN
*Europe inc. Britain, N. America.*
**F** 75–150 cm (30–60 in); acid/wet; evergreen.

Long, creeping black rhizomes, much branched, give rise to fronds at intervals, these being light green, singly or doubly pinnate with stems as long as the blades. The sterile fronds are produced in the spring, the stouter fertile ones in the early summer. Useful as a colonizer only in very wet acid conditions.

### *Thelypteris phegopteris.* See *Phegopteris connectilis.*

269

*Polystichum setiferum* 'Foliosum' is one of the very many
cultivars of soft shield fern showing intricately cut lace-like
fronds with the soft texture of velvet.

*Matteuccia struthiopteris*, the shuttlecock or ostrich feather
fern. The depth of these 'shuttlecocks' is about 75 cm (30 in),
but they can vary from 45–150 cm (18–60 in).

## WOODSIA

### Woodsia obtusa    BLUNT-LOBED WOODSIA
*N. America*
**F** 15–25 cm (6–10 in); alkaline; deciduous
A small deciduous kind with bipinnate fronds. It does well in shaded well-drained soil, either neutral or somewhat limy.

## WOODWARDIA

### Woodwardia areolata    CHAIN FERN
*N. America*
**F** 50–90 cm (20–36 in); acid/wet; evergreen and deciduous.
Could easily be mistaken for a related *Blechnum* species. The paired pinnae form a series of ladder rungs. The strong, glossy-textured fronds form clumps that grow well in moist acid soils where they stand more sun than most ferns.

### Woodwardia fimbriata    GIANT CHAIN FERN
*Mexico, N. America.*
**F** 1–2 m (3–6½ ft); acid/alkaline; deciduous.
A robust, large fern with airy, wide triangular bipinnate fronds. Grows best in a moist, shaded spot and there forms upright dark green masses.

### Woodwardia orientalis    ORIENTAL CHAIN FERN
*N. India, China, Japan*
**F** 1–2.3 m (3–7½ ft); acid, deciduous.
The large, long, widely triangular fronds are tough-textured and a rich green. They arch over and even approach the ground. As fronds age some will give rise to a series of many plantlets sprouting light green fronds, an easy means of increase.

### Woodwardia radicans    EUROPEAN CHAIN FERN
*Europe, Asia*
**F** 45 cm–2.1 m (1½–7 ft); acid; deciduous.
An impressive long-cultivated, robust fern with arching, shining green fronds. Bipinnate. Needs placing to rear of fernery with room to grow. Substantial bulbils borne at apex of the fronds provide easy method of increase.

### Woodwardia virginica
*N. America*
**F** 25–60 cm (10–24 in); acid/wet; deciduous.
Creeping rhizomes are often under water and given the right conditions spread quickly. Rich green fronds, 30–45 cm (12–18 in) long, are oblong in shape and bronzed in youth. Plants can look very ornamental in a boggy bit of ground.

**This fern border consists of *Asplenium scolopendrium*, *Dryopteris filix-mas* and *Athyrium filix-femina*.**

# Large-Leaved Perennials

## Myles Challis

*Gunnera manicata*, the largest-leaved hardy perennial of all, for majestic foliage by the pool or lakeside.

# Introducing Large-Leaved Perennials

Big leaves are in – or, at least, becoming more widely appreciated! As with all things, fashions change and different styles and tastes evolve, and gardening and plants are no exception.

Who among us on seeing for the first time the great towering, spreading leaves of *Gunnera manicata* under which we could stand to shelter from the rain, could not fail to be impressed? Not many plants it is true, especially perennials, are built on such a Brobdignagian scale, but nevertheless there is a wealth of large and handsome leaves of every shape and form imaginable to be found among herbaceous plants. No one of course would want to fill their garden with gunneras, but one or two strategically placed in the right setting, preferably by a pond or lake, would be a showstopper. Some people have a fixed idea that only large gardens can accommodate large-leaved plants but, as we shall see, large leaves can act as an effective contrast to smaller-leaved specimens and actually enhance the design of a small garden. But for many gardeners, the boldness of large-leaved plants is something of an acquired taste.

There are, of course, exceptions to every rule and surely this must apply to hostas, appreciated probably by almost every gardener. Indeed, I am hazarding a guess here, but the popularity of hostas may have played an important role in the increasing interest in the use of foliage, if not large leaves in particular. They are first-class plants which no garden should be without. Hostas have become so popular that specialist societies have been formed in many countries and hosta breeders, especially in the USA, appear to have gone berserk, and consequently the number of varieties available nowadays is enormous. For a detailed account of hostas, see pages 6–96 – only the largest-leaved varieties are dealt with in this part of the book.

My aim here is to introduce the merits and advantages, and not least the beauty, of large-leaved perennials, and their potential and value in the garden. I am not suggesting, of course, that you should fill your garden with them, but by careful selection and positioning of some of them, great interest and beauty will undoubtedly be added to your garden.

Large leaves are an essential part of the garden scene, and a satisfactory one cannot be completed without them. They not only emphasize the smaller leaves, but are an important contrast (especially those of rounded outline) to the vertical shapes of plants such as grasses or the laciness of ferns.

Garden styles, like the plants in them, wax and wane in popularity. I am myself a great advocate of the informal garden, because I feel that gentle curves rather than straight lines and geometric shapes best accommodate the natural forms of plants. However, formal gardens are certainly enjoying a resurgence in popularity, and leaves, especially large ones, are invaluable in helping to soften the harshness of angular paving or brickwork. International flower shows often make extensive use of paving in the garden exhibits and then give inspiration in the use of bold plantings to soften contours.

In informal gardens the generous shapes of large-leaved plants emphasize the rounded curves of beds and the more architectural forms provide a focus in the way a statue or sundial might in a more formal setting.

While speaking of 'points of focus' and 'style', why shouldn't the same principles of interior design be applied to gardening? Plants are as important in the garden as furniture is in the house, and their positioning, relation to one another, background etc., can equate to furniture, curtains, carpets and wall-paper. Plants can be used to create atmosphere in the garden just as effectively as any interior designer's materials in the house and it is perhaps here that the large leaves play an especially important role, as they so often possess 'architectural' qualities.

There will always be those who crave a rainbow of colour in the garden, but the restful qualities and more subtle tints of foliage do, I feel, give much more lasting pleasure. The gardener who concentrates on foliage in his or her garden for interest, and indeed colour, will be rewarded and satisfied far more than the individual who relies on short-lived annuals, for the period of interest which foliage gives is far greater – a particularly important factor to consider in the case of those who have smaller gardens.

The selection available is a varied one, as large leaves come in many forms, from the solid simple round shapes of hostas, ligularias or peltiphyllum to the much divided and toothed leaves of aruncus or melianthus, or the sword-like blades of phormium. Why nature has produced this profusion of shapes is difficult to answer, as plants, just like animals, birds or insects, have evolved over millions of years. We can, however, be fairly certain why some have larger leaves than others. The leaf, after all, is what enables a plant to function, given light, soil and water. Different plants have evolved to adapt to different conditions and, where water is concerned, the larger the leaf the greater the degree of transpiration because of the larger surface area. Thus, one way in which plants have developed to suit their environment is to produce large leaves where they can afford to lose moisture and small ones where they have to conserve it. Gunneras and lysichitons, for example, will thrive best in boggy conditions where there is a constant supply of moisture at the root; on the other hand, plants found growing in arid areas where little moisture is available usually have much smaller leaves.

If you look at the vegetation across the globe, it is very evident that the concentrations of plants with large leaves are not only to be found in the warmer regions, but also in areas of high rainfall such as the tropical forests. By studying the leaves of a gunnera or a banana, for example, you will see how the rain collected is directed to their centre to land on the soil where the main concentrations of root are.

As well as the hardy large-leaved perennials, I have selected a few tender ones. These have been included both for their great beauty and especially for their value in creating an atmosphere of tropical climes, as discussed on pages 307–321.

Perhaps, like me, you will catch the 'big leaf bug', something which can lead to extraordinary results. A visitor to my garden once remarked: 'you feel as Alice must have done when she ate the piece of mushroom which the Caterpillar gave her to reduce her size. Huge and wonderful leaves are above and all around you.'

I caught the 'big leaf bug' at the tender age of seven when I was taken for the very first time to Kew Gardens. Stepping into the Aroid House I was engulfed and enveloped by a jungle of gigantic leaves of every shape and form: I was mesmerized by it all, and hooked from that moment on.

# The Value of Architectural Plants in the Garden

Nature is amazing for her apparently limitless scope in producing variety of form both in the animal and plant worlds. She is the greatest designer that ever was, and ever will be, and much inspiration has been sought from her creations from time immemorial.

I cannot help but be reminded, when I stand under the vast leaf of a gunnera, of the vaulting of some great cathedral. Look at the segmented canes of a colony of giant bamboo and you have the strength and structure of stone buttressing.

The Greeks and the Egyptians decorated their buildings with the strong architectural forms of acanthus leaves, and plants such as the lotus were deemed sacred by them. In more recent times Art Nouveau drew complete inspiration from form of leaf and flower.

In the garden the value of plants with strong architectural shapes cannot be underestimated, particularly where modern hard landscaping has produced severe straight lines and geometric shapes. These can be broken or at least softened by natural plant forms, and this is most easily achieved with large-leaved subjects or groupings of plants with strong leaf character.

**Here the fineness of the ivory, feathery plumes of *Aruncus sylvester* (*A. dioicus*) are set off by the huge leaves of *Gunnera manicata*.**

## Softening a hard landscape

The materials used in many modern buildings have a harshness which can be unattractive on its own. A modern house is often best complemented by a contemporary garden design, but a garden, after all, is not like an office or waiting room – it should possess an atmosphere which is conducive to relaxation and entertaining. The necessity, therefore, to use plants with architectural yet softening qualities is much greater in the case of modern, hard-landscaped gardens than with those of a more informal or 'natural' design, where their value is more for contrast in size, texture, colour and so on.

The greater the evidence of hard landscaping the larger the number of architectural plants will be required to obtain a satisfactory picture. This presents no problem as there is such a wealth and range of material to choose from, and naturally the greater the variety incorporated into the planting the better, and evergreens such as phormiums, play an important role here.

*Phormium tenax*, the New Zealand flax, consists of a great tuft of stiff, sword-like leaves standing 2 m (6 ft) high which are topped (in good summers) by even taller flower spikes which are equally architectural though not very colourful. This is an invaluable plant for instant effect, a landscaper's favourite.

Large plants such as phormiums should not be confined to large gardens. If they are combined with smaller-leaved plants in a small garden they will not

Bold architectural plants can be used to
accentuate the shape of a border:
1. *Phormium tenax*
2. *Rodgersia pinnata* 'Superba'
3. *Ligularia dentata* 'Desdemona'
4. Ferns
5. Pampas grass
6. *Hosta sieboldiana elegans.*

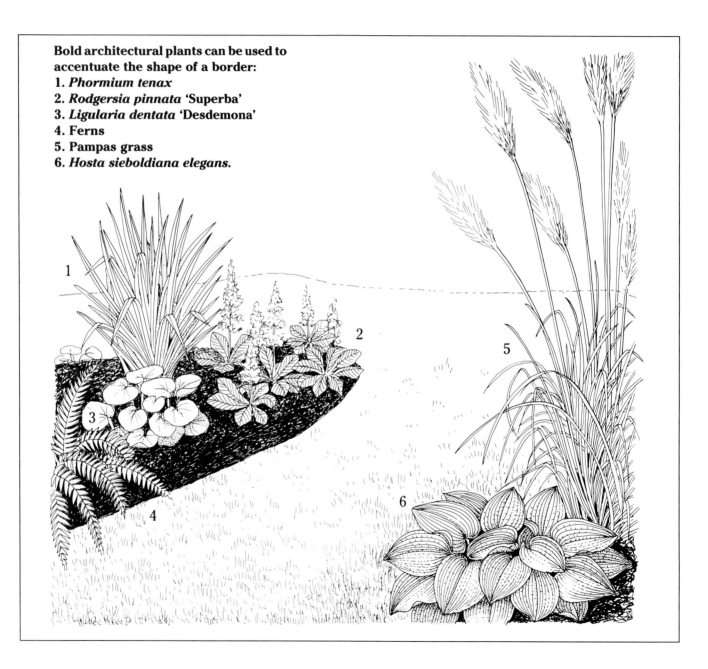

only be of value for contrast in size and variation of shape, but give an illusion of size to the garden. Small plants on their own will do nothing to make a small garden seem bigger; equally a collection of purely large or large-leaved ones, no matter how varied, beautiful or architectural, will not be as effective as where they are combined with smaller or more delicately leaved plants. Where space is limited it is better to have fewer different plants, rather than to reduce too much the size of each individual clump, as then the character, and to a certain extent the beauty, of the plants is lost.

# Providing emphasis

One of the greatest values of plants with strong architectural shapes is their use in emphasizing the design of the garden itself. Trees and shrubs obviously also play an important role here as they form the 'bones' of the garden, but bold architectural plants also give it structure.

Even in ordinary gardens regardless of their size architectural plants are of value. The eye is naturally drawn to them and because of this gives emphasis or draws attention to an area or feature. For example, steps can be marked or accentuated, or the location of a little bridge over a stream would be much more evident if architectural plants were situated by it.

If a large border swings out into the lawn to give shape to the garden, then this purpose is achieved more satisfactorily if this area of the border contains bold plants, which will give strength to the shape. This is particularly important where distance is concerned. Plants with strong, clearly defined shapes can be distinguished and appreciated from afar, whereas those with small or finely cut foliage must be observed close to. This variation of leaf size creates contrast and

therefore interest, the small leaves accentuating and complementing the large and vice-versa. The larger the garden the greater the necessity for use of plants of strong character, to add variation if nothing else.

# Considering texture and colour

Variety is what creates interest and this is achieved also with contrast of shape, texture and colour.

First, colour. Certain colours do not harmonize, but nevertheless colours which people would not dream of putting together in a room or even with their clothes, are often used side by side in the garden. Similarly, where only two or three colours may be considered sufficient in a room, all hell is let loose in the garden, as a kind of colour blindness seems to take over. Some beautiful effects can be created with colourful planting, but gardens which rely on their beauty solely through the use of flower colour cannot ever be as successful as those where greater emphasis is put on plant character and leaf shape.

We do not have to omit colour by any means to achieve this, as even foliage comes in many shades – purples, pinks, yellows, reds, white as well as the many tints of green itself. Many plants with bold architectural leaves also possess beautiful flowers. Take the acanthus, for example. Apart from having the most sculptural leaves, it also possesses dramatic flower spikes of purple and white which are themselves an architectural feature of the plant. But if a plant does not have attractive foliage as well as flowers, then when the flowers have finished there is nothing worthwhile left to look at. The leaf is around usually far longer than the flower and is really therefore of greater importance.

It is leaf shape and size that basically gives large-leaved perennials their architectural qualities and we

281

should create as many contrasts with them as space allows. What could be more contrasting than, say, the spikiness of a yucca or phormium with the roundness and smoothness of a hosta, or the huge solidity of a gunnera leaf next to the much divided one of a heracleum or an aruncus. The round, scalloped leaves of peltiphyllum would be perfectly set off by the spears of a bog iris, while the serrated leaves of melianthus contrast well with those of the banana-like leaves of the canna.

Texture, too, adds another dimension of interest. At one extreme we have the acanthus with its highly glossy leaves, at the other the verbascum with its very woolly ones, and there are a whole host of variations in between. The leaves of ligularias are often described as oily smooth, and those of gunnera as puckered. Those of blue hostas can be glaucous and a rheum is matt. So in addition to the wide variety of leaf shape, we also have colour and texture increasing still further the value of these plants in the garden.

## A tropical atmosphere

The Victorians realized at a very early stage the merits of these large-leaved plants. One can understand their enthusiasm when one realizes that many of the plants were new to them, having been recently introduced, but nevertheless they certainly appreciated their potential. Writers of the time, especially William Robinson, greatly influenced the style of gardening and the use of the new plants that the Victorians grew both in their gardens and their conservatories and greenhouses. The fashion of 'sub-tropical' gardening, which was a new and highly fashionable occupation of the time, was largely his innovation, and although it involved the use of a lot of greenhouse plants and hardy exotics such as bamboos, phormiums and so on, it also incorporated many large-leaved perennials because of their great usefulness in creating a tropical atmosphere.

Palms, cordylines and yuccas might be under-planted with acanthus, while an Abyssinian banana (*Ensete ventricosum*) might be given a fringe of hostas. The same style was used in the public parks of the time. Sometimes, both in private and public gardens, plants would be used on their own as lawn specimens. This is a very attractive way of displaying a highly architectural plant where the space is available. Plants which require as much sun as is available would obviously benefit from this kind of position.

Treated as specimens, the full individuality and character is best appreciated with large subjects such as bamboos or pampas grass, the giant reed, *Arundo donax*, or *Aralia cachemirica*, which, although a perennial, is 2m (6ft) high.

Tender bedding plants such as cannas are effective in bold clumps, and if the beds are raised they will do even better as the sun's heat is retained longer than in the surrounding level ground. Plants of lesser stature can provide a similar effect if planted in a bold group; as a lone specimen their character would be lost.

The potential of architectural plants is only realized when one has used them. What you have never had you do not miss, but try them and you will be enlightened!

*Phormium tenax* **'Variegatum', one of the most architectural of plants, good for creating exotic effects.**

**Large-leaved perennials can be used to 'accent' a spot. Here rheums (along with pampas grass) are used as sentinels to accent a bridge.**

# Companion Planting

The exact arrangement of the plants in a garden may not seem vital to the inexperienced, but the precise position of a tree, shrub, climber and even an herbaceous plant can contribute as much to the final effect as the positioning of furniture, pictures and ornaments can in a room. And, like planning a room, a well-thought-out colour scheme can make a world of difference in the garden.

The 'art' of landscaping and planting demands even greater skill than that of the interior decorator, as he or she has to possess a combination of talents: that of horticulturalist and draughtsperson with an artist's eye for perspective and colour sense, married with imagination and vision. And so unless you are employing the skills of such an expert, it will necessitate much thought before planting, whether dealing with a virgin site or one already partially planted.

What follows can only be guidelines as every garden is different and should, indeed, be individual. Nevertheless much experience lies behind these suggestions, which I hope will save time and unnecessary mistakes, and although an entire garden cannot be planned by them the suggested companions and groupings should be of considerable help.

By creating contrast, by using plants of different sizes, forms, colours and textures, we achieve variety and therefore interest and, with the exception of colour, we need put no limits on these things. Because we are considering here companions specifically for large-leaved perennials I have excluded certain groups such as conifers, heathers, alpines, annuals and the cottage garden-type flowering plants. This is partly for aesthetic reasons and also simply because this book would need to be a good deal larger to include them. Companions for bog and waterside perennials are covered in the following chapter, and more tender plants such as banana, ginger, cannas etc. are discussed on pages 307–321, because it is the sub-tropical style of garden to which they are best suited.

## Deciding on a colour scheme

I consider the choice of colour the first decision to make when planning an area of the garden. A small area should be thought of as one 'room' and therefore have one colour scheme consisting of, at most, three colours plus green. The larger the garden, the larger number of colour schemes which can be employed for different areas or 'rooms' in the garden.

Ideally, we should use together colours from the same areas of the colour spectrum, combining hot colours like reds and oranges or planting cool blues with mauves, but this is not always possible or necessary providing we do not place colours which clash next to one another. Nature never does this, even when employing some if the most vivid hues whether it be in the plant or animal worlds.

### YELLOWS

Colour in the garden, even green (though this is not always realized), provides continuity, and it is important to achieve this. Green apart, yellow or yellow variegation occurs in leaves more often than any other colour and therefore offers a greater choice in trees, shrubs, herbaceous including grasses and even climbers. Most people tend to use yellow-leaved specimens individually for contrast with purples and blues; they can be used to even greater effect when grouped together in their many contrasting forms, and will light up an area of the garden as if in sunshine, even on a dull day. Picture the lovely tree *Robinia pseudoacacia* 'Frisia', with its slightly pendant branches heavily clothed with small oval leaves. The golden cut-leaved elder, *Sambucus racemosa* 'Plumosa Aurea' would be a good contrasting shrub with a large-leaved perennial alongside, perhaps the variegated New Zealand flax, *Phormium tenax* 'Variegatum'. A little lower could be the yellow-leaved form of *Choisya ternata*, called 'Sundance', and the pretty and slow-growing Japanese maple, *Acer japonicum* 'Aureum'. Finally, at the foot of the group, another large-leaved perennial, the golden-leaved *Hosta* 'Sum and Substance' would provide contrast with the little gold-striped bamboo *Arundinaria viridistriata* or one of the golden grasses such as *Hakonechloa macra* 'Alboaurea', or *Molinia caerulea* 'Variegata'. In this grouping we have achieved continuity of colour with contrast and variation in leaf form and size.

## WHITE

White with a green background will give a similar 'lighting up' effect but this will largely be achieved with flowers. A good background subject would be the shrub *Viburnum plicatum* 'Mariesii', with its horizontal layered branches and white lace-cap flowers. The large-leaved perennial this time could be *Crambe cordifolia* and perhaps a group of arum lilies, *Zantedeschia aethiopica* 'Crowborough'. Additional white could be in the form of white variegated shrubs such as *Cornus sibirica* 'Variegata' or *Aralia elata* 'Variegata' with its elegant arching sprays of pinnate white-edged leaves, and finally a clump of white-edged hostas such as *H.* 'Thomas Hogg'.

Almost any colour can be added to white and is often desirable to relieve any coldness. Purples and pinks work particularly well. For a sunny spot the purple smoke bush, *Cotinus coggygria* 'Royal Purple' would make a lovely background for anything white but especially the rather tender variegated reed, *Arundo donax* 'Variegata'. The purple *Phormium tenax purpureum* would give contrast of form, along with another large-leaved perennial, *Acanthus mollis* 'Latifolius' with its mauve and white flower spikes and perhaps in front the little heuchera, 'Palace Purple'.

In light shade we could add those beautiful shrubs, *Hydrangea aspera* or *H. sargentiana*, with their sumptuous velvety leaves and mauve and white lace-cap flowers. The large-leaved perennial here could be *Rheum palmatum tanguticum*, whose leaves are carmine underneath and tinged red on top. A group of turk's cap lilies, *Lilium martagon*, with their soft pinkish purple flowers, would accentuate this, perhaps together with a drift of *Polygonum bistorta* 'Superbum', with their similarly coloured flowers but contrasting poker shape. For bolder contrast we could use another large-leaved perennial, *Ligularia dentata* 'Desdemona', with its heart-shaped leaves whose stems and undersides are intense purplish red, but we would have to remove its orange flowers later in the summer to maintain our colour scheme. In a sunny spot the leaves would also be tinged with purple on top. If more pink is desirable then one of the more subtly hued pink astilbes could be added.

## USING PURPLE

Glaucous blue-grey or grey-green is difficult to mix with ordinary greens but is stunning with purples. In a sunny position, with some of the purple plants just mentioned we could have, for example, a eucalyptus tree such as *Eucalyptus niphophila* or *Eucalyptus*

**Veratrum viride, pleating at its finest in the vegetable world.**

*gunnii*, which can be pruned to form a bush. Two more large-leaved perennials, neither of which we should be without, can be included in such a scheme: the semi-tender *Melianthus major*, with its bold serrated leaves, and *Hosta sieboldiana elegans* with its oval, strongly ribbed leaves. The plume poppy, *Macleaya cordata*, is another glaucous large-leaved perennial, its three-lobed leaves, of a similar but less intense hue, are not so good with purples, but the bronzy colouring of its flowers is heightened when it is planted with a fairly recently introduced bronzy grass called *Deschampsia caespitosa* 'Golden Dew'.

Even more beautiful with purple, perhaps, is silver. A purple rheum, for example, would contrast beautifully with an underplanting of the creeping *Lamium maculatum* 'Beacon Silver', and a purple phormium would look stunning with a skirt of the silver filigree foliage of *Artemesia arborescens* or *A. canescens* and perhaps the new heuchera, *H.* 'Snow Storm', with its silvery white leaves and dazzling red flowers. Artemisias and heucheras require reasonable drainage, as do the magnificent silvery thistle-like plants like the cardoon, *Cynara cardunculus*, or *Onopordum acanthium*, both in the 2 m (6 ft) range. Slightly smaller are the eryngiums such as *E. giganteum*. If spiny plants are not to your taste, then *Verbascum olympicum* with its big rosettes of silvery woolly leaves and tall yellow flower spikes, rising to 2.5 m (8 ft), should appeal. Again, it is a plant for a well-drained spot, perhaps in gravel.

We can of course add reds to our purples – subjects like *Crocosmia* 'Lucifer', for example, would be admirable. This would be a change from the norm of mixing reds with oranges and yellows.

## SHADES OF GREEN

Yellows and purples are more plentiful than any other colours when it comes to foliage, but we should not forget that there are many diverse and subtle shades of green itself to be exploited, and ever greater variety is supplied by the different textures of leaves. *Rodgersia (Astilboides) tabularis*, for example, has huge circular leaves of the palest green. These are not only a lovely contrast to the star-shaped crinkly bronze leaves of, say, *Rodgersia podophylla* but are a beautiful foil to the turquoise blue flowers of the Himalayan poppy, *Meconopsis sheldonii*. The ostrich fern, *Matteuccia struthiopteris*, is an equally fresh pale green. The greeny yellow flowers heads of marsh spurge, *Euphorbia palustris*, if planted with them, will heighten the gold of these pale greens like sun shining through them. All would thrive together as they like moisture and dappled shade.

Preferring the same conditions are two more large-leaved perennials, *Smilacina racemosa* and *Aruncus dioicus* (syn. *A. sylvestris*): both have divided leaves and creamy coloured flower plumes. The latter is best used for waterside planting where it is of great value for the variety of form it adds, but the fresh green leaves of *Smilacina racemosa*, looking like some exotic solomon's seal, is more suited to woodland. Although a beautiful and architectural plant, it needs some stronger colours alongside to enhance it, preferably pink and blue or mauve. A Turk's cap lily would

**A group of yellow-foliaged plants showing the diversity of leaf shape to be found:**
1. *Robinia pseudoacacia* 'Frisia'
2. *Phormium tenax* 'Variegatum'
3. *Sambucus racemosa* 'Plumosa Aurea'
4. *Choisya ternata* 'Sundance'
5. *Acer japonicum* 'Aureum'
6. *Arundinaria viridistriata*
7. *Hosta* 'Sum and Substance'
8. *Hakonechloa macra* 'Alboaurea'.

be ideal here, as would Himalayan poppies (*Meconopsis* spp) or, at a lower level, even in front of the smilacina, could be the salmon-hued *Primula pulverulenta* and the water forget-me-not, *Myosotis scorpioides* 'Mermaid'.

## Shady spots

*Trachystemon orientale*, is the ideal large-leaved perennial for those difficult shady dry spots and makes very good ground cover. It looks most attractive when planted with cranesbills whose finely divided leaves relieve the solidness of those of the trachystemon. Other good companions for it would be *Dicentra formosa*, again with ferny foliage, or the lush-leaved *Dicentra spectabilis* (bleeding heart).

The veratrums are also best when grown in dappled shade, for although they will grow in full sun their splendid pleated foliage often gets scorched. Lilies, especially the turk's cap variety, are again some of the best companions for the bland-flowered veratrums, although a bold group of the black-flowered *Veratrum nigrum* would be quite dramatic on its own.

## Matching like with like

Because the foliage of veratrums is so striking, it is best when grouped with other architectural subjects where it would add variety and contrast, plants such as rheums and ligularias, perhaps this time the huge *L. wilsoniana* or *L. veitchiana*, with their big almost triangular leaves. The butter yellow variegated *Polygonum cuspidatum* 'Spectabile', would be a good

**Rheum palmatum tanguticum, the leaves tinged purple and blue when young are produced further into the season than other kinds.**

background and rodgersias such as *R. podophylla* but especially *R. pinnata* 'Superba' with feathery pink flower spikes, would be suitable additions to such a group. The so-called poke weeds, *Phytolacca americana* and *P. clavigera* seem to succeed best in a fairly open situation, though they will tolerate light shade. Although quite substantial in leaf they are most attractive when closely planted with other things. *P. clavigera* is the better of the two, both for its rose pink flowers and its red stems, and its companions need to be quite bold in order to hold their own against the strong robust shape, but should all be shorter so that it sits among them like a candelabrum. The evergreen bergenias – good forms are *B.* 'Ballawley' or *B.* 'Eric Smith' – would be admirable both for their rose pink flowers in summer and their bronzed leaves in winter and would more or less cover the gap left by the phytolacca at that time. *Bergenia cordifolia* 'Purpurea' is even more colourful in winter than the two varieties cited above, the whole plant turning a purplish red.

While on the subject of bergenias, the most beautiful of all this genus must not be forgotten. The ordinary evergreen kinds just mentioned are perfect for under-planting or on the edge of curved or island beds to give additional emphasis, but *Bergenia ciliata*, though deciduous, is too lovely a plant to be obscured by any others. With its round hairy leaves reaching 30 cm (1 ft) across, it should be given pride of place somewhere in dappled shade, perhaps on the edge of a pool with rodgersias and ligularias for company. The only instance in whch I would use it for underplanting is with a large tree-fern, *Dicksonia antarctica*, or a Chusan palm, *Trachycarpus fortunei*, whose fronds would be held high enough above the bergenia. A shady dell occupied by the former would certainly be a very beautiful sight. An alternative to the bergenia would be the lovely Chatham Island forget me not,

291

*Myosotidium hortensia*, with its equally large but strongly ribbed round shiny leaves and sprays of little blue flowers.

## Bold bulbs

A dell would certainly be the perfect setting for one of the most dramatic perennials, the bulbous giant lily, *Cardiocrinum giganteum*. It is not an easy plant but if you can provide the conditions it needs, that of a very deep acid humus, and you can afford to buy sufficient bulbs of varying ages which will be necessary to give an annual show, then you will be rewarded by a breathtaking experience when your colony or group comes to fruition. Certainly this plant is too much of a showstopper to have its limelight stolen by any lesser ones and as such we cannot seriously consider companions for it unless we simply frame it with something as humble as ferns.

Almost equal in stature though less dramatic than *Cardiocrinum giganteum*, is another bulbous perennial, the eremurus, or foxtail lily. When considering companions for these the main thing to bear in mind is the gap they will leave when finished. The long strap-like leaves are also somewhat untidy and the stately flower spikes need a dark background to set them off. The back of a sunny border is where they are usually planted and because of their stature should be given largish companions. Herbaceous plants such as *Crambe cordifolia* would be fine in summer but an evergreen shrub such as a phormium or yucca would be better, as then the hole left in winter would be less evident. Another important consideration would also be that of colour. The purple *Phormium tenax purpureum*, for example, would make an excellent companion for the largest eremurus, *E. robustus*, with its 3 m (10 ft) high ivory spikes.

Eucomis is another group of dramatic bulbous plants but except in mild regions with good sunshine I consider it to be far more suitable for pot culture (see pages 323–326) as the plants benefit from the extra soil warmth supplied this way.

## Some like it hot

There are a few rather tender but interesting large-leaved plants which I would like to include here, because although they share a love of warmth with the species on pages 307–321, they also require drier conditions than the lush, jungly habitat discussed later.

Heat is something which is certainly appreciated by that most extraordinary and exotic-looking of plants, *Beschorneria yuccoides*, looking more like some rain forest bromeliad than a member of the *Amaryllis* family, which it is. This likes to be thoroughly baked and the best way to achieve this is to plant it in a sunny rockery, in paving or in a pot. It is such a dramatic plant when in flower with its 2.5 m (8 ft) arching flower spikes of coral pink bracts and green bells, that it is difficult to mix with other subjects but perhaps the giant mauve-flowered *Echium pinniana* would hold its own here.

The yuccas certainly seem very tolerant of drought. It is said that this is the best way to get both yuccas and phormiums to flower, but I think myself it is more a question of warmth. I also find yuccas most unattractive when not in flower and this is the first thing to remember when considering companions for them. I have found white variegated or white-flowered shrubs the most suitable candidates here; they both detract from the dullness of the foliage of the yucca, and enhance it when in flower. Liking the same conditions of full sun and good drainage, *Crambe cordifolia* would suit, but in an ordinary sunny border with more moisture the white variegated shrubs *Cornus sibirica* 'Variegata' or *Cornus alba* 'Elegantissima' would be better. They could then be combined with such perennials as arum lilies (*Zantedeschia* spp.) and white variegated hostas. Once sufficient white has been provided, warmth could be added to the scheme in the form of pink and purple.

*Cautleya spicata*, though hardy, is quite exotic-looking, with its deep yellow and maroon bracts and ginger-like foliage. It will grow in sun or dappled shade, and the latter will suit one of the lovelier companions for it. *Lilium canadense* is a very elegant lily with golden yellow trumpets whose mouths have maroon spots. Of similar colouring but with the turk's cap shape is another lily, one of the Bellingham hybrids called 'Shuksan'.

# The invaders

The giant hogweed, *Heracleum mantegazzianum*, would be best confined to an island in the middle of a large pond or lake, but if you have some rough wood-land then this stately plant with its huge umbrellas of tiny white flowers and enormous cut leaves will soon colonize it. Of lower stature but equally invasive, *Petasites japonicus giganteus* is the ideal ground cover plant for a large area of heavy wet clay in shade. The huge kidney-shaped leaves 1 m (3 ft) across collapse in sun even in boggy soil. Again rough woodland, especially if there is a stream or river, will have its banks covered in the wink of an eye if this is planted on them, any weeds in its path will be smothered.

While on the subject of invasive plants it would be amiss of me not to include here the giant knotweeds. The largest of them, *Polygonum sachalinense*, is not decorative enough for the garden proper but again for rough ground will make a fine show, growing to around the 3.5 m (12 ft) mark. Far lovelier is the smaller cream and butter-yellow variegated *Polygonum cuspidatum* 'Spectabile' at 2–3 m (6–9 ft). But beware, for although the original plant will not seem to spread that rapidly it has the unfortunate habit of sending out long runners which can pop up quite a way from the main clump. Despite this, this plant's beauty, especially in spring when its canes are reddish pink, make it rather desirable. One method of controlling its spread is that used for bamboos, whereby a length of old conveyor belt about 1 m (3 ft) wide is buried around it. The coloration of this knot-weed deems it suitable as a companion to a grouping of yellow-leaved or variegated plants (see page 285), but its size dictates that they should be large enough to hold their own with it. Perhaps *Inula magnifica* or the similarly looking but smaller *Buphthalmum speciosum* which would make a nice footnote.

# Variations on a theme

Although I mentioned some of the rodgersias earlier these noble plants deserve wider mention. Because of their variety of leaf form and colour, they contrast well not just with other plants but with each other. For example, *Rodgersia tabularis* (syn. *Astilboides tabularis*) with its round pale green leaves could be planted successfully either with *Rodgersia podophylla* with star-shaped bronzy leaves, or with ferns or astilbes. In turn *R. podophylla*, or for that matter *R. pinnata* 'Superba', would fit in well with ferns or astilbes. Near water these species would combine happily with bog primulas and others, but more of that in the next chapter. *Rodgersia sambucifolia* is not often seen, but is an attractive and individual plant, different in appearance from the other rodgersias in that the pinnate segments are arranged in a half rather

293

than full circle. Given the space, it would be satisfying to grow all these plants, but we could change the partnerships in different areas of the garden.

The ligularias, although not possessing such varied leaf shapes, do have flower spikes of different forms. The dramatic 3 m (10 ft) yellow spires of *Ligularia wilsoniana* with its big green, heavily veined leaves are a real feature of the landscape and even if planted not far from, for example, *Ligularia dentata* 'Desdemona' would not be repetitive as this has candelabra spikes of orange flowers and smooth dark green leaves with purple stems and undersides.

The almost endless variety of size, shape and leaf colour available in the hosta family means that they have a book of their own in this series. I would only suggest a few examples here, with a note that the colour of their leaves should be the prime consideration when choosing companions for them.

The much sought-after *Hosta sieboldiana* 'Frances Williams' with its glaucous grey leaves with greeny gold margins make it a little easier to place than the plain glaucous green kinds; it deserves an important spot as it remains in pristine condition well into the autumn. The bronze-leaved *Rodgersia pinnata* 'Superba' would be a beautiful companion to it, as it is to any of the blue-leaved hostas. These blue-leaved varieties are complemented by a substantial clump of *Heuchera* 'Palace Purple' or even a perimeter of *Ajuga reptans* 'Purpurea' with its little bright blue flowers.

The suggestions I have made for companion planting may seem at first glance a little restrictive, especially in terms of colour, but once the different groupings are brought together the possibilities will be more evident. You may follow them to the letter, but the fun is to experiment until a satisfying result is obtained.

I have so far recommended companions or groupings with which my main aim has been to achieve variety of form and harmony of colour. These plant groups and associations will in themselves be more attractive if installed into a garden with a good framework or bones.

# Planting ideas

Herbaceous plants are largely deciduous and so it is essential to incorporate evergreens to avoid undue bareness in winter. Small conifers are often used but are really only suitable where heathers and alpine plants are concerned. The larger growing forms are useful for screening or dividing areas. For our purpose, however, evergreen shrubs are more suitable.

The best method when dealing with beds or borders is to divide them into compartments and shrubs are the best subjects for this. It is not essential that they are all evergreen but the more that are the more attractive the winter picture will be. These shrubs will largely act as a framework to a grouping, and those with coloured foliage – yellow and purple for example – can be incorporated into the groups themselves as previously suggested. Even hedging shrubs such as laurel and elaeagnus can be used but allowed to grow naturally and only pruned with secateurs to keep them in check. If more colour is desirable or if there is not sufficient space to include shrubs in the groupings themselves, the shrubs appropriate to the groupings of herbaceous plants can be used as a background or as dividers instead. For example use a pink camellia for a pink or pink, purple and white group, a *Choisya ternata* for a white or white and cream group, or a yellow rhododendron for a yellow or yellow and white group. If there is insufficient space for shrubs as a backcloth,

**Acanthus mollis 'Latifolius'. The flowers surprise the uninitiated by being hard and prickly.**

walls or fences can be covered with suitable climbers.

One thing to bare in mind at this stage is that some of the perennials will benefit from light shade and where possible one or two trees should be included. The choice and size of subjects will be dictated by the size of your garden, but division or compartmenting with shrubs informally this way is far more attractive than a continuous run of purely herbaceous material. Another but less obvious advantage is the protection from wind that is given by the shrubs.

Remember that some of the herbaceous perennials die back earlier in the season than others and so should be situated such that they do not leave too obvious a gap. Such plants as rheums or eremurus are usually best placed more to the back of the border.

To a certain extent this bareness can also be avoided by using ground cover plants, which can also give a nice finish to the front of a bed or border. In winter plants like hellebores are especially good as even when their flowers have finished their foliage remains attractive. In spring bulbs can be used between the shrubs or perennials as they will have more or less finished and died back by the time the perennials have developed.

## Positioning of herbaceous plants in the border

It is standard practice with beds and borders (even island beds) to place the shortest plants in front and grade up to the tallest at the back. This can sometimes look a trifle monotonous, understandably one does not want to hide any plants from view, but this need not be the case if the right kind of taller plants are placed in more forward positions: plants with 'see through' type foliage which may be feathery or ferny such as fennel and even the taller grasses. Remember also that some plants, although tall in flower, sometimes have a low-growing basal clumps of leaves. By occasionally using taller subjects this way we relieve the regularity.

It is also important to be able to use large subjects sometimes near the front of borders to emphasize their shape, and where hard landscaping is concerned to be able to use their foliage to soften any hard lines by breaking them up. Where beds or borders are fronted by grass, large subjects should be far enough back that their leaves do not flop over the edge and become a nuisance when the lawn is mown. Where borders meet gravel or paving this does not matter; in fact where gravel is concerned a few plants over-spilling on to it gives a very attractive and natural effect.

## Arranging perennials

One of the advantages of perennials is that they can be moved at almost any time of the year, unlike trees and shrubs which can only be moved in the dormant season. Providing they are well watered before being dup up, and lifted with a reasonable amount of soil and replanted immediately they should not suffer. It is wise however to avoid moving them on hot sunny days, when many plants are apt to wilt in the heat, or when they are at vigorous stages of growth and their leaves expanding.

This enables us to rearrange them should we wish to experiment with new associations, an advantage so far as time is concerned. A garden is never *finished* in the true sense as most of us are continually making changes even if they are only subtle ones. We may discover new plants or tire of old ones. Change is desirable as our interest and enthusiasm is thereby retained. Even the greatest plants people of our time have worked this way and spent many years achieving a personally satisfying result. The suggestions I have given should be considered as basic guidelines and further inspiration should be sought by visiting some of the great gardens and plant collections around the country. This and reading are the best ways of self educating, the greatest benefits of which are the reduction in mistakes and so a saving of time.

When visiting gardens make notes of plant associations or groupings which particularly please you, it is very easy to forget such things especially when plants can have such long and difficult names. If you take photographs remember to note down the names of the plants you have snapped; there will not always be someone who can identify them for you.

# Planning your garden

I have already stressed the value of such things as water in the relevant chapters, but I feel it important to give mention especially for the garden novices amongst you, as to some practical points when considering the design or general layout of gardens, which if nothing else will save time and error. As I have already mentioned trees and shrubs are not as easily moved as herbaceous plants especially when they are well established. Therefore careful consideration should be given before planting these things which will form the framework or 'bones' of the garden.

The best method is to do a scale drawing as the size and shape of a garden can be very deceptive when you are in it. Note the direction your garden faces. This will affect the amount of sun and shade you will have and will influence the number of trees (if any) you may choose or require, remember many plants benefit from partial shade.

You should also at this stage consider your boundaries as they should be thought of as part of the framework. Hedges are the most attractive form of boundary but take several years to establish, especially if they are required to be a reasonable height to give wind protection. Gardens vary tremendously so far as shelter is concerned and exposed gardens should have the shelter established before serious planting is undertaken.

The next decision is the layout of your paths, beds and borders, water features and so on, after which you are then (and not before) at the stage to consider your planting plans.

The simplest method is to think of the plants as consisting of four layers as follows: 1 – trees. 2 – Shrubs. 3 – Herbaceous plants. 4 – Ground cover, and they should really be planted in that order.

If your garden is not on a level site this can be an advantage as further interest can be created by accentuating the different levels with steps, and the lower levels or hollows which are usually the dampest used for the more moisture loving plants or as a natural looking situation for a pond.

Whatever the size and shape of your garden it will be far more interesting if it is planted in such a way that it cannot *all* be seen at a single glance. This is easily achieved by winding paths and strategically placing large shrubs for example to mask your view and thereby arouse interest and curiosity so that new or different vistas appear one by one.

It is worth some time and effort in carefully planning all these things as the final result will be vastly more satisfactory than a mere jumble of plants. Individual plants may be very beautiful in themselves but it is the context in which they are used (i.e. their companions and siting etc) within the whole which can display them to best effect and whereby their full beauty can be appreciated.

# Large-Leaved Perennials and Water

Water, more than any other element, adds life, interest and beauty to the garden. The sound as well as the sight of it, especially on a warm summer's day, is both peaceful and relaxing.

Some of the most attractive features to be found in gardens are those assocated with water. It is such a versatile element, in formal use as a fountain or trickle from a statue, to informal natural features – a dramatic waterfall or cascade, a bubbling stream or a 'secret' silent pool. In whichever of these forms it appears it should always form the focal point of the garden and as such there should be somewhere close by where you can sit and enjoy it.

Water is of particular importance where large-leaved perennials are concerned as so many of them require the conditions it creates to sustain them and enable them to grow to their full glory and perfection. It is also beside water that their full beauty can be appreciated as it is such a natural setting for them. A variety of plants with large foliage planted on the margins of water give a lush, luxuriant feel and the reflections they cast in the water add further beauty and enhancement.

## Water features

I will always remember the very first time I saw the Great Waterfall at Chatsworth House. At the foot of the fall on either side are two great clumps of gunnera which receive the spray from it. Waterfalls and cascades are the most beautiful and spectacular of water features, whether natural or man-made, and with the addition of lush and luxuriant planting around them can be breathtaking. Vegetation is naturally rich around them because of the moisture and humidity that is created. A crashing waterfall may not be to everyone's taste but a silent pool can be just as beautiful.

One of the best examples of water gardens that I have seen is Longstock Park, in southern England. It is a large flat piece of land, dissected by a series of lagoons and channels crossed by plank bridges. The banks and margins of the water are richly planted with a wide range of foliage and flowering plants – one tiny lagoon is fringed entirely with hostas. The plantings are broken by the turf paths which occasionally come to the water's edge. It is important whether you have a lake, pond, river or stream that you can reach the water in this way, as then you can fully appreciate at close quarters the beauty of the plants on the margins.

Whatever the size of your garden ideas such as these can be used from such places. You do not have to possess a lake in order to grow a gunnera, but where space is limited, an alternative would be the umbrella plant, *Peltiphyllum peltatum*, or perhaps a rheum.

Whether by an informal pond or stream, or a formal terrace pool or swimming pool, large-leaved

**A bold clump of *Gunnera manicata* backed here by a magnificent red Japanese maple lit by the sun.**

perennials can be used to good effect. On a formal terrace, large pots on the paving with plants with bold shapes like acanthus or ligularias and hostas would do much to enhance and relieve the flatness of the area. In the pool itself pots or baskets of water dock (*Rumex*) or arum lilies alongside irises and so on would be reflected in the water and break up the straight edges.

Large areas of paving round an outdoor swimming pool should be broken with beds for plants or a collection of pots, the number depending on the dimensions of the area. Here, I feel, a slightly more exotic feel would be appropriate and more exciting, and a combination of large-leaved perennials and hardy but tropical-looking plants like palms, bamboos and phormiums would certainly achieve this (see pages 307–321).

Just as owners of small gardens should not be deterred from growing large plants, neither should

**Pots or baskets with bold foliage enhance and soften formal ponds by breaking up the hard straight edges.**
**1. Bog iris**
**2. *Zantedeschia aethiopica***
**3. *Senecio smithii***
**4. *Caltha polypetala*.**

they deprive themselves of a water feature. Once you have introduced a water feature into the garden you will never want to be without it. It is so easy these days – with plastic and butyl liners a pond can be installed in a matter of hours, unlike the days when ponds had to be made of concrete or puddled clay and even then were prone to leaks.

## The range of waterside habitats

When water is incorporated into the garden's design it greatly expands the range of plants that can be grown, and these fall into several categories.

There are, first, the plants which actually live in or under the water, such as the water lilies, but as we are dealing here specifically with large-leaved perennials, the only subjects which will apply are those which normally grow in just a little water, and are usually close to the banks – plants like *Senecio smithii*, giant water dock (*Rumex hydrolapathum*) or giant marsh marigold (*Caltha polypetala*). In natural or informal ponds these would be planted out in the shallow water, but in formal ponds could be grown in pots or baskets and would therefore help to mask some of the concrete or stonework.

Next are the bog plants, subjects which do not like their crowns submerged but which must have permanently moist or wet conditions. The British native butterbur, *Petasites hybridus*, and its Japanese equivalent, *P. japonicus giganteus*, are rampant indeed. Less invasive is the umbrella plant, *Peltiphyllum peltatum* which, if planted at the water's edge, will grow both up the bank and down into the water. The arum lily, *Zantedeschia aethiopica*, in its hardiest form 'Crowborough' can also be grown in the water providing it is planted at least 15 cm (6 in) below the surface.

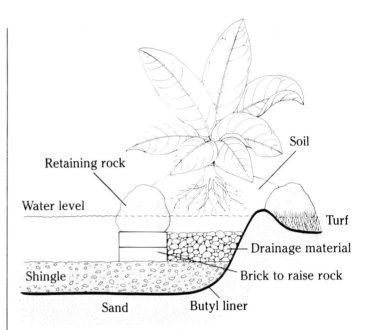

**A section of a marginal bed at a poolside.**

Then there are those most magnificent of waterside plants, the bog arums, *Lysichiton americanum* (yellow), *L. camtschatcensis* (white) and the gunneras, *G. manicata* and *G. scabra* (*G. chilensis*). I must stress here that these plants would be happy in natural boggy conditions where the water flows through the soil, but when a bog area has been artificially created, such as with a butyl liner, it is necessary first to have a layer of drainage material about 15–20 cm (6–8 in) thick of broken brick or gravel and to replace the soil every three to four years as it eventually becomes sour and would rot the roots of even bog plants such as these.

Lysichitons and gunneras can also be planted in our final waterside setting, the damp border, but may not grow quite as luxuriantly as where their roots can reach down to water.

301

The damp border is where ligularia, rodgersia, rheum, filipendula and aruncus will all flourish. Most will also benefit from a little shade to prevent scorching or wilting of the leaves. They can all be planted on the water's edge, and indeed are more attractive there, but they must either be planted in marginal beds or outside the pond liner. Where there is natural water they should be above the flood plain as they will not tolerate either being submerged or having water stagnating around their roots. The ground therefore should be built up before planting where necessary to prevent this happening.

# A flower for every season

Although the large-leaved perennials suitable for association with water are chosen predominantly for the variety of leaf shapes, we should not forget the interest and attraction by way of flowers they also supply.

Early in the spring the floral rosettes of petasites emerge before the leaves; the strange frilled flower heads which sit on the ground are very popular with flower arrangers. A month or so later the lysichitons produce their magnificent yellow or white spathes as the leaves begin to emerge, these are beautiful when reflected in the water. Incidentally, there is a hybrid (as yet unnamed) between *L. americanum* and *L. camtschatcensis*, which has even larger leaves, up to 2 m (6 ft) of a lovely glaucous pale green, and handsome creamy coloured spathes which can be as much as 45 cm (18 in) high. About the same time the umbrella plant, *Peltiphyllum peltatum*, pushes up its little pink flower heads on tall hairy stalks, a rather strange sight, and these are almost over before the leaves begin to appear.

Colourful and decorative in summer are the fluffy flower spikes of the rhubarb-like rheums. Those of the ordinary *Rheum palmatum* are creamy white but those of *R. p.* 'Atrosanguineum' are a lovely cherry red. Both top 2 m (6 ft). The flowers of *Aruncus dioicus* are also creamy white through the summer, but less fluffy and more like an astilbe. Filipendulas have similar but much flatter-topped heads; in *F. camtschatica* they are ivory white, but in *F. palmata* 'Rubra' they are a glistening rosy red.

The flowers of ligularias, which appear later in high summer, are predominantly orange or yellow of varying shades but very variable in form. Those of *L. dentata* 'Desdemona' or *L. dentata* 'Gregynog Gold', for example, are of candelabra form, while those of *L. przewalskii* 'The Rocket', *L. veitchiana* or *L. wilsoniana* are tall spikes, slender in the case of 'The Rocket'.

More daisy-like flowers, but this time large and yellow, are produced by *Inula magnifica* in a candelabra-like spike 2.5 m (8 ft) high above the huge paddle-shaped leaves. The rodgersias again provide more astilbe-like, feathery plumes, ivory in *R. pinnata* 'Elegans' and brilliant pink in *R. pinnata* 'Superba', an effective tone with its bronzy leaves.

In late summer the arum lilies (*Zantedeschia*) always stand out, their white spathes with yellow spadixes backed by their shining dark green leaves. For flower arrangers the variety 'Green Goddess' with its green and white flowers would be a must.

Down almost in the water *Senecio smithii* is a very decorative subject when carrying its yellow-eyed white daisies, and the giant water dock, *Rumex hydrolapathum*, produces its brownish pink flowers in late summer.

**A successful trio of form and colour – the blue-leaved *Hosta tokudama* backed by (LEFT) *Ligularia dentata* 'Desdemona' and red primulas.**

Although not at all colourful the huge flowers spikes or, more descriptively, seed heads, of the gunneras are very architectural and dramatic, and those of *G. scabra* (*G. chilensis*) are retained well into the autumn, making quite a feature on the landscape.

# Effective planting

When planting up a pond or stream side, remember as well as combining other waterside plants, to use large-leaved perennials of both contrasting shape, colour and texture together. The huge paddle-shaped leaves of *Lysichiton americanum*, for example, would be a good contrast of shape and texture with those of *Gunnera manicata* and yet would hold their own. Next to the lysichiton could be *Rodgersia podophylla* which would give a further contrast of form, colour and texture with its star-shaped, crinkly bronze leaves.

To give height again we could then have either *Filipendula palmata* 'Rubra' or *F. camtschatica* (syn. *F. gigantea*), or *Aruncus dioicus* (syn. *A. sylvestris*), whose pale green divided leaves would contrast well with those of *Ligularia dentata* 'Desdemona', which are kidney-shaped, dark green and purple underneath. A drift of arum lilies, *Zantedeschia aethiopica* 'Crowborough', with their white sails would be set off by the purple and finally a carpet of *Primula pulverulenta* with their salmony pink flowers.

The lovely bog primulas come in various colours from white to purple, the bog irises in even greater variety of colour. The astilbes, with their fluffy flower spikes and ferny leaves, contrast well with the perpendicular outline of the iris.

Drifts of one type of plant by the waterside are far more effective and attractive than a jumble of different ones; where space is limited reduce the variety rather than the numbers of each plant. If you study plants in the wild you will see that they adopt these habits naturally. In Africa, for example, arum lilies (*Zantedeschia aethiopica*) colonize the banks of rivers and streams. In Britain the native butterbur (*Petasites hybridus*) does the same. So in a way we are simply copying nature! Obviously something as large as a gunnera could only be massed by a lake, but certainly three rheums could be planted together by a reasonably sized pond. Bold groups of plants like ligularias will need to be planted in numbers to give a massed effect but the individual clumps can, and indeed should, be divided occasionally to increase the size of the patch and also to maintain the health of the plant. Peltiphyllums, on the other hand, will naturally expand to form a colony and therefore can be left alone. Do not forget that hostas or *Inula magnifica*, although usually associated with a border, will do well by the waterside.

One of the greatest advantages of having water in the garden is that it is not only attractive in itself but it increases the beauty of many plants that can be associated with it. The great number and variety of large-leaved perennials that we have to choose from for use in this situation means that we need never tire of what we have or grow short of ideas for new schemes or changes.

**A wide diversity of leaf shape and form by the waterside:**
1. *Lysichiton americanum*
2. *Rodgersia pinnata* 'Superba'
3. *Ligularia dentata* 'Desdemona'
4. *Zantedeschia aethiopica*
5. *Peltiphyllum peltatum*
6. *Gunnera manicata*
7. *Aruncus sylvestris* (*dioicus*)
8. Bamboo.

# The Tropical Touch

It is large leaves above all that convey that air of tropical lushness that we usually associate with warmer climes. When thinking of somewhere as exotic the West Indies, we may be forgiven for first visualizing the dazzling colours of such exotic blooms as hibiscus and orchids, but it is also the leafy lushness of these places, the bananas, gingers and palms, which completes the picture – together, of course, with the wonderful sand, sea and sunshine.

We cannot reproduce the climate, except under glass, but you may be surprised how exotic a picture can be painted, even in an uncertain and relatively cool climate. Believe it or not, it is possible to create the kind of scene where, on a hot summer's day, you may be seen sitting in the shade of the banana or palm tree with the flower of a hibiscus in your hair (or on your hat), dangling your toe in a pool to be tickled by the root of the water hyacinth, while the bamboo rustles in the gentle breeze which carries the intoxicating scent of the datura!

Exotic-looking plants seem to have the effect of making it seem warmer than it really is. Another of their great qualities is that they prolong the period of interest. Come late summer, and the traditional bedding plants are beginning to look jaded, dry and frazzled, the exotics are at the peak of their perfection, still fresh and making vigorous growth, which in most cases continues until the frosts. I use the term 'exotic' here loosely, for I am speaking of plants that are merely exotic in appearance not necessarily in origin.

*Rodgersia pinnata* **making a strong contrast to the lovely golden grass** *Hakonechloa macra variegata.*

## The nineteenth-century innovators

With the introduction of lots of newly discovered plants, the fashion of so called sub-tropical gardening arose, involving the planting out in summer of many exotic plants kept under glass in winter. A great industry arose to satisfy the demand both for plants and conservatories, or Winter Gardens as they were called. Mistakes were made by people at the time due to lack of knowledge and experience of the plants, but we have of course since learnt and in the following pages I shall only recommend plants that are either hardy (though exotic looking), or in a few cases frost tender but which still thrive making vigorous growth outdoors in summer. An exotic looking garden can be created without the tender subjects, but if you have a frost-free conservatory or greenhouse and can accommodate them they will do much to enhance your garden.

For anyone looking for a change who is thoroughly bored by traditional forms of gardening with the usual herbaceous and shrub borders, roses and clematis scrambling over pergolas, potted geraniums and hanging baskets of petunias, then the sub-tropical look is for you. Say goodbye to the days of backbreaking trudgery, hours of weeding, staking, pruning, dead-heading and planting of countless annuals. Dust the deck chair and prepare it for the summer, for it will be thoroughly used – weather permitting – in an 'exotic' garden. The plants may be unusual, but they are easy to grow, and a garden of this type requires far less maintenance than a traditional one.

# The foundations

Generally, because the large-leaved perennials only occupy the lower planting levels, it is necessary to add structure, in this case not just trees or shrubs but palms, bamboos, bananas etc. – a stark contrast to a traditional garden. But first it is important to create the kind of setting in which such exotics will thrive and which suits them aesthetically. Shelter is paramount, as large leaves of any kind become tattered when battered by wind and their beauty destroyed.

In large gardens, tall, preferably evergreen hedges should be grown; in small ones, walls or fences can be topped with trellis covered with fine plastic mesh or evergreen climbers such as ivy.

The second consideration is water. A joy in any garden, it is, I feel, an essential feature in a sub-tropical setting, even if only a small pond or stream with the water splashing over rocks or cobbles. Remember, when deciding where the water will be, that it should be a focal point of the garden and as such there should be somewhere close by for you to sit and enjoy it.

Next come the hard structural elements: paths and paved areas. Never lead a path straight to an area of interest, but curve and twist it, diverting it with large shrubs or clumps of bamboo so that interest and curiosity is aroused. Even in small gardens mystery can be achieved this way. A point of good garden design is that you should never be able to take in or view a whole area at once, but that it should be revealed little by little.

A patio does not have to be the usual paving of stone slabs or bricks. Why not have wooden decking? It is far more comfortable to walk on and very much in keeping with this type of planting. It is also easy to maintain and no more expensive than, say, York stone or old stock bricks. It can be used in a totally informal setting such as by a lake or in a formal area around a swimming pool. Remember, however, to take into account the style or period of the house it would be connected with. These same rules would apply when choosing a conservatory.

Your outdoor furniture should, of course, first and foremost be comfortable. Style is very personal, but furniture of a contemporary or 'Colonial' design is probably more appropriate for this kind of garden and white, although less practical, does add a tropical note.

White is often associated with hot countries, especially for walls and buildings, where it is used to reflect the sun's heat. Certainly it would be appropriate to have white walls around a patio area or swimming pool. Exotic-looking plants in large tubs or terracotta pots would stand out well against the white walls (see also pages 323–326).

There are lots of natural construction materials available now which should be used more often. There are, for example, some lovely white and coloured Italian cobbles to be had which could be used in or out of water. Beds of plants, especially those of an exotic nature, look very attractive when covered with cobbles, when adjoining patio areas or swimming pools. They give a clean modern look ideal for contemporary settings and complement both paving and wooden decking. They are often used, along with gravel, in oriental designs.

Gravel comes in a number of varieties and is probably the best material to use for covering the

**A Mediterranean feel can be created at the poolside with hardy exotics and large-leaved perennials:**
1. Bamboo – *Phyllostachys aurea*
2. Palm – *Trachycarpus fortunei*
3. *Hosta sieboldiana elegans*
4. *Phormium tenax* 'Variegatum'
5. *Ligularia dentata* 'Desdemona'.

309

bottom of artificial ponds, extending out of the water to form a beach – sand is attractive and comfortable but, I think, impractical in view of the wind, even in sheltered spots.

Several different kinds of rock are available and large smooth boulders can be very decorative.

Other items, such as barbecues, will be added attractions, but I should like to mention one latest innovation: the 'hot tub', surely appropriate here in terms of both the plants and the climate.

In view of the plumbing and convenience in reaching it, it should be situated relatively close to the house. It could for example be installed in an area of wooden decking where it could be easily reached and the lush tropical setting appreciated from the warm water. Hot tubs, though expensive to buy and install are thereafter reasonable to run and maintain. One of their greatest assets is that they can be used all year round, and they are terrific fun for families with children. They originated from the United States where they are very popular.

# Creating the exotic look

### TEMPERATE TREES WITH A TROPICAL LOOK

The trees and shrubs described below are perfect companions to large-leaved perennials. When planted with them they make even familiar things such as hostas look more unusual. Large-leaved perennials are in themselves a trifle exotic, but when mixed with such things as palms and bamboos their lushness is accentuated, and they take on a totally new look.

***Rodgersia tabularis** (**Astilboides tabularis**) is a plant of great beauty and grace; at the peak of perfection it requires careful culture.*

It seems only natural to begin with the largest things, as these are normally the 'bones' of the garden and as such their position needs careful consideration.

There are few trees of an exotic nature, but as space in most gardens normally only permits a few, this is of little consequence. They all have large leaves which gives them an exotic or sub-tropical look and are mentioned in order of merit.

The Indian horse chestnut, *Aesculus indica*, is a medium-sized tree to about 10 m (30 ft) possessing smooth dark green seven-lobed leaves (those of the common kinds are much coarser). It produces large panicles of pink flowers in late summer. The Japanese poplar, *Populus lasiocarpa*, has 30 cm (1 ft) long heart-shaped leaves with red veins and stalks and is of rather open habit and is also of medium height. The familiar tree of Heaven, *Ailanthus altissima*, with its pinnate leaves would be too big for most gardens, but if pollarded each winter (i.e. cut to within 15 cm (6 in) of the ground), can be accommodated more easily and will produce larger leaves if treated this way (up to 90 cm (3 ft) long).

The same treatment should be given to the foxglove tree, *Paulownia imperialis* (syn. *P. tomentosa*), which is a fine contrast, having almost unlobed leaves 60 cm (2 ft) or more across (if pollarded). It must, however, have full sun and shelter from strong wind.

The eucalyptuses are valuable for being evergreen. One of the best is *E. niphophila*, the snow gum, with broad sickle-shaped leaves and trunk marbled cream, grey and green. A fast-growing, tall but light tree to approximately 20 m (60 ft).

The Chilean fire tree, *Embothrium coccineum*, will be more of a large shrub for most of us, and is dazzling when clothed with its orange-red flowers in early summer. It is evergreen and somewhat tender, though the variety *E. c. lanceolatum* 'Norquinco Valley' is said to be hardier.

311

## PALMS AND BAMBOOS

The first of our truly exotic subjects is the Chusan or windmill palm, *Trachycarpus fortunei*. Though slow growing it will eventually reach some 6 m (20 ft) or more, and is one of the largest of exotic-looking trees that can be grown in a cool climate. Sometimes it is to be seen in ordinary plantings, where it looks quite out of place, but with equally foreign-looking subjects such as bamboos and phormiums, it is in perfect keeping. Happy in sun or dappled shade, the large fan-like segmented leaves 90 cm (3 ft) across are very distinctive and handsome, suiting both informal and formal situations, such as paved areas or alongside swimming pools along with other architectural plants. It can also be grown in a large pot, though this will slow its rate of growth as it likes to be kept permanently moist at the roots. Although hardy, it should be positioned out of strong winds which will otherwise dishevel its appearance; it is worthwhile going to some trouble to keep a Chusan palm in good fetter as it is undoubtedly one of the best for producing an exotic effect outside a tropical climate. Although expensive to procure, it is well worth the expenditure in view of the charm added to a planting. There *are* a few other palms which have proved to be reasonably hardy, but they do not have the rate of growth of the Chusan palm, and would therefore take even longer to attain a reasonable size.

Next in importance for effect after the Chusan palm I would place the bamboos. Despite their exotic appearance the majority of the kinds available are quite hardy, originating from eastern Asia and Japan. Their graceful character and beauty, especially when planted by water makes them indispensable. Because of their upright habit and grass-like appearance they are also a lovely contrast to the more solid or horizontal forms of other plants. They vary mainly in the size of the leaf and the colour of their canes and their height can be from as little as 60 cm (2 ft) to 7 m (20 ft) or so. Many grow much taller in their native habitat.

One of the smallest but most colourful is *Arundinaria viridistriata*, growing only 60–90 cm (2–3 ft), its leaves are striped lemon yellow. It should be cut to ground level at the end of each winter to produce the best growth the following season.

For small gardens or containers *Arundinaria murielae* and *A. nitida* at about 2–3 m (6–10 ft) are similar to each other and easy to grow.

*Sasa palmata* 'Nebulosa', though only 2 m (6 ft) high is distinct in having much larger leaves than most bamboos at 30–40 cm (12–16 in) long. It is, however, rather invasive and best confined to containers in smaller gardens.

The taller kinds, growing up to 6 m (20 ft) or so, more in warmer countries, usually belong to the *Phyllostachys* group. *P. mitis*, *P. aurea* and *P. nigra* are the ones usually available. The first two are similar of yellowish green coloration, but *P. nigra* has jet black canes making it more desirable and decorative. These big bamboos need shelter from strong winds to do their best.

## PHORMIUMS AND CORDYLINES

Of the New Zealand flax, *Phormium tenax*, the plain green form is the hardiest. The stiff fans of sword-like leaves 2 m (6 ft) high are overtopped several feet by the architectural if not very colourful flower spikes in good summers. The creamy yellow variegated *P. t.* 'Variegatum', and the purple *P. t. purpureum* of the same proportions are a little less hardy. The smaller *P. cookianum* forms variously coloured pink purple cream and green with more lax foliage are even more tender and are probably only suitable for containers which can be wintered under glass. All phormiums like full sun.

The cordylines or inappropriately named 'cabbage' palms, like the phormiums are valuable for the additional variety of form they introduce into this type of garden.

The hardiest, C. australis, has a fountain of narrow leaves about 1 m (3 ft) across which eventually rises on a tall trunk. The very handsome smaller dark purple leaved C. a. atropurpurea is sadly too tender for an outdoor life but makes a super container plant for the conservatory.

## DECORATIVE SHRUBS

Aralia cachemirica, being completely deciduous, is classed as a perennial and included in the Plant Directory (see page 329), but A. elata produces tall woody spiny stems clothed with whorls of huge pinnate leaves about 70 cm (2½ ft) long, giving a lush appearance especially when planted in groups. There are white and yellow variegated forms, A. e. 'Variegata' and A. e. 'Aureovariegata' respectively. They are both slower growing and expensive to procure. Aralias like dappled shade. Fatsia japonica, often incorrectly called the castor-oil plant, is very handsome with its big lobed shiny evergreen leaves. Often sold as a house plant it is much happier in a shady spot.

Less familiar is the loquat, Eriobotrya japonica, which has long crinkly serrated evergreen leaves. It can be grown free standing or as a wall shrub. In hot summers it will produce small orange fruits which are an acquired taste.

Most of you will have seen Magnolia grandiflora with its almost rubber tree-like dark green shiny evergreen leaves, but rarely seen and more beautiful and refined is the evergreen Magnolia delavayi which has larger grey-green leaves. Two attractive but deciduous magnolias, even rarer, are M. tripetala and M. macrophylla, the largest leaved of all magnolias with thin papery leaves to 60 cm (2 ft) long.

For shade are two sumptuous and exotic-looking hydrangeas, H. aspera and H. sargentiana. Both are similar in that they have velvety leaves and mauve and white lace-cap flowers. H. aspera is probably the best as it is bushier, (H. sargentiana is inclined to become leggy) and of darker coloration.

Other more familiar shrubs such as camellias, pieris and mahonia are all evergreen and associate well with tropical-looking plants.

## EXOTIC CLIMBERS

Clematis armandii should be grown more often. Though less showy than some in flower, its large dark green shiny sickle-shaped evergreen leaves deserve space in any garden. Similar but smaller in leaf is the exotic Lapageria rosea with large waxy rosy-red bells unfortunately far too tender except for the mildest gardens.

Almost as exotic looking but hardy is Campsis tagliabuana 'Madame Galen' with ferny foliage and large, orangey-red trumpet flowers.

## TENDER PLANTS

Some of the tender plants I have selected are perennials, but all have large and handsome leaves, and although an exotic-looking garden can be achieved without them, their inclusion will add great beauty and interest with little extra trouble, especially for those who possess a conservatory or greenhouse. These plants will need to be moved under glass from about mid autumn until late spring, and kept frost-free at about 7°–10°C (45°–50°F).

We all have our favourites and mine, since I first discovered it, has been the great Abyssinian banana, Ensete ventricosum (Musa ensete). Its leaves are huge, beating even the great gunnera for area of leaf. It has to be grown from seed as it does not produce offsets like other bananas, but once germinated these will

313

grow into 1 m (3 ft) plants in six months. Of a much stockier build than most bananas, its thick leaves with their striking red midrib are much less prone to laceration by the wind. It is a very fast grower – in 18 months it will reach 3 m (10 ft) in height if regularly potted on and well fed and watered. By then it will have leaves about 2 m (6 ft) long and 45 cm (18 in) wide. Ultimately it will reach 6 m (20 ft) in height with leaves 4.5 m (14 ft) long by 75 cm (2½ ft) wide, but it would have to be planted out to achieve this. It would then be necessary before the first frost to cut off its leaves, wrap the trunk generously in straw and cover it with sheets of corrugated iron to keep it dry. Alternatively, of course, when it became too big to move indoors, one could easily replace it with a smaller specimen, which, after all, would only cost the price of a packet of seed. This may all seem a great deal of trouble, but the visual effect of such a plant is staggering, and visitors will rub their eyes in astonishment.

There is one other so-called hardy banana, *Musa basjoo*, the Japanese banana. This can be grown permanently out of doors in sheltered or town gardens in mild areas, though I recommend wrapping its trunk in bracken in case of a severe winter, but even when cut down by frost it will usually shoot again from the ground. Although a tall-growing kind it is very slender, with the more usual papery leaves which tear very easily. Its comparative hardiness is to be commended, and it would be a good candidate for a sheltered spot.

Of similar appearance, leaf-wise, to the bananas but of smaller stature are the cannas. Their foliage reaches the 2 m (6 ft) mark while their flowers add another 45 cm (18 in) or so. One of the most beautiful is *Canna* × *generalis* 'Wyoming', valued on account of its dark purple leaves. The flowers of apricot orange, reminiscent of a gladiolus, are a trifle garish for my taste, but the foliage is a stunning contrast to the glaucous grey serrated, divided leaves of *Melianthus*

*major*. This combination of foliage is probably one of the choicest that can be made, and would be a high spot in any exotic-style garden. Another equally desirable canna, a little taller at 3 m (10 ft), is *C. iridiflora ehrmanii*. This has huge banana-like leaves 1 m (3 ft) long (green this time) and elegant drooping spikes of rose-coloured flowers. A beautiful companion for this would be *Ricinus communis* 'Gibsonii', a purple-leaved form of the true castor-oil plant. This is an annual which has to be raised from seed sown in the greenhouse in late winter and planted out in late spring.

Most cannas have to be treated rather like dahlias, the tubers lifted in late autumn and dried off in a frost-proof place. They then need to be potted up in early spring and given a little heat, about 15°C (60°F) in the greenhouse to start them into growth to be planted out after the last frosts. *Canna iridiflora ehrmanii*, however, when lifted, should simply be potted up in fresh soil and kept with the other cannas to be planted out with them the following spring.

For sheer exotica, even the cannas are beaten by the daturas. These fast-growing shrubs with their soft downy leaves are an absolute show-stopper when hung with their huge trumpet-shaped blooms. The one usually seen is *Datura cornigera*, which has semi-double white flowers 20 cm (8 in) long with (especially at night) an intoxicating scent. There are other varieties to be had, in shades of cream, pink and orange. All are easy to grow providing they are fed and watered regularly; they strike easily from cuttings and usually flower in their first year. Always keep them in their containers, re-potting or top-dressing annually and keep cool but frost-free, 7–10°C (45–50°F), in winter. Hard prune in early spring to

**Cana × generalis 'Wyoming', a tender perennial, valued for its dark purple leaves.**

ensure good flowering the following season. Daturas make lovely patio subjects, but if put in the garden proper their pots should be sunk in the ground. They prefer light shade to full sun, which tends to wilt the foliage.

The gingers are another group of exotic flowered plants. The herbaceous foliage consists of canes to about 2 m (6 ft) with opposite rows of long fleshy leaves, which are topped with spikes of almost orchid-like blooms. The most beautiful is *Hedychium gardnerianum*, which has yellow petals with orange stamens in a 20 cm (8 in) long spike. This can only be planted out permanently in very mild areas, where it will be deciduous; otherwise it should be kept in a tub and moved to the conservatory or greenhouse for the winter. There are other similar varieties, such as *H. coccineum* 'Tara', which is hardier, but the hardiest of all is *H. forrestii*. Although deciduous, this is probably the tallest-growing kind, producing 2.5 m (8 ft) canes topped with 15 cm (6 in) spikes of flowers with white petals and orange stamens. When it dies down in the autumn its roots should be covered with a thick mulch.

Although there are some hardy forms of hibiscus, they are by no means as flamboyant and exotic looking as the tropical ones. There is, however, one exception: *Hibiscus moscheutos*. Unlike the tropical kinds, which are evergreen, this is deciduous, in fact, really herbaceous, the stems dying back to the ground each winter. The flowers, which are 15 cm (6 in) across, are spectacular, and come in either red, pink or white according to variety. My favourite, the red form, is 'Southern Belle'. These can be planted out permanently in a sunny position preferably against a wall, but must be given a thick mulch in winter. Their only drawback is that they are late to flower, usually not until the end of the summer, but they are surely a must on account of their very exotic appearance.

A true shrub is *Tibouchina urvilliana* (syn. *T. semidecandra*). The angular stems are clothed with 8 cm (3 in) ovate leaves which are covered in fine white pubescent hairs. The flowers, which are like those of an African violet, are an almost electric blue, 5 cm (2 in) across and freely produced later in the summer. It requires to be kept in the conservatory or greenhouse in winter and when put out for summer should be placed in dappled shade.

Returning to foliage now, the very beautiful lobed leaves of the rice paper plant, *Tetrapanax papyriferus* are 60 cm (2 ft) across, rather the shape of *Fatsia japonica*, and are covered in a fine white down. It can be left out all year but will be deciduous, so it would be better to overwinter it under glass so that it will add instant beauty when put out in late spring. Light shade is preferable, though it will tolerate full sun, but the leaves will be smaller. It it gets too leggy it can be cut down and will shoot from base or below ground.

The tree ferns always attract attention and admiration, the hardiest of which is *Dicksonia antarctica*. A large specimen, which can be 3 m (10 ft) across, is breathtaking. Even small specimens are difficult and expensive to acquire but well worth the effort. They like a shady spot and must be kept moist at all times. The big crown of fronds begins at ground level and gradually forms (after several years) a trunk, hence its name. They are too precious to risk losing by leaving

**A bed in a paved area within a walled garden can be planted up with bold leaved perennials and other architectural plants, for a clean, modern and Mediterranean look.**
1. Palm (*Trachycarpus fortunei*)
2. *Acanthus mollis* 'Latifolius'
3. *Ligularia dentata* 'Desdemona'
4. *Phormium tenax* 'Variegatum'.
5. Fig (*Ficus carica*)

out all winter, and should be grown in tubs so that they can be moved indoors at the approach of frost.

My last subject is a very beautiful variegated reed, *Arundo donax* 'Variegata' – along with *Aralia elata* 'Variegata', I consider it to be the most beautiful of all white variegated plants. The striped canes reach about 2 m (6 ft) and are clothed with drooping leaves 30 cm (1 ft) long which have a broad white margin. They eventually become tatty lower down and should be cut down each or every other winter to encourage new shoots. Although it grows quite well permanently out of doors in mild areas it is far better to grow it in a tub and take it in during the winter. A position in full sun and free-draining soil is best.

## Planting for harmony and effect

All the large-leaved perennials I have listed will take on a more exotic and unusual character when mixed and planted with the trees, shrubs and climbers described in this chapter. Wherever space permits, they should be planted in bold groups of a minimum of three or five for proper impact. Herbaceous plants, even large-leaved ones, should never be dotted about. Large clumps or groups convey the beauty and character of the plant far more fully, and it is better to have a smaller number of varieties where space is limited, than to reduce too much the size of the individual clumps. They will appear scaled-down anyway in some instances, especially when used as companions to large subjects such as palms and bamboos and even phormiums.

**Ligularia dentata 'Desdemona' will, as here, produce purplish tints on top of its leaves if grown in the sun. In the shade they will be greener but bigger.**

319

The number of options open when selecting plants for grouping together is immense, and so the suggestions I make here do not have to be firmly adhered to by any means: they are simply combinations which I know from experience work well. Remember, too, when planning a grouping that it is not just simply which plant looks good with another, but whether they are happy with the same types of conditions – sun, shade, moisture etc.

## PLANTING WITH PALMS

The Chusan palm, *Trachycarpus fortunei*, rates first among my choice of desirable large plants and when small – up to 2 m (6 ft) – would be best encircled or underplanted with either the evergreen fern *Blechnum tabulare* or the deciduous ostrich fern, *Matteuccia struthiopteris*. Rodgersias such as *R. podophylla* or *R. tabularis* (or both) would look good, as would *Hosta sieboldiana elegans* and *Ligularia dentata* 'Desdemona'. All would benefit from the light shade that the palm fronds would supply.

## THE BEAUTY OF BAMBOOS

Bamboos should be situated either close to water or so that they screen part of the view, creating mystery, or perhaps diverting a path. For this the taller *Phyllostachys* varieties would be best. They are most beautiful when they arch over water or can be planted both sides of a path to create a tunnel effect. As regards companions, they are very versatile and any of the large-leaved herbaceous plants look good when planted around them. When close to water they are particularly well matched when placed alongside clumps of gunnera. Bamboos make very attractive woodland plants as an underplanting for trees, providing they only receive light shade. The large-leaved *Sasa palmata* looks especially good in this situation and could be grown with *Fatsia japonica* or any other of the woodland shrubs.

*Phyllostachys nigra* should be grown in an open sunny position such as in the middle of a lawn to retain the blackness of its stems, and the little golden-striped *Arundinaria viridistriata* must also have sun for good coloration. This, grouped with the golden-leaved *Hosta* 'Sum and Substance' and the golden cut-leaved elder *Sambucus racemosa* 'Plumosa Aurea' makes a lovely splash of sunshine.

## PHOTOGENIC PHORMIUMS

Where there are palms there should always be bamboos and phormiums, their size merits them as the 'bones' of an exotic garden. The lovely purply-leaved *Phormium tenax purpureum* with *Hosta sieboldiana elegans* planted around its feet cannot be beaten for beauty of colour combination and architectural contrast. The creamy yellow-striped *Phormium tenax* 'Variegatum' would also prove spectacular planted with hostas with cream or yellow-edged leaves. Other good companions for phormiums are the acanthus and *Crambe cordifolia*. A group of all three would give a very distinctive and interesting picture both in leaf and flower, the white gypsophila-like flower heads of the crambe harmonizing with the white and purple flower spikes of the acanthus, and the great blackish purple flower spikes of the phormium. All require an open sunny situation and so would be happy together.

## A TRULY EXOTIC COLLECTION

For those possessing a conservatory or greenhouse the following arrangement of tender plants would be a *pièce de résistance*. Such an assemblage would be the envy of neighbours and the height of exoticism.

The focus of this collection of treasures would be the majestic Abyssinian banana, *Ensete ventricosum*

(*Musa ensete*), with at its feet a ginger, *Hedychium gardnerianum*. The stunning combinations of *Melianthus major* with *Canna×generalis* 'Wyoming', and *Canna iridiflora ehrmanii* with *Ricinus communis* 'Gibsonii' should also be included. On the other side of the purple-leaved canna we should have the white variegated reed *Arundo donax* 'Variegata', and last but not least the sumptuous *Hibiscus moscheutos* 'Southern Belle'. On the perimeter of this group but still in full sun we should have a couple of hardier specimens: *Eucalyptus niphophila* and *Paulownia tomentosa*, and perhaps *Cordyline australis* underplanted with purple- and white-variegated pittosporums. Close by but lightly shaded, perhaps by a Japanese poplar, *Populus lasiocarpa*, could be the huge white pendulous-flowered *Datura cornigera* and the rice paper plant, *Tetrapanax papyriferus*.

## SUB-TROPICAL SHADE

Deserving a dell of its own is the breathtaking tree fern, *Dicksonia antarctica*, perhaps sharing its privilege with the treasured *Rodgersia tabularis* with (for contrast) *R. podophylla*. Nearby could be a few more familiar shade-loving plants: *Fatsia japonica*, camellias, pieris, and those aristocratic hydrangeas, *H. aspera* and *H. sargentiana*, underplanted with that lovely partnership of *Hosta sieboldiana elegans* and *Ligularia dentata* 'Desdemona'.

These examples have brought together the best of both worlds in terms of hardy and non-hardy subjects. There are, of course, countless other possibilities, and the great fun is to experiment and to try alternatives until you reach an individual, personally satisfying result.

# Large-Leaved Perennials in Containers

We generally think of flowers when planning plants for outdoor containers, but foliage can be equally effective, especially when bold and decorative.

The range of containers available now is probably greater than ever, all shapes and sizes, plain or fancy and in a number of different materials. Pots and containers especially when grouped together greatly enhance an area of paving or terrace, whatever the situation, and are much more effective than when scattered about individually.

## Siting

A patio area is of course the first situation to come to mind when thinking of placing containers, but they can be placed virtually anywhere in the garden to good effect. Corners and edges of terrace or paved areas are more clearly defined when pots are placed on them. The areas around swimming pools or formal ponds are enhanced by groups of pots. If placed either side of doorways or steps they give definition, and add a decorative note if placed either side of garden benches. Very small gardens of only a few square metres are best paved and the plants confined to pots which can be alternated, and enclosed courtyards which are usually paved or gravelled are very appro-

priate areas for them. A pot placed at the side of the start or the end of a path makes a note. In general containers, especially if planted with striking subjects, can do much to emphasize the design of the garden.

## Which plants?

Some plants are actually happier in containers than in the open ground, enjoying the freer drainage which is provided, and can be given special soil if need be. They also obtain increased soil warmth which is beneficial to tender plants, which can then be moved under glass for the winter. Incidentally arum lilies (*Zantedeschia aethiopica*) if grown in pots and overwintered in the conservatory or greenhouse will begin flowering in midwinter.

Lilies and other bulbous plants often do better in pots where a suitable well-drained sandy soil or humus can be provided, and where they are less prone to damage by slugs or other bulb-eating pests. One bulbous family, *Eucomis*, is particularly attractive in a pot because this raises it to a higher level where it can be appreciated more easily, and the leaves, which would normally lie untidily on the ground, hang over the edge of the pot.

Naturally the pots and containers themselves make the plants more decorative but the smaller plants in particular benefit from being raised to a higher level. Take hostas, for example: the big-leaved varieties obviously look distinctive in pots, but it is the smaller

**Bold leaves of contrasting shape *and* texture: (LEFT) *Peltiphyllum peltatum* and (RIGHT) *Hosta sieboldiana elegans* by the waterside.**

323

leaved ones which benefit most from closer inspection. Incidentally, hostas are certainly among the most attractive of foliage plants for containers, and they come in so many varieties of different size and leaf colour that there is one suitable for any pot.

Big-leaved perennial plants are not often chosen for pot culture, which is a pity as many, such as acanthus, ligularias and phormiums make very handsome pot plants. One of the greatest advantages of having plants in containers is that they can be moved around so that the groupings or their positions can be changed if we get bored, and it also enables us to move any tender plants into the conservatory or greenhouse for the winter.

Containers can be used to grow a plant which we like but which is too invasive to be planted out. Petasites, for example, is a wonderful foliage plant but not one which most of us would want to smother the whole garden. Grown in a pot and kept damp, its huge leaves can be enjoyed without fear of it taking over.

## Other plants in containers

Container gardening is practised more widely than ever now, and it is probably the most practical form where very small gardens are concerned and is some-

**Pots accentuate steps far better when planted with bold architectural plants such as arum lilies and purple cordylines.**

times the only method available in some instances such as with roof gardens.

In these situations it is obviously still desirable to grow as *wide* a range of plants as possible to create sufficient interest.

There are many shrubs and even trees which can be grown in pots and tubs, which, added to the herbaceous plants (including of course some large-leaved perennials), and, if desirable, such things as bulbs, means that there is no reason why a container garden should be a dull one.

Trees and shrubs will naturally be restricted in growth and in some instances may benefit from pruning so their root systems can maintain their stem and leaf structure, but the most important thing to ensure is that they are watered and fed regularly to compensate for the root restriction.

If pots are grouped together it makes watering much easier and is certainly more practical if automatic irrigation systems are used. Other advantages are that some shade or protection may be given to some of the plants, and, as when house plants are grouped together they create a microclimate around themselves. The same guidelines for plant association and groupings which I have given for beds or borders can be used here, and as the plants are in pots can be easily changed around or experimented with if desirable.

It is just as important with containers as with the border to include some evergreen plants and shrubs, as a collection of empty pots in winter is just as gloomy as an empty border. Plants such as phormiums and bergenias, and shrubs like camellia, choisya and *Fatsia japonica*, and even some bamboos such as *Arundinaria murielae* are invaluable. Remember too that some plants are only semi-deciduous. In mild or average winters, plants such as acanthus and many ferns remain almost evergreen. There are even a few evergreen climbers such as *Clematis armandii* and ceanothus which could be grown on fan-shaped trellis panels in pots. The wide range of ivies, some of which are variegated, can also be useful. The larger forms are best used as climbers while the smaller varieties make very attractive trailing plants useful for softening the edges or sides of containers.

So, as we see, the scope for creating beauty and interest when using containers is quite large.

# Arranging containers and plant care

When grouping pots of plants together we should follow the same rules as we would when using them in the border and consider contrast of shape, form, colour and, if possible, texture. One advantage over planting in a border is that differing soil requirements are no longer a problem, as each pot can be filled with a suitable mixture.

Using a phormium as a background subject in the biggest pot, for example, it could be fronted by an acanthus, a ligularia and finally a hosta. Here we have achieved variety of form, colour and texture. Continuity could be provided by planting them in pots of all the same design but of different sizes.

When considering containers for plants, the size of the plant will dictate the size of the container but allow for plants to increase in size and remember that the larger the container the less quickly it will dry out.

You will need to provide a good soil for your containers (garden soil will not do). A special tub and pot compost is available, but most plants also require or benefit from liquid feeding, usually once a fortnight. Give a top dressing of fresh soil once a year (removing the top few inches of the old soil and replacing with new) and where possible every four years or so

325

remove the plant from its container (in winter with deciduous plants and spring for evergreens), remove as much of the old soil from around the roots without damaging them and repot in fresh compost.

## Which pot?

If a plant is very ornate or architectural in its leaf shape then it is more likely to be set off in a pot of relatively simple design, whereas a plant of simple shape might look better in a fancy pot, but these are not hard and fast rules and individual taste will obviously play an important part. It would be a pity, however, to destroy the beauty of a plant with a pot of too elaborate a design, therefore simpler designs are usually safer.

Cost obviously plays a part when choosing containers but other things must be taken into consideration. Weight, for example, can differ enormously, especially with the larger sizes. A 75 cm (30 in) diameter terracotta pot will probably require two people to lift it even empty, whereas the fibreglass look-alikes are only a fraction of the weight, and also a fraction of the price. Terracotta pots breathe and so will dry out more quickly than fibreglass or plastic and therefore suit plants liking free drainage. Moisture lovers are happier in plastic or other non-porous pots.

There are, however, some disadvantages. Small pots will dry out very quickly in summer and will need watering every day, so an automatic drip-feed watering system is something to consider if you are going away. Another disadvantage is that during severe weather the soil may freeze. Again, the small pots are most vulnerable, the larger ones may only freeze on the outside. This can be prevented to a certain degree by tying sacking round them.

In severe weather it may be advisable to group *all* your containers together. This way they will not only protect each other but it will be more practical and easier to give them some additional protection of straw or sacking. Another method is to bury the pots in the soil. Pots will also be given some protection if placed against the wall of the house, and this way will be even easier to give additional protection.

These problems are few, though, when compared to the pleasure we may get from growing plants this way. From the tiniest paved yard to the grandest of terraces or swimming pool areas, containers play an essential part in completing an attractive picture which can only be enhanced if our large-leaved perennials are added to the normal choice of flowering and other plants.

**Large leaves may be solid or finely divided and contrast well together, as here with the hybrid *Lysichiton* and the royal fern *Osmunda regalis* with primulas in the foreground.**

# Plant Directory

**ACANTHUS** (Acanthaceae) BEAR'S BREECHES

The combination of handsome leaves and beautiful flowers make the acanthus one of the best herbaceous foliage plants. Not surprisingly, its strong architectural leaf shape has been used from Greek and Roman times in decorating buildings, and this quality should be exploited when positioning this plant in the garden.

### *Acanthus mollis*   *Italy*

Long in cultivation, this plant has long, deeply lobed dull green leaves and the usual prickly flower spikes of pinky mauve and white about 90 cm (3 ft) tall, which are quite plentifully produced. More handsome is the variety *A. m.* 'Latifolius', which has larger, arching leaves 90 cm (3 ft) long of deep dark glossy green, but the flowers are not so freely produced.

### *Acanthus spinosus*   *S. Europe*

The dark green leaves, 60–90 cm (2–3 ft) long, are deeply divided and have spiny points. This is probably the most free-flowering. *A. spinosissimus* has even more finely cut and prickly leaves but, like other available species, *A. balcanicus* and *A. perringii*, is less garden worthy.

**Bold large-leaved perennials grouped in pots show contrast of form, shape and texture:**
1. *Phormium tenax*
2. *Ligularia dentata* 'Desdemona'
3. *Acanthus mollis* 'Latifolius'
4. *Hosta sieboldiana elegans.*

Acanthus are happiest in full sun where they will flower in any good but fairly well-drained soil. Best planted when young, they do not move well when established, sending down long tap roots which inevitably break off in the process.

*A. m.* 'Latifolius' is probably the best of the bunch. Though not over generous with flowers it is certainly the most handsome in leaf. Flower arrangers should use gloves when cutting the flowers which have hard very prickly calyxes.

**AMICIA** (Leguminosae)

### *Amicia zygomeris*   *Mexico*

A very individual looking tender handsome foliage plant, with strong stems to over 2 m (7 ft) carrying large tri-lobed leaves. The large yellow flowers with maroon markings are a tell-tale indication of its family. It likes good soil and plenty of sun but will only succeed in sheltered gardens in mild areas.

**ARALIA** (Araliaceae)

### *Aralia cachemirica*   *Kashmir*

Huge rosettes of rich green and much divided leaves topped in summer with a panicle of ivory flowers (which are followed by maroon-black berries), give this plant a very lush, almost tropical appearance. At nearly 2 m (6 ft), this plant should be given a prominent position such as on the curve or the centre of a border. It would make a beautiful focus point by a pond or waterfall where the climate does not permit a tree fern (*Dicksonia antarctica*).

### *Aralia racemosa*  N. America

Of slightly smaller stature than the previous aralia, and of more upright habit, this carries greenish white flower heads on dark stems. Though graceful it does not possess the lushness of *A. cachemirica*.

These species will grow in sun or dappled shade in any good soil. They die down to the ground in winter whereas the other kinds, though mostly deciduous, retain their stems.

### ARISAEMA  (Araceae)

### *Arisaema speciosum*  Himalayas

I have only included this one species as the others are of rather small stature and this has probably the best leaves: three-lobed, bright green with maroonish edges supported on mottled brown stems standing about 60 cm (2 ft) high. The flowers, or correctly spathes, which are the main attraction of these plants are, in this species, deep purplish maroon inside, striped with the same outside on short stalks so that they are held beneath the leaves. The ivory spadix has a thin purplish extension 50 cm (20 in) long giving the plant a very strange appearance. Arisaemas require a sheltered position preferring humusy soil and dappled shade.

**Ligularia wilsoniana. This is one of the largest leaved ligularias and also one of the tallest in flower, often producing its yellows spires 2.5 m (8 ft) in length.**

**ARUNCUS**   (Rosaceae)   GOAT'S BEARD

***Aruncus dioicus***   *Northern Hemisphere*

Often listed under the synonym *A. sylvester*, this huge ferny plant is like a giant astilbe. The thick mound of bright green leaves 1.2 m (4 ft) high is overtopped in summer by a further 60 cm (2 ft) of great plumes of ivory coloured flowers making it a great feature plant, especially for the waterside. The finely divided leaves are a splendid contrast to the huge solid ones of gunneras and lysichitons and their fresh green colouring a lovely foil for the purple-leaved *Ligularia dentata* 'Desdemona' or *Rheum palmatum tanguticum*.

It tolerates most conditions but is happiest in good moist soil, sun or dappled shade and is easily propagated by division.

**ASPIDISTRA**   (Liliaceae)

***Aspidistra lurida***   *China*

This tender but tough evergreen plant will be familiar as a houseplant. The broad dark green leaves are hardly beautiful but its stemless maroon flowers are a curiosity. It likes shade in any good soil.

**BEGONIA**   (Begoniaceae)

***Begonia evansiana***   *Japan, China, Malaysia*

Yes, a hardy begonia, and the only one. It is every bit as attractive as its tender companions. The glistening waxy leaves have pinky red-tinged undersides, and stems and the flower buds of the same hue open to sprays of pale pink. It reproduces by little bulbils and, though modest in height at 45 cm (18 in), is worthy of any garden in a warm spot in sun or dappled shade. There are white and large-flowered forms.

**BERGENIA**   (Saxifragaceae)   ELEPHANT'S EARS

***Bergenia ciliata***   *Nepal, Kashmir*

By far the most beautiful in leaf of all the bergenias, the huge round leaves, 30 cm (1 ft) across, are very hairy on both sides and quite different from the other leathery leaved bergenias. They are, however, frost-tender, making it a deciduous species, whereas the others are evergreen. The stems are hardy and soon push up large heads 30 cm (1 ft) high of pale shell pink flowers in spring.

*B. ciliata* makes stunning underplanting for the tree fern (*Dicksonia antarctica*), appreciating the dappled shade of its crown of fronds, but is too beautiful and unusual to use as ground cover under ordinary shrubs or for the edges of borders or beds, for which the other kinds are more suited. It seems to thrive particularly well when grown on a slope.

***Bergenia cordifolia*** 'Purpurea'   *Siberia*

Vastly superior to the ordinary form, the greatest asset of *B. cordifolia* 'Purpurea' is that its bold round leaves take on purplish tints in winter. The tall strong stems of magenta flowers in spring make this one of the tallest of the tribe, in the 60 cm (2 ft) region.

HYBRIDS

**'Bellawley'**
An excellent plant in foliage and flower. Less stiff oval leaves 30 cm (1 ft) long, shining green are topped by sprays of crimson flowers 60 cm (2 ft) high. Though not so colourful in winter it is one of the best for summer display but should be given a little shelter and dappled shade to do its best.

**'Silberlicht'**
One of the few white-flowered varieties with handsome leaves make this a useful alternative to the

usual purple-flowered kinds. The snowy white flowers, around 30 cm (1 ft) tall, turn pale pink with age.

**'Sunningdale'**

A feature of this plant is the coral red flower stalks supporting vibrant carmine flower heads. The foliage assumes rich winter colouring. Growing about 30 cm (1 ft), it is considered by some to be the best yet available.

The richest winter coloration of the foliage is achieved in positions exposed to sun and wind and often poorish soil which makes them valuable plants for difficult positions. Their greatest asset, however, must be their value in softening the hard lines of paving and brickwork and for accentuating the curves of beds or borders where their spreading rhizomes form carpets of excellent groundcover foliage. The clumps are easy to divide for propagation.

## BESCHORNERIA    (Amaryllidaceae)

**Beschorneria yuccoides**    *Mexico*

This extraordinary plant has always reminded me of those wonderful rain-forest plants, the bromeliads but, as we see, it belongs to the amaryllis family. A large tuft of slightly flaccid sword-like blue-grey-green leaves 60 cm (2 ft) high after a few years throws up an enormous arching flower spike 2.5 m (8 ft) long, consisting of coral pink bracts from which dangle apple green bells, a breathtaking sight.

It needs to be thoroughly 'baked' to flower well and by far the best position would be on a sunny rockery or in paving. I have seen a dramatic example planted high up on a rock face. A most exotic-looking plant, but unfortunately only suitable for warm gardens.

## BUPHTHALMUM    (Compositae)

**Buphthalmum speciosum**    *S.E. Europe*

A rather coarse plant with paddle-shaped leaves and large deep yellow daisies which last for several weeks. It is useful for rough ground where it will spread rapidly to form ground cover and rise to 1.5 m (5 ft) level. I much prefer the similar looking but less invasive *Inula magnifica*, which is even larger.

## CALTHA    (Ranunculaceae)
GIANT MARSH MARIGOLD

**Caltha polypetala**    *Caucasus*

For bog or shallow water. Tall succulent stems 60 cm (2 ft) high carry the almost water-lily-like veined leaves and the buttercup flowers. Intriguingly, legend has it that this plant was originally stolen from the Vatican gardens, though I cannot imagine why. However, it is most suited to the margins of large ponds or lakes, where it spreads by long runners.

## CANNA    (Cannaceae)

**Canna indica**    *S. America, W. Indies*

The so-called Indian shot, with coppery-green leaves and small reddish flowers is the least exciting of these tender plants. It reaches 1.2 m (4 ft).

**Canna iridiflora ehrmanii**    *Peru*

A choice and desirable plant, and possibly the hardiest, thriving in warm gardens in our climate. The huge banana-like blue-green leaves, 90 cm (3 ft) long, are overtopped by elegant arching spikes of beautiful small rich rose pink flowers, making the whole plant often as much as 2.5 m (8 ft) high. It is one of the most exotic-looking things we can grow here and as such one of the best for creating a tropical effect. It survives

333

334

**Rockwork by a small pond with (LEFT)** *Peltiphyllum peltatum*
**and (RIGHT)** *Rodgersia podophylla* **which, growing in a sunny
position, has taken on purplish tints.**

**Lagoon with backcloth of *Lysichiton americanum* (LEFT) and
*Gunnera manicata*.**

in the warmest gardens if given a good mulch at the end of the autumn, but is best lifted and potted up, and placed in a frost-free conservatory or greenhouse until late the following spring. This way it will shoot forth and flower by midsummer. It is stunning when placed alongside purple-leaved subjects such as the annual *Ricinus communis* 'Gibsonii' or the shrub *Cotinus* 'Grace'.

HYBRIDS

**'Malawiensis'**

A very striking variety, the leaves having narrow stripes of lemon yellow and the usual large gladiolus-like flowers, a bronzy orange.

**'Le Roi Humbert'**

A feature of the famous Red Border at Hidcote, Gloucestershire, England. Its foliage is a rich purple with a faint green feathering, and the flowers are like bright red gladioli, around 1.8 m (6 ft).

**'Wyoming'**

The best of the purple-leaved kinds, though not the most vigorous, with broad leaves of a deep rich purple. The flowers in apricot orange clash a trifle for my taste but the foliage makes the most beautiful possible foil to *Melianthus major*. Like all cannas it should be grown in full sun in rich moist soil.

Cannas have been used as summer bedding for formal plantings in public parks since Victorian times and are still commonly seen today. But their beauty is marred when used this way in straight rows or blocks.

Although their roots are not frost hardy they are as tough as old boots and need no more attention than dahlia tubers. Lift them in late autumn, store them in a dry frost-free place until early spring, then divide and pot up and start them into growth at about 15°C (60°F) and harden off before planting out in late spring.

## CARDIOCRINUM    (Liliaceae)

### *Cardiocrinum giganteum*    W. China

A real showstopper if ever there was one, growing 1.8–3 m (6–10 ft). Thick stems taper from a basal rosette of huge arum-like leaves above which long greenish white trumpets with maroon throats 20 cm (8 in) long hang down from the visible stem. It was once remarked on as being 'like a woman whose great beauty is marred by her having thick ankles!' It needs deep leaf mould in woodland and the bulbs (which should be planted with their noses just below the surface) should be planted in groups of different ages to achieve annual flowering, because they take about seven years to flower. An expensive practice, but if you can afford it, and can supply the conditions this plant requires then you will be well rewarded.

## CAUTLEYA    (Zingiberaceae)

### *Cautleya spicata*    Himalayas

One of the few hardy gingers, not as exotic-looking as its tender relatives, but none the less a very attractive subject when grown in a bold group. The stems of opposite rows of long green blades are topped with maroon bracts with deep yellow flowers about 60 cm (2 ft) high, perhaps taller in very rich soil.

Sun or dappled shade suit best and as a precaution a good mulch in winter. This should be grown at the front of the border and is particularly nice when grown with a group of *Lilium candidum* whose flowers of similar coloration accentuate those of the cautleya.

## CLEMATIS    (Ranunculaceae)

### *Clematis × heracleifolia*    China

There is always doubt on first sight of this plant as to its correct labelling. A herbaceous clematis? Yes, indeed.

Not a spectacular plant but one whose foliage seems to draw attention, which is why I have included it.

The large divided leaves have wiry stems and taller leafy stems bear little blue scented flowers 90 cm (3 ft) high, which are followed by fluffy silvery seed heads. Any soil in sun will do. Attractive with hostas.

## CRAMBE    (Cruciferae)

### *Crambe cordifolia*    *Caucasus*

Even if the huge mound of rather coarse puckered heart-shaped leaves are not to everyone's taste, the great sprays of tiny white, scented gypsophila-like flowers usually are. At 2 m (6 ft) high and nearly as much across, they are a great sight especially when swarming with butterflies. It will not (infuriatingly) succeed in rich moist soil, insisting on poor and well-drained earth in which it sends down its long tap roots. It prefers full sun. The very brittle roots can be divided for propagation as long as each piece has a crown.

## CURTONUS    (Iridaceae)

### *Curtonus paniculatus*    *S. Africa*

Looking like a giant crocosmia, this individually striking plant has broad ridged blades 90 cm (3 ft) long and arching sprays of fiery orange trumpets topping 1.2 m (4 ft). Like crocosmia it prefers full sun and is not fussy as to soil. The foliage almost merits it as a subject for 'exotic' plantings but the flowers are not quite up to scratch for that purpose. Propagation by division.

## DRACUNCULUS    (Araceae)   DRAGON PLANT

### *Dracunculus vulgaris*    *Mediterranean*

I include this plant as a novelty more than for any other reason, though it does possess rather large coarse divided leaves on 60 cm (2 ft) spotted stems. But undoubtedly its main feature, albeit a monstrous one, is the enormous crimson spathe 45 cm (18 in) high with its maroon-black spadix. To top it all it smells most foully of rotting flesh. The large tubers should be planted 15 cm (6 in) deep in well-drained soil in full sun. It suits pot culture well. Of similar curiosity are the smaller and less offensive arisaemas.

## EREMURUS    (Liliaceae)   FOXTAIL LILY

### *Eremurus robustus*    *Turkestan*

All the foxtail lilies, of which this is the largest, are very similar in appearance, differing only in colour and size. The untidy long limp strap-like leaves lay on the ground and have begun to wither by the time the flower spikes develop. The pale pink, small starry flowers of *E. robustus* are massed on a spike 3 m (10 ft) tall and shaped like a giant lupin. They are best set off with a dark background. The huge star-fish shaped roots, which are very brittle, should be buried just beneath the ground in well-drained soil in full sun. They leave a hole when they die back and are therefore best placed at the back of the border. There are other smaller species in other shades and some splendid hybrids, notably 'Shelford' and 'Highdown', some of rich colouring.

## EUCOMIS    (Liliaceae)

### *Eucomis pole-evansii*    *Transvaal*

Very rare in cultivation, this strikingly unusual bulbous plant is only suitable for the warmest gardens. From long glossy 15 cm (6 in) wide leaves arises a stout central stem 1.5 m (5 ft) high with a huge pineapple-shaped flower head consisting of a mass of tiny star-shaped flowers topped with a tuft of leaves 25 cm (10 in) across like a pineapple – an unforgettable sight.

It is probably best grown in pots (in full sun) and would make a decorative patio subject and grown this way it benefits from the additional soil warmth in summer and could be moved under cover in extreme weather in winter. There are smaller more easily obtainable kinds: *E. bicolor*, which is one most frequently met with, and *E. punctata*. The unusual and exotic character of these plants deems them appropriate for the 'exotic' garden (see pages 307–321).

### FILIPENDULA (Rosaceae) MEADOW SWEET

#### *Filipendula camtschatica* (syn. *gigantea*) *Kamchatka*

Lording it over all the other waterside plants with exception of the gunnera, the 3 m (10 ft) straight stems clothed with jagged palmate leaves are crowned with large flat frothy flower heads of either ivory or pale pink, 30 cm (1 ft) across. A truly grand plant, ideal for mixing with other noble plants for bog and waterside. Dappled shade and acid soil is where it is at home.

#### *Filipendula rubra* *E. United States*

The queen of the prairies, though of lesser stature than *F. camtschatica* at around 2 m (6 ft), is none the less dramatic in that it forms very substantial leafy clumps of the same palmate leaves, and has generous flat heads of pink flowers, best in the form 'Venusta'. This form is more vigorous than *F. camtschatica* but would make a superb waterside plant in any large garden.

**A stream-lined planting showing a variety of strong leaf forms: (TOP) *Peltiphyllum peltatum*, (BOTTOM LEFT) *Lysichiton americanum*, and (RIGHT) *Rheum palmatum*.**

The coloration of its flowers renders it a lovely companion to both purple-leaved ligularias, white arum lilies and the blue-grey-leaved hostas such as *H. sieboldiana elegans*. The smaller *F. purpurea* has flowers of a vibrant cerise, a bit overpowering for most gardens. All these plants prefer very moist, even boggy conditions in good soil and dappled shade.

## GLAUCIDIUM    (Glaucidiaceae)

### *Glaucidium palmatum*    *Japan*

Something of a treasure but requiring cool acid soil in woodland. The delicate pale mauve poppy-like flowers 60 cm (2 ft) tall are held above big lobed fresh green leaves.

## GUNNERA    (Haloragidaceae)

### *Gunnera manicata*    *S. Brazil*

'Lovely big rhubarb' was the last comment I over-heard of this plant, and quite descriptive at that. The first experience of meeting this plant is always memorable, even to non-gardeners.

In spring from huge creeping rhizomes, the leaves push skyward, great prickly stems with their folded umbrellas to ultimately rise and expand to 2 m (6 ft) or more high and the same across, deeply lobed and as rough as sandpaper. The flowers consist of huge cones 1 m (3 ft) high of rusty brown when their seed is ripe. In all a plant of unparalleled drama, requiring a position by water or in marshy ground. It reaches its ultimate size if well fed and grown in light shade, though it is quite happy in full sun. The crowns should be covered in winter first with bracken and then by the plant's dead leaves which should be turned upside down and folded on top of it.

### *Gunnera scabra*    (syn. *chilensis, tinctoria*)

Of smaller stature having smaller leaves (to 1.5 m (5 ft) across), more puckered and serrated, on shorter stalks. The flowers remain for some weeks after the leaves have died down, a strange sight!

## HEDYCHIUM    (Zingiberaceae)    GINGER LILY

These noble plants with their banana-like leaves and almost orchid-like blooms are truly exotic and as such best fitting in association with others of similar character – bananas, palms, bamboos, cordylines, cannas, phormiums and the like (see pages 307–321). They are only suitable for very mild gardens; although their roots will survive colder areas they do not make sufficient growth to flower, coming up too late in the season. They like a rich moist soil in full sun and their roots, which are thick fleshy rhizomes, should be planted just beneath the surface. In winter when the stems die down they should be covered with a thick mulch. Propagation is by division.

### *Hedychium coccineum*    *India, Burma*

The strong stems carry opposite pairs of narrow fleshy leaves terminating in flower spikes with coral red petals and red stamens 90–120 cm (3–4 ft) high. The variety 'Tara' which originated from Wakehurst seems a trifle hardier.

### *Hedychium densiflorum*    *E. Himalayas*

In this species the 90 cm (3 ft) spikes have rich orange petals and coral red stamens. The best variety is 'Assam Orange' of slightly larger proportions.

### *Hedychium forrestii*

This is the hardiest of the bunch, and makes lush and leafy clumps over 2 m (7 ft) high. The flower spikes, though smaller and less dramatic than the others, are a change in that they have white petals with projecting orange stamens.

### Hedychium gardnerianum   *N. India*

This is the most majestic of the race, bearing huge stems clothed with broad blue-green blades 38 cm (15 in) long. The 25 cm (10 in) flower spikes have long yellow petals and orange-red projecting stamens. In rich soil in a warm spot this plant will attain 1.8 m (6 ft). If it is grown in a tub in a frost-free greenhouse for the winter it will remain evergreen and flower earlier as a result the following year. Stunning when planted at the foot of the great Abyssinian banana (*Ensete ventricosum*).

### Hedychium greenii   *Bhutan*

The distinctive foliage is dark blue-green and at only 60 cm (2 ft) adds interesting variety to the race.

### Hedychium × raffillii

This is a hybrid between *H. gardnerianum* and *H. coccineum*, and a fine plant. The 1.5 m (5 ft) stems with broad leaves have brilliant orange petals and dark red stamens, finer than *H. coccineum* but not as hardy.

## HERACLEUM   (Umbelliferae)   GIANT HOGWEED

### Heracleum mantegazzianum   *Caucasus*

An exciting plant but one with a notorious reputation. Like a giant cow parsley towering 3 m (10 ft), sometimes 4 m (12 ft) in the air, its great cartwheels of tiny white flowers on stems like huge sticks of celery make a magnificent show in woodland or rough places. But it is not suitable for the average garden in that it seeds invasively and the large leaves, 1 m (3 ft) across and much divided, die back early, leaving a huge hole. One can control it by removing the flower heads before they set seed. Heracleums give a wonderfully exotic effect, especially when grown with other statuesque plants. The notorious reputation I mentioned earlier is due to the fact that if roughly handled in strong sunshine heracleum can cause blistering and sometimes a most unpleasant purple staining of the skin. I once saw an old church graveyard which had become entirely engulfed in a forest of heracleum, making it rather reminiscent of *The Day of the Triffids*!

## HOSTA   (Liliaceae)   PLANTAIN LILY

As mentioned earlier, for a more detailed account of these first-class popular plants, see pages 6–96. Here, I shall just describe briefly those which have particularly large leaves.

Hostas are one of the best plants for ground cover, growing in sun or shade but usually preferring dappled shade in good moist soil where their leaves will be largest. They are a splendid contrast to sword-shaped leaves, grasses and ferns and are lovely in association with waterside plants. The leaves of many of them remain in pristine condition throughout the season but the glaucous-leaved kinds should be placed away from the drip of trees. They are very prone to slug and snail damage and poison should be spread when the leaf spikes appear. Most have spikes of lilac coloured flowers but the foliage is the main beauty of these plants.

### Hosta crispula   *Japan*

Large dark green leaves with wavy edges, broadly margined white. One of the best and most striking of the white-variegated kinds when well grown. It is more beautiful when grown in shade, and reaches around 75 cm (2½ ft).

*Zantedeschia aethiopica* 'Crowborough'. The familiar arum
lily will succeed if heavily mulched in winter.

An unusual use of *Hosta sieboldiana elegans* entirely
fringing a small lagoon.

### *Hosta fortunei* 'Albo-picta'   *Japan*

At its most beautiful in spring when the leaves are bright yellow with dark green margins. These colours eventually tone down to two soft shades of green in summer. 75 cm (2½ ft).

### *Hosta fortunei* 'Marginata Alba'

Less striking than *H. crispula* but of softer beauty, with sage green corrugated leaves with bold white margins. 75 cm (2½ ft), happiest in shade.

### *Hosta fortunei* 'Obscura Marginata'

Broad leaves, this time with a creamy yellow margin (which gave it its old name 'Yellow Edge') which is retained through the season. 75 cm (2½ ft).

### *Hosta* 'Fringe Benefit'

An American introduction with large puckered leaves with a broad white margin. Happy in sun or shade. 90 cm (3 ft).

### *Hosta* 'Honeybells'

A descendant of *H. plantaginea* but of lesser stature. The pale lilac flowers have inherited the perfume of its parent but the leaves have more undulating margins. A first-class plant, staying in good fetter well into the autumn. 75 cm (2½ ft).

### *Hosta* 'Krossa Regal'

Large, glaucous green arching leaves with undulating margins. Forms a lush and impressive clump at 90 cm (3 ft).

### *Hosta plantaginea*   *China*

A rare and noble plant with large, arching glossy bright green leaves. In autumn it produces large white beautifully scented trumpet flowers. This plant requires a warm sheltered spot in dappled shade to succeed. 75 cm (2½ ft).

### *Hosta* 'Royal Standard'

Similar to but a little smaller than *H. plantaginea,* one of its parents. 90 cm (3 ft).

### *Hosta sieboldiana*   *Japan*

Very large broad grey-green leaves to 40 cm (16 in) form a lush mound, the flowers barely rising above the leaves.

### *Hosta sieboldiana elegans*

The most sumptuous of hostas and infinitely superior to the ordinary form, with almost round blue-grey, strongly ribbed and puckered leaves 30 cm (1 ft) wide, forming huge striking clumps. It is stunning with purple-leaved plants such as *Ligularia dentata* 'Desdemona' and is happiest in dappled shade 90 cm (3 ft).

### *Hosta sieboldiana* 'Frances Williams'

In effect, a gold-edged *H. s. elegans*. In good clones the margins are of an almost mustard yellow; in poor sorts they are more beige. A first-class and desirable plant, whose foliage remains in pristine condition well into the autumn. 75 cm (2½ ft).

### *Hosta* 'Snowden'

Large pointed sage-green leaves form a mound sometimes 90 cm (3 ft) in height, overtopped by a further 30 cm (1 ft) of strong spikes of white green-tinged flowers. One of the most impressive of all hostas both in leaf and flower. Best in dappled shade.

## Hosta 'Sum and Substance'

The leaves, which are reminiscent of *H. sieboldiana*, start green but mature to a beautiful golden yellow, making it the largest in leaf and one of the most spectacular of all yellow-leaved hostas. It will grow in sun or shade but is probably best in light shade where the leaves will be partly greeny gold. The usual lilac flowers rather clash.

## Hosta ventricosa    *E. Asia*

An impressive plant, the shiny handsome dark green leaves being strongly veined and heart-shaped, with undulating margins. The flowers are of much richer colouring than is usual among hostas. 1.2 m (4 ft).

## Hosta ventricosa 'Variegata'

The *ventricosa* leaves are here boldly margined with deep cream, making it a very striking plant. It is not as vigorous as some and should be encouraged by feeding and watering.

## INULA    (Compositae)

### Inula magnifica

A stately plant magnificent for the bog garden or waterside. Huge paddle-shaped 1.2 m (4 ft) long leaves form basal clumps above which strong stems rise to 2.5 m (8 ft), forming branched heads of deep yellow daisies 12 cm (5 in) across. *I. racemosa* is a larger but coarser plant only suitable for rough wild places. Happiest in sun, these plants will tolerate dry conditions but prefer soil where their deep tap roots can reach moisture. Easily propagated by division.

## KIRENGESHOMA    (Saxifragaceae)    *Japan*

A much over-rated plant. The leaves, which remind me of those of the plane tree on dark wiry stems, are topped in late summer with sprays of pale yellow flowers at the 90 cm (3 ft) level. It prefers dappled shade and moisture.

## LIGULARIA    (Compositae)

A distinctive race of plants which we should not be without where water is present. They prefer rich damp or boggy soil, where they soon form very substantial clumps which benefit from division every few years. They are best grown in dappled or light shade as full sun often wilts their leaves. They are much loved by slugs and snails so precautions will need to be taken early in the season as growth starts.

## Ligularia dentata 'Desdemona'    *China*

Probably the most popular of all the ligularias, the striking leaves dark green on top while their undersides and stems are a rich dark reddish purple. In sun the tops of the leaves are often tinged the same. The branched daisy heads, at 1.2 m (4 ft) tall are a rich orange. This is a beautiful companion to *Hosta sieboldiana elegans* and makes a stunning contrast to white variegated bog irises.

## Ligularia 'Gregynog Gold'

A noble plant of grand proportions, bearing large round leaves with toothed margins and great conical spikes of vivid orange flowers 1.8 m (6 ft) high.

## Ligularia macrophylla    *Orient*

A desirable and rare plant quite different from all the other ligularias, having large grey-green horseradish-like leaves 75 cm (2½ ft) long with prominent central white ribs. The dense short spikes of yellow flowers are most handsome at around 1.5 m (5 ft).

345

**Variety of form with (FROM LEFT)** *Miscanthus, Osmunda regalis* **and** *Hosta sieboldiana* **by the water.**

**A tropical glade featuring the Abyssinian banana** *Ensete ventricosum* **as a centrepiece.**

### Ligularia × palmatiloba

A hybrid between *L. dentata* and *L. japonica* and a great improvement on both, having handsome broad leaves with deeply toothed margins and candelabra spikes of orange daisies 1.2 m (4 ft) high.

### Ligularia przewalskii    *N. China*

The triangular, deeply incised, dark green leaves have wiry black stems and flower spikes 1.8 m (6 ft) high carrying narrow spines of small yellow daisies. 'The Rocket' is the best form and *L. stenocephala* is a similar but less striking plant of lesser stature. These plants must have shade even in boggy soil as the leaves flag with the least bit of sun, giving the plant a very untidy appearance.

### Ligularia veitchiana    *China*

Large, slightly triangular, heavily veined leaves 30 cm (1 ft) across are borne on stout triangular stems and the 1.5 m (5 ft) high columnar flower spikes consist of small yellow daisies.

### Ligularia wilsoniana    *China*

Similar to *L. veitchiana* but when established becomes a larger and more handsome plant. The slightly smoother leaves stand 90 cm (3 ft) high on hollow triangular stems and the flower spikes, clothed for 90 cm (3 ft) of their length can reach 2.5 m (8 ft) high. Dappled shade will prevent the huge leaves from collapsing and a good rich soil should be provided. The flowers are followed by fluffy seed heads. One of the most dramatic plants for the waterside.

## LYSICHITON    (Araceae)    SKUNK CABBAGE

Along with the gunneras these are among the most architectural plants for the waterside, bog garden or streamside. They have to be planted in the young state as they strongly object to being moved once established, sending down their great tap roots 90 cm (3 ft) or more. Their huge leaves damage easily and they should be placed out of strong winds in a hollow or where they would be protected by other plants. They should be planted in very rich soil in which plenty of manure has been incorporated and fed annually.

### Lysichiton americanum    *N. America*

In spring just as the leaves are emerging the large striking yellow spathes with their green spadixes appear, 30 cm (1 ft) high. The rosette of huge shiny paddle-shaped leaves when the plant is mature can reach 1.2 m (4 ft) and makes a handsome companion to gunneras. The leaves retain their beauty until the autumn.

### Lysichiton camtschatcensis    *Kamchatka*

The whole plant is of somewhat smaller proportions than *L. americanum* but the flowers are snowy white and the leaves a beautiful pale glaucous green. In gardens where both have been growing for a number of years a hybrid (still unnamed) has arisen. This supersedes both in vigour, resulting in a plant often reaching 1.8 m (6 ft) in height. The 45 cm (18 in) tall spathes are a beautiful cream with green spadixes and the leaves a lovely pale glaucous pea-green, obviously inherited from *L. camtschatcensis*. A spectacularly beautiful and dramatic plant which always draws attention and admiration.

## MACLEAYA    (Papaveraceae)    PLUME POPPY

### Macleaya microcarpa    *China*

An impressive foliage plant forming bold clumps of 2.1 m (7 ft) felty white stems clothed with fig-shaped grey-green leaves white underneath. The whole is topped with branched plumes of flesh or coppery-buff fluffy flowers. 'Coral Plume' is a variety of richer coloration and *M. cordata* has white flowers.

These plants make a lovely tall accent among lower growing species. They are said to do best in sun but I have known them to luxuriate in shade. However, they do prefer reasonably well-drained soil. Propagation is simple in that it runs quite freely at the root.

## MELIANTHUS   (Melianthaceae)

### *Melianthus major*   S. Africa

A plant needing no introduction to foliage lovers and undoubtedly one of the most beautiful. The gracefully poised stems are clothed with divided deeply serrated leaves, the whole of a lovely grey-green. In mild areas the plant produces its flowers with dark maroon bracts and green stamens in autumn or winter, but these are of no great beauty and by this time the plant is usually losing its lower leaves. Although it does best in warm gardens (as it is tender) where it will remain evergreen, it is far better to cut the stems down each winter, when it will shoot vigorously in the spring to form a bushier, more compact plant. The coloration of this plant makes it a stunning companion to purple foliage, such as *Cotinus coggygria* 'Royal Purple' but especially the tender *Canna×generalis* 'Wyoming'. It should be grown in full sun and protected with a thick mulch of forest bark in winter.

## MUSA   (Musaceae)   BANANA

### *Musa basjoo*   Japan

The only banana which will survive our winters, and then only in the very warmest parts. The slender trunk is topped with the huge paddle-shaped blue-green papery leaves which unfortunately tear in the wind. At 3 m (10 ft), it is undoubtedly impressive especially when grown (which indeed it should be) with other exotic-looking things such as palms, bamboos, cordylines and phormiums. This plant should be placed in the most sheltered position possible but in sun and in rich moist soil. It will greatly benefit from regular feeding and watering and often flowers as a result. As with most bananas when this happens the plant begins to die but produces several offsets or side shoots. It should be well wrapped up with bracken or straw in winter but if the winter is severe, and it is cut to the ground it may still shoot forth from the ground again in summer.

## MYOSOTIDIUM   (Boraginaceae)

CHATHAM ISLAND FORGET-ME-NOT

### *Myosotidium hortensia*   Chatham Islands

A distinct and highly individual-looking plant and one to be treasured. The leaves, reminiscent of *Hosta sieboldiana elegans*, are rich green and glossy, 25 cm (10 in) across and long. The sprays of tiny flowers are forget-me-not blue. It is a notoriously difficult plant, only thriving in warm gardens and even so it must be covered with cloches for the winter. The secret in less favourable gardens is to grow it as a pot plant, feeding it regularly with seaweed fertilizer and keeping it in a frost-free greenhouse or conservatory for the winter. A worthwhile effort. It is usually grown from seed.

## PELTIPHYLLUM   (Saxifragaceae)

UMBRELLA PLANT

### *Peltiphyllum peltatum*

This plant has recently been re-named *Darmera peltata*, but is still generally listed by nurseries and reference books under *Peltiphyllum*.

349

*Hosta sieboldiana elegans*, one of the largest and possibly
the most splendid of all hostas.

351

*Melianthus major,* possibly the finest foliage plant, here displaying its maroon flowers. It should always be accompanied where possible by *Canna×generalis* 'Wyoming'.

Sometimes called the poor man's gunnera, this is a first-class big or waterside plant, forming wonderful lush clumps of its bog round scalloped leaves each 38 cm (15 in) across. The whole plant often standing 1.5 m (5 ft) high. The thick snaky rhizomes are a strange sight, especially in spring when they send up long bristly flower stalks topped with heads of almost bergenia-like flowers. These are almost over before the leaves appear.

It likes a rich peaty moist or boggy soil at the water's edge where its rhizomes will form a colony. Though it is happy in sun it grows taller in the shade and is easy to multiply by lifting sections of the rhizomes with a spade, ensuring that each has a growing point. This is an indispensable plant for any collection of waterside plants and would be a good substitute for a gunnera where there is not sufficient space for one of these giants.

## PETASITES (Compositae)

Along with the big polygonums, these are among the most invasive of plants, making them unsuitable candidates for all but the largest gardens. They make ideal ground cover, smothering everything in their path and they will grow particularly well in heavy wet clay in shade where little else will flourish and so are valuable for that purpose.

### Petasites hybridus    Britain

The native British butterbur can be seen on long stretches of river banks, the huge kidney-shaped leaves 90 cm (3 ft) across often stand 1.2 m (4 ft) high and are glaucous with ivory veins and serrated margins.

### Petasites japonicus giganteus    Japan

More refined than the previous species, of the same proportions but with fresher green leaves of cleaner shape. If you have a rough patch of bog or stream in woodland or a shady bank of a lake then this will add beauty and variety if added to the other waterside giants, gunneras, lysichitums and peltiphyllums, soon forming a huge colony.

The flowers of both these species, which appear in early spring before the leaves, consist of rosettes of pale mauve or white flowers sitting on the ground, a curious sight and popular with flower arrangers.

## PHORMIUM    (Liliaceae)    NEW ZEALAND FLAX

Among the most architectural of herbaceous plants, valuable as evergreens but especially for creating a sub-tropical effect. The most colourful forms are unfortunately the most tender and even the plain green form, *P. tenax*, can be killed in severe winters. The base of the plant is most vulnerable and should be surrounded with a thick mulch of forest bark in winter and the leaves tied up to prevent snow damage. They like full sun and shelter from strong winds and a good moist soil. The flowers, which overtop the leaves by a good margin, are reminiscent of *Strelitzia reginae* (bird of paradise flower), but of dark dull coloration, none the less very dramatic and architectural. They are easy to propagate by separating one of the fans of leaves, ensuring it has some root, and potting in well-drained sandy soil in as small a pot as will contain it, retaining it under glass until established.

### Phormium cookianum    New Zealand

Suitable for the most sheltered gardens only. This and its varieties differ from the *P. tenax* forms in that they are of more modest height, 90–120 cm (3–4 ft) and have more lax leaves. The best variety is 'Tricolor', which is striped red, yellow and green. The flowers are brownish with reddish filaments but are less often produced than on the bigger *P. tenax* forms.

### Phormium tenax  *New Zealand*

In mild, sheltered gardens the leaves alone can reach 3 m (9–10 ft), while the dark blue flowers, which have a whitish bloom, will overtop them by a further 1 m (3 ft) or so. The form 'Goliath' is a vigorous clone with wider leaf blades.

### Phormium tenax purpureum

In this the leaves are of a reddish purple hue but this varies greatly, some plants being almost green and so a good colour form should be sought. 'Dark Delight' is the richest and darkest of the purple forms but is a hybrid between *P. tenax* and *P. cookianum* and so has shorter, more lax leaves. 'Purple Giant' is the largest, with bronze-purple foliage.

### Phormium tenax 'Variegatum'

A much over-used plant but none the less attractive for its boldly cream and yellow striped leaves which give more of a contrast to the dark red flowers covered in a white bloom. Because of their very tough consistency the flowers remain a decorative feature many months after they have finished. There is a more beautiful yellow-variegated form called 'Williamsii', whose leaf blades contain more yellow than green but it is sure to be more tender. Crosses between *P. tenax* and *P. cookianum* have resulted in a number of very colourful variegated offspring in shades of salmon pink, orange, red and yellow.

## PHYTOLACCA  (Phytolaccaceae)  POKEWEED

These large, lush, leafy plants make a bold accent in the border and have an individual though slightly coarse character. They do best in sun or light shade and should be underplanted with ground cover such as bergenias to complement them. They develop huge thick rhizomes and should not be moved when large.

These plants seed quite readily and are fast-growing; they appear to live to a considerable age. The whole plant is poisonous.

### Phytolacca americana  *Florida*

In this species candelabra-like stems terminate in small spikes of white flowers which are followed by dark maroon berries.

### Phytolacca clavigera  *China*

More attractive than *P. americana*, in that the flower spikes are pink, and in autumn the stems turn bright crimson, constrasting with the yellow leaves and jet black berries.

## POLYGONUM  (Polygonaceae)  KNOTWEED

I have included these largely on account of the size of their leaves; although *P. cuspidatum* 'Spectabile' is undoubtedly beautiful, they are all disastrously invasive and should be confined to little islands in large lakes.

### Polygonum cuspidatum 'Spectabile'  *Japan*

It is easy to be lured by the beauty of this plant, whose 2.5 m (8 ft) succulent stems, pinky red in spring, are clothed with eye-catching alternate large heart-shaped leaves marbled cream, butter-yellow and green. It is less invasive than the plain green kinds but will still run amuck causing havoc in a small garden. It must have dappled shade or the leaves will scorch.

### Polygonum sachalinense  *Sakhalin Islands*

The worst culprit, forming forests of 3.5 m (12 ft) high canes almost like bamboo, and sending underground runners several metres or yards at a time. The male plant has attractive small vertical ivory white fluffy flower spikes between the huge green heart-shaped leaves, which are each 25 cm (10 in) long.

***Ensete ventricosum*** (syn. ***Musa ensete***), the Abyssinian banana, is a giant but tender perennial which can be grown from seed.

*Hedychium gardnerianum*, a member of the ginger family, is
best pot grown and overwintered under glass to guarantee
flowers the following year.

**RHEUM**   (Polygonaceae)   ORNAMENTAL RHUBARB

A bold, highly decorative plant, both in leaf and in flower, especially beautiful when planted by the waterside, and a possible substitute for a gunnera where space does not allow. They like a rich, moist but not boggy soil in sun or dappled shade and if space permits should be planted in threes to produce a really lush effect. They should always be included with rodgersias, ligularias and the like for contrast and variety of leaf shape. They are best propagated by removing the side crowns (which they freely produce) in winter or early spring. (The common rhubarb is *R. officinale.*) Most flower in late spring.

### Rheum australe (syn. emodi)   *Himalayas*

A rare species with huge entire heart-shaped leaves with red veins and undulating margins. The erect flower spikes, over 2 m (7 ft) high may be white or red.

### Rheum palmatum   *China*

The most frequently seen, with large, deeply cut and serrated leaves standing 1.8 m (6 ft) high, topped by crimson flower spikes.

### Rheum palmatum 'Atrosanguineum'

In this form of the above, the leaf buds and emerging leaves are bright red and the leaves retain a reddish coloration underneath when mature. The flower spikes are great fluffy panicles in cherry red.

### Rheum palmatum tanguticum

The best form, producing new leaves further into the season which are purple tinted on top when young as well as retaining colour underneath, and with less deeply serrated margins. The flower spikes, though less vivid, are most handsome – usually ivory (contrasting well with the purple) or sometimes pink.

Beautiful when planted with a margin of silver lamium (*Lamium maculatum* 'Beacon Silver').

**RODGERSIA**   (Saxifragaceae)

Indispensable plants for the waterside, especially streams and ponds where their splendid, characterful leaves and beautiful astilbe-like flowers add invaluable variety to the other noble and architectural subjects. They like moist or marshy ground in sun or dappled shade, especially thriving in acid soil rich in leaf mould. They spread fairly freely and are easily propagated from the creeping rhizomes.

### Rodgersia aesculifolia   *China*

The leaves are like those of a horse-chestnut, bronzy five-lobed but about 45 cm (18 in) across. The branched flower spikes can be ivory or pale pink.

### Rodgersia pinnata   *China*

Leaves are similar to the above, but arranged in pairs; the flowers are soft pink. Well known is *R. p.* 'Superba', one of the best, with very bronzy leaves and bright, slightly salmon pink flowers on dark stalks. A stunning contrast to *Hosta sieboldiana elegans*.

### Rodgersia podophylla   *Japan*

Big, distinctive star-shaped leaves with jagged edges sometimes 60 cm (2 ft) across. They are bronze when young and if grown in a sunny position take on purplish tints in summer. The rather sparsely produced flowers are creamy ivory. A good contrast to *R. tabularis*.

### Rodgersia sambucifolia   *China*

Less often seen, but a very handsome plant with distinctive pinnate leaves gracefully poised, and elegant sprays of creamy white flowers.

***Rodgersia tabularis***   *China*

The choicest of the race and much sought after. It is said that the huge circular pale green, scalloped leaves can reach 90 cm (3 ft) across, but they are more usually 60 cm (2 ft). The small ivory flowers are held well above the leaves, 1.5 m (5 ft) high. *R. tabularis* must have dappled shade or the leaves will scorch. A plant to be treasured and a lovely companion to *R. podophylla*, *Ligularia dentata* 'Desdemona' or the fern *Matteuccia struthiopteris*. This plant is sometimes called *Astilboides tabularis*, incomprehensibly as it bears no resemblance to an astilbe whatsoever.

**RUMEX**   (Polygonaceae)   WATER DOCK

***Rumex hydrolapathum***   *Britain*

A rather coarse but handsome plant with great spear-shaped leaves of some architectural quality. However, this plant's greatest value lies in the russet colour of the flower heads produced in late summer and the crimson autumn coloration of the foliage. It should be grown in shallow water, preferably on the margins where its foliage can give contrast to other waterside subjects.

**SENECIO**   (Compositae)

***Senecio smithii***   *S. Chile*

Another subject for shallow water but of more handsome appearance, with thick dark green, spear-shaped leaves and branched heads of white, yellow-eyed daisies 1.2 m (4 ft) high. These are followed by fluffy seed heads. Can also be grown in a damp border but is happiest with its feet in water. Propagation is by division.

**SILPHIUM**   (Compositae)   PRAIRIE DOCK

***Silphium terebinthinaceum***   *N. America*

The weedy daisy-like flowers let down what is otherwise a noble plant. The mound of long-stalked, big dark green leaves 90 cm (3 ft) high is topped by a further 60 cm (2 ft) of flower stems, which I would cut off as they destroy the beauty of the plant's handsome leaves. It likes sun and any good soil.

**SMILACINA**   (Liliaceae)   FALSE SPIKENARD

***Smilacina racemosa***   *N. America*

Like some exotic solomon's seal, a deservedly popular plant. Dense clumps of arching stems terminate in creamy ivory fluffy flower spikes, like small astilbes but beautifully scented. It likes shade and acid humusy soil, preferably with plenty of leaf mould. It can be divided for propagation but it is a shame to spoil large established clumps.

**TRACHYSTEMON**   (Boraginaceae)

***Trachystemon orientale***   *Caucasus*

This plant's greatest quality must be that it will grow in dry shade. A good ground cover plant with large rough rounded leaves the size of *Hosta sieboldiana*. It must be sheltered from wind or its leaves will bruise each other. The strong rhizomes spread quickly along the ground. Lovely electric blue flowers appear in early spring just as the leaves begin.

**VERATRUM**   (Liliaceae)

Noble plants prized for their beautiful pleated foliage. They take a number of years to mature and should be planted when young as they resent movement when established. They require deep rich moist soil and

357

*Myosotidium hortensia*, the Chatham Island forget-me-not,
is a much prized plant – tender but thrives if fed on seaweed.

***Beschorneria yuccoides***, exotic and dramatic, but somewhat
tender, has to be baked to flower well.

shade to prevent scorching of their splendid foliage. They mix well with most bold foliaged plants but are especially attractive when grown with groups of turk's cap lilies.

### Veratrum album    Europe, Siberia

The leaves of all species are very similar being large – 30 cm (1 ft) – long, oval and pointed, and heavily pleated, encircling strong stems. The flowers are the easiest means of identification; those of *V. album* are greenish white in a dense narrow spike up to 1.8 m (6 ft) high.

### Veratrum nigrum    Europe, Siberia

The most striking in flower, with spikes of maroonish black 1.8 m (6 ft) high. Large clumps make a stately and dramatic sight and are much to be treasured. If space were limited then this should be the choice, but otherwise all three listed here are first-class plants.

### Veratrum viride    N. America

Nature displaying her great colour harmony in an all-green plant, flowers and all. This has possibly the best and largest leaves but is usually of lesser stature than the two above, reaching about 1.2 m (4 ft) but occasionally more.

## VERBASCUM    (Scrophulariaceae)    MULLEIN

### Verbascum vernale    unknown

The huge rosettes of silvery white furry leaves are of sufficient beauty in themselves and are complemented by the 1.8 m (6 ft) tall stately spikes of vivid yellow flowers. Like all furry leaved plants it abhors wet, liking a well-drained soil. To keep the splendid leaves in mint condition it is best grown in gravel and as a foreground subject in full sun. It seeds quite readily.

## YUCCA    (Liliaceae)    PALM LILY

These plants are barely herbaceous but since we have included phormiums which are similar, architecturally speaking, it seems only fair to include the best species, which certainly qualify as large-leaved. I should warn the unwary, however, that most possess stiff and viciously pointed leaves making them totally unsuitable candidates for gardens with children, and adults should beware, too! All the species are exotic in effect but only of great beauty when in flower as the foliage on its own, with the possible exception of *Y. recurvifolia*, is rather dull. All require full sun and free-draining soil, and freely produce side shoots which can be separated, potted and rooted under glass.

### Yucca filamentosa    S.E. United States

The usual rosette of stiff grey-green leaves 90 cm (3 ft) across is well cleared by the equally stiff flower spike which bears lustrous creamy bells, beautifully fragrant, 1.5 m (5 ft) high.

### Yucca flaccida    S.E. United States

With narrower leaves than *Y. filamentosa*, and less dangerous, being limp and having drooping tips. The flowers, which have longer side branches, are generously produced.

### Yucca gloriosa    S.E. United States

The most frequently met with of the species and one of the largest. The stiff rosette of leaves is topped by flower stems often 2.5 m (8 ft) high but they often appear so late in the season that they become damaged by frost.

### Yucca recurvifolia    S.E. United States

Foliage-wise a splendid plant. Probably the best and most magnificent of the species, it combines the qualities of laxer, longer leaves and more elegantly poised flower spikes rising 2.5 m (8 ft) high. Happily, these are produced enough in the season to avoid frost.

## ZANTEDESCHIA (Araceae) ARUM LILY

### *Zantedeschia aethiopica* *S. Africa*

The well-known lily of the Nile, a handsome plant both in foliage and flower, is unfortunately disliked by some due to its decorative use at funerals. When in flower, clumps or drifts of them by streams or ponds, with their big white sails lit up by the glossy dark green leaves, are a wonderful sight. It should always be included in waterside plantings; though succeeding in the border it does seem to prefer to have its feet in the mud. Can also be grown in water providing the crowns are at least 15 cm (6 in) below the water (and frost) level. The form 'Crowborough' is said to be hardier but I often wonder if there is any difference. For the collector there is a beautiful green-throated form called 'Green Goddess', which has larger glaucous green leaves. It beats *Z. aethiopica* in height, often reaching 1.5 m (5 ft) and is certainly hardier. I am sure it is popular with flower arrangers.

Zantedeschias should be grown in rich soil for good flowering and their crowns protected with a thick mulch in winter. If grown in pots in a frost-free conservatory or greenhouse they will flower in midwinter.

# Index

Page numbers in *italics* indicate illustrations

*Acanthus*, 279, 281, 282, 300, 320, 324, 325, 329; *A. mollis*, 329; *A. m.* 'Latifolius', 286, 294, 317, 328, 329; *A. spinosus*, 329
*Acer japonicum* 'Aureum', 286, *288*; *A. negundo* 'Flamingo', *66, 160*
*Achnatherum brachytrichum*, *135*, 140
Acid soils, 221, 232
*Adiantum pedatum*, 201, *205*, 213, 223, 228, *230–231*, 244, *246*; *A. reniforme*, 232; *A.* × *tracyi*, 244; *A. venustum*, 213, 223, 245
*Aesculus indica*, 311
*Agropyron magellanicum*, *96–97*, 104, 116, 140; *A. pubiflorum*, 115, 140
*Agrostis canina* 'Silver Needles', 115, 116, 137, 140–142, *185*; *A. nebulosa*, 142
*Ailanthus altissima*, 311
*Aira elegantissima*, 142
*Ajuga reptans* 'Purpurea', 294
*Alchemilla mollis*, 38; *A. xanthochlora*, 38
*Alopecurus alpinus glaucus*, 116, 142; *A. lanatus*, *101*, 104, 142; *A. pratensis* 'Aureovariegatus', *105*, 113, 137, 142
Alpine beds, 31
Alpine lady fern, 248
Alpine water fern, 228, 249
American glade fern, 249
American maidenhair, 228, 224
*Amicia zygomeris*, 329
Anderson's holly fern, 265–268
*Andropogon scoparius*, 142
*Aralia cachemirica*, 282, 313, 329–330; *A. elata*, 313; *A. e.* 'Aureovariegata', 313; *A. e.* 'Variegata', 286, 313, 319; *A. racemosa*, 330
*Arisaema speciosum*, 330
*Arrhenatherum elatius bulbosum* 'Variegatum', 116, 143

*Artemesia arborescens*, 288; *A. canescens*, 228
*Arum italicum* 'Pictum', 15
*Aruncus*, 277, 302; *A. aethusifolius*, 20; *A. dioicus*, 278, 288, 302, 304, *305*, 332; *A. d.* 'Glasnevin', 35
*Arundinaria murielae*, 312, 325; *A. nitida*, 312; *A. viridistriata*, 286, *289*, 312, 320
*Arundo donax*, 143, 282; *A. d.* 'Variegata', 143, 286, 319, 321; *A. pliniana*, 143
*Aspidistra lurida*, 322
*Asplenium adiantum-nigrum*, 209, 228, 232, 245; *A. ceterach*, *205*, 208, *209*, 228, 232, 245; *A. fontanum*, 232; *A.* × *hybridum*, 245; *A. resiliens*, 232; *A. rhizophyllum*, 232; *A. ruta-muraria*, 188, 208, 228, 232, 245; *A. scolopendrium*, 188, *205*, 207, 210, 211, *224*, 228, *230–231*, 232, 237, 245–248, *259*, *273*; *A. trichomanes*, 198, *205*, *209*, 228, 232, 248; *A. viride*, 228, 232, 248
*Astilbe simplicifolia* 'Sprite', *66*
*Astilboides tabularis*, see *Rodgersia tabularis*
*Athyrium*, 236; *A. deltoidofrons*, 248; *A. distentifolium*, 248; *A. filix-femina*, *201*, 204, *205*, 207, 210, 213, *225*, 228, 233, 248–249, *254*, *273*; *A. frangulum*, 249; *A. niponicum pictum*, 43, 223, 249; *A. pycnocarpum*, 249
Autumn fern, 228, 257
*Avena sterilis*, 143

Bamboo, 26, *51*, 279, 282, 293, 300, *305*, *308*, 309, 312, 320, 325
Bananas, 282, 313–314, 320–321, *347*, 349
Bark, shredded, 238
Bead fern, 261
Beech fern, 264

*Begonia evansiana*, 332
*Bergenia*, 325; *B.* 'Ballawley', 232, 291; *B. ciliata*, 232, 291; *B. cordifolia* 'Purpurea', 232, 291; *B.* 'Silberlicht', 332–333; *B.* 'Sunningdale', 333; *B.* 'Eric Smith', 291
Berry bladder fern, 253
*Beschorneria yuccoides*, 292, 333, *359*
Black spleenwort, 209, 228, 245
*Blechnum*, *193*; *B. penna-marina*, 227, 228, 249; *B. spicant*, 210–213, 252; *B. tabulare*, 228, 320; *B. vulcanicum*, 252
Blue gardens, 32
Blunt-lobed woodsia, 272
Borders, 10–13, 23
*Bothriochola caucasica*, 143, 146
*Bouteloua curtipendula*, 146; *B. gracillis*, 146
Bracken, 188, 193, 214, 240
Brittle bladder fern, 253
*Briza*, 106; *B. maxima*, *108*, 119, 146; *B. media*, 115, 119, 146; *B. minor*, 119, 146
Broad buckler fern, 202, 207, 209, 256, *262*
*Bromus brizaeformis*, 146; *B. macrostachys*, 146; *B. madritensis*, 146; *B. ramosus*, 146
Buckler ferns, 202, 207, 209
Bulbils, 237
*Buphthalmum speciosum*, 293, 333

*Calamogrostis* × *acutiflora* 'Karl Foerster', 119, 147; *C.* × *a.* 'Stricta', 119; *C. arundinacea* 'Overdam', 115, 147
*Caltha polypetala*, 35, 301, 333
*Camassia*, 28
Camellias, 321, 325
*Campsis tagliabuana* 'Madame Galen', 313
*Canna*, 282; *C.* × *generalis* 'Wyoming', 314, *315*, 321, 336, *351*; *C. indica*, 333;

*C. i. ehrmanii*, 314, 321, 333–336; *C.* 'Malawiensis', 336; *C.* 'Le Roi Humbert', 336
*Cardiocrinum giganteum*, 292, 336
*Carex albula*, 115, 147; *C. atrata*, 147; *C. berggrenii*, 115, 147; *C. buchananii*, 111, 115, 137, 147; *C. comans*, *51*, 148; *C. c.* 'Bronze Form', 115, 148; *C. conica* 'Snowline', 115, 148; *C. dipsacea*, 111, *112*, 148; *C. elata* 'Aurea', 104, 111, *117*, 148; *C. firma* 'Variegata', 148; *C. flagellifera*, 115, *120*, 148; *C. fraseri*, 148; *C.* 'Frosted Curls', 115, 148; *C. grayi*, 148–150; *C. kaloides*, 111, 150; *C. morrowii* 'Fisher's Form', *112*, 150; *C. m.* 'Variegata', 150; *C. muskingumensis*, 113, 150; *C. m.* 'Wachtposten', 150; *C. ornithopoda* 'Variegata', 150; *C. oshimensis* 'Evergold', 115, *125*, 150–151; *C. o.* 'Variegata', 113, 151; *C. pendula*, 113, 151; *C. petriei*, 115, 151; *C. pilulifera* 'Tinney's Princess', 151; *C. plantaginea*, 151; *C. riparia* 'Variegata', 113, 151; *C. saxiatilis* 'Ski Run', 151; *C. secta*, 151; *C. s. tenuiculmis*, 115, 151; *C. siderosticta* 'Variegata', 115, *129*, 137, 151; *C. testacea*, *59*, 113, 151, 154; *C. trifida*, 154; *C. umbrosa* 'The Beatles', 154; *C. uncifolia*, 154
*Cautleya spicata*, 293, 336
Chain fern, 272
Chalky soils, 232
*Chasmanthium latifolium*, 154
*Chionochloa conspicua*, 154–155; *C. flavescens*, 155; *C. rubra*, 111, 137, 155
*Choisya*, 325; *C. ternata*, 294;

*C..t.* 'Sundance', 286, *298*
Christmas fern, 228, 265
Chromosomes, 235
*Chusquea couleou*, 155
Clay soils, 230
*Clematis armandii*, 313, 325;
    *C.* × *heracleifolia*, 336–337;
    *C. jouiana* 'Praecox', *79*
*Coix lacryma-jobi*, 155
Colour, 32–43, 202, 223
Containers, 44–45, 49, 137, 216
*Cordyline*, 282, *324*; *C. australis*,
    313, 321; *C. a. atropurpurea*,
    313
*Cornus alba* 'Aurea', *59, 90*;
    *C. a.* 'Elegantissima', 36, *51*,
    293; *C. sibirica* 'Variegata',
    286, 293
*Cortaderia fulvida*, 155;
    *C. richardii*, 155; *C. selloana*,
    *133*, 155, 158; *C. s.* 'Gold
    Band', 111, *136*, 158; *C. s.*
    'Monstrosa', 158; *C. s.*
    'Pumila', *f. c.*, 158; *C. s.*
    'Rendatleri', 158; *C. s.* 'Rosea',
    158; *C. s.* 'Silver Stripe', 113,
    158; *C. s.* 'Sunningdale Silver',
    158
*Corynephorus canescens*, 158
*Cotinus coggygria* 'Royal
    Purple', *164*, 286
*Crambe cordifolia*, 286, 292,
    320, 337
Crested buckler fern, 256
*Crocosmia* 'Lucifer', 288
*Cryptogramma crispa*, 230, 232,
    252
Cultivation: of hostas, 47–57; of
    ornamental grasses, 106,
    138–139
*Curtonus paniculatus*, 337
*Cynara cardunculus*, 288
*Cyperus eragrostis*, 158;
    *C. longus*, 158
*Cyrtomium falcatum*, 232, 252;
    *C. fortunei*, 253;
    *C. lonchitoida*, 253
*Cystopteris bulbifera*, 232, 253;
    *C. fragilis*, 232, 253

*Dactylis glomerata* 'Variegata',
    116, 158
*Dactylorhiza elata*, *22*
*Datura cornigera*, 314–316, 321

*Davallia mariesii*, 253
Derris, 241
*Deschampsia caespitosa*, 119,
    159; *D. c.* 'Bronzeschleier',
    119, 159; *D. c.*
    'Goldgehaenge', 119, 159;
    *D. c.* 'Goldschleier', 159; *D. c.*
    'Goldtau', 159, 288;
    *D. c. vivipara*, 159;
    *D. flexuosa*, 159; *D. f.* 'Tatra
    Gold', 113, 159
*Dicentra formosa*, 291;
    *D. spectabilis*, 291; *D. s.* 'Alba',
    *20*
*Dicksonia antarctica*, 206, 291,
    316–319, 321
*Digitalis lutea*, 37
Diseases, 55–56, 139, 241
*Dracunculus vulgaris*, 337
*Dryopteris*, 233, 236; *D. aemula*,
    207, 253; *D. affinis*, *198–199*,
    205, 207, 210, 228, 253–256,
    260; *D. atrata*, 256;
    *D. carthusiana*, 256;
    *D. clintoniana*, 256;
    *D. cristata*, 256; *D. dilatata*,
    202, 205, 207, 209, 223, *224*,
    228, 256–257, *262*;
    *D. erythrosora*, 201, 202, 223,
    228, 257; *D. filix-mas*, 15, 188,
    *190*, 202, 205, 210, 213, 223,
    *224*, 228, 233, *255*, 257, 260,
    *263*, *273*; *D. f.* 'Linearis', 37;
    *D. goldieana*, 228, 260;
    *D. ludoviciana*, 232;
    *D. marginalis*, 228, 260;
    *D. oreades*, 260; *D. sieboldii*,
    260; *D. wallichiana*, 202, 223,
    228, 260
Dwarf ferns, 228

*Echium pinniana*, 292
*Elaeagnus ebbingei*, 43, *59*
*Elymus arenarius*, 113, *136*,
    159, 160
*Embothrium coccineum*, 311;
    *E. c. lanceolatum* 'Norquinco
    Valley', 311
*Ensete ventricosum*, 282,
    313–314, 320–321, *347, 354*
*Eragrostis curvula*, 159
*Eremurus*, 292, 296; *E. robustus*,
    292, 337
*Eriobotrya japonica*, 313

*Eriophorum* 106;
    *E. angustifolium*, 159–160;
    *E. vaginatum*, 160
*Eryngium giganteum*, 228
*Eucalyptus gunnii*, 286–288;
    *E. niphophila*, 286, 311, 321
*Eucomis*, 292, 323; *E. pole-
    evansii*, 337–339
*Euphorbia amygdaloides
    robbiae*, 15; *E. palustris*, 283
European chain fern, 272
Evergreen maidenhair, 245

*Fatsia japonica*, 313, 320, 321,
    325
Feeding: ferns, 238; hostas, 48
Ferns: choosing, 232–233; cold
    weather and, 229; colonizing,
    210–213; design and,
    198–202; division of, 236–237;
    drainage, 221, 232; dry areas
    and, 208–209; fertilizers, 238;
    fronds, *192*, 193–195; frost
    and, 229; germination of, 236;
    humus, 230, 240; life cycle of,
    *233*; lime and, 230, 232;
    maintenance of, 238–243;
    microclimates and, 207, 218;
    mulching, 230, 232, 238, 240;
    mutations of, 188–189;
    nitrogen and, 238; pH levels
    of soils, 221; plant
    associations and, *212, 225*;
    planting, 221–228, 232–233;
    plantlets, 188, 237; pruning,
    240; reproduction of, 188,
    196; rhizomes, 196, 236–237;
    roots of, 196, 217, 229, 236;
    sori, 195, 235; sporangia, 195;
    spores, 188, 195–196,
    235–236; stoloniferus shoots,
    188; texture and, 201–202,
    223; thinning, 240; tissue
    culture and, 237; tubers, 237;
    walls and, 208; watering, 238;
    weeding, 240; winds,
    protection from, 229
Ferneries: 189, 217–228; paths,
    221, 232; ravines, 218, 221,
    232; sites, 218
*Festuca amethystina*, 160;
    *F. erecta*, 115, 160; *F. eskia*,
    160; *F. filiformis*, 160;

*F. glacialis*, 161; *F. glauca*
    'Azurit', *161*; *F. g.* 'Blaufuchs',
    115, 161; *F. g. coxii*, 161; *F. g.*
    'Harz', 115, 161; *F. g.*
    'Merrblau', 161; *F. g.* 'Minima',
    161; *F. g.* 'Seeigel', 161; *F. g.*
    'Silbersee', 115, 162;
    *F. mairei*, 162; *F. paniculata*,
    162; *F. punctoria*, 162;
    *F. vivipara*, 162
*Filipendula*, 302;
    *F. camtschatica*, 302, 304,
    339; *F. palmata* 'Rubra', 302,
    304; *F. rubra*, 339–340
Flower arranging, 45–46
*Fritillaria meleagris*, *28*
Fungi, 241

*Geranium macrorrhizum
    album*, 15; *G. phaeum album*,
    37
Giant chain fern, 272
Giant wood fern, 260
*Glaucidium palmatum*, 340
*Glyceria maxima* 'Variegata',
    113, *141*, 162
Gold gardens, 38
Green gardens, 37
Green-ribbed spleenwort, 228,
    248
Ground cover, 26, 130–132
*Gunnera*, 277, 279, 282, 298,
    320, 337; *G. manicata*, 274–275,
    276, *278, 299*, 301, 304, *335,
    335*, 340; *G. scabra* (*chilensis*),
    301, 304, 340
*Gymnocarpium dryopteris*, 260;
    *G. d. plumosum*, 228;
    *G. robertianum*, 232, 260

*Hakonechloa macra*
    'Alboaurea', *59*, 286, *289*,
    *H. m.* 'Aureola', *11*, 111, 137,
    *144*, 162–163; *H. m. variegata*,
    *306*
Hanging baskets, 216
Hard fern, 252, 265
Hare's foot fern, 253
Hart's tongue fern, 188, 193,
    198, 201, 207, 208, 210, *211*,
    214, 223, 228, *230–231*, 237,
    245, *247, 258, 259*
Hay-scented buckler fern, 207,
    253

*Hedychium*, 340; *H. coccineum*, 340; *H. c.* 'Tara', 316; *H. densiflorum*, 340; *H. forrestii*, 316, 340–341; *H. gardnerianum*, 316, 321, 341, *355*; *H. greenii*, 341; *H. × raffillii*, 341
*Helictotrichon sempervirens*, 111, 115, 137, 163
*Helleborus foetidus*, 15, 36–37
*Heracleum*, 282; *H. mantegazzianum*, 293, 341
*Heuchera* 'Palace Purple', 286, 294; *H.* 'Snow Storm', 288; *H. cylindrica*, 20
*Hibiscus moscheutos*, 316; *H. m.* 'Southern Belle', 321
*Holcus mollis* 'Albovariegatus', 115, 137, *145*, 163
Holly fern, 268
*Hordeum jubatum*, 163
*Hosta* 'Abiqua Moonbeam', 60; *H.* 'Allan P. McConnell', 59–60; *H.* 'Amanuma', 31, 60; *H.* 'Amber Maiden', 63; *H.* 'Antioch', *14*, 60; *H.* 'Aphrodite', 85; *H.* 'August Moon', *14*, 50, 60; *H.* 'Barbara White', 53, 60; *H.* 'Bennie MacRae', 60; *H.* 'Betsy King', 64; *H.* 'Bianca', 89; *H.* 'Big Daddy', 53, 60; *H.* 'Big Mama', 50, 60; *H.* 'Bill Brincka', 60; *H.* 'Birchwood Parky's Gold', 69; *H.* 'Black Hills', 37, 61; *H.* 'Blond Elf', 31, 61; *H.* 'Blue Angel', 15, 37, 53, 61; *H.* 'Blue Belle', 58, 61; *H.* 'Blue Blush', 31, 61; *H.* 'Blue Boy', 15, 23, 61; *H.* 'Blue Cadet', 53, 61; *H.* 'Blue Danube', 61; *H.* 'Blue Dimples', 59, 61, 63; *H.* 'Blue Moon', 23, 31, 58, 61–62; *H.* 'Blue Seer', 37, 89; *H.* 'Blue Skies', 31, 62; *H.* 'Blue Umbrellas', 53, 62; *H.* 'Blue Wedgewood', 15, 59, 63, 68; *H.* 'Bold Ribbons', 63; *H.* 'Bold Ruffles', 53, 63; *H.* 'Borwick Beauty', 68; *H.* 'Bouquet', 81; *H.* 'Bright Glow', 63; *H.* 'Bright Lights', 12, 63; *H.* 'Brim Cup', 63, *79*;

*H.* 'Buckshaw Blue', 63; *H.* 'Candy Hearts', 15, 63, 81; *H.* 'Carol', 68; *H.* 'Carrie Ann', 31, 37, 63; *H.* 'Celebration', 31, 46, 63; *H.* 'Change of Tradition', 79; *H.* 'Chartreuse Wiggles', 31, 64; *H.* 'Chelsea Babe', 65; *H.* 'Chelsea Ore', 85; *H.* 'Chinese Sunrise', 38, 64, 68; *H.* 'Christmas Tree', 23, 46, *51*, 53, 64; *H. clausa normalis*, 26, 64; *H.* 'Colossal', 64; *H.* 'Colour Glory', 68; *H. crispula*, *22*, 36, 55, 64, 341; *H.* 'Dawn', 31, 76; *H.* 'Daybreak', 64; *H. decorata*, 64; *H.* 'Diamond Tiara', 72; *H.* 'Dick Ward', 94; *H.* 'Dorset Blue', 23, 31, 58, 62, 64–65; *H.* 'Duchess', 31, 65; *H.* 'Elfin Power', 31, 65; *H.* 'Emerald Isle', 37, 89; *H.* 'Emerald Skies', 62; *H.* 'Emerald Tiara', 72; *H.* 'Emily Dickinson', 65; *H.* 'Emma Foster', 81; *H.* 'Eric Smith', 58; *H.* 'Evening Magic', 84; *H. fluctuans* 'Variegated', 35, 45, 53, 65, *82*; *H. fortunei*, 26, 45, 50, 65; *H. f.* 'Albo-marginata', 65; *H. f.* 'Albo-picta', 65, 344; *H. f.* 'Aurea', 38, 65–66; *H. f.* 'Aureo-marginata', *12*, *14*, 26, 35, 37, 53, 66; *H. f.* 'Hyacinthina', 15, 66–67; *H. f.* 'Hyacinthina Variegata', 67; *H. f.* 'Marginata Alba', 344; *H. f.* 'Obscura Marginata', 344; *H.* 'Fragrant Bouquet', 67; *H.* 'Fragrant Gold', 67; *H.* 'Francee', 9, 15, 20, 26, 32, 35, 36, 37, 44, 45, 50, 68, *83*; *H.* 'Frances Williams', 12, 32, 38, 43, 50, 53, 57, 68, *75*, *90*, 294, 344; *H.* 'Fresh', 31, 68; *H.* 'Fringe Benefit', 23, 26, 53, 68, 344; *H.* 'Frosted Jade', 23, 68; *H.* 'Geisha', *11*, 68; *H.* 'George Smith', 68–69; *H.* 'Ginko Craig', 9, 15, 20, 31, *46*, 69; *H.* 'Gloriosa', *46*, 69; *H.* 'Gold Edger', 26, 38, 53, 69; *H.* 'Gold Haze', 66, 73; *H.*

'Gold Leaf', 66; *H.* 'Gold Regal', 38, 53, 69; *H.* 'Gold Standard', 32, 38, *39*, 44, 45, 69, 72; *H.* 'Goldbrook', 45, 60, 69; *H.* 'Goldbrook Gift', 93; *H.* 'Goldbrook Glimmer', *62*, 76; *H.* 'Goldbrook Gold', 69; *H.* 'Goldbrook Grace', 31, 69; *H.* 'Golden Age', 73; *H.* 'Golden Bullion', 72; *H.* 'Golden Medallion', 38, 72; *H.* 'Golden Nakaiana', 69; *H.* 'Golden Prayers', 13, 31, 38, 45, 72; *H.* 'Golden Scepter', 20, 72; *H.* 'Golden Sculpture', 53, 72; *H.* 'Golden Sunburst', 50, 69, 72, *75*; *H.* 'Golden Tiara', 12, 45, 72; 'Goldsmith', 73; *H. gracillima*, 76; *H.* 'Granary Gold', 73; *H.* 'Great Expectations', 73; *H.* 'Green Fountain', 44, 45, 53, 73; *H.* 'Green Pastures', 84; *H.* 'Green Piecrust', 53, 73; *H.* 'Green Sheen', 53, 73; *H.* 'Green with Envy', 31, 76; *H.* 'Ground Master', 20, 26, 73; *H.* 'Ground Sulphur', 73; *H.* 'Hadspen Blue', 23, 26, *66*, 73, 76; *H.* 'Hadspen Heron', 31, 76; *H.* 'Hakujima', 31, 88; *H.* 'Halcyon', 10, 15, 23, 26, *42*, 43, 45, 50, 57, 59, 68, 76; *H.* 'Happy Hearts', 81; *H.* 'Harmony', 31, 76; *H.* 'Harvest Glow', 81; *H.* 'Heartsong', 63; *H.* 'Helen Doriot', 89; *H. helonioides* 'Albo-picta', 85; *H.* 'Holly's Honey', 76; *H.* 'Honeybells', 26, 57, 76, 344; *H.* 'Hydon Sunset', 31, 38, 45, 76; *H. hypoleuca*, 53, 76–77; *H.* 'Inaho', 64, 68, 77; *H.* 'Invincible', 26, 45, 77; *H.* 'Iona', 23, 77, *86*; *H.* 'Iron Gate Glamour', *30*, 77; *H.* 'Jade Scepter', 37, 72; *H.* 'Janet', 77; *H.* 'June', 57, 77, *78*; *H. kikutii*, 45, 77; *H. k.* 'Pruinose', 37, 53, *78*; *H.* 'Krossa Regal', 9, 35, 45, 53, 57, *70*, 78, 344; *H. lancifolia*, 15, 26, 45, 78–79; *H.* 'Leather

Sheen', 79; *H.* 'Lemon Lime', 31, 79; *H.* 'Little Aurora', 31, 72; *H.* 'Little Blue', 80; *H.* 'Little White Lines', 31, 80; *H. longipes latifolia hypoglauca* 'Hachijo Urajiro', 80; *H. longissima*, 80; *H.* 'Louisa', 37, 89; *H.* 'Love Pat', 37, 53, 80; *H.* 'Lunar Eclipse', 60; *H.* 'Maekawa', 77; *H.* 'Marquis', 81; *H.* 'Mayan Moon', *see H.* 'Abiqua Moonbeam'; *H.* 'Midas Touch', 24, 38, 50, 53, 80; *H.* 'Mildred Seaver', 67, 80; *H. minor*, 31, 45, 80–81; *H. montana*, 26, 37, 81; *H. m.* 'Aureo-marginata', 20, 70, 81; *H.* 'Moon Glow', 81; *H.* 'Moonlight', 38, 81; *H.* 'Moorheim', 60; *H.* 'Mountain Snow', 81; *H. nakaiana*, 45, 58, 81; *H.* 'Neat Splash', 63; *H.* 'Neat Splash Rim', 63; *H.* 'New Tradition', 79; *H.* 'Nicola', 81; *H. nigrescens*, 53, 81; *H.* 'North Hills', 68; *H.* 'Northern Halo', 84; *H.* 'Northern Lights', 84; *H.* 'On Stage', 84; *H. opipara*, 55, 60; *H.* 'Osprey', 37, 84; *H.* 'Pastures New', 84; *H.* 'Pearl Lake', 62, 81, 84; *H.* 'Phyllis Campbell', 65; *H.* 'Piedmont Gold', 38, 50, 84; *H.* 'Pizzazz', 43, 53, *62*, 84; *H.* 'Pixie Power', 31, 65; *H. plantaginea*, 9, 23, 37, 85, 344; *H.* 'Platinum Tiara', 72; *H.* 'Po Po', 94; *H. pycnophylla*, 85; *H.* 'Regal Splendour', 12, 43, 57, *66*, 85; *H.* 'Resonance', 73; *H.* 'Reversed', 45, 58, 85; *H.* 'Richland Gold', 72; *H. rohdeifolia*, 85; *H.* 'Roseanne', *14*; *H.* 'Royal Standard', 23, 26, 36, 37, 85, *87*, 344; *H.* 'Royalty', 31, 85; *H. rupifraga*, 53, 85; *H.* 'Saishu Jima', 31, 85; *H.* 'Samurai', 68; *H.* 'Sea Dream', 88; *H.* 'Sea Drift', 88, *91*; *H.* 'Sea Gold Star', 38, 88; *H.*

'Sea Lotus Leaf', 15, 37, 53, 88; *H.* 'Sea Monster', 88; *H.* 'Sea Octopus', 88; *H.* 'Sea Sprite', 55; *H.* 'September Sun', 32, 60; *H.* 'Shade Fanfare', 23, 26, 35, *71*, 88; *H.* 'Shining Tot', 31, 88; *H. sieboldiana*, *6–7*, 20, 26, 37, 45, 48, 50, 53, 344, 346; *H. s.* 'Elegans', 24, *34*, 37, 58, 88–89, *280*, 288, 308, 320, 321, 322, 328, *343*, 344, 350; *H. sieboldii*, 26, 31, 45, 56, 89; *H. s.* 'Alba', 37, 89; *H. s.* 'Kabitan', 89; *H. s.* 'Silver Kabitan', 31, 89; *H.* 'Silver Lance', 89, *95*; *H.* 'Snow Cap', 12, 37, 43, 53, *62*, 89; *H.* 'Snowden', 36, 37, 44, 45, 89, 92, 344; *H.* 'Snowflakes', 89; *H.* 'So Sweet', 9, 23, *30*, 37, 45, 92; *H.* 'Spinners', 60, 69; *H.* 'Spritzer', 53, *59*, 68, 92; *H.* 'Squiggles', 31, 89; *H.* 'Stiletto', 92; *H.* 'Sugar and Cream', 23, 26, 35, 37, 45, 57, 92; *H.* 'Sum and Substance', 10, 13, *14*, 24, 26, 38, 44–45, 53, *74*, 92, 286, 289, 320, 345; *H.* 'Summer Fragrance', 23, 45, 92; *H.* 'Sun Power', 92; *H.* 'Sundance', 77; *H.* 'Sunset', 31, 76; *H.* 'Tall Boy', 26, *54*, 92; *H.* Tardiana group, 53, 58; *H. tardiflora*, 31, 53, 58, 93; *H.* 'Thomas Hogg' *see H. undulata* 'Albo-marginata'; *H.* 'Thumb Nail', 31, 93, 94; *H.* 'Tiny Tears', 31, 93, 94; *H. tokudama*, 15, 37, 45, 53, 93, 303; *H. t.* 'Aureonebulosa', 12, 38. 43, 93; *H. t.* 'Flavo-circinalis', 93; *H. undulata*, 45; *H. u.* 'Albo-marginata', 15, 26, 32, 64, 93, 286; *H. u.* 'Erromena', 24, 26, 93; *H. u.* 'Univittata', *15, 19*, 26, 93; *H.* 'Valentine Lace', 81; *H.* 'Vanilla Cream', 31, 93–94; *H. ventricosa*, 26, 94, 345; *H. v.* 'Aureo-maculata', 94; *H. v.* 'Variegata', 73, 94, 345; *H.* 'Venus', 85; *H. venusta*, 31, 48, 94; *H. v.*

'Variegated', 31, 94; *H.* 'Vera Verde', 94; *H.* 'Weihenstephan', 89; *H.* 'White Shoulders', 85; *H.* 'Wide Brim', 26, 35, 61, 94; *H.* 'Winning Edge', 93; *H.* 'Wogon Gold', 76; *H.* 'Yellow River', 94; *H.* 'Yellow Splash Rim', 63; *H.* 'Zounds', 53, 69, *90*, 94
*Hydrangea*, *51*; *H. aspera*, 286, 313, 321; *H. sargentiana*, 286, 313, 321
*Hystrix patula*, 163

*Imperata cylindrica* 'Rubra', 104, 111, *149*, 163
*Indocalamus tessellatus*, 163
*Inula magnifica*, 293, 302, 304, 345
Irises, 282, 300, *300*, 304; *Iris foetidissima* 'Variegata', 15, 36; *I. pseudacorus* 'Variegatus', *27*, 35
Ivies, 325

Japanese holly fern, 252
Japanese painted fern, 249
*Juncus concinnus*, 166; *J. decipiens* 'Curly Wurly', 166; *J. effusus* 'Spiralis', 166; *J. inflexus* 'Afro', 166; *J. xiphiodes*, 166

King fern, 210
*Kirengeshoma*, 345
*Koeleria cristata glauca*, 115, 166; *K. vallesiana*, 166

Ladder fern, 210–213
Lady ferns, 193, 207, 210, 213, 214, 228, 233, 248–249, *254*
*Lagurus ovatus*, 119, 166
*Lamarckia aurea*, *152*
*Lamium maculatum* 'Beacon Silver', 288
*Lapageria rosea*, 313
Leathery polypody, 264
*Ligularia*, 277, 282, 300, 302, 324, 325, 345; *L. dentata* 'Desdemona', *280*, 286, 294, 302, 303, 304, *305, 308, 317, 318–319*, 320, 321, *328*, 345; *L. d.* 'Gregynog Gold', 302, 345; *L. macrophylla*, 345;

*L. × palmatiloba*, 348; *L. przewalskii*, 348; *L. p.* 'The Rocket', 35, 38, 302; *L. veitchiana*, 291, 302, 348; *L. wilsoniana*, 291, 294, 302, *330–331*, 348
*Lilium canadense*, 293; *L. martagon*, 286
Limestone oak fern, 260
*Liriope muscari*, 43
*Luzula alopecurus 166*; *L. × borrerii* 'Botany Bay', 166–167; *L. nivea*, 113, 167; *L. pumila*, 167; *L. sylvatica forma*, 167; *L. s.* 'Hohe Tatra', 113, 167; *L. s.* 'Marginata', 15, 113, *153*, 167; *L. s.* 'Select', 167; *L. s.* 'Tauernpass', 167; *L. ulophylla*, 104, 167
*Lysichiton*, 277, 302, *326*, 348; *L. americanum*, 301, 302, 304, *305, 335, 338–339*, 348; *L. camtschatcensis*, 301, 302, 348
*Lysimachia ephemereum*, 43; *L. nummularia* 'Aurea', *11, 149*

*Macleaya cordata*, 288; *M. microcarpa*, 348–349
*Magnolia delavayi*, 313; *M. grandiflora*, 313; *M. macrophylla*, 313; *M. tripetala*, 313
Maidenhair: American, 228, 244; evergreen, 245
Maidenhair spleenwort, *209*, 228, 248
Male ferns, 188, *190, 194, 198–199*, 202, 207, 210, 213, 214, *218–219*, 223, *225*, 228, 233, *247, 250*, 257
Marginal shield fern, 228, 260
Marsh buckler fern, 207
*Matteuccia orientalis*, 260; *M. struthiopteris*, 20, 193, 202, *205*, 210, 223, 228, 232, 236, 240, 261, *266, 271*, 288, 320
*Meconopis*, 291; *M. sheldonii*, 288
*Melianthus*, 277, 282; *M. major*, 288, 314, 321, 349, *351*
*Melica altissima* 'Atropurpurea', 167; *M. nutans*, *131*, 167;

*M. uniflora*, *156*; *M. u.* 'Variegata', 167, 170; *M. u.* var. *albida*, 170
*Milium effusum* 'Aureum', 104, 111, *157*, 170
*Miscanthus*, *346*; *M. floridulus*, 170, *181*; *M. sinensis*, 119, 170; *M. s.* 'Caberet', 170; *M. s.* 'Flamingo', *170*; *M. s.* 'Goldfeder', 170; *M. s.* 'Goliath', 170; *M. s.* 'Gracillimus', *f. c.*, 113, 119, 170; *M. s.* 'Graziella', 119, 171; *M. s.* 'Kascade', 119, 171; *M. s.* 'Kleine Fontane', 119, 171; *M. s.* 'Malapartus', 119, 171; *M. s.* 'Morning Light', 171; *M. s.* 'Nippon', 171; *M. s.* 'Punktchen', 171; *M. s. purpurascens*, 111, 119, 171; *M. s.* 'Rotsilber', 119, 171; *M. s.* 'Silberfeder', *6–7*, 114, *161*, 171; *M. s.* 'Silberspinne', 119, 171; *M. s.* 'Sirene', 171; *M. s.* 'Strictus', 171; *M. s.* 'Variegatus', 36, 115, 119, *164*, 171; *M. s.* 'Zebrinus', *f. c.* 38, 111, 171; *M. tinctoria* 'Nana Variegata', 171; *M. yakushimensis*, 171
*Molinia caerulea*, 35, *90*; *M. c.* 'Heidebraut', 172; *M. c.* 'Moorhexe', 172; *M. c.* 'Variegata', 115, *165*, 172, 286; *M. c. arundinacea* 'Bergfreund', 172; *M. c. a.* 'Karl Foerster', 119, 172; *M. c. a.* 'Skyracer', 172; *M. c. a.* 'Windspiel', 119, 172; *M. c. a.* 'Zuneigung', 172
Mountain male fern, 260
*Muhlembergia japonica* 'Cream Delight', 172
*Musa basjoo*, 314, 349
*Myosotidium hortensia*, 292, 349, 355
*Myosotis scorpioides* 'Mermaid', 291

*Narcissus* 'Thalia', 13, *24*, 37
Narrow buckler fern, 256

Oak fern, 228, 260
*Onoclea sensibilis*, 228, 261

*Onopordum acanthium*, 288
Oriental chain fern, 272
Ornamental grasses: dried arrangements of, 137; flowers, 100–102, 104–106, 107, 116–121; foliage colour, 102, 104, 107, 109–116, 121–130; form of, 103–104, 107; indoor arrangements of, 137; lawns of, 137; shady sites and, 134; siting, 99–100; sunny sites and, 134; wet sites and, 134–137
*Osmunda banksifolia*, 261; *O. japonica*, 261; *O. regalis*, 188, 197, 204, *205*, 209, 223, 228, *239*, 261, *326*, *346*; *O. spectabilis*, 228, 261
Ostrich feather fern, 193, 201, 202, 210, 223, *225*, 228, 236, 240, 261, *266*, *271*

*Pachysandra terminalis* 'Green Carpet', *30*
Palms, 282, 300, 308, 312, *317*, 320
Pampas grass, *280*, 282, *284*
*Panicum clandestinum*, 172; *p. miliaceum*, 173; *P. m.* 'Violaceum', 173; *P. virgatum* 'Haense Herms', 173; *P. v.* 'Rehbraun', 173; *P. v.* 'Rotstrahlbusch', 173; *P. v.* 'Rubrum', 173; *P. v.* 'Strictum', 119, 173
Parsley fern, 230, 252
*Paulownia imperialis*, 311, 321; *P. tomemtosa*, 321
*Pellaea atropurpurea*, 232
*Peltiphyllum*, 277, 282, 304; *P. peltatum*, 298, 301, 302, *305*, *322*, *334*, *338–339*, 349–352
*Pennisetum alopecuroides*, 119, 173–174; *P. a.* 'Hameln', 174; *P. a.* 'Woodside', 174; *P. macrourum*, 174; *P. orientale*, 119, 174; *P. setaceum*, 174; *P. villosum*, *168*, 174
Pests, 52–53, 139, 241
*Petasites*, 302, 324, 352; *P. hybridus*, 301, 304, 352;

*P. japonicus giganteus*, 293, 301, 352
*Phalaris arundinacea* 'Feesey's Form', 113, *169*; *P. a. luteopicta*, 174; *P. a.* 'Picta', 174; *P. a.* 'Tricolor', 174; *P. canariensis*, 174
*Phegopteris connectilis*, 264
*Phleum pratense*, 175
*Phormium*, 277, 282, 288, 292, 300, 320, 324, 325, 352; *P. cookianum*, 312, 352; *P. tenax*, 279, *280*, 312, 328, 353; *P. t. purpureum*, 286, 292, 312, 320, 353; *P. t.* 'Variegatum', *283*, 286, *289*, *308*, 312, *317*, 320, 353
*Phragmites australis giganteus*, 175; *P. a.* 'Variegatus', 111, 175; *P. a.* 'Karka', 175
*Phyllostachys*, 320; *P. aurea*, 175, *308*, 312; *P. a.* 'Holochrysa', 175; *P. mitis*, 312; *P. nigra*, 175, 312, 320
*Phytolacca*, 353; *P. americana*, 291, 353; *P. clavigera*, 291, 353
*Pleioblastus humilis pumilis*, 175; *P. pygmaeus*, 175; *P. variegatus*, 175; *P. viridistriatus*, 104, 111, *173*, 178
*Poa acicularifolia*, 178; *P. buchananii*, 178; *P. chaixii*, 178; *P. colensoi*, 115, 178; *P. ×jemtlandica*, 178; *P. labillardieri*, 178
*Polygonum*, 353; *P. bistorta* 'Superbum', 186; *P. cuspidatum* 'Spectabile', 291, 293, 353; *P. sachalinense*, 293, 353
*Polypodium australe*, 232, 264; *P. scouleri*, 264; *P. vulgare*, 198, *205*, *206*, 208, 213, 214, 228, 232, *242–243*, *255*, 264–265
*Polypogon monspeliensis*, 178
*Polystichum acrostichoides*, 228, 265; *P. aculeatum*, 228, 232, 265; *P. andersonii*, 265–268; *P. braunii*, 38, *67*, 268; *P. cystostegia*, *268*; *P. imbricans*, 268;

*P. munitum*, 268; *P. polyblepharum*, *267*, 268; *P. retroso-paleaceum*, 268; *P. richardii*, 268; *P. setiferum*, *186–187*, 189, *194*, 201, 210, *215*, 223, *224*, *225*, 228, *234–235*, 237, 240, 242, 268–269, *270*; *P. tsus-simense*, 228, 269
Ponds, 23–26
*Populus lasiocarpe*, 311, 321
Potassium, 240
Prickly buckler fern, 256
Prickly shield fern, 228, 265
*Primula*, *303*, 304, *327*; *P.* 'Dawn Ansell', 20; *P. pulverulenta*, 291, 304
Propagation: of ferns, 229, 235–237; of hostas, 56–57; of ornamental grasses, 139
*Pseudosasa japonica*, 178–179
*Pteidium aquilinum*, 188
*Pulmonaria mollis* 'Royal Blue', *62*
Pyrethrum, 241

Regal fern, 197
*Rheum*, 282, *284*, 288, 291, 296, 298, 302, 304, 356; *R. australe*, 356; *R. palmatum*, *27*, *186–187*, 302, *338–339*, 356; *R. p.* 'Atrosanguineum', 302, 356; *R. p. tanguticum*, 286, *290*, 356
*Rhyncheltyrum repens*, 179
*Ricinus communis* 'Gibsonii', 314, 321
*Rodgersia*, 302, 356; *R. aesculifolia*, 356; *R. pinnata*, *306*, 356; *R. p.* 'Elegans', 302; *R. p.* 'Superba', *280*, 291, 293, 294, 302, *305*, 356; *R. podophylla*, 288, 291, 293, 304, 320, 321, *334*, 356; *R. sambucifolia*, 293, 356; *R. (Astilboides) tabularis*, 288, 293, *310*, 320, 321, 357
Royal fern, 188, 200, 202, 204, 207, 209, 223, 228, *239*, 261

*Rubus thibetanus* 'Silver Fern, *66*
Rumex, 300; *R. hydrolapathum*, 301, 302, 357
Rusty-back fern, 188, 208, *209*, 228, 245

*Saccharum ravennae*, 179
*Sambucus racemosa* 'Plumosa Aurea', 286, *289*, 320
*Sasa palmata*, 320; *S. p.* 'Nebulosa', 312; *S. veitchii*, *176*, 179
Scaly male fern, 207, 210, 228, 253
*Schoenus pauciflorus*, 111, 179
*Scirpus lacustris* 'Albescens', 179; *S. l. tabernaemontani* 'Zebrinus', 179
*Senecio smithii*, *300*, 301, 302, 357
Sensitive fern, 228, 261
*Sesleria caerula*, 116, 179, 182; *S. heufleriana*, 182; *S. nitida*, 115, 182
Shade, hostas and, 13–23
Shaggy shield fern, 256
*Shibataea kumasasa*, 182
Shuttlecock fern, 210, 213, 223, 261, *266*, *271*
*Silphium terebinthinaceum*, 357
*Sinarundinaria mureilae*, 182; *S. nitida*, 182
Slugs and snails, 52–53, 241
*Smilacina racemosa*, 288, 357
Soft shield fern, 189, 201, 210, *215*, 223, 228, 237, 240, 268–269
Soils, 221, 230–232, 238
*Sorghastrum avenaceum*, 182
*Sorghum halepense*, 182
Southern polypody, 264
*Spartina pectinata* 'Aureomarginata', 111, *177*, 183
Specimen ferns, 209–210
Spleenwort, 198; black, 209, 228, 245; green-ribbed, 228, 248; maidenhair, *209*, 228, 248; wall, 209, 245
*Spodiopogon sibiricum*, 183
*Stenotaphrum secundatum* 'Variegatum', 183
*Stipa*, 106; *S. arundinacea*, 183;

*S. a.* 'Autumn Tints', 183; *S. a.* 'Golden Hue', 183; *S. calamagrostis*, 119, *180*, 183; *S. gigantea*, 113, *181*, 183; *S. pennata*, 183–184; *S. tenacissima*, 184; *S. tenuissima*, 184
Sword fern, 268

Tatting fern, 202
*Tellima grandiflora*, 15
*Tetrapanax papyriferus*, 316, 321
*Thelypteris palustris*, 207
*Tibouchina urvilliana*, 316
*Trachycarpus fortunei*, 291, *308*, 312, 317, 320

*Trachystemon orientale*, 291, 357
Tree ferns, 188, *206*
*Typha angustifolia*, 184; *T. latifolia*, 184; *T. l.* 'Variegata', 184; *T. minima*, 184

*Uncinia rubra*, 104, 111; *U. uncinata*, 111

*Veratrum*, 357–360; *V. album*, 360; *V. nigrum*, 23, 291, 360; *V. viride*, *287*, 360
*Verbascum*, 282; *V. olympicum*, 288; *V. vernale*, 360

*Viburnum plicatum* 'Mariesii', 286
Vine weevils, 55
*Viola labradorica*, 23

Wall spleenwort (wall rue), 188, 209, 228, 245
Water ferns: alpine, 228, 249; wedge, 252
Water gardens, 204–208, *224*
Wedge water fern, 252
White gardens, 35–37
Woodland gardens, 208
*Woodsia obtusa*, 228, 272
*Woodwardia areolata*, 272; *W. fimbriata*, 272;

*W. orientalis*, 272, *W. radicans*, 228, 272; *W. virginica*, 272

*Yucca*, 282, 292, 360; *Y. filamentosa*, 360; *Y. flaccida*, 360; *Y. gloriosa*, 360; *Y. recurvifolia*, 360–361

*Zantedeschia*, 293, 302; *Z. aethiopica*, *300*, 301, 304, *305*, 323, 361; *Z. a.* 'Crowborough', 286, 301, 304, *342*
*Zea mays*, 184; *Z. m.* 'Amoro', 184; *Z. m.* 'Harlequin', 184; *Z. m.* 'Multicolor', 184; *Z. m.* 'Quadricolor', 184